Inflation and
the Income Tax

Studies of Government Finance

Inflation and the Income Tax

HENRY J. AARON *Editor*

*A Report of a Conference Sponsored by
the Fund for Public Policy Research
and the Brookings Institution*

Studies of Government Finance

THE BROOKINGS INSTITUTION

WASHINGTON, D.C.

Copyright © 1976 by
THE BROOKINGS INSTITUTION
1775 Massachusetts Avenue, N.W., Washington, D.C. 20036

Library of Congress Cataloging in Publication Data:

Main entry under title:
Inflation and the income tax.

   (Studies of government finance; 2d ser., no. 4)
   Includes bibliographical references and index.
   1. Inflation (Finance) and taxation—United States—
Addresses, essays, lectures.   2. Income tax—United
States—Addresses, essays, lectures.   I. Aaron, Henry J.
HJ4652.I54   336.2′4′0973   76-25875
ISBN 0-8157-0024-5
ISBN 0-8157-0023-7 pbk.

9 8 7 6 5 4 3 2 1

THE BROOKINGS INSTITUTION is an independent organization devoted to nonpartisan research, education, and publication in economics, government, foreign policy, and the social sciences generally. Its principal purposes are to aid in the development of sound public policies and to promote public understanding of issues of national importance.

The Institution was founded on December 8, 1927, to merge the activities of the Institute for Government Research, founded in 1916, the Institute of Economics, founded in 1922, and the Robert Brookings Graduate School of Economics and Government, founded in 1924.

The Board of Trustees is responsible for the general administration of the Institution, while the immediate direction of the policies, program, and staff is vested in the President, assisted by an advisory committee of the officers and staff. The bylaws of the Institution state: "It is the function of the Trustees to make possible the conduct of scientific research, and publication, under the most favorable conditions, and to safeguard the independence of the research staff in the pursuit of their studies and in the publication of the results of such studies. It is not a part of their function to determine, control, or influence the conduct of particular investigations or the conclusions reached."

The President bears final responsibility for the decision to publish a manuscript as a Brookings book. In reaching his judgment on the competence, accuracy, and objectivity of each study, the President is advised by the director of the appropriate research program and weighs the views of a panel of expert outside readers who report to him in confidence on the quality of the work. Publication of a work signifies that it is deemed a competent treatment worthy of public consideration but does not imply endorsement of conclusions or recommendations.

The Institution maintains its position of neutrality on issues of public policy in order to safeguard the intellectual freedom of the staff. Hence interpretations or conclusions in Brookings publications should be understood to be solely those of the authors and should not be attributed to the Institution, to its trustees, officers, or other staff members, or to the organizations that support its research.

Foreword

THAT INFLATION makes the fair distribution of tax burdens more difficult is clear to all. How and whether to correct the distortions caused by inflation—that is, how and whether to index the tax system—is far less obvious. To deal with these questions, the Brookings Institution and the Fund for Public Policy Research organized a conference on inflation and the income tax system that was held on October 30 and 31, 1975. The papers presented at the conference, together with formal comments and summaries of the discussions, appear in this volume.

Although the conference participants did not resolve the problems of how to correct tax distortions caused by inflation, several points of general consensus emerged. Inflation distorts both the rate structure and the tax base. Discretionary changes in tax laws enacted by Congress have more than offset the tendency of inflation to push wage earners into higher rate brackets. They have had a weaker offsetting effect, however, on recipients of income from capital. The principal distortions affect the tax base: at the onset or during an acceleration of inflation, inflation-adjusted business income would probably be higher than income as currently calculated, but it would be lower in the long run.

The participants divided almost evenly on whether inflation adjustments are warranted or desirable. Some expressed the view that adjustments for inflation should be added to the agenda for tax reform and deserved no higher priority than other items already on the agenda. Some believed that the objective of indexing the tax system is, and should be, merely to make the tax laws—which have been written as if for a world with stable prices—operate as intended. Others suggested that certain provisions of the tax code are justified in part as counterweights to the imbalances caused by inflation and would need to be changed if the tax system were explicitly indexed. Still others believed that the problems created by inflation strengthened the arguments for replacing the income tax with a consumption, or expenditure, tax. Most felt that the desirability of adjustments for inflation hinged significantly on rates of inflation expected in the future.

The conference discussion made clear that at least two problems required additional attention. If an indexed tax system became necessary or desirable, how should the transition—a process that would significantly reallocate tax burdens—be arranged? Is it possible to make any further partial adjustments for inflation that would avoid some of the difficulties of full adjustment?

The papers, which were revised in light of the conference discussion and, in some cases, to include new data or information, were edited by Henry J. Aaron, a Brookings senior fellow, and checked for factual accuracy by Evelyn P. Fisher, assisted by Carol Gurvitz and Thang Long Ton That. Valerie J. Harris provided secretarial assistance throughout the project; Tadd Fisher edited the manuscript for publication; and the index was prepared by Florence Robinson. The project was supported by the Fund for Public Policy Research.

This is the fourth publication in the Brookings Studies of Government Finance second series, which is devoted to examining issues in taxation and public expenditure policy. The views expressed in this volume are those of the authors and discussants and should not be ascribed to the trustees, officers, or other staff members of the Brookings Institution; to the Fund for Public Policy Research; or to any of the organizations with which the authors and other conference participants are affiliated.

GILBERT Y. STEINER
Acting President

Washington, D.C.
June 1976

Contents

Comments by George Perry *188*
Comments by Robert J. Gordon *190*
Comments by Ray C. Fair *191*
Discussion *191*

7. Adjusting Taxable Profits for Inflation: The Foreign
   Experience   195
   George E. Lent

   Nature and Coverage of Plans *196*
   Revaluation Techniques *204*
   Mandatory versus Elective Revaluation *207*
   Taxation of Revaluation Gains *208*
   Annual versus Periodic Revaluations *209*
   Administrative Problems *210*
   Summary and Conclusions *211*

8. Adjusting Personal Income Taxes for Inflation:
   The Foreign Experience   215
   Vito Tanzi

   Analytical Description of Adjustment Schemes *216*
   Some Problems with Adjustment Schemes *218*
   Practical Applications of Indexing in Foreign Countries *222*
   Conclusion *226*
   Discussion *227*

9. Price Series for Indexing the Income Tax System   233
   Edward F. Denison

   Why One Index Should Be Used for All Taxpayers *236*
   The Selection of an Appropriate Index *243*
   Some Points of Detail *258*
   Comments by Alan Blinder *261*
   Comments by Robert J. Gordon *264*
   Discussion *266*

10. The Economic and Budgetary Effects of Indexing
    the Tax System   271
    Edward M. Gramlich

    The Present Mixed System *272*
    The Effect of Underindexing the Tax System *278*
    Conclusions *290*

Tables

Figures

CHAPTER ONE

Inflation and the Income Tax: An Introduction

HENRY J. AARON

'Tis the Night Before Xmas, and all through the nation
Your bonus means nothing because of inflation.

—*MAD*, January 1975

INFLATION not only erodes the value of income, it also raises the taxes of many people and businesses and lowers others. The recent increase in inflation has elevated the question of whether and how the tax system should be adjusted to cope with rising prices from a matter of academic curiosity to a live political issue. Many nations, having long experienced high rates of inflation, years ago adopted rules for altering their tax systems automatically as prices rise.[1] Should the United States do so today? If so, which adjustments should be made automatically and which should be left to ad hoc remedy by periodic legislation?[2]

1. See chapters 7 and 8, and the discussion at the end of chapter 8 for a description of current practices.

2. For other studies of these questions, see M. F. Morley, *The Fiscal Implications of Inflation Accounting* (London: Institute for Fiscal Studies and Chartered Accountants Trust for Education and Research, 1974); and Thelma Liesner and Mer-

These questions raise a host of considerations involving fairness, economic efficiency, and politics: fairness, because inflation alters the relative tax burdens among individual taxpayers, among businesses, and between these groups; economic efficiency, because the tax system alters the impact of inflation on interest rates, saving, and investment; and politics, because the choice between automatic and discretionary adjustments in tax laws may affect the size, rate of growth, and composition of public expenditures.

The authors of the chapters in this book address all these questions. In addition they examine some of the practical problems legislators must address if they index the tax system.[3] The essays are not comprehensive in their coverage, however, but focus on selected major issues. This introduction provides an overview of these issues and summarizes the conclusions of each of the authors. In some places the introduction raises matters and takes stands on issues not treated in the papers but discussed during the conference at which these papers were presented. A summary of the conference discussion follows most of the chapters.

The Problem

Inflation operates in three distinct ways to change economic decisions, real incomes, and tax liabilities. First, inflation directly alters economic decisions and before-tax incomes. It discourages households and businesses from holding assets in the form of cash or demand deposits and encourages them to hold other assets or to increase consumption.[4] These decisions in turn alter real interest rates, and this further affects savings and investment. Furthermore, the excessively rapid growth of the money supply necessary to fuel sus-

---

vyn A. King, eds., *Indexing for Inflation* (London: Heinemann Educational Books for the Institute for Fiscal Studies, 1975).

3. Throughout this book an "indexed tax system" will refer to one in which the impact of inflation on the real tax liabilities imposed on any real income are automatically removed by legislated formulas. "Real" tax liabilities and "real" income refer to income expressed in current units of purchasing power deflated by an appropriate price index.

4. The cost of holding cash and demand deposits is the difference between their rate of return (the loss of value due to inflation) and the rate of return on other assets (the rate of interest on financial assets or the change in price of real assets and of corporate equity, less the rate of inflation).

tained inflation often results from increases in government expenditures not matched by higher taxes. Through all these channels, inflation affects real incomes and would do so even if no taxes were imposed. But the way tax laws are written alters the size and nature of the changes in real income because tax liabilities may be affected by inflation, and taxes influence economic decisions.[5]

Second, inflation alters the tax base (1) by reducing the real value of deductions based on historical cost for depreciation and materials used in production, (2) by reducing the real burden (for debtors) and the value (for creditors) of debt repayment, and (3) by distorting the computation of capital gains.

Third, inflation alters the structure of income tax rates—the real width of tax brackets and the real value of all exemptions, credits, deductions, and allowances fixed in nominal terms.

The second and third effects of inflation on tax liabilities flow from the mundane fact that inflation reduces the real value of any dollar magnitude contained in private contracts or public laws. A 10 percent increase in prices with complete impartiality lowers by 10 percent the real values of a business loan, a congressional appropriation, a checking account, personal exemptions under the personal income tax, depreciation deductions based on historical cost that a business may claim in computing its profits or its tax liability, and the historical-cost basis used in computing capital gains.

In some cases markets adjust automatically for *anticipated* inflation. A private lender, for example, may require borrowers to pay more interest to compensate, at least in part, for the fact that he will be repaid in dollars of reduced value. In other cases adjustments can be made for inflation that has already occurred. Congress has repeatedly amended personal income tax laws to take account of the increased taxes caused by inflation so that today total federal tax liabilities are smaller than they would have been if tax laws had been left unchanged and no inflation had occurred.[6]

As recent history dramatically proves, however, not all inflation is

5. See Martin J. Bailey, "The Welfare Cost of Inflationary Finance," *Journal of Political Economy,* vol. 64 (April 1956), pp. 93–110; and Martin Feldstein, Jerry Green, and Eytan Sheshinski, "Inflation and Taxes in a Growing Economy with Debt and Equity Finance," Discussion Paper 481 (Harvard Institute of Economic Research, 1976).

6. See chapter 5.

anticipated, and in many cases no adjustments can be or are made to take account of it.[7] For example, the value of cash depreciates as prices rise; since interest is not paid on cash balances, and accordingly cannot be increased, holders cannot be compensated as a practical matter.

One could imagine a world in which all the effects of inflation were neutralized. In such a world all nominal quantities in laws or contracts would be adjusted automatically and frequently for changes in prices that had occurred since the preceding adjustment. When prices rose 10 percent, the borrower who previously owed $1,000 would owe $1,100; the congressional appropriation that had been $1 million would become $1.1 million; the personal exemption under the income tax that has been $750 would become $825; the bank account balance that had been $100 would become $110; each $10 bill would be exchanged for an $11 bill; and so on through all contracts and all laws. While such a world is conceivable, some have questioned its desirability, and in any case, it does not exist.[8]

Some parts of the economy are already adjusted automatically for inflation, that is, indexed. Some wage contracts contain cost-of-living escalators. The wage ceiling under the social security payroll tax is now automatically increased as wages rise. Social security benefits, civil service retirement pensions, and the wages of many federal employees are adjusted automatically by more than the increase in prices.[9] Ad valorem or proportional taxes are self-adjusting because they are defined as percentages rather than as nominal amounts.

The operational question now being debated is whether Congress should enact legislation that will permit, or require, the automatic adjustment of nominal dollar magnitudes in certain kinds of contracts and in certain laws. In particular, should the personal and corporation income tax liabilities be indexed? If so, how should it be done? It is important to recognize that this question will be resolved within an institutional framework that does not automatically revalue

7. On the distinction between anticipated and unanticipated inflation, see chapters 2, 10, and 11.

8. Milton Friedman, long an advocate of indexing the tax system, holds that only items that involve a "substantial time dimension" need to be indexed. See round table discussion in Eileen Shanahan, moderator, *Indexing and Inflation* (American Enterprise Institute for Public Policy Research, 1974), p. 14.

9. For a more complete enumeration of the aspects of the U.S. budget already subject to automatic adjustment, see chapter 10.

all private contracts and that modifies only some government expenditures and taxes. It is even more important to realize that indexing would undo only the second and third effects of inflation on tax liabilities. It would modify but not prevent the effects of inflation on disposable income.

An Inflation-Proof Tax System

All tax systems distort economic decisions. Indexing makes these distortions the same regardless of the rate of inflation. An inflation-free, or indexed, income tax system is one that imposes the same real tax burden on a particular amount of real before-tax income regardless of the rate of inflation. For given real before-tax income the real tax base and the rate structure must be unaffected by inflation. Whether indexing is desirable depends on whether in its absence inflation improves or worsens the particular set of distortions a tax system contains.[10] Indexing the tax system cannot eradicate, although it may offset, consequences of inflation not related directly to the tax system, such as the reduction in the demand for money and the consequent effects on interest rates, savings, and investment.

Inflation affects income tax liabilities in two distinct ways. First, inflation distorts the tax base—the measures of current-dollar business and personal income from which personal exemptions and deductions are subtracted and to which personal and corporate income tax rates are applied in order to compute tax liabilities. Second, inflation changes the rate structure, loosely defined to include the real value of all nominal quantities in the Internal Revenue Code, most notably personal exemptions and dollar-limited credits, the standard deduction, the low-income allowance, the refundable credit on earnings, and the size of the income brackets to which the personal income tax applies. It also lowers real profits exempt from the corporation surtax.[11]

In general the distorting effects of inflation on the tax base are important because they cause a taxpayer to pay a different amount of tax than he would pay on the same real income in a noninflationary world. Moreover, this distortion will vary among taxpayers. In contrast, the distorting effects of inflation on the rate structure are im-

10. For a discussion of this point, see chapter 11.
11. Other nominal quantities in the personal and corporation income taxes are listed in chapters 2 and 5.

portant principally because they change the relative tax liabilities of taxpayers who would be in different brackets in a noninflationary world.

Tax Base

Economists generally define income as the sum of consumption plus additions to real net worth (for individuals) or as the excess of receipts over costs, where costs include the replacement of capital consumed (for businesses). Some individuals receive both business income—in the form of dividends, profits, rents, interest, or capital gains—and earnings, in the form of salaries and wages.

Inflation negligibly distorts the measurement of earned income but creates serious problems in the measurement of business income. Business income is the residual after subtracting from receipts a variety of expenses. Since receipts and associated expenses may occur at widely separated times, the purchasing power of the dollars in which they are measured may differ widely. When inflation is occurring, earnings received at the beginning and end of the year also are denominated in dollars of different purchasing power and are not strictly comparable; but in most cases these effects are relatively small. Earnings paid evenly throughout the year are denominated *on the average* in midyear dollars. Unless some earners are paid mostly at the beginning of the year or mostly at the end, *relative* earnings will not be affected by inflation.

In principle, the definition of income just enunciated requires that all changes in real net worth be taxed as accrued. In fact, the Internal Revenue Code generally requires realization of gains or losses on capital assets before they become subject to tax, but permits (and generally requires) businesses to accrue receipts and expenses in measuring business net income. Whether this distinction should be preserved if adjustments are made for inflation (or if they are not) raises difficult questions, because inflation simultaneously affects current expenses and receipts and the value of capital assets.

Inflation-sensitive elements of income include (1) capital gains and losses and interest payments and (2) business deductions for depreciation and the cost of materials used.

CAPITAL GAINS AND LOSSES AND INTEREST PAYMENTS. The United States now taxes the difference between the selling price of an asset and the purchase price of the asset (or its value at acquisition), reduced by any depreciation that has been claimed for tax purposes.[12] All net gains from the sale of assets held less than six months and half the net gain on assets held more than six months are taxed; in addition some taxpayers face a minimum tax on the excluded half of capital gains on assets held more than six months. In no case, however, is the tax imposed before the asset is sold, and if the asset is donated to a charity or held until death, the gain is not taxed at all.

Part of capital gains may be due to a general increase in the price level. In fact, after adjusting for the change in prices, apparent gains may be revealed as actual losses.[13] What if anything should be done about the impact of inflation on the measurement of capital gains?

Certain recently proposed remedies should *not* be adopted. In chapter 4, Roger E. Brinner shows that proposals to reduce the fraction of capital gains included in taxable income as the holding period lengthens are ill-conceived if the objective is to adjust the tax system to reach only real gains. First, in a world of stable inflation the inclusion proportion should rise, not fall, in order to achieve this objective.[14] Second, and of greater practical significance, the rate of inflation is not stable, an awkward fact that rules out any simple adjustment formula. The variability of inflation also renders ineffective such other proposals to adjust capital gains equitably for inflation as an automatic increase of the basis (purchase price less depreciation) by 1 percent a year or by a fraction that varies with recent inflation.

12. This brief statement does not indicate the highly complex rules and numerous special cases concerning the taxation of capital gains. For a fuller description, see Joseph A. Pechman, *Federal Tax Policy* (rev. ed., Brookings Institution, 1971), especially pp. 96–99, 107–08, 138–39.

13. An investor who buys a bond for $800 and sells it for $1,000 five years later has a $200 apparent, or nominal, gain; but if prices have risen 50 percent, he has a real loss of $200 calculated in current prices at the time of sale, that is, $1,000 − (1.5) $800 = −$200.

14. Brinner presents formal proof in chapter 4. But a numerical example may make this counterintuitive finding plausible. If prices rise 10 percent a year and an asset purchased at a price of 1 appreciates in real terms by 10 percent a year, the nominal value increases 21 percent a year. The real gain in current prices—the difference between the current nominal value and the purchase price adjusted for inflation is 1.21 − 1.1, or 0.11. Just over half of the apparent gain is real and should be included in taxable income if realized. At the end of, say, three years, the nominal value is $1.21^3 = 1.772$, and the purchase price in current dollars is $1.1^3 = 1.331$. The real gain measured in current prices is therefore 0.441. Fifty-seven percent of the gain is real and should be included. For holding periods of ten and twenty years the proper inclusion fractions are 72 and 87 percent, respectively. The proper inclusion rate increases with the holding period.

Brinner then presents an administratively feasible method for adjusting capital gains so that only real gains are taxed. The method requires multiplication of the historical cost of the asset, less depreciation based on historical cost, by the ratio of the general price level at the time of sale to the price level at the time of purchase. There is no need to adjust depreciation claimed at different times for different amounts of inflation. Then the adjusted basis is subtracted from the selling price. The difference between the adjusted basis and the selling price is the properly taxable gain.[15]

The application of such an adjustment raises three difficult questions that can be perceived best with a numerical example. Suppose that an individual buys a new twenty-year $1,000 bond yielding 5 percent interest. The individual holds the bond two years and receives $50 in interest a year. During the first year, prices rise 10 percent and interest rates rise sufficiently to reduce the market value of the bond to $800. During the second year, prices rise an additional 10 percent and the market value of the bond remains $800. How should the individual be taxed? How should the firm issuing the bond be taxed?

At least three answers to these questions received some support at the conference. First, under strict realization accounting, the individual would report $50 in interest income each year. When he sold the bond after two years, he would realize a $410 capital loss in current dollars ($800 less the purchase price of $1,000 adjusted to $1,210 for the 21 percent increase in prices). The business would deduct $50 in interest each year until the bond matured (or was repurchased). At that time the firm would realize a capital gain equal to the difference between the $1,000 issuing price adjusted for inflation and the $1,000 actually repaid at maturity.[16]

The second approach involves partial accrual. The individual would report $50 in interest income as before, but he also would be allowed a deduction equal to the rate of inflation multiplied by the face value of the bond, or $100 in the numerical example. His net income from holding the bond would be $50 − $100, a $50 loss. Symmetrically, the firm issuing the bond would be entitled to deduct

15. This method is satisfactory if depreciation is based on historical cost. If depreciation is based on replacement cost, then more complex adjustments would be necessary.

16. For example, if inflation averaged 10 percent a year for 20 years, the gain would be $1,000 $(1.1)^{20}$ − $1,000 = $5,727.50.

$50 of interest expense, as before, but it would also be required to report as income the rate of inflation times the face value of the bond and would have a net income of $50 from the bond. It would have to make a similar adjustment each year prices rose. The additional item represents the change in the purchasing power of the face value of the bond during the year. If the bondholder sold the bond after two years, he would realize a loss of $200, the purchase price of $1,000 less the current market value of $800. From then through eventual repayment of the bond at $1,000, other holders of the bond would realize a net gain of $200. When the bond matured, the firm would realize no gain or loss. This approach is embodied in the exposure draft of proposed financial accounting standards of the Financial Accounting Standards Board.[17]

The third approach involves complete accrual. In addition to the adjustments made under partial accrual, it would require bondholders and bond issuers to report the change in the market value of bonds (and other assets) held in portfolios. In the numerical example, the bondholder after the first year would report a loss of $200 due to the decline in the market value of the bond, in addition to the $100 loss due to inflation and the $50 of interest income. The firm would report an equivalent gain. The justification of this adjustment is that the firm could repurchase its outstanding debt, and the difference between face and market value would be taxable.[18]

No consensus emerged on which of these three approaches is preferable, but there was a strong consensus that whichever course might be chosen, symmetrical adjustment of business and personal taxes would be essential. During inflation the real value of all assets denominated in fixed terms declines. Such assets include bonds, debentures, notes, mortgages, bank deposits, and cash. The decline in value of all private debt symmetrically affects private borrowers and lenders. Whatever lenders lose, borrowers gain. If inflation adjust-

17. Financial Accounting Standards Board, *Financial Reporting in Units of General Purchasing Power,* Proposed Statement of Financial Accounting Standards, Exposure Draft (Stamford, Conn.: FASB, December 31, 1974), p. 8. The FASB subsequently decided not to issue guidelines embodying these proposals. See also chapters 2 and 3 of this volume.

18. See John B. Shoven and Jeremy I. Bulow, "Inflation Accounting and Nonfinancial Corporate Profits: Financial Assets and Liabilities," *Brookings Papers on Economic Activity, 1:1976,* pp. 15–57.

ments are made for losses suffered by lenders, they should also be made for inflation gains enjoyed by borrowers.

A central requirement for deciding what form of inflation adjustment, if any, should be made in the computation of capital gains is the choice of the form of taxation that would be considered ideal in a world of stable prices. Those who believe that the present treatment of capital gains (50 percent exclusion on long-term gains held until death) is excessively generous would favor adjustments to remove inflation gains only if one or more of the existing concessions is removed. By contrast, those who feel that capital gains should be taxed less than now (either as an investment incentive or because the proper definition of income would exclude capital gains entirely) would favor adjustment for inflation, even if no other changes are made.

DEPRECIATION. Businesses deduct the cost of goods or services sold from gross revenues to calculate net income. Some advocates of inflation adjustment hold that correct measurement of net income requires that all receipts and expenses must be recorded in dollars of the same purchasing power. If all costs are calculated in dollars with midyear purchasing power, adjustment of wage payments for inflation is unnecessary unless the period of production is lengthy. Wages and salaries are paid and revenues are received in dollars of approximately the same period.[19] The costs of materials used and of depreciation on assets pose more serious problems if all items are adjusted for inflation. Under current law, businesses may deduct a portion of the original cost of most durable assets, based on the estimated life of such assets. Given these lives, a few standard formulas ordinarily are used to apportion the deductions across time.

This procedure is subject to criticism even if the average of all prices is stable but becomes progressively more deficient the higher the rate of inflation. At least three alternative procedures might be employed if the aggregate price level is stable but relative prices change. First, the Samuelson method would require businesses to deduct the actual change in market value of depreciable assets in calculating the cost of goods sold.[20] Any appreciation of a certain kind

---

19. Alternatively, all costs and receipts may be expressed in end-of-year dollars. In that case, wages and salaries must be multiplied by $(1 + \pi)^{1/2}$, where π is the annual inflation rate. See chapter 3.

20. See Paul A. Samuelson, "Tax Deductibility of Economic Depreciation to Insure Invariant Valuations," *Journal of Political Economy*, vol. 72 (December 1964),

of asset relative to the general price level would be offset against the decline in the value due to aging and obsolescence. This procedure is equivalent to taxing accrued capital gains as ordinary income. For example, assume that average prices are stable and that widgits last five years and lose one-fifth of their original value during the first year. If in 1975 new widgits cost 100 and the depreciated value of one-year-old widgits is 80, while in 1976 new widgits cost 120 and the depreciated value of one-year-old widgits is 96, the Samuelson rule would permit the owner to take 4 in depreciation, the difference between the purchase price in 1975 and the value of one-year-old widgits in 1976. In effect, the owner is required to deduct 20 in depreciation and report a gain of 16 on his one-year-old widgits. A second approach would allow depreciation based on replacement cost. In the example above, the firm would be allowed to deduct 24, because based on a replacement cost of 120, widgits lose one-fifth of their value in becoming a year old.

In contrast to both of these approaches, current law permits firms to deduct 20 (assuming widgits are valueless after five years and that firms use straight-line depreciation) or more (if they adopt one of various accelerated depreciation rules that permit larger deductions in earlier years and smaller ones in later years).

Assume now that all prices, including those of widgits, rise 10 percent during the year in question so that in 1976 new widgits cost 132 and the depreciated value of one-year-old widgits is 105.6. The Samuelson rule would permit depreciation of 4.4 and the replacement-cost approach would allow 26.4, the same amounts as before, adjusted for the 10 percent rise in prices. Several conference participants suggested instead that depreciation be based on "inflated historical cost"—that is, a historical cost of 20 inflated to 22 because of the 10 percent rise in prices. Current law allows no explicit adjustment. But provisions that permit accelerated (that is, faster than straight-line) depreciation, and recent amendments to the Internal Revenue Code shortening depreciable lives and abandoning the reserve ratio test,[21] are frequently defended on the ground that inflation erodes the value of straight-line depreciation on historical cost and causes taxes to be excessively high.

---

pp. 604–06. This rule guarantees that depreciation under an income tax will not change the ranking of investments according to rates of return.

21. The reserve ratio test was a device to assure that depreciable lives used for computing taxes were not materially shorter than actual depreciable lives.

In chapter 10, Edward M. Gramlich shows that accelerated depreciation based on historical cost is worth about as much to firms as straight-line depreciation based on replacement cost when prices rise about 5 percent a year.[22] Thus explicit recognition of inflation through the adjustment of historical cost by the change in aggregate prices would be an alternative to the various forms of accelerated depreciation, shortened depreciable lives, and disregard of the relation between tax depreciation and actual depreciation. In the preceding numerical example, adjusted historical-cost depreciation would permit firms owning widgits to deduct 22, one-fifth of the historical cost of 100 raised by the 10 percent change in the price level.

The problem of what to do about depreciation deductions thus consists of three parts: (1) whether depreciation should be based on historical costs or whether historical costs should be adjusted for changes in the general price level; (2) whether depreciation should take account of changes in relative prices; and (3) whether accrued capital gains and losses from changes in relative prices should be included in depreciation (as they are in the Samuelson rule) or ignored (as they are when replacement cost or inflated historical cost is used).

Many conference participants who favored replacement-cost depreciation as an ultimate goal felt that a jump in historical-cost depreciation by the percentage change in the average price level since the depreciable asset was acquired was a desirable initial step.

MATERIALS USED. Measuring the cost of materials used in production during inflation poses problems similar to those concerning depreciation. If explicit adjustment for inflation is made, how should inventories be handled? In particular, should general inflation be ignored or taken into account, and how should the change in relative prices be handled?

At present most firms use one or both of two methods of computing the cost of materials used. Under first-in-first-out (FIFO) accounting, materials are valued at the price first paid for similar items then in stock. Under last-in-first-out accounting (LIFO), materials are valued at the price last paid for similar items then in stock. As recently as 1973 a survey found that FIFO was used by more than two times

22. See also chapter 2 for more detailed calculations of the impact of inflation on required rates of return on alternative investments under conventional accounting and inflation adjustment.

as many surveyed firms as used LIFO, and the fraction was rising, despite the fact that a shift to LIFO would have reduced taxes for nearly all firms.[23] But many firms abruptly shifted to LIFO in 1974 in the face of the sharply higher rates of inflation.

The two accounting conventions embody different views of the impact of inflation on the value of the firm and of the time and circumstances under which gains or losses due to changes in the relative prices are realized. FIFO accounting treats the change in the price of materials between purchase and use as a realized gain and an element of business profit subject to tax in the same way historical-cost depreciation does.[24] If the average price level is stable, FIFO accounting treats as profit (or loss) any increase (or decrease) in the price of the firm's inventory relative to the general price level. In effect, the change in the liquidation value of the firm is made subject to tax. By contrast, LIFO accounting treats any change in the value of inventories as unrealized and not subject to tax so long as the holdings of each category of inventory do not decrease. In this case replacement cost is used for measuring the value of materials used. If inventories decline, however, the cost of materials used is computed on the basis of earlier and lower prices, leading to the realization of deferred gains similar to and possibly larger than under FIFO.[25] So long as inventories of each item are maintained, any change in the liquidation value of the firm due to increases or decreases in the relative value of its inventories is ignored. If inventories are maintained, LIFO functions very much like replacement-cost depreciation in its domain. The two approaches would be strictly parallel if materials used were valued at current prices whether or not inventories actually declined—"strict LIFO." Ordinary LIFO is indistinguishable from strict LIFO if inventories are not depleted.

23. Survey reported by Robert G. Skinner in "Capital Recovery and Inflation," *Tax Revision in an Inflationary Era,* Proceedings of Tax Foundation's 26th National Conference (Tax Foundation, 1975), p. 23. Many of the firms surveyed used other accounting methods, including valuation of materials according to actual invoices, but this method generally is impractical for large firms.

24. For example, if materials purchased at 100 are now valued at 150 and if prices reflect that current products are priced on the basis of the present cost of materials, profits are 50 higher than they would be if materials were valued at replacement cost.

25. Consider a firm whose inventories turn over annually but have not decreased for thirty years. If the firm now dips into inventories, LIFO accounting will value materials used at prices prevailing thirty years ago, generating large book profits. By contrast, the FIFO firm will have been allowed to deduct the costs of materials used based on prices that were at most a year out of date.

Thus LIFO accounting automatically adjusts the costs of materials used for inflation unless inventories decline, and strict LIFO would do so regardless of the change in inventories. A third possible approach to indexing materials costs would start from FIFO accounting but would adjust historical cost by the *average* change in all prices since the item entered the inventory. Such "current-price-FIFO" accounting (like inflated historical-cost depreciation) would inflate historical costs to dollars of the current year and would save the firm from the large tax liabilities generated under FIFO (or by historical-cost depreciation) by wholly fictitious "gains" from inflation. Unlike LIFO or strict LIFO, it would not insulate the firm from the tax consequences of appreciation or depreciation in the value of its inventory *relative* to the general price level. Such changes in relative prices would be regarded as realized gains subject to taxation as ordinary income (unlike capital gains that are subject to lower rates).[26]

Only current-price FIFO and strict LIFO represent full adjustments for inflation. The former subjects to tax any gain or loss in the liquidation value of the firm due to changes in relative prices. The latter is appropriate if the firm is assumed to remain in the same activities forever, using the same inventories to produce final output. Neither rule is entirely appropriate. Firms rarely liquidate, but output mixes and technology change. Both, however, protect firms against taxation of illusory inflation gains.

RELATION AMONG ADJUSTMENTS. The various adjustments are clearly related to one another. For example, if a firm has borrowed to finance machinery, a rise in prices under current law will generate an offsetting gain and loss. The gain is the decline in the real value of outstanding debt; it equals the nominal value of outstanding debt multiplied by the rate of inflation. The loss is the decline in the real value of depreciation that can be claimed for tax purposes; it equals the value of the machinery times the rate of inflation. If the debt matures at the same rate as the machinery depreciates, the loss and the gain exactly offset one another.[27] Because of these interactions, care is necessary to ensure that tax burdens will be the same after adjustments for inflation have been made as they would be in a noninflationary world *for given real transactions*.

26. For a proposal along these lines, see William Fellner, Kenneth W. Clarkson, and John H. Moore, *Correcting Taxes for Inflation* (American Enterprise Institute for Public Policy Research, 1975).

27. See Arthur Okun's comments, chapter 11. If inflation changes the interest rate at which the firm can borrow, then the loss and gain will not equal one another.

Table 1-1. **Alternative Methods of Adjusting for Inflation**

	Adjustment	
Item	Changes in *relative prices ignored*	Adjustments made for changes in *relative prices*
Capital gains	Inflate acquisition cost (for creditor) or sale proceeds (for debtor)[a]	
Inventories	Use inflated FIFO accounting	Use strict LIFO accounting
Depreciation	Use inflated historical-cost method	Use replacement-cost method

a. Adjustment may be made annually (semi-accrual) or when either asset is sold or liability is liquidated (realization). Changes in the nominal market value of assets may also be recognized (complete accrual).

This objective can be approximated with either of two sets of adjustments (see table 1-1 and the appendix at the end of this chapter). The same objective can be achieved roughly if no adjustment is made for net debt and for depreciation on an equal amount of depreciable capital. Except for the difference between the rate at which capital depreciates and debt matures, this omission will be offsetting.[28]

THE INDEX. The correct measurement of capital gains, depreciation, and the cost of materials used during inflationary periods, and possibly during periods of stable prices as well, cannot depend on historical costs. As a practical matter advocates of indexing must decide by what price index to multiply historical values in order to reach current market value. Even those who favor replacement-cost depreciation must face this issue because exact replicas of machines or buildings produced several years ago may no longer exist. Should the same index be used for adjusting all categories of accounts—depreciation, capital gains, and cost of materials? If not, should the same or different indexes be used within categories—for example, should the same index be used for correcting all capital gains (or all depreciation)? This choice entails issues of policy and of administrative cost and feasibility.

The case of depreciation illustrates these problems. Two extreme approaches are possible. The simpler would update historical costs by an aggregate price index. But which? The GNP deflator? A na-

28. This procedure is equivalent to basing depreciation on the Samuelson rule for assets equal in value to the net debt of the firm and eliminating the debt adjustment. (See appendix.)

tional income or net national product index? The consumer price index? An index of prices of reproducible investment goods? A more complex alternative would increase the historical costs of each depreciable asset according to an index specific to it or to a narrow category of goods. This approach would approximate depreciation by replacement cost. Other alternatives lie between these extremes; for example, two indexes might be used, one for structures, one for machinery.

The use of a single economy-wide index ignores any change in the price of reproducible investments relative to other prices. Should the price of reproducible investments rise (fall) relative to other prices, this gain (loss) would be taxed as ordinary income (loss) at the applicable rate of tax. The use of a price index based only on depreciable products would prevent this result but would ignore changes in the relative price of different business assets unless the firm liquidated. Any small number of indexes would inevitably ignore changes in the relative replacement costs of various assets, however.

A similar set of considerations arises with respect to capital gains. In this case the use of separate price indexes for each kind of asset, if carried to the extreme, would define capital gains out of existence. While such a procedure is absurd if capital gains are to be taxed at all, the question of what index or indexes should be used to revalue the depreciated bases of assets remains. There seems to be no plausible justification for defining away any part of the capital gains of individuals by using two or more partial indexes. Whether a variety of indexes should be used for adjusting capital gains of businesses is less clear, however, particularly if one feels that the cost of materials used should be measured by LIFO (or strict LIFO) and depreciation should be based on replacement costs, because following these procedures is equivalent to using a separate price index for each inventory category and depreciable asset.

EFFECT ON REVENUE OF INDEXING THE TAX BASE. Indexing the tax base will reduce the amount of tax collected in the aggregate, but many firms would pay more in taxes for many years. No comprehensive estimate exists of the impact of indexing the tax base on Treasury revenues.

Adjustments to the tax base fall into two broad categories: those that depend only on inflation during the current year but are independent of inflation in previous years, and those that depend on inflation both in the current and in preceding years. The first category includes only the accrual adjustment for gains (losses) from the decline in the real value of net debt (credit) position in fixed nominal values assets. These adjustments depend only on the change in prices during the current year and terminate as soon as price stability is achieved. The second category includes all other capital gains (including those on net debt if the realization method is used) and materials used (if some form of FIFO accounting is used). These adjustments depend on the change in the price level since the asset was acquired.[29]

When inflation commences, adjustments in the first category rise abruptly, but those in the second category are small. As time passes, adjustments of the second type grow in importance and continue to be necessary even after inflation has ceased. The greater the proportion of a firm's capital financed by borrowing, the more durable the firm's capital stock is; and the higher the ratio of the firm's capital stock to its annual receipts, the more pronounced these effects are.

In the aggregate, indexing the tax base will reduce Treasury revenues. The adjustment for the declining real value of privately issued debt will change the taxable income of debtors and creditors by offsetting amounts. Revenues will change to the extent that the average tax rate on the income of creditors differs from that on the income of debtors. The adjustment for the declining value of debt issued by governments or foreigners held by U.S. taxpayers will unambiguously reduce taxes. Similarly, any increase in depreciation or materials costs allowed in calculating income will reduce income subject to tax.

The impact of indexing on tax liabilities differs dramatically across firms and through time. According to Sidney Davidson and Roman L. Weil, the overall impact on the 1974 taxable income of fifty-four corporations—the thirty Dow Jones industrials and twenty-four utilities listed in the Dow and Standard & Poor's averages—would have been quite varied.[30] They apply the system of indexing put forward by the Financial Accounting Standards Board that ignores changes in relative prices in the accounting for depreciation, debt, and capital gains but permits firms to use LIFO accounting. Among the thirty industrial firms, taxable incomes would have risen for nine firms and

29. See chapters 2 and 3.
30. See chapter 3.

fallen for twenty-one if all inflation adjustments had been made. The total taxable income of the group would have risen a small amount, largely because of a massive increase in the profits of AT&T. The taxable profits of most firms would have been increased by adjustments for the decline in the real value of net debt.[31] Whether a firm gains or loses overall depends on the ratio of debt to equity finance, the age structure of the firm's capital stock, and the methods of inventory accounting used.[32]

Among utilities full inflation adjustment would clearly have increased net income in 1974. Utilities finance a much larger proportion of their total investment from bonds (which would be subject to inflation adjustment) than do industrial firms that rely more heavily on stock (which would not be subject to inflation adjustment). Among the twenty-four utilities, net income would have been increased for all by inflation adjustment; net income would have at least doubled for seventeen.[33]

Davidson and Weil show the impact on taxes in a single year when the tax base is indexed after a history of inflation. T. Nicolaus Tideman and Donald P. Tucker present complementary estimates that show the difference in taxes between the current tax system and an indexed system from a single burst of inflation and from sustained inflation.[34] They show both the first-year and long-term effects of a single 10 percent burst of inflation. If a sudden 10 percent burst of inflation occurred after protracted price stability, all industry groups but one would pay more taxes in the year the inflation occurred if the tax base were indexed than they would pay under prevailing law, but

31. Davidson and Weil adjust net liabilities on an accrual basis. The results would be quite different if such adjustments were made on a realization basis. In that case no adjustments would occur until debts were paid off, at which time the full adjustment would be recorded. For an argument that such gains and losses should be subject to tax as accrued, see chapter 2.

32. Among the thirty industrial firms, the big gainers and losers as shown by profits without adjustment and with adjustment (in parentheses) are AT&T, $2.5 billion ($4.6 billion); Du Pont, $483 million ($254 million); General Motors, $1.1 billion ($254 million); Sears Roebuck, $421 million ($116 million). See chapter 3, table 3-5.

33. For estimates of the impact of inflation adjustment in 1973, see Sidney Davidson and Roman L. Weil, "Inflation Accounting: What Will General Price Level Adjusted Income Statements Show?" *Financial Analysts Journal,* vol. 31 (January-February 1975), pp. 27–31, 70–84; and Davidson and Weil, "Inflation Accounting: Public Utilities," ibid., vol. 31 (May-June 1975), pp. 30–34, 62.

34. See chapter 2, tables 2-2 through 2-5.

in the long run all industry groups but one would pay less taxes than they would pay under current law.[35] The effects are large. The first-year increase in taxes under an indexed system would exceed 1 percent of gross assets in seven industry groups, reaching 2.2 percent for electric and gas utilities. Over the long run, the cumulative reduction in taxes from indexing is sufficient to wipe out the first-year increase and further reduce taxes by amounts that average 0.5 percent of total assets for all firms. Measured against 1972 tax liabilities the effect of indexing is even more dramatic. In the first year the taxes of railroads and airlines would have nearly quintupled; those of electric and gas utilities would have nearly tripled, and those of communications would have more than doubled. In the long run, the taxes of railroads would turn negative, indicating that inflation adjustment would convert apparent profits into losses, and the taxes of all firms would decline about 18 percent.

The impact on tax revenues from indexing if 10 percent inflation were sustained is even more dramatic. Taxes would be 25 percent lower than under current law, and railroads would record losses instead of profits. Nevertheless, roughly 26 percent of all firms would pay more taxes if the tax base were indexed than they would under current law if 10 percent inflation persisted.

In interpreting those results two qualifications must be kept in mind. First, real operations of each industry vary from year to year. These estimates assume that the operations carried out in 1972 would be carried out forever. Second, indexing would almost certainly change the capital structure of firms and affect interest rates. For those reasons, the empirical results of chapters 2 and 3 must be regarded as rough approximations rather than as exact estimates of the effects of indexing the tax base on corporation tax liabilities.

Despite these qualifications, it is clear that if the corporation income tax were adjusted for inflation, some firms would gain and some would lose as inflation begins. If inflation continued but did not accelerate, indexing would reduce tax liabilities for most firms below those under current law. If inflation decelerated or stopped, then all firms would gain; the cessation of inflation would terminate the adjustment for debt items, but increased depreciation allowances would

35. The one gainer in the first year is the finance, insurance, and real estate group; the one loser in the long run is services.

persist until all depreciable assets purchased during the inflation had been replaced.

Whether indexing the tax base would raise or lower total individual income taxes is unclear. There can be little doubt, however, that indexing the tax base would redistribute tax burdens. The most important adjustment for most households would be the tax treatment of home mortgages. As with all other fixed debts, inflation reduces the real value of home mortgages, a gain to homeowners, a loss to mortgage lenders. A decision would have to be made whether (1) to tax this gain on an accrual basis, perhaps by reducing the allowable mortgage interest deduction by the rate of inflation times the mortgage balance; (2) to tax this gain upon realization, where realization is deemed to occur as the mortgage is paid off; or (3) to tax the gain upon realization, where realization is deemed to occur only when the house is sold. The first approach would significantly and immediately increase taxes on homeowners. The second approach would increase taxes on new homeowners negligibly at first because only a small part of mortgage principal is repaid in early years, but the increase in taxes would grow and in later years would exceed that of accrual adjustment. The third approach would defer the tax increase still longer; if the gain on the mortgage were regarded as a reduction in the basis of the house and taxed as are other capital gains on owner-occupied houses, the tax increase might be negligible.[36]

A second set of adjustments would be made for financial assets—bonds and savings accounts. The value of these assets is eroded and this loss should be deducted from income if the tax base is indexed. These adjustments would be of benefit primarily to upper-income households, in contrast to those related to mortgages that would affect homeowners in all brackets. In combination, adjustment of the individual income tax base seems likely to shift tax burdens from upper-income households to middle- and lower-income homeowners. The redistribution among income brackets can be offset by changes in bracket rates. The result would then be a shift in tax burdens from renters to homeowners and from savers to nonsavers.

Rate Structure

Once income has been measured, taxable income and actual tax liabilities are calculated by applying a structure of rates, exemptions,

36. For a discussion of these issues, see chapter 4.

credits, allowances, and deductions. Many of these provisions are expressed in fixed nominal amounts. For example, married couples pay 14 percent of the first $1,000 of taxable income in tax; the personal exemption is $750; the per capita credit is $30; corporations pay 20 percent on the first $25,000 of profits, and 22 percent on the second $25,000; the low-income allowance is $1,900 and the maximum standard deduction is $2,600.[37] The real value of those and other quantities is reduced when prices rise. Through this channel inflation unambiguously increases income tax liabilities on both individuals and corporations. When prices rise, say, 20 percent, the real value of $750 exemptions, $30 credits, and all other provisions expressed in nominal amounts declines 20 percent. If, at the same time, corporate and individual incomes increase by 20 percent and thus remain unchanged in real terms, effective tax rates increase because the rate structures are progressive.

The increase in real income tax collections on individuals due to inflation may be sizable. A 10 percent inflation will increase real tax liabilities roughly by 1 to 2 percent of after-tax income.[38] The effect is largest on those with incomes of $50,000 to $250,000 and smallest on those with incomes of $12,000 to $25,000, based on 1975 rates. By contrast, the impact on corporations, except for the very smallest, is negligible because most corporate profits are subject to proportional taxation at 48 percent, the rate applicable to profits above $50,000 a year.

If Congress had not modified income tax laws, then the combination of inflation and growth would have increased personal income tax collections from 10.7 to 16.2 percent of adjusted personal income between 1960 and 1975.[39] Real growth alone would have increased revenues from 10.7 percent to 12.2 percent of adjusted personal income. In fact, personal income taxes rose from 10.7 to 11.3 percent of adjusted personal income between 1960 and 1975, indicating that tax changes enacted periodically by Congress counteracted not only the increase in revenues generated by inflation but also part of that caused by economic growth.

37. For a complete list of provisions in nominal dollars under the individual income tax, see chapter 5.

38. See ibid.

39. See ibid., table 5-3. Also see George M. von Furstenberg, "Individual Income Taxation and Inflation," *National Tax Journal,* vol. 28 (March 1975), pp. 117–25.

The practical question is whether these adjustments should be made automatically by formula or periodically by Congress.

TECHNICAL PROBLEMS: THE FORMULA. All nominal quantities in the tax law would be inflated by the change in prices; tax liabilities then could be calculated directly. If prices have doubled, for example, the bracket widths, exemptions, standard and minimum standard deductions, and other nominal quantities would be doubled.[40]

Two other approaches that seem effective in removing the effects of inflation actually do not do so. As Vito Tanzi shows in chapter 8, both an equiproportional reduction in tax rates and the exclusion from taxation of increases in earnings due to inflation fail to remove equitably the effects of inflation on tax liabilities.

TECHNICAL PROBLEMS: THE INDEX. What price index or indexes should be used to adjust the bracket widths and other nominal quantities in the tax system? The answer depends on the objectives sought. If the goal is to enable an individual whose income has risen as much as consumer prices to buy the same bundle of current consumption goods or to meet the same consumption standards as before, then the proper index to use would be a consumer price or cost-of-living index. If the objective is to hold the ratio of taxes to national income the same regardless of the price level, then a broader index based on national income or net national product, along the lines advocated in chapter 9 by Edward F. Denison, is indicated. The latter approach is also consistent with the rationale that a proper adjustment for inflation should take account of the option to save as well as to consume; this can be done, as a practical matter, by incorporating the price of investment goods into the index. Denison argues that it is not legitimate to use any index related to gross national product; such an index would overweight investment goods because it would include investments that replace depreciation, an item not included in taxable income. Denison also considers the use of separate indexes

40. Under an alternative procedure the bracket widths are left unchanged, all income items are deflated from current dollars to dollars of the year for which the tax law was designed, tax liabilities are calculated, and then the amount of tax due is inflated to current year prices. For example, if prices have doubled since the tax law became effective, all income items, deductions, and so on would be cut in half; tax liability would be computed and then doubled to restore quantities to current year prices. This approach yields the same results, but the one described in the text is far easier for taxpayers since the Treasury carries out the extra computations; under the first, the taxpayer must do the calculations himself. See comments by Alan Blinder, chapter 9.

for different classes of taxpayers both impractical and undesirable. He finds the question of whether indirect taxes should be included in the price index to be of negligible practical importance for the United States, a position that contrasts with the attention lavished on this question in other countries.[41]

An alternative to all of the above would be to use an index of per capita national income, per capita earnings, or some other measure that comprehends both inflation and the growth of real per capita income. Such an index would hold constant both real per capita income tax collections and the ratio of taxes to real income regardless of inflation or economic growth and therefore would not be indexing in the usual sense. This form of automatic nominal adjustment recently became law in Denmark, the first and only country to have adopted it. Since 1960 U.S. tax collections have differed negligibly from those that would have been yielded by a system indexed by per capita income.

What Should Be Done?

As Denison observes, "A government's decision to eliminate either of the two types of inflation effect is logically independent of its decision with respect to the other. It may choose to index the tax system so as to tax income expressed in the prices of some former year instead of in current prices, however the latter may be measured [rate structure adjustment]; to eliminate distortions in the measurement of income in current prices [tax base definition adjustment]; to do neither of these things; or to do both of them."[42] In fact, some nations have followed each of these courses, although none has comprehensively corrected the definition of income.[43] Not only are the two forms of adjustment logically independent, they also raise quite different technical and political issues.

41. See chapter 8. See also Organisation for Economic Co-operation and Development, *The Adjustment of Personal Income Tax Systems for Inflation* (Paris: OECD, 1976), p. 29.
42. See chapter 9, p. 235.
43. See chapters 7 and 8. See also OECD, *The Adjustment of Personal Income Tax Systems for Inflation;* and Sheila A. B. Page, "International Experience of Indexing," in Liesner and King, eds., *Indexing for Inflation*, pp. 97–109.

Tax Base

Anticipated inflation increases interest rates and affects savings and investment, although the nature of the effect is unclear.[44] When inflation is unanticipated, borrowers enjoy gains and lenders suffer losses; whether inflation is anticipated or not, owners of depreciable assets suffer losses. The result of unanticipated inflation led Robert J. Gordon to state that "the basic argument in favor of indexing is simply fair play."[45] These losses and gains refer to a comparison between a world with inflation and one with stable prices *under the same set of tax laws*. But some existing provisions were enacted or are retained, at least in part, to offset the effects of inflation and would be harder to defend if prices were stable; such provisions include accelerated depreciation, the investment tax credit, and the exclusion of half of long-term capital gains. Furthermore, as Edward Gramlich and Martin J. Bailey stress in chapters 10 and 11, the tax system does not fall neutrally on all income and would not do so if prices were stable. They also point out that anticipated inflation may alter the incentives and distortions of the tax system, but by definition it springs no surprises on borrowers or lenders. For this reason the reestablishment of fair play is *not* an argument for offsetting the effects of anticipated inflation. Indeed the contrary is true. If taxpayers based all their investment decisions on correctly anticipated inflation and the current tax law, the unexpected indexing of the tax base would violate fair play. In deciding whether to adjust the tax base for inflation, one must consider whether the distortions of inflation offset or aggravate the distortions that the tax system imposes in an inflation-free world and whether taxpayers have adjusted to prevailing rates of inflation.

While recent U.S. history has led most people to worry about the effects of the onset of unanticipated inflation, the possibility that inflation may subside equally unexpectedly should be kept in mind. Should the rate of inflation decline below expected levels, borrowers will lose and lenders will gain. The losses suffered by owners of depreciable assets will be increased dramatically to the extent that they borrowed to buy those assets. On balance, whether to adjust the tax base for inflation hinges on the weight attached to two sets of factors.

44. See chapter 11. See also Feldstein, Green, and Sheshinski, "Inflation and Taxes in a Growing Economy with Debt and Equity."

45. Round table discussion in Shanahan, *Indexing and Inflation*, pp. 4–5.

First, how damaging is the added uncertainty about after-tax rates of return generated by a tax system that ignores inflation? How important are changes in real saving and investment decisions, the qualitative nature of which are unclear? And what is the impact on the sense of tax justice when the tax system focuses on nominal rates of return although real rates of return are changing. The second set of factors concerns the distributional fairness of letting inflation increase the rate of taxation on capital incomes relative to earnings. If a decision is made explicitly to adjust the tax base for inflation, it seems desirable to reexamine whether income from capital is properly taxed when prices are stable.

Rate Structure Adjustment

Whether nominal quantities in the tax code should be indexed raises one economic issue—the impact of indexing on economic stability—and a host of political issues.

The long-held view that a tax system in which nominal quantities are *not* indexed promotes economic stability has been shown to be incomplete. While such a tax system may help curtail inflation triggered by excessive domestic demand, it may aggravate unemployment when inflation is due in part to such external events as the United States has experienced in recent years. Furthermore, John Bossons and Thomas A. Wilson have shown that inflation-caused rises in revenues may occur only after the rate of inflation has slowed, but unemployment is on the rise.[46] Using the Social Science Research Council-MIT-Penn (SMP) model, James L. Pierce and Jared J. Enzler report simulations in chapter 6 that suggest that automatic adjustment of the rate structure and partial correction of the tax base (by removing inflation-caused capital gains) will have little effect on the overall stability of the U.S. economy.

All other considerations concerning the desirability of nominal adjustment for inflation are political.[47] Congress, in fact, has offset the growth in tax revenues from inflation by periodic amendments to the tax code; there is no reason why such adjustments could not be made in the future. The most rapidly increasing federal expenditure, social security, is financed by a tax that did not keep pace with infla-

46. John Bossons and Thomas A. Wilson, "Adjusting Tax Rates for Inflation," *Canadian Tax Journal*, vol. 21 (May-June 1973), pp. 185–99.
47. These issues are treated at length in chapters 10 and 11.

tion until the Social Security Act was amended in 1973, and even now increases in the social security tax rate require discretionary action by Congress. Based on this record, as Bailey observes in chapter 11, it is difficult to take seriously the contention that inflation-caused growth in revenues will tend to increase the size of the federal government.

During inflation Congress now must act periodically to offset the effects of rising prices, not only on taxes, but also on expenditures. The central issue, as Gramlich points out, is whether such periodic reexamination results in better or worse tax and expenditure policy than would result if automatic adjustment freed Congress from the need to reexamine these programs. A case can be made either way. On the one hand, each tax bill has further complicated the tax code, a point stressed by Bailey. On the other hand, Congress has elected to distribute tax reductions differently from the patterns automatic adjustments for inflation would have generated, a fact that suggests national priorities have shifted. Furthermore, annual or biennial re-examination of tax rates would give Congress increased flexibility in setting fiscal policy.

A second political issue, long debated but unresolved, concerns the impact of adjusting the rate structure on the government's resolve to refrain from policies that increase inflation and to undertake policies that will curtail it. According to one view, adjusting the rate structure by protecting individuals from higher taxes during inflation will weaken their resolve and that of their democratically elected representatives to resist inflation. Another issue centers on the fact that governments can increase tax collections by expanding the money supply excessively, thereby causing inflation and avoiding the political chore of increasing tax rates. Would indexing that prevents such an increase in taxes reduce or increase the propensity of governments to countenance monetary expansion that makes sustained inflation possible?[48]

Conclusion

In general the case for adjusting the tax system rests heavily on the anticipated course of inflation. If inflation is expected to abate and return to rates experienced during the 1950s and early 1960s, the

48. See the debate between Milton Friedman and William Fellner in Shanahan, *Indexing and Inflation*, pp. 2–26.

issues concern who should bear the gains and losses caused by the price rises of the past few years. The higher the expected future rate of inflation and the greater the anticipated fluctuations in that rate, the stronger the case for adjusting the tax base becomes, particularly if other provisions introduced or retained partly to offset the effects of inflation are reexamined. The case for adjusting the rate structure automatically at any expected rate of inflation seems far weaker, more dependent on political judgments, and less dependent on the volatility of the inflation rate than does the case for indexing the tax base.

The relative importance of the two kinds of indexing was discussed extensively at the conference. No participant attached much intrinsic importance to indexing the rate structure. Some felt that it would advance acceptance of indexing the tax base; some that it would retard it. All conference participants felt that indexing the tax base was a major change in the tax structure. They also agreed that it would be desirable at sufficiently high rates of inflation but could not agree whether it was desirable at existing or expected future rates of inflation. They also could not agree whether indexing the rate structure, though less important, was desirable at any rate of inflation.

A major issue, raised at the conference but not resolved, concerned the framework within which the debate over indexing the tax base should take place. Should this debate include a reconsideration of other aspects of the tax code, particularly those relating to income from capital? According to one view, indexing should guarantee that tax provisions are not capriciously changed by inflation. The Internal Revenue Code, for better or worse, is the democratic outcome of the pulling and tugging of various interests. While particular provisions may be contrary to some person's preferences and may not accord with an economist's definition of income, it is this system that the political process has produced and which should (or should not) be defended against the consequences of inflation. According to another view, there is no reason why the particular distortions caused by inflation should rank ahead of other distortions on the tax reformer's agenda. To do so is to put form before substance. One version of this argument stresses that inflation vaguely resembles a wealth tax at a rate equal to the product of the rate of inflation and the taxpayer's marginal tax rate.[49] For those who feel that income from capital is too

49. The resemblance would be precise if accrued capital gains were taxed and all capital gains were taxed at ordinary income rates. In that case k percent of the

lightly taxed because of various loopholes, this inflation tax improves the distribution of tax burdens and may improve economic efficiency. According to this view, indexing the tax base might be unacceptable standing by itself but desirable if combined with other changes in the tax law.

Another issue raised at the conference concerned the manner in which indexing should be introduced if a decision is made to go ahead with it. The problem is that indexing the tax base involves massive redistribution of tax liabilities among businesses and individuals. If these changes were introduced abruptly, they would cause large changes in the market values of such assets as bonds, common stocks, and homes, creating large windfall gains and losses for some households. A variety of methods for cushioning or spreading out these effects—grandfather clauses for existing assets, a deferred effective date for currently enacted legislation, or a gradual shift from the current to an indexed base—were suggested.[50] But the conference discussion made clear that problems of transitional equity, although possibly serious, were only vaguely understood.

Finally, the conference papers and discussion underscore the fact that there are different ways to index the tax base. Choices must be made, not only between accrual and realization and between taking into account or disregarding changes in relative prices, as explained above, but also between complete and partial indexing. In addition to the complete indexing schemes described above, two partial schemes were mentioned. Under one, all the adjustments described above would be made except on capital financed by debt. Investors who have borrowed to buy depreciable assets or inventories suffer losses from historical-cost depreciation or FIFO accounting identical to the gains they enjoy from the fall in the real value of debt, provided that debt matures at the same rate as the assets lose their value.[51] On this ground William Fellner and Arthur M. Okun suggest that inflation adjustments, if they are made at all, should be made only for depreciation or the cost of materials financed by equity.[52]

---

initial net worth of an individual would be an illusory capital gain, but one subject to tax, where k is the rate of inflation. See chapter 4.

50. See Stanley Fischer's comments, chapter 4.

51. Since debt does not mature at precisely the same rate as assets depreciate, the identity is not exact. Whether the difference is important or trivial is not clear.

52. See Fellner, Clarkson, and Moore, *Correcting Taxes for Inflation*, pp. 5–8; and comments by Arthur Okun, chapter 11.

Alternatively, indexing the tax base can be approximated if depreciation is adjusted for inflation, but no other change is made. Gramlich discusses this approach at length but does not advocate it. The present tax code, by permitting LIFO accounting, allows firms in effect to index materials costs. Gramlich shows that the market brings about adjustments in interest rates that leave borrowers and lenders with the same after-tax incomes whether or not inflation adjustments are allowed for debt, provided that borrowers and lenders are in the same tax bracket. Not all borrowers and lenders are in the same tax bracket, however, and this method of indexing causes interest rates to fluctuate more than they would under full indexing or no indexing.[53]

Unfortunately, the operational details of none of the varieties of adjustments to the tax base have been explored. The tax code and the countless regulations that interpret it constitute a jungle of complexity. Indexing would affect thousands of provisions in ways that remain only vaguely understood. It is not clear, for example, whether partial indexing would be easier or harder to administer than full indexing. Past experience suggests that whatever form of indexing might be adopted would require changes in numerous provisions of the tax code and in countless regulations and years of costly litigation. Several conference participants expressed the fear that well-conceived proposals might emerge as monstrosities from this tortuous process.

Appendix: Derivation of Inflation Adjustments

Within a simplified profit and loss statement, let profits, Z, be equal to the difference between sales proceeds, S, on the one hand, and the sum of labor costs, L; materials, M; depreciation, D; and interest expense, I, on the other. Net interest expense equals the firm's net debt, B, multiplied by the interest rate, i. For simplicity, the firm's borrowing and lending rates are assumed to be the same, and firms are assumed to employ FIFO accounting and to keep enough mate-

---

53. On this issue, see chapters 10 and 11. George Terborgh advocates adjustments similar to those discussed by Gramlich, in *Inflation and the Taxation of Business Income* (Machinery and Allied Products Institute, 1976). This approach to indexing received no support at the conference.

rials in stock to satisfy needs during one accounting period. For a particular set of transactions in a world of completely stable prices

(1) $$Z = S - L - M - D - iB.$$

If all commodities rise in price equally and at the same rate, all items in equation 1 may be adjusted. The objective of such an adjustment is to cause taxable income to rise in the same proportion. If prices rise by $\dot{P}/P = \dot{p}$, then profits after adjustment should become $Z^* = Z(1 + \dot{p})$, where $\dot{P}$ is the absolute change in the price level, P, and $\dot{p}$ is the proportionate change in prices; in that case real taxable income will be unaffected by inflation.

If inflation raises all prices proportionately, before-tax receipts rise to $S(1 + \dot{p})$; labor costs rise to $L(1 + \dot{p})$; interest costs rise to $[(1 + i)(1 + \dot{p}) - 1] B$;[54] but neither materials costs nor depreciation change if the firm uses FIFO accounting and is compelled to base depreciation on historical cost.

In that case, profit calculated on the basis of historical-cost depreciation and of FIFO inventory accounting yields taxable profits, Z', where

$$
\begin{aligned}
(2) \quad Z' &= (1 + \dot{p})(S - L) - (M + D) - [(1 + i)(1 + \dot{p}) - 1] B \\
&= (1 + \dot{p})(S - L - B) - (M + D + \dot{p}B).
\end{aligned}
$$

This result differs from the correct result by the amount

(3) $$Z^* - Z' = -\dot{p}(M + D - B).$$

In other words, three adjustments are necessary: materials costs and depreciation must be increased by the rate of inflation, and the reduction in the real value of debt must be added to ordinary income. Note that the depreciation deduction is increased only by inflation in the current period because depreciable assets are assumed to be correctly valued in prices of the immediately preceding period. If inflation has gone on for some time and the book value of assets is expressed in prices of an earlier period, proper adjustment requires that book depreciation be increased by all inflation that has occurred since its book value was entered.

---

54. The loan repayment must exceed the loan by $\dot{p}B$ to maintain the lender's real capital intact; the interest payment must equal $i(1 + \dot{p})$ to maintain the real value of the interest payment. The sum of these two adjustments equals the mathematical expression in the text.

These adjustments concern ordinary income. In addition, the historical-cost basis used in computing capital gains must be adjusted in current prices before capital gains are computed.

The same result may be obtained in two other ways. The first does not require firms to include nominal gains on net debt in income, provided that all borrowers and lenders confront the same marginal tax rate, expect the same rate of inflation, and are allowed to measure depreciation and materials costs in current prices. In that case, the market interest rate becomes not $[i(1 + \dot{p}) + \dot{p}]$, but $[i(1 + \dot{p}) + \dot{p}/(1 - t)]$. Net income is unchanged. The second disallows the adjustment on net debt and on an equal amount of depreciation and/or materials.

If nominal interest rates change by more or less than enough to keep real interest rates intact, the procedures just described will not keep real taxable income invariant to the price level. Because of various differences between taxable and economic income, actual nominal interest rates may not change in the manner shown in equation 2. If so, real income may be affected by inflation even if all the suggested adjustments are made. Businessmen ordinarily bear a variety of risks, however, and the set of adjustments seems suitable, although it does not protect firms from the added variability in real interest rates that might exist in a fully indexed, inflationary world.

CHAPTER TWO

The Tax Treatment
of Business Profits
under Inflationary Conditions

T. NICOLAUS TIDEMAN *and* DONALD P. TUCKER

INFLATION distorts the comparison of dollar magnitudes from different periods of time. When dollars from different periods are combined to measure business income, using conventional accounting practices, the result is an accounting income that differs significantly from real income when there is inflation. If the inflation is rapid, the difference can be substantial. Furthermore, this distortion will vary, depending on the durability of capital, the relative proportions of debt and equity in the financial structure of firms, and inventory accounting practices. Therefore under conventional accounting prac-

The first section of the text and appendix A were done by Tideman. The second section and appendix B were done by Tucker. Both authors contributed to the final section. The empirical estimates reported in the discussion of adjustment procedures were made possible through the cooperation of the Office of Tax Analysis, U.S. Treasury Department, with extensive help from Thomas Vasquez and Linden Smith. Sherrie Ledford and Carol Keyt carried out excellently the heavy programming requirements of this study.

tices and tax rules, inflation produces incentives for unnecessary and inefficient alterations in these business decisions. These incentives can be eliminated by appropriate revisions in tax accounting practices.

The first section of this chapter describes the allocative effects of inflation under present tax law. The fraction of taxes borne by income from capital increases. The cost of debt relative to the cost of equity declines. Firms are encouraged to use long-lived rather than short-lived assets and, if last-in-first-out (LIFO) accounting is used, to increase inventories relative to depreciable assets. If first-in-first-out (FIFO) accounting is used, inventory investment is discouraged. Mergers are encouraged.

The next section describes the effects of three corrections to business income. The first is an adjustment to inventory profits; the second is an increase in depreciation charges to allow for the fall in the value of dollars between the time an asset was purchased and the time the allowance is taken; and the third is an addition to income equal to the firm's gain from the decline in the real value of its net monetary obligations. The significance of these adjustments depends on past inflation, the durability of a firm's assets, its inventory accounting procedures, and its capital structure. When inflation is just beginning, the monetary correction dominates. As inflation progresses, the depreciation correction becomes more important, and it remains significant for many years after inflation ceases.

When inflation begins, an inflation-adjusted tax law would initially cause the average nonfinancial firm to pay more taxes than under current law. Over the long run, however, the inflation-adjusted tax law would result in lower taxes than under current law, with an average reduction in taxes of over one-half of 1 percent of assets if inflation averaged 10 percent a year. The effects of such a tax law would vary greatly from firm to firm. While over half of nonfinancial firms would enjoy tax decreases of up to 2 percent of assets for each year of 10 percent inflation, some would enjoy even larger tax decreases and some would experience tax increases.

The final section of the paper addresses problems in implementing inflation corrections. Some effects of inflation corrections may be regarded as inequitable, but they are relatively minor. Departures from full correction are shown to be undesirable.

Effects of Inflation without Corrections

Economists define household income as consumption plus net increase in wealth and business income as dividends plus the before-tax increase in shareholders' equity (excluding any changes arising from the sale or retirement of shares). If no allowance is made for inflation, these measures of income include nominal increases in the value of assets. For example, if all prices rise 10 percent, then nominal income will include the 10 percent increase in asset prices due to inflation. If this rise in nominal value were taxed, it would reduce the real worth of the asset holder by the amount of the tax. Thus inflation converts an ordinary income tax into a kind of wealth tax. In fact, the U.S. individual and corporation income taxes do not subject accrued gains to tax, as this example presumes, but fall only on realized gains, defined as selling price plus depreciation less purchase price. And the depreciation schedules are intended to be accurate when prices are stable. Thus changes in asset values generated by inflation are not taxed until the assets are sold. If the assets are used in production, the inflationary increases in their value are taxed when they are reflected in the higher prices of the products made with the assets.

Inflation gives firms an incentive to shift to production methods that make greater use of assets with inflation gains that are deferred for longer periods or not taxed at all. For example, a firm that uses LIFO accounting for materials is not taxed on the inflation gains on inventories but is taxed on the difference between the replacement cost of depreciable assets and the deductions for depreciation (based on historical costs) that the firm is permitted to claim. As a result, inflation will encourage firms to carry large inventories and to use less equipment than they would use if prices were stable. To the extent that these changes in investment are motivated by tax considerations, they generally reduce economic efficiency.

Inflation also encourages firms to borrow more than they otherwise would as long as interest rates do not rise sufficiently to increase the after-tax cost of borrowing. The key to this distortion is the deductibility of interest and the nondeductibility of dividends. This distortion also reduces economic efficiency and probably increases the risk of bankruptcy.

The Higher Allocative Cost of Inflation-Induced Taxes

It might seem that the extra taxes generated by inflation are not important because they can be returned through reduced tax rates. Unfortunately, this simple solution does not exist. First, under current accounting practices inflation changes the relative costs of different investments because of the way the tax base is measured, not because of tax rates. Second, legislators may well not perceive the extra revenues from inflation as a tax increase and may use them to increase spending, not to cut taxes. Third, if the extra revenue is used to cut tax rates (or to avoid increasing them), labor income will generally share in the boon. Taxes on labor income also rise with inflation, but less than do taxes on capital. Therefore inflation will tend to increase the fraction of taxes borne by capital even if the total tax revenue is kept constant by a reduction in tax rates.

Effect of Inflation on Capital Structure

Under conventional accounting procedures, inflation encourages firms to satisfy a larger share of capital needs by borrowing and a smaller share by the sale of equities than would be chosen when prices are stable. This bias stems from the fact that interest payments are deductible, but dividends are not. When inflation occurs, interest rates usually increase, but the deductibility of interest payments means that the government pays part of any increase in interest expense that firms incur. With a 48 percent corporation income surtax rate, the federal government pays 48 cents out of each additional dollar of interest and the firm pays 52 cents.[1] If the corporation sells equity to raise $1,000, the extra profits earned during inflation will be subject to tax.

A numerical example illustrates this process. Assume that prices are stable and that a firm may borrow $1,000 if it pays $40 interest or sells $1,000 in stock to buyers who expect dividends of $90.[2] The firm retains no earnings and hence stock prices are not expected to grow. For numerical simplicity, assume that the corporation tax rate is 50 percent and that 5 percent inflation becomes universally ex-

1. Actually, the firm pays less if it is also subject to state corporation income tax. If the state taxes 10 percent of income after federal tax, then the state pays 5.2 cents and the firm pays 46.8 cents out of the extra dollar of interest expense.

2. As net profits fluctuate, so do dividends, making stock prices vary. Because of risk aversion, stock buyers demand a larger expected yield.

pected. If the firm now wishes to provide potential buyers of bonds and equities with the same real before-tax yields, then after the first year it must pay $92 in interest and $94 in dividends. The $92 interest payment consists of $50 necessary to offset the 5 percent decline in the value of $1,000 the lenders will suffer during the year and a $42 interest payment that has the same purchasing power after a 5 percent price increase as the original $40. The $94 in dividends is a 5 percent increase over the original $90 in dividends. Stockholders also have a $50 nominal capital gain in the expectation that dividends will remain higher by 5 percent. If the firm was indifferent between issuing bonds or stock when prices were stable, it will prefer to issue bonds when there is inflation under these assumptions. The after-tax cost of borrowing $1,000 is 0.5 ($92) = $46. But the firm may repay its debt with 1,000 depreciated dollars that have a real value of $50 less than those it borrowed. The total after-tax cost of borrowing in this example is −$4. The total after-tax cost of $94 in dividends is exactly $94. In real terms the cost of equity is unchanged, while the cost of debt has actually become negative.

This result hinges on the assumption that interest rates rose only enough to maintain the real before-tax incomes of lenders. Interest costs may well rise by a larger amount, offsetting the additional taxes that inflation imposes on lenders. How much they will rise is a complex problem of economic analysis that is beyond the scope of this study. But even if they rise enough to maintain the real after-tax incomes of lenders, the qualitative result of the foregoing example— that inflation increases the relative attractiveness of debt—will carry over. This conclusion follows from the fact that the marginal tax rates of lenders are lower than the marginal tax rates of borrowers on the average. So long as this is true, a rise in interest rates sufficient to leave the real after-tax income of lenders unaffected by inflation will result in a fall in the real after-tax interest costs of borrowers.[3]

An increase in interest rates large enough to increase the after-tax

3. Let t and u be the marginal tax rates of lenders and borrowers, respectively. Let $(1-t)r$ be the after-tax income of lenders when prices are stable. When inflation occurs at the rate of $100i$ percent per year, the interest rate must rise to r' to leave real after-tax income unchanged, where (abstracting from the fact that interest is usually paid quarterly rather than continuously) r' satisfies the relation $(1-t)r = (1-t)r' - i$. Solving for r' yields $r' = r + i/(1-t)$. In the same manner, the interest rate that leaves the after-tax cost of borrowing, r'', unchanged is $r'' = r + i/(1-u)$. But $r'' > r'$ because $i/(1-u) > i/(1-t)$.

interest costs of borrowers seems unlikely without some change in economic conditions independent of inflation. If, as seems more likely, the after-tax interest costs of borrowers decline, firms will be apt to raise more capital by borrowing and less by selling stock. This is inefficient because it leaves stockholders and bondholders with a different allocation of risk than they would have chosen in the absence of taxes. The more they leverage their firm with a high debt ratio, the lower their taxes will be. So they increase their leverage up to the point where the additional tax reduction barely offsets the lower utility of an undesired allocation of risk. But this adjustment on their part merely reduces their taxes without producing any social gains. One of the consequences of the greater leverage induced by profits taxes is an increased risk of bankruptcy. This risk is probably increased further by inflation. Firms are induced to borrow more, but real interest costs would fall if real interest rates declined by a greater percentage than borrowing increased. Nominal interest expenses will rise, however, so that the ability of a firm to meet its fixed obligations will become more dependent on its ability to stay in the bond market and borrow on the inflationary increases in the prices of its assets. A further factor that increases the risk of bankruptcy is that times of high inflation are often times of high variation in the rate of inflation. If the rate of inflation drops suddenly and interest rates drop correspondingly, a firm will face a cash squeeze unless it can repay its loans without penalty and reborrow at the new, lower interest rates.

Inflation and Required Rates of Return

Because inflation distorts profits computed under conventional accounting rules, it increases the required rate of return on investments. Table 2-1 illustrates these increases for a variety of assets of varying durability at different rates of inflation. The procedures used in computing table 2-1 are set forth in appendix A. Five kinds of assets are analyzed: equipment, structures, inventories, point input-point output (PIPO) investments (such as forests or scotch whiskey that entail an initial cost and eventually yield revenue with essentially no cost in between), and expensable investments. These investments differ in their durability, as indicated in table 2-1, and in the assumed pattern of depreciation. Equipment is assumed to depreciate exponentially at one and one-half times its straight-line depreciation rate. Structures

Table 2-1. Real Before-Tax Rates of Return Required to Yield a 6 Percent Real Return after Business Taxes, by Type of Asset
Percent

Asset, investment tax credit, and life or holding period	No inflation or full correction	2 percent inflation	7 percent inflation
Equipment[a]			
Investment tax credit = 0			
Life			
5 years	9.4	10.4	12.7
12 years	9.6	10.5	12.4
20 years	9.9	10.7	12.4
Investment tax credit = 7 percent			
Life			
5 years	6.1	7.2	9.5
12 years	7.1	8.0	10.0
20 years	8.0	8.9	10.6
Investment tax credit = 10 percent			
Life			
5 years	4.8	5.8	8.1
12 years	6.0	7.0	8.9
20 years	7.3	8.1	9.8
Structures			
Life			
25 years	10.0	10.7	11.8
50 years	10.0	10.4	11.0
Inventory			
Holding period			
1 year	11.5	13.3	17.6
30 years	11.5	12.0	12.5
100 years	11.5	11.6	11.6
Point input–point output investment			
Holding period			
10 years	9.5	10.1	11.1
50 years	7.3	7.3	7.3
Expensable investment			
Life of any length	6.0	6.0	6.0

Source: See appendix A. Figures are rounded.
a. Assumed to depreciate at one and one-half times the straight-line depreciation rate.

are assumed to deliver constant real services over their lives. The one-year inventory holding period would correspond to FIFO accounting, the longer periods to LIFO accounting. PIPO investments appreciate. The pattern of returns on expensable investment does not matter.

A tax system that did not affect the ranking of investments would produce equal required real rates of return among investments. This condition is met if there is no investment tax credit and if tax depreciation or appreciation exactly equals economic depreciation or appreciation, or if all investments are expensable, in which case new investments are effectively relieved of any tax burden. Even if prices are stable, the existing tax system fails this test. The figures below the "no inflation" heading in table 2-1 establish this point. Quite apart from variations in the investment tax credit, the required rates of return differ widely among investments. Figures under the next two headings show the increase in required rates of return necessitated under conventional accounting at 2 percent and 7 percent inflation. The required rates of return with full corrections are the same as with stable prices.

Expensable investments have very low required returns because they are effectively tax exempt. Long-term PIPO investments also have low required returns because taxes on the capital gains they generate are deferred. The failure to tax accrued capital gains is similar to accelerated depreciation, which equipment and structures receive to some extent. Inventory investments require the highest returns, even when prices are stable, because they receive no accelerated depreciation. When there is inflation, the required return on inventory falls with the holding period because of the value of deferral of taxes. The investment tax credit has a potent effect on the required rate of return, especially for short-lived equipment.

Some inequalities in required rates of return are reduced by inflation, but most are increased. The figures below the "7 percent inflation" heading in table 2-1 show this. The already high return on short-lived inventory rises. And the differential between short-lived and long-lived inventory increases, encouraging firms to shift to LIFO inventory accounting, which provides long holding periods for inventory. Inflation reduces the real value of depreciation allowances. The effect of this on required rates of return is proportional to the change in the present value of depreciation allowances multiplied by the sum of the real cost of funds and the depreciation rate. The impact is greatest on assets with short lives even though their depreciation allowances change by less because depreciation is so much larger for them. This bias from inflation toward long-lived equipment happens to partly offset a bias in the other direction from the investment tax credit. However, raising the investment tax credit from 7 percent to 10 percent (as happened in 1975) restores the bias toward short-lived equipment to what it is with a low rate of inflation.

The required rates of return with corrections for inflation are the same as when prices are stable. The operative corrections are adjustments in depreciation allowances and inventory profits for the change in the value of money The most dramatic effect of the corrections is the 3 to 5.5 percentage point decline in the required return to short-lived inventory investment. The tax incentive for LIFO inventory accounting disappears. Required returns for equipment fall by about 3 percentage points. The bias toward short-lived equipment is unfortunately increased but could be eliminated by better calibration of the investment tax credit to asset life.[4] The required returns to structures are reduced slightly by indexing. The already low returns to expensable and long-term PIPO investments are unchanged.

The figures in table 2-1 are based on the same real cost of funds under differing inflation rates. In fact, there are two reasons for thinking that the real cost of funds will be lower when there is more inflation. The first is that with higher required rates of return there will be less investment. To equate supply and demand for investment, a lower cost of funds will be needed. The second reason is that the lack of a monetary correction will tend to reduce the cost of funds for the reason stated earlier. Thus if all corrections except the monetary correction were instituted, there would be a drop in all required rates of return from the lower cost of funds (and lower total tax collections). In this event there would also be a greater bias toward debt financing than at present.

Effect of Inflation on Incentives for Mergers

Among the factors influencing decisions to conclude business mergers and acquisitions, tax considerations are generally of minor importance. In two situations, however, the opportunity to reduce taxes may provide a significant tax incentive for two firms to combine.

The first and widely recognized circumstance is the existence of a large loss carry-forward in one firm with little or no prospect of

---

4. If depreciation allowed for tax purposes is true depreciation, an investment tax credit of $x/(R - i + \delta)$, where R is the nominal cost of funds, i is the inflation rate, δ is the depreciation rate, and x is any number, will provide uniform required rates of return for all equipment, regardless of durability.

enough income in the near future against which to offset the accumulated losses. In such a case the tax benefit of the accumulated losses can be captured by combining this firm with another that has sufficient taxable income.

The second circumstance in which a merger confers tax benefits arises during inflation when a firm that uses LIFO inventory accounting and has done so for a number of years plans to liquidate its inventory. Because its inventories are carried on its tax accounting records at values far lower than their current market value, liquidation of its inventories will result in abnormally large income and corresponding tax liabilities levied at the ordinary corporate income tax rate. If this firm is combined with another firm in a taxable combination, on the other hand, then the acquiring firm can value these inventories at the cost of acquiring them, presumably their current market value, thereby incurring a much lower tax liability when they are liquidated. Furthermore the selling firm owes no corporation income tax on the accounting profit derived from selling the inventories if two conditions are met. The selling firm must be liquidated within one year, and the inventories must all be sold in a single bulk purchase to a third party. Both of these conditions could easily be met in a planned purchase of the entire business by another firm. Finally, whatever gain the stockholders of the liquidated business derive from this transaction will be taxed only at the long-term capital gains rate.

A switch to inflation-corrected accounting for income would increase opportunities for the first type of merger because on the average it would reduce income and increase losses, increasing loss carry-forwards and reducing future incomes against which they could be offset. It would eliminate the second incentive for merger, however, because all inventories would be revalued to reflect current price levels; hence there would no longer be any large tax on inventory profits to be partially escaped through merger.

The Impact of Inflation Adjustment Procedures on Taxable Income

To eliminate tax-related distortions in incentives and in the distribution of income due to inflation, real taxable income must, in an accounting sense, be independent of inflation. This requires three basic adjustments to the standard computation of income for tax purposes.[5] First, spurious "inventory profits" must be eliminated. All sales receipts and current expenses must be restated to current dollars by increasing them by the percentage increase in the general price level since the expenditure or sale date. Because costs are incurred before sales, costs will be increased more than sales. Second, depreciation charges based on the original cost of depreciable assets must be increased to reflect changes in the general price level since the purchase dates of the assets. Third, the decline in the real value of monetary assets (such as cash, bonds, and accounts receivable) due to inflation must be included as a cost, and the decline in the real value of monetary liabilities (such as bank loans, bonds, and accounts payable) due to inflation must be included as income. This third adjustment is equivalent to specifying that only real interest paid (calculated at the nominal interest rate less the inflation rate) can be deducted as a cost and that only real interest earned needs to be included in income.[6] Whether inflation is anticipated or not does not affect this adjustment, although it does affect both the nominal and real rates that are observed in the financial markets.

These adjustments take no account of changes in relative prices or relative values of assets. They do not produce a perfect measure of income, but merely one from which distortions arising from general price inflation have been eliminated. If prices of inventory stocks or depreciable assets change more or less than average, their accounting values are not adjusted for these deviations. In general this procedure does not record the income that accrues from changes in the real market value of all assets and liabilities (real capital gains on land, inventories, depreciable capital, and financial assets). Consequently the inventory adjustment is not equivalent to the use of LIFO inventory accounting under present tax law.

The first and third steps of the inflation adjustment procedure, if followed literally, would substantially increase corporate bookkeep-

5. In substance, these adjustments are the ones that were proposed and later withdrawn by the Financial Accounting Standards Board in *Financial Reporting in Units of General Purchasing Power,* Proposed Statement of Financial Accounting Standards, Exposure Draft (Stamford, Conn.: FASB, December 31, 1974).

6. This equivalence holds true only if a negative real rate of interest is assigned to monetary items whose nominal rate of interest is less than the inflation rate. In particular, cash and other noninterest-bearing assets must then be assigned a real interest rate of minus the inflation rate in accounting for income. Note that changes in the market prices of financial instruments, arising from changes in interest rates, for example, are not included in this adjustment.

ing costs, and this is one practical disadvantage of using inflation-corrected income as the base for corporate income taxation. This added burden could be eased significantly by permitting certain arbitrary rules of thumb to be used. For example, all transactions during the year (or quarter) might be assumed to have been made at the midpoint of the year (or quarter). As an alternative, the inflation-corrected income for the firm can be approximated closely from a computation that requires neither the dating of labor and materials purchases nor the periodic recording of the net credit or debit position on monetary items. This computation is based on the notion of inflation-corrected income as the increase in the inflation-corrected book value of equity (excluding any equity changes due to the issuance or retirement of equity shares) plus the inflation-corrected value of dividends and income taxes paid.[7]

Illustration of Inflation Adjustments over Time

Let Y and Y' be the conventional and the inflation-corrected measures of current-dollar income for a firm, respectively, and let the difference $(Y-Y')$ be called the income error due to inflation. Then $\tau(Y-Y')$ is the "tax overpayment" due to the effect of general inflation on the conventional accounting measure of income used for tax purposes, where τ is the tax rate. This overpayment is the excess of the firm's tax liabilities under present tax accounting over the tax liabilities the firm would have if the tax base were its price-level-adjusted income.

Figure 2-1 shows the effect of inflation on this tax overpayment for five hypothetical firms. It plots the ratio of $\tau(Y-Y')$ to total assets for four manufacturing firms and a representative firm from the transportation-communication-utility (TCU) group, using a value of 0.48 for τ.[8] The manufacturing firms differ from each other only in their capital structures, which are 75 percent equity and 25 percent debt, 55 percent equity and 45 percent debt (the mean proportion in

7. This alternative computation method is derived and explained in an unpublished appendix available on request from Donald Tucker.

8. In principle, the ratio of tax overpayment to net assets (shareholders' equity) rather than to total assets might provide a better measure of the importance of the tax overpayment both in figure 2-1 and in the succeeding empirical estimates. The characteristics of the data, however, required the use of gross rather than net assets in the empirical estimates below. For the sake of uniformity, the same asset concept is used here.

the 1970 *Statistics of Income*),[9] 45 percent equity with 55 percent debt, and 35 percent equity with 65 percent debt. In other respects they and the TCU firm have balance sheet and income statement proportions that are representative of their respective industries as shown in the 1970 *Statistics of Income.*

In this illustration it is assumed that there is no inflation before year 1. Then, prices rise by 2.5, 5.0, 7.5, and 10.0 percent respectively in the first four years (the first shaded area in figure 2-1), by 10 percent annually for the next eleven years, and then by 7.5, 5.0, 2.5, and zero percent in years sixteen through nineteen (the second shaded area). An extended period of constant prices follows. Throughout this inflation every firm's sales, investment, noninterest costs, and balance sheet items are assumed to grow 3 percent faster than the current rate of inflation. Only interest costs fluctuate with inflation.[10] These assumptions are economically naive, but this illustration is an accounting exercise and not an economic one. It illustrates four important points.

First, the correction for monetary items, which accounts in this example for all the differences between the tax overpayments of the manufacturing firms, is present only when inflation is occurring currently, and its magnitude depends only on the current inflation rate. Hence the differences between the manufacturing firms due to their different capital structures rise and fall with the inflation rate and disappear when the inflation stops. Furthermore, the tax *underpayment* experienced by the firms with the greatest excess of monetary liabilities over monetary assets (the fourth manufacturing firm and the TCU firm) persists only so long as inflation remains at or near its peak.

Second, the depreciation correction, by contrast, reflects past as well as present inflation and hence must continue long after inflation has ceased. Each year's inflation widens the gap between the *nominal* original costs, on which the *conventional* depreciation allowances are based, and the *inflation-corrected* costs, on which the *inflation-corrected* depreciation is based. Thus after inflation has ceased, inflation corrections of depreciation must continue to be made until all equipment and structures on the books in the last year of inflation have

9. U.S. Internal Revenue Service, *Statistics of Income—1970, Corporation Income Tax Returns* (Government Printing Office, 1974), p. 37.
10. See the note to figure 2-1.

Figure 2-1. Excess of Actual Taxes over Taxes Based on Inflation-Corrected Income, as a Percentage of Assets, for Four Representative Manufacturing Firms and a Representative Transportation-Communication-Utility Firm

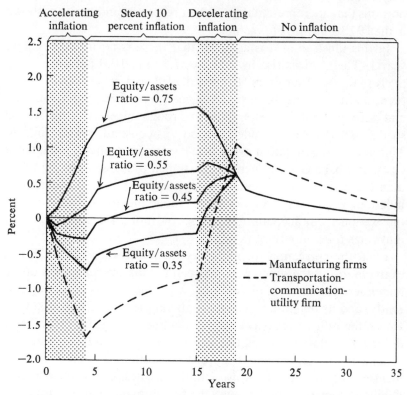

Source: Derived using the assumptions that follow. Initial values assumed for the manufacturing and transportation-communication-utility (TCU) firms, respectively, are total assets 100 and 210, monetary assets 25 and 17, short-term debt 20 and 30, annual equipment investment 3.27 and 10.90, annual structures investment 1.40 and 4.67, sales 100 and 100, cost of sales 70 and 55, and other costs 20 and 18. The long-term debt of the TCU firm is initially 85, while the long-term debts of the four different manufacturing firms are initially 5, 25, 35, and 45. All these magnitudes are assumed to grow at a constant 3 percent real rate. The tax accounting life of equipment is twelve years in manufacturing and twenty-five years in the TCU firm; all firms use a forty-year life for structures. Equipment and structures are depreciated by the 200 percent and the 150 percent declining balance methods, respectively. Inventories are turned over three times a year in manufacturing and six times a year in the TCU firm. The nominal interest rate on short-term debt adjusts completely to the current inflation rate within one year, while the average rate on outstanding long-term debt depends on an average of inflation rates over the past twenty years.

been fully depreciated, sold, or scrapped. The depreciation correction can continue to be of major importance for ten to fifteen years after inflation has ceased; for firms with relatively new structures when inflation ends, some correction may be required for thirty to forty years after inflation has ceased. This is illustrated by the continuing tax overpayments shown in figure 2-1 in years 19–35 when there is no inflation.

Third, the depreciation correction gradually builds up over time, and it takes many years of steady inflation for it to reach its maximum. This accounts for the rising trend of the curves during the steady 10 percent inflation of years 4–15 in figure 2-1.

Fourth, in the early years of a new inflation, the tax underpayment experienced by a net debtor firm arising from the lack of correction for monetary items can easily exceed the tax overpayment from failure to adjust historical-cost inventories and depreciation. This is most likely to occur if a firm is heavily leveraged, has a high ratio of long-lived fixed assets to inventories (such as the TCU firm), or has inventories with a very short turnover period. For net debtor firms with particularly durable assets, inflation-corrected income, although initially greater than conventional income, will generally be smaller in many subsequent years after the depreciation correction has built up from the continuation of inflation or after the correction for monetary items has declined or disappeared because of the decline or disappearance of inflation.

For these reasons it is not possible to determine the general effects of inflation on most firms' incomes by examining their inflation-corrected incomes for only one or two individual years. This point bears on the interesting figures reported by Sidney Davidson and Roman L. Weil comparing the reported and inflation-corrected incomes of a number of large industrial and utility firms for 1973 and 1974.[11] All the utilities and several of the industrial firms they examined had higher inflation-corrected incomes than their reported incomes in 1973 and 1974. To conclude from these figures, however, that a large percentage of firms would actually have higher tax liabilities in the long run if taxed on their inflation-corrected income would be a mistake (Davidson and Weil have not made this mistake). The years 1973 and 1974 correspond roughly to years 3 and 4 in figure 2-1 in the sense that they are the final two years of an accelerating inflation. They contain the corrections for monetary items but little of the de-

11. See chapter 3. See also Sidney Davidson and Roman L. Weil, "Inflation Accounting: What Will General Price Level Adjusted Income Statements Show?" *Financial Analysts Journal,* vol. 31 (January-February 1975), pp. 27–31, 70–84; idem, "Inflation Accounting: Public Utilities," ibid., May-June 1975, pp. 30–34, 62; and idem, "Impact of Inflation Accounting on 1974 Earnings," ibid., September-October 1975, pp. 42–54.

preciation corrections that will be spread over a number of future years. A few firms in the Davidson-Weil sample might be worse off even over the long run if taxed on their inflation-corrected income, but the list of those firms would be much shorter than the list of those whose 1973 and 1974 inflation-corrected income was greater than reported income.

In order to take proper account of both the immediate and the delayed effects of inflation that are pointed out in this illustration, it is necessary to analyze the effect of one year's inflation in isolation. This can be done, regardless of the pattern of inflation in preceding and subsequent years, by taking a discounted sum combining the current with all the future effects of one year's inflation. This is the analytical approach followed in deriving the empirical estimates that follow.

Empirical Estimates of Distributive and Aggregate Impacts

Empirical estimates of the extent to which corporate tax liabilities are altered by using the present conventional accounting measure of income rather than inflation-corrected income (general-price-level-adjusted income) as the tax base can be derived from the Treasury Department's corporate tax model file. This file contains information from balance sheets and income statements of a representative sample of corporate returns, most recently for 1972.

The main results of this estimation are presented in tables 2-2 through 2-5. These results show that tax liabilities on the average would be sharply reduced by a switch to inflation-corrected income for tax purposes. They also show a substantial variation across firms in the distribution of this effect. Most firms now pay substantially more than 48 percent of their inflation-corrected taxable income in taxes, but a few pay significantly less.

Each firm's current tax overpayment due to general inflation—the amount by which its current tax liabilities exceed the tax it would owe if taxed on its inflation-adjusted income—is the sum of an overpayment (possibly negative) due to current inflation and an overpayment due to past inflation. Similarly, as explained above, current inflation has not only an immediate effect but also deferred effects on income. Tables 2-2 through 2-4 report estimates of both the immediate and the long-term differences in tax burdens between an inflation-corrected and a conventional tax basis.

Table 2-2. Average Tax Overpayments as Percentage of Assets for Firms with Assets of at Least \$1 Million in 1972, Assuming 10 Percent Inflation[a]

Industry	10 percent inflation in one year		Steady-state overpayment, 10 percent inflation in every year (3)
	First-year overpayment (1)	Discounted total over-payment[b] (2)	
Mining	−0.90	0.27	0.41
Contract construction	−0.61	0.25	0.31
Food and related products	−0.62	0.57	0.71
Petroleum refining	−0.47	0.62	0.78
Chemicals, rubber	−0.52	0.84	0.98
Other nondurables	−0.56	0.67	0.80
Primary metals	−1.02	0.30	0.48
Fabricated metals, nonelectrical machinery	−0.39	0.69	0.78
Electrical equipment	−0.71	0.15	0.24
Transportation equipment	−0.41	0.57	0.65
Other durables	−0.42	0.89	1.02
Railroads	−1.51	0.54	0.94
Airlines	−1.94	0.23	0.48
Other transport	−1.60	0.02	0.21
Communication	−1.90	0.50	0.81
Electric, gas utilities	−2.22	0.07	0.53
Trade	−0.53	0.65	0.74
Finance, insurance, real estate	0.14	0.19	0.20
Services	−1.53	−0.38	−0.21
All nonfinancial industries	−0.96	0.46	0.66

Source: U.S. Department of the Treasury, 1972 corporate tax model file.

a. Overpayment is the excess of tax liabilities based on conventional income over tax liabilities based on inflation-corrected income.

b. Future overpayments resulting from one year's inflation were discounted at 5 percent in deriving column 2.

Table 2-2 shows the estimated tax overpayment due to inflation for twenty industrial groups, measured as a percentage of assets. Column 1 shows the immediate effect of inflation. The minus signs indicate underpayment, which means that inflation adjustment would increase taxes in the first year of a new inflation because firms are net debtors on the average. Column 2 shows the present value of all tax overpayments (including the first-year underpayment) occasioned by a single burst of inflation of 10 percent in one year, discounted at 5

Table 2-3. Average Tax Overpayments as Percentage of Tax Liabilities for Firms with Assets of at Least $1 Million in 1972, Assuming 10 Percent Inflation[a]

Industry	10 percent inflation in one year		Steady-state overpayment, 10 percent inflation in every year
	First-year overpayment	Discounted total over-payment[b]	
Mining	−15	4	7
Contract construction	−35	14	18
Food and related products	−18	17	21
Petroleum refining	−23	31	39
Chemicals, rubber	−12	19	22
Other nondurables	−16	19	23
Primary metals	−78	23	36
Fabricated metals, nonelectrical machinery	−10	18	20
Electrical equipment	−24	5	8
Transportation equipment	−11	15	17
Other durables	−10	21	25
Railroads	−374	134	233
Airlines	−374	45	92
Other transport	−73	1	9
Communication	−111	29	48
Electric, gas utilities	−198	6	48
Trade	−21	26	29
Finance, insurance, real estate	46	64	68
Services	−94	−23	−13
All nonfinancial industries	−37	18	25

Source: U.S. Department of the Treasury, 1972 corporate tax model file.

a. Overpayment is the excess of tax liabilities based on conventional income over tax liabilities based on inflation-corrected income. An overpayment greater than 100 percent indicates that the industry earned an inflation-corrected loss although it earned a conventional profit.

b. Future overpayments resulting from one year's inflation were discounted at 5 percent in deriving the figures in this column.

percent.[12] These figures incorporate the depreciation and inventory corrections that do not arise until the second and later years. Column 3 shows the eventual steady-state annual overpayment of taxes if inflation persists indefinitely at 10 percent.[13] Table 2-3 shows the

12. Five percent was chosen to represent an after-tax real rate of return on corporate capital.

13. The estimates for steady-state inflation are based on the assumption that corporations, on the average, would have the same balance sheet proportions under steady-state inflation as they had at the end of 1972. Although probably valid for fully anticipated steady inflation of 5 percent or less, this assumption may be subject to question when the inflation rate is 10 percent.

Table 2-4. Distribution of Nonfinancial Firms by Their Tax Overpayments as Percentage of Assets, Assuming 10 Percent Inflation in One Year

Size of firm (total assets in millions of dollars)

Percentage of assets	1–10		10–50		50–250		Over 250		All sizes	
	First year[a] (1)	Total[b] (2)	First year[a] (3)	Total[b] (4)	First year[a] (5)	Total[b] (6)	First year[a] (7)	Total[b] (8)	First year[a] (9)	Total[b] (10)
Overpayment										
2.0 to 5.0	4.1	16.9	2.2	14.7	0.3	7.2	0.2	2.3	3.9	16.4
1.5 to 2.0	4.4	10.4	2.8	11.5	0.8	11.4	0.3	6.2	4.2	10.5
1.0 to 1.5	6.5	13.1	5.4	14.3	2.7	15.0	0.3	13.6	6.3	13.2
0.5 to 1.0	10.0	15.0	9.0	15.4	6.7	16.8	2.5	22.5	9.9	15.1
0.0 to 0.5	11.7	15.7	15.1	14.9	13.8	17.9	8.2	30.6	12.0	15.8
Underpayment										
−0.0 to −0.5	12.9	11.2	15.8	10.4	19.5	12.7	19.1	13.2	13.2	11.2
−0.5 to −1.0	12.6	6.3	13.8	7.0	17.8	9.1	22.6	5.9	12.9	6.4
−1.0 to −1.5	10.8	4.0	11.1	4.8	12.9	4.3	12.9	3.9	10.9	4.1
−1.5 to −2.0	8.5	2.6	9.0	3.1	8.9	3.2	9.9	1.6	8.6	2.7
−2.0 to −5.0	17.6	4.3	15.3	3.6	16.4	2.4	24.0	0.3	17.5	4.2
Less than −5.0	0.7	0.3	0.2	0.1	0.1	0.0	0.0	0.0	0.6	0.3
All firms	100.0	100.0	100.0	100.0	100.0	100.0	100.0	100.0	100.0	100.0
Weighted mean percentage of assets	−0.60	0.65	−0.65	0.58	−0.83	0.46	−1.11	0.41	−0.96	0.46
Addenda										
Number of firms	66,120		5,134		1,396		645		73,295	
Percentage of assets[c]	5.7		4.0		7.0		27.5		44.3	
Percentage of taxes[d]	13.7		9.2		14.0		50.4		87.4	

Source: Derived as explained in appendix B from data in U.S. Department of the Treasury, 1972 corporate tax model file. Figures are rounded.
a. Percentage of firms for which the ratio of first-year overpayments to assets lies in the indicated range.
b. Percentage of firms for which the ratio of discounted total overpayments to assets lies in the indicated range; the overpayments caused in future years by one year's inflation are discounted at 5 percent.
c. Percentage of all business assets held by all firms covered in the sample that are accounted for by the firms in each column.
d. Percentage of all taxes paid by all firms covered in the sample that are accounted for by the firms in each column.

Table 2-5. Distribution of Nonfinancial Firms by Their Tax Overpayments in Every Year as Percentage of Assets, Assuming 10 Percent Steady-State Inflation[a]

Percentage of assets	Size of firms (total assets in millions of dollars)				
	1–10	*10–50*	*50–250*	*Over 250*	*All sizes*
Overpayment					
2.0 to 5.0	18.6	17.3	9.7	3.4	18.2
1.5 to 2.0	11.0	12.4	12.2	8.2	11.1
1.0 to 1.5	13.9	14.6	16.5	18.9	13.6
0.5 to 1.0	15.4	15.5	17.3	30.7	15.6
0.0 to 0.5	15.8	13.5	17.8	20.9	15.7
Underpayment					
−0.0 to −0.5	10.2	10.2	9.6	8.7	10.2
−0.5 to −1.0	5.8	6.1	8.5	4.5	5.8
−1.0 to −1.5	3.7	4.3	3.5	3.0	3.8
−1.5 to −2.0	2.1	2.6	2.6	1.4	2.1
−2.0 to −5.0	3.5	3.1	2.2	0.3	3.4
Less than −5.0	0.3	0.1	0.0	0.0	0.3
All firms	100.0	100.0	100.0	100.0	100.0
Weighted mean percentage of assets	0.77	0.70	0.60	0.64	0.66
Addenda					
Number of firms	66,120	5,134	1,396	645	73,295
Percentage of assets[b]	5.7	4.0	7.0	27.5	44.3
Percentage of taxes[c]	13.7	9.2	14.0	50.4	87.4

Source: Derived as explained in appendix B from data in U.S. Department of the Treasury, 1972 corporate tax model file. Figures are rounded.

a. Percentage of firms in each size class for which the ratio of yearly overpayments to assets lies in the indicated range.

b. Percentage of all business assets held by all firms covered in the sample that are accounted for by the firms in each column.

c. Percentage of all taxes paid by all firms covered in the sample that are accounted for by the firms in each column

same overpayments expressed as a percentage of 1972 tax liabilities rather than as a percentage of assets. Tables 2-4 and 2-5 show the variation among firms in the size of the overpayment.

Additional empirical estimates and an explanation of the procedures used in deriving them are contained in appendix B. The basic method was to derive an algebraic expression for the tax overpayment $\tau(Y-Y')$, deflate this by a price index to express it in real terms, and then to calculate the change in the present and future values of this real tax overpayment associated with an increase in the price index. This calculation was performed for every firm with at least $1 million in assets in the Treasury Department's 1972 tax model file.

The inflation assumptions underlying these empirical estimates differ from those on which the illustration shown in figure 2-1 is based. The illustration shows the tax overpayment in each year arising from the combined effects of several years of variable inflation, whereas these empirical estimates examine the immediate and long-run consequences of a single year's inflation and of steady-state inflation. These may be compared because the first-year overpayment in the tables corresponds to the results for year 1 in figure 2-1, and the steady-state overpayment in the tables corresponds roughly to the overpayments shown for year 15 in figure 2-1.[14] The discounted total overpayment resulting from a single year's inflation has no direct counterpart in figure 2-1.

The industry averages reported in tables 2-2 and 2-3 clearly show that inflation causes the average firm's current taxable income to exceed its inflation-corrected taxable income by a substantial margin. Since inflation-corrected income approximates true income more closely than does the current income measure, these results show that inflation raises the tax rate of the average firm under present tax law. That is, inflation raises the ratio of taxes to true income. The total tax overpayment from one year of 10 percent inflation is at least 15 percent of one year's taxes in most industries, and substantially more in some (table 2-3).

These results should not be interpreted as comprehensive estimates of the aggregate revenue consequences of basing the corporate income tax on inflation-corrected income. Firms with less than $1 million in assets in 1972 were excluded from the sample. The 1972 data were not adjusted in any way to represent 1975 or future years. Losses, loss carry-overs, capital gains, and foreign-source income were not adequately treated. The estimates used for the relative proportions of LIFO and FIFO inventories are undoubtedly obsolete. Finally, and most important, firms would behave differently if taxed on their inflation-corrected income—they would make different investment, financing, and pricing decisions—and these estimates make no allowance for the behavioral consequences of altering the definition of taxable income. For all these reasons, these results do not show the change in revenues from a switch to an inflation-corrected corporation income tax base.

14. Strictly speaking, the steady-state overpayments in tables 2-2, 2-3, and 2-5 correspond to the positions the lines would approach in figure 2-1 if inflation continued indefinitely at 10 percent.

These results also do not apply directly to a situation of variable inflation of the kind experienced recently in the United States. The best that can be said is that numerical estimates of the compounded effect of several years' inflation at different rates could be obtained using the same kind of analysis employed here.

Even after making a liberal allowance for error, however, it is clear that a change to inflation-corrected income as the tax base would reduce taxes. In many industries it would be roughly equivalent to a reduction in the 48 percent corporation tax rate of about 1 percentage point for each percent of inflation, with no change in the tax base.

The variations among firms in the tax consequences of inflation shown in tables 2-4 and 2-5, and the variations across industry groups, as seen in tables 2-2 and 2-3, are as important as the averages. These variations are substantial and are present within every industry and industry group.[15] These results demonstrate that the surtax imposed by inflation is arbitrarily and inequitably distributed. Table 2-4 shows, for example, that while 25 percent of the 645 largest nonfinancial firms pay less taxes than they would on the basis of their inflation-adjusted income, another 22 percent of these firms are overtaxed by at least 1 percent of their assets for every single year of 10 percent inflation. Among nonfinancial firms with assets between $1 million and $50 million in 1972, the variation is even greater: over 28 percent of these firms now pay less tax than they would pay on inflation-corrected income, while over 16 percent of them are overtaxed by at least 2 percent of their assets for each year of 10 percent inflation.[16]

15. The variation is probably greater than shown because these results were derived without information about each firm's inventory valuation method or the purchase dates of its depreciable assets. It was necessary to rely on industry-wide averages, thus excluding two important sources of variation among firms. Tables 2-6 and 2-7 in appendix B and other results not reported here show that the distributional differences shown in tables 2-4 and 2-5 are present in every major industry with the partial exception of finance, insurance, and real estate. Although the dispersion of overpayments for financial firms relative to their *assets* is less than it is for nonfinancial firms, the dispersion of overpayments relative to *income* is significantly greater there than it is for nonfinancial firms on the average. The variations across firms within each of the nineteen industries shown in tables 2-2 and 2-3 are available from Donald Tucker.

16. It would not be correct to conclude from these results that 25 percent of the largest nonfinancial firms and 28 percent of the smaller firms would have to pay more taxes if the definition of taxable income were changed to correct for inflation. These firms now underpay because of their substantial net debt positions. If faced with a tax on their monetary gains from debt, they might substitute some equity for debt, thereby reducing or eliminating the tax increase that would otherwise have occurred.

The results of tables 2-2, 2-3, and 2-4 also underscore the difference between the first-year and the long-run effects of inflation on tax liabilities shown graphically in figure 2-1. Table 2-2 shows, for example, that conventional accounting understates the income of most firms when inflation begins because conventional accounting ignores the gain on net debt, but the inventory and depreciation corrections in later years more than offset this first-year effect.[17]

This difference in size between the first-year and the long-run effects implies that the present corporate profits tax is procyclical. The rate of tax paid under present tax law, figured as a percentage of inflation-corrected income, declines below 48 percent in a year of new or increased inflation and then rises above 48 percent in future years after the inflationary stimulus has stopped accelerating or has subsided. A tax based on inflation-corrected income, by contrast, would have a distinct countercyclical impact in the year inflation occurs. Relative to present tax rules, inflation correction of the income base would be equivalent to a prompt inflation surtax on conventional income of about 12 percentage points (that is, an increase in the surtax from 48 to 60 percent) at the onset of 10 percent inflation, accompanied by an even larger tax reduction in subsequent years as inflation subsides.[18]

Foreign Income and Tax Credits

The estimates just described are based on the assumption that remitted foreign income and tax credits for foreign taxes paid would be unaffected by inflation correction. This assumption, although certainly not true for every firm, has some general validity.

Foreign income of U.S.-owned foreign subsidiaries is taxed only when remitted to the U.S. parent. At that time the foreign taxes paid on this income can be claimed as a credit against U.S. taxes.[19] In

17. In manufacturing, less than 15 percent of the total increase in depreciation allowances that would arise from a switch to inflation-corrected income occurs in the first year. Also, the inventory correction is not recorded until the finished products containing the inflated inventories are sold, and thus a substantial portion of the inventory correction occurs in the second year. These factors account for the difference between the first-year effect of inflation and the long-run effect.

18. It is essential to recall that these estimates ignore the probable change in the behavior of firms in response to the introduction of inflation-corrected accounting.

19. This rule does not apply to income from certain "tax haven" subsidiaries, nor does it apply to foreign branches, but it covers much of the foreign-source income of U.S. firms. See George F. Break and Joseph A. Pechman, *Federal Tax Reform: The Impossible Dream?* (Brookings Institution, 1975), pp. 83–85.

general, the U.S. parent firm can claim as a tax credit a portion of foreign taxes equal to the ratio of remitted income to total foreign income, measured according to accounting principles accepted by U.S. tax authorities. The inflation-corrected foreign income of most firms would be lower than the conventional measure. Therefore if remittances were unchanged, the tax credit from foreign taxes paid would tend to increase.

The amount of tax credit, however, that can be claimed by any firm is subject to some overall limitations. Total credits for foreign taxes paid cannot exceed U.S. taxes before any credits multiplied by the ratio of all remitted foreign income to domestic plus remitted foreign income, and this ceiling would not necessarily be changed significantly by a change in domestic taxable income. Since many firms with a tax liability for foreign-source income are already claiming all the tax credit permitted under their ceilings, the practical effect on the tax revenues derived from foreign subsidiary operations of making an inflation correction may be rather small, assuming firms continue to remit the same amount of foreign income.

Issues in the Implementation of Inflation Corrections

A move to inflation-corrected taxes would be relatively free of inequities, partly because it would reduce taxes on balance. Even general tax reductions hurt those who would have benefited from the additional expenditures that additional revenues would have paid for, or those who would have benefited from alternative tax reductions. But these injuries are highly amorphous. The one identifiable redistribution that would be caused by inflation corrections would be a redistribution from debtors to creditors. The monetary correction would impose on debtors an additional tax by reducing their interest deduction, in effect permitting only real interest to be deducted, and creditors would receive an equivalent reduction in taxes. Debtors could reasonably say that they would not have agreed to interest rates so high if they had known that only real interest would be deductible.

This injustice is less severe than it appears. First, many loans were contracted before the recent inflation at interest rates that creditors would not have accepted had they known inflation was coming. Those who benefited from unanticipated inflation have little cause to complain if tax reform eliminates some of their windfall benefits.

Second, many loans can be repaid early with little or no penalty. If interest rates decline when inflation adjustment is introduced, many borrowers will be able to renegotiate their loans at the new lower rates that reflect the changed tax rules. Finally, anyone who borrowed without the option of early repayment and at an interest rate that was advantageous only with continued inflation was taking a definite risk that the rate of inflation would fall, to his disadvantage. If instead of reduced inflation this borrower were faced with an unfavorable change in the tax deductibility of interest, he would simply have to absorb the loss from reduced deductibility, as he would have had to absorb the loss from a fall in market interest rates. In any event, inflation adjustment might be limited to debts contracted after a certain date.

Partial Correction Schemes

Legislators might be tempted to enact the depreciation and inventory adjustments because they reduce taxable income, while skipping the correction for monetary items because it usually raises the taxable income of firms. Although under certain conditions the monetary correction is not required to eliminate the distorting effects of inflation on relative rates of return among investments,[20] it is required to yield a meaningful concept of income. In particular, its omission would cause creditor firms to be taxed more heavily on their true income than debtor firms. Furthermore, when applied to both borrowers and lenders, the monetary correction reduces the uncertainty about the real return to debt arising from uncertainty about how much actual inflation will deviate from the inflation expected by borrowers and lenders.

The gain from the decline in the real value of outstanding monetary liabilities due to inflation superficially resembles an unrealized capital gain, as it does not give rise to any current cash flow. Therefore it might be argued that even if this income is taxed, the tax should be deferred until realization, as is the tax on unrealized capital gains. This position is likely to be defended stoutly by firms with large monetary liabilities if serious consideration is given in Congress to basing the corporation income tax on inflation-corrected income, because deferral until realization would lower current and total long-run tax liabilities.

20. See chapter 10.

The resemblance between monetary gains on debt and capital gains is only skin deep, however. The three major arguments for deferring the tax on capital gains until realization do not apply to inflation-related gains on monetary liabilities.

The first argument for deferral of the tax on certain types of capital gains rests on the difficulty of obtaining reliable valuations if the assets are not converted to cash. Basing a firm's current tax liability on gains that can only be guessed would introduce an element of arbitrariness into the tax system. But there is no valuation problem with monetary liabilities. The inflation correction is obtained by applying a standard and general inflation index to a nominal par value.

The second argument rests on the indivisibility of certain capital assets that cannot be sold piecemeal to raise cash to meet the tax bill on some accrued capital gains. The piecemeal sale of other assets that are technically divisible may give rise to substantial transaction costs —for example, because total ownership is worth more than the sum of partial interests. A taxpayer may therefore have to choose between selling the entire asset and borrowing to pay his taxes, and for someone without access to low-cost credit, a tax on accrued capital gains can impose a severe hardship. But indivisibility is less of a problem with monetary liabilities than with an asset since one does not sell part of an indivisible liability in order to raise cash. Instead, if anything, one issues a new liability.

A third argument against accrual taxation of capital gains rests on the incontrovertible fact that capital gains are often transitory. A firm without sufficient other income against which to offset the subsequent capital losses will not be able to obtain a tax benefit from these losses as large as the tax already paid on the transitory gains. Consequently accrual taxation would discourage investment in risky assets unless the period for loss carry-backs and carry-forwards were extended, with interest accrued on deferred tax benefits from loss carry-forwards. In sharp contrast, changes in general price levels are seldom transitory. Consequently they can be taxed without fear that subsequent losses will go uncompensated.

Four additional considerations support the immediate taxation of gains on monetary liabilities. First, the present tax system contains a bias in favor of debt finance and against equity finance by firms, a bias that arises from the deductibility of interest costs while dividends are not deductible. Deferral of the tax on gains on monetary liabilities would reduce the extent to which inflation adjustment corrects this bias. Second, in an important sense the gain on monetary liabilities *is* realized, or is at least realizable, if the value of the firm's stock rises with inflation or if the value of its outstanding bonds declines with inflation.[21] In that case inflation reduces the firm's debt-equity ratio and thereby increases the firm's capacity to take on new debt. Third, if the taxes due on gains on monetary liabilities are deferred, inflation will confer an advantage on debt-heavy firms relative to creditor firms that they would not have in the absence of inflation. Fourth, the accounting profession's proposal for inflation-neutral financial reporting states that "no portion of the general purchasing power gain or loss [from monetary items] shall be deferred to future periods."[22]

Another departure from full inflation correction that has been proposed would be to eliminate the monetary correction and to adjust depreciation and inventories only to the extent that they are financed by equity. It is argued that the gain from the reduced value of the debt would be offset by the declining value of the depreciation allowances on debt-financed assets and by the tax liability on the inflation gains on debt-financed inventory.

The vagueness of this proposal leaves room for several possible interpretations,[23] and the proposal appears to have serious weaknesses. First, it would introduce a serious distortion if it excluded all correction for monetary assets. Monetary assets offset by debt need no correction, but many firms are net creditors, and this proposal appears to deny them a monetary correction that would work to their advantage. Second, the current years' inflation gives rise to depreciation corrections in a number of future years, whereas it generates a monetary correction for debt only in the current year. Because of this timing difference, the two inflation corrections being proposed as offsets are not equivalent. The immediate benefit is worth more than the loss of future depreciation allowances. Furthermore, the firm that sells its capital before depreciating it fully would permanently

21. Such an increase in stock prices cannot be taken for granted, however. See Zvi Bodie, "Common Stocks as a Hedge Against Inflation" (Massachusetts Institute of Technology, 1975; processed).

22. FASB, "Financial Reporting," p. 15.

23. For example, would one assign to each asset a permanent classification as debt- or equity-financed according to the financial arrangements at the time of its purchase? Or would its classification be determined each year on the basis of the firm's current financial structure?

escape taxation on part of its income under this proposal. For these reasons, this proposal is a partial, not a complete, adjustment for changes in the general price level. Finally, it might be extremely diffi-cult to administer this proposal in a reasonable way. Firms mingle funds and change their financial structures continually, and it is not clear how the debt-financed portions of inventory and capital would be identified.

What can be said in favor of this proposal is that if the adminis-trative problem can be solved, it might be a reasonable second-best solution if the monetary correction were unattainable.

Conclusion

Because of the inadequacies of the income measure currently used as the base for the corporation income tax, inflation introduces sev-eral distortions into the investment and financing decisions of firms and inequities into the distribution of the tax burden across firms. Furthermore, inflation increases the average tax rate collected on the true income of firms, but it does this in a procyclical way by col-lecting tax at a *reduced* rate in the year in which inflation occurs and at higher rates for a number of years after the inflation has occurred. The interfirm inequities and the procyclical alterations in tax rates caused by even a moderate inflation of 10 percent are sufficiently great to suggest that a switch to inflation-corrected income as the tax base for the corporation income tax would significantly alter the dis-tribution of income among firms and the cyclical properties of the tax system.

Appendix A: Real Rates of Return Required to Yield a Given Real Return after Business Taxes

The formula for the required real rate of return used in table 2-1 is

(1) $$\rho = [(R - i + \delta)(1 - k - uz)]/(1 - u) - \delta,$$

where ρ is the real rate of return net of depreciation, δ; k is the rate of investment tax credit; u is the marginal corporation income tax rate; z is the present value of depreciation deductions discounted at the rate, R, the firm's required after-tax return on funds; and i is the rate of increase in prices. R, in turn depends on the nominal cost of borrowed capital, r_d, and the anticipated nominal return on equity (dividend plus anticipated nominal capital gain), r_e, according to equation 2.

(2) $$R = fr_d(1 - u) + (1 - f)r_e,$$

where f is the fraction of debt in the capital structure of the firm. Equation 1 closely resembles the standard formula for the user cost of capital developed by Hall and Jorgenson, $c = q\,[\rho(1-u) + \delta]$ $(1-k-uz)/(1-u)$, where $c/q = \rho + \delta$, and $\rho\,(1-u) = R$.[24]

The values of the variables used to generate values of ρ that are reported in table 2-1 are as follows:

The low inflation rate of 0.02 corresponds to average annual inflation between 1948 and 1966. The high inflation rate of 0.07 corresponds roughly to price change in 1975. It was assumed that 30 percent of capital is debt ($f = 0.3$). At low inflation, $r_d = 0.04$, the average for the 1948–66 period, and $r_e = 0.11$, the sum of dividends of 0.04, a real capital gain of 0.05 (midway between the 0.08 average annual gain on the Standard and Poor's 500 stocks between 1948 and 1966 and the 0.02 gain between 1933 and 1974), and an inflationary capital gain of 0.02 yielding $R = 0.08$. At high inflation, $R = 0.13$, to preserve $R - i = 0.06$. It was assumed that $\delta = 1.5/T$, where T is the asset life for tax purposes. This corresponds to declining balance depreciation at 150 percent of the straight-line rate for the assigned life. The investment tax credit, k, takes on one of three values—0, 0.7, or 0.10; for assets with five-year lives, the credit is two-thirds of these values. The corporation income tax rate, u, is 0.48. The present value of depreciation allowances for equipment is calculated according to the formula

(3) $$z = 2\,[T(e^R - 1) - 1 + e^{-TR}]/[T(T + 1)\,R(e^R - 1)].$$

With inflation corrections, depreciation allowances are based on the same formula, but with $(R-i)$ substituted for R. Structures are ineligible for the investment tax credit and are assumed to behave like "one-hoss shays," yielding uniform services until they suddenly collapse. These assumptions yield the following equation for structures:

24. See Robert E. Hall and Dale W. Jorgenson, "Application of the Theory of Optimum Capital Accumulation," in Gary Fromm, ed., *Tax Incentives and Capital Spending* (Brookings Institution, 1971), p. 16.

(4) $\rho/(1 - e^{-\rho T}) = (R - i)(1 - uz)/[(1 - e^{-(R-i)T})(1 - u)].$

The maximum permissible depreciation deductions for structures are obtained using declining balance depreciation at 150 percent of the straight-line rate. Taxpayers find it advantageous to switch over to straight-line depreciation at the point T^*, that is, one-third of the life of the asset, rounded up to an integer. Letting X equal the undepreciated value after one year $(1-1.5/T)$, the present value of depreciation on structures is

(5) $z = 1.5(e^R - 1)[1 - (X/e^R)^{T^*}]/[TR(e^R - X)]$
          $+ X^{T^*}(e^{-T^*R} - e^{-TR})/[(T - T^*)R].$

The required returns for structures in table 2-1 were computed by using values of z from equation 5 and then solving equation 4 for ρ by successive approximations.

The required rate of return for inventories is $\rho = (R-i)[1+u(e^{ih}-1)/(e^{Rh}-e^{ih})]/(1-u)$, where h is the holding period for inventories. With inflation correction, this relation simplifies to $\rho = (R - i)/(1 - u)$.

For an investment with a point input, and a point output after the period h, the required rate of return is $\rho = \{\ln[(e^{Rh} - u)/(1 - u)]\}/h - i;$ with inflation corrections, $(R - i)$ replaces R, and the i at the end drops off.

Appendix B: Derivation of Estimates of Distributive and Aggregate Effects of Inflation on Tax Liabilities

Nominal income before taxes (conventional measure), Y, equals gross operating profit, GOP, minus depreciation, $DEPR$, minus interest expense, INT:

(1) $Y = GOP - DEPR - INT,$
          $GOP = S_t(p_{s,t} - w_{t-a}n - p_{m,t-b}m) - OC_t,$

          $DEPR = \sum_{j=1}^{L} \alpha_j I_{t-j},$

          $INT = r_t D_t,$

where all t subscripts refer to period t, and
    a = average time lag between labor inputs into production and sale of the resulting product ($a = 0$ under LIFO for a growing firm);
    b = average time lag between purchase of material inputs and sale of the associated product ($b = 0$ under LIFO for a growing firm);

D = average debt during the year;

I = new investment assumed for tax purposes to have been purchased at the end of the year;

L = accounting life of depreciable assets;

m = direct materials input per unit of sales;

n = direct labor input per unit of sales;

OC = other costs (for example, advertising, rent, repairs, salaries of nonproduction employees);

p_m = price of materials;

p_s = price of sales;

r = nominal interest rate on debt;

S = sales of product in real units;

w = wage rate;

α_j = depreciation fraction for assets purchased j years ago.

Inflation-corrected income before taxes, indicated by a prime and stated in end-of-year dollars, equals gross operating profit (restated) minus depreciation (restated) minus interest expense (restated) minus losses on monetary items ($MONL$):

$$(2) \quad Y' = GOP' - DEPR' - INT' - MONL,$$

$$GOP' = \frac{X_t^*}{X_t}(p_{s,t}S_t - OC_t) - \frac{X_t^*}{X_{t-a}} w_{t-a}nS_t - \frac{X_t^*}{X_{t-b}}p_{m,t-b}mS_t,$$

$$DEPR' = \sum_{j=1}^{L} \alpha_j \frac{X_t^*}{X_{t-j}^*}I_{t-j},$$

$$INT' = \frac{X_t^*}{X_t}r_t D_t,$$

$$MONL = \left(\frac{X_t^*}{X_{t-1}^*} - 1\right)(C_t - D_t),$$

where

C = average monetary assets during the year, including cash, accounts receivable, debt securities, etc.;

X = average value of index of prices during the year;

X^* = value of price index at end of year.

This formulation ignores the distinction between equipment depreciation and structures depreciation and omits additional first-year depreciation, but both are taken into account in the actual empirical estimates. This definition of income corresponds to that proposed by the Financial Accounting Standards Board.

The error in the conventional income measure because of inflation is $(Y-Y')$; in real terms this error is $(Y-Y')/X^*$.

Transitory Inflation

In analyzing the consequences of a single year's inflation, we have assumed that the price index follows

$$X_t = (X_t^* X_{t-1}^*)^{\frac{1}{2}},$$
$$X_{t-a} = X_t^{1-a} X_{t-1}^a, \quad X_{t-b} = X_t^{1-b} X_{t-1}^b;$$

that inventories are not held for more than a year on the average; that changes in the current year's inflation rate do not influence the rate of price change in future years; and that all real prices and the real value of the firm's net credit position on monetary items are unaffected by inflation. Finally, we have chosen to analyze the consequence of a small amount of inflation in a context where there would otherwise have been no inflation. This assumption makes it unnecessary to specify the effect of inflation on the nominal interest rate.

With these assumptions, the effect of inflation in introducing error into the measure of current income is shown by

$$(3) \quad \frac{d}{dX_t^*}\left(\frac{Y_t - Y_t'}{X_t^*}\right) = \frac{1}{2}\left\{\begin{matrix}S_t[-p_{s,t} + (1+a)nw_{t-a} + (1+b)mp_{m,t-b}] \\ + r_t D_t + OC_t\end{matrix}\right\}$$

$$+ \sum_{j=1}^{L} \alpha_j I_{t-j} + (C_t - D_t).$$

The term in braces is the inventory correction, plus a general inflation error that does not drop out if the firm uses LIFO inventory accounting. The second and third terms are the depreciation correction and the correction for monetary items on the balance sheet.

One year's change in the price level also affects the real value of this error in several future years. Inflation creates a differential between the conventional and inflation-adjusted book values of all the firm's depreciable capital held at the time the inflation occurs, and this differential gives rise to a depreciation component in the error $(Y-Y')$ for as long as any of this capital remains on the firm's books. In the first year following the price-level change there is also a spillover inventory adjustment effect that is exhausted before the end of the second year, assuming that the lag between material and labor inputs and product sales does not exceed one year. Therefore the impacts of the current year's inflation on the error in the second year and in all succeeding years, respectively, are

(4) $\quad \dfrac{d}{dX_t^*}\left(\dfrac{Y_{t+1} - Y'_{t+1}}{X_{t+1}^*}\right) = \displaystyle\sum_{j=2}^{L} \alpha_j I_{t+1-j} + \dfrac{S_{t+1}}{2}(anw_{t-a} + bmp_{m,t-b}),$

(5) $\quad \dfrac{d}{dX_t^*}\left(\dfrac{Y_{t+i} - Y'_{t+i}}{X_{t+i}^*}\right) = \displaystyle\sum_{j=i+1}^{L} \alpha_j I_{t+i-j}, \qquad i = 2, 3, \ldots, L-1.$

The discounted present value of the tax overpayment, $OPAY$, due to incorrect measurement of the tax base, assuming a single 10 percent increase in the price level and assuming a marginal tax rate of 48 percent, is

(6) $\qquad OPAY = 0.048 \displaystyle\sum_{i=0}^{L-1} \dfrac{1}{Z^i}\dfrac{d}{dX_t^*}\left(\dfrac{Y_{t+i} - Y'_{t+i}}{X_{t+i}^*}\right),$

where Z is a real rate of discount.

Steady-state Inflation

The analysis of steady-state inflation and the tax overpayments that result from it requires a slightly different framework. Let π be the annual rate of steady-state inflation. In this case it is necessary to look at only one year's income measures to derive the effect of an increase in π on the real error $(Y - Y')/X^*$. Taking the derivative of the real error in one year with respect to π and evaluating the derivative at $\pi = 0$ and $X_t^* = 1$ gives

(7)
$$\dfrac{d}{d\pi}\left(\dfrac{Y_t - Y'_t}{X_t^*}\right) = \tfrac{1}{2}\left\{ \begin{matrix} S_t\,[\,-p_{s,t} + (1 + 2a)nw_{t-a} + (1 + 2b)mp_{m,t-b}] \\ + r_t D_t + OC_t \end{matrix} \right\}$$

$$+ \displaystyle\sum_{j=1}^{L} j\alpha_j I_{t-j} + (C_t - D_t).$$

Note the similarity between this expression and equation 3. Note further that if investment and sales have grown at a constant geometric rate, g, such that $I_{t-j} = I_t/(1 + g)^j$, and $S_{t+1} = (1 + g)S_t$, and if the real rate of discount Z employed in equation 6 in evaluating the long-run effect of a single increase in the price level satisfies $Z = (1+g)$, then the sum of the derivatives in equation 6 is identically equal to the derivative in equation 7. Hence it is unnecessary to estimate equation 7 separately. Instead, we evaluated the effect of steady inflation by employing a discount rate of 3 percent (where 3 percent is an assumed average real growth rate of individual firms) in the procedure for estimating the discounted total effect (equation 6) of a single year's inflation.

Derivation of Numerical Estimates

Numerical estimates of the values of these expressions were made, using a number of simplifying assumptions, for every individual firm with assets of at least $1 million in the Treasury's 1972 tax model file. The first-year overpayment, $FYOPAY$, resulting from 10 percent inflation in one year, the first term of the sum in equation 6, can be evaluated from reported year-end balance sheet and income statement figures as

$$(8) \qquad FYOPAY = 0.048 \, \frac{d}{dX_t^*} \left(\frac{Y_t - Y_t'}{X_t^*} \right)$$

$$= 0.024 \begin{bmatrix} 0.96 \text{ (FIFO inventories)} \\ + \text{(cost of sales)} \\ - \text{(sales)} \\ + \text{(interest expense)} \\ + \text{(other costs, excluding depreciation)} \\ - \text{(other taxable receipts, excluding capital gains)} \end{bmatrix}$$

$$+ 0.048 \begin{bmatrix} \text{(depreciation deduction)} \\ - (1 - \alpha_1) \text{ (additional first year depreciation)} \\ + 0.96 \text{ (net credit position on monetary items)} \end{bmatrix} .$$

This uses the approximation that, under conditions of 4 percent annual real growth and 4 percent inflation, (0.96) (FIFO inventories) $= (a)$ (nominal cost of sales) $+ (b-a)$ (nominal materials cost). The factor α_1 is the depreciation fraction applied to equipment investment in its first year.

We have ignored the fact that the tax value of an operating loss deduction from previous years' losses is greater to a firm under inflation-adjusted accounting than under conventional accounting. We have also assumed that all firms whose inflation-corrected income is lower than conventional income will be able to capture the tax advantage that arises from the reduction of their tax base. In fact, this downward restatement of income will cause some firms to report losses instead of income (or increased losses) whose tax benefit they may never be able to capture if they never have enough income against which to offset these losses. These two biases are partially off-setting.

In principle, inflation correction should encompass capital gains, but capital gains were excluded because they are a very small portion of corporate income and because the data necessary to compute the correction are unavailable. A compromise was also necessary in the treatment of inventories. Since the tax model file does not report the inventory accounting procedure of each firm, we assumed that all firms in an industry had the same ratio of FIFO inventories to total inventories. We used industry-average ratios derived from 1970 Commerce Department data.

Estimating the future overpayments based on equations 4 and 5 required a further set of assumptions. The spillover inventory terms in equation 4 were evaluated assuming $S_{t+1} = 1.04S_t$. The discounted sum of the depreciation terms in equations 4 and 5 was estimated for each firm by estimating an industry-wide average ratio, *DSUM*, of discounted to undiscounted future depreciation to be taken on the industry's current capital stock, and then by applying that ratio to the reported depreciated book value of each firm's depreciable capital. Then the discounted sum, *OPAY*, of all present and future tax overpayments for each firm, represented by equation 6, was computed as

$$(9) \quad OPAY = FYOPAY + \frac{0.024}{Z} \text{(FIFO inventories)} - FAFYD(Z)$$

$$+ 0.048 \, DSUM(Z) \left[\left(\begin{matrix} \text{depreciable} \\ \text{capital at cost} \end{matrix} \right) - \left(\begin{matrix} \text{accumulated} \\ \text{depreciation} \end{matrix} \right) \right].$$

The values used for the discount factor Z were 1.03 in the steady-state inflation case and 1.05 in the case of 10 percent inflation in one year. The term *FAFYD* represents the future effect of the additional first-year depreciation taken in the past.

In deriving each industry average value, *DSUM*, of discounted future depreciation over undiscounted future depreciation, the vintages and original-cost values of the industry's current capital stock were assumed to match the aggregate industry investment totals reported by the Commerce Department. The proportions of annual in-

Table 2-6. Distribution of Nonfinancial Firms by Their Tax Overpayments as Percentage of Assets, Assuming 10 Percent Inflation in One Year, by Industry

Percentage of assets	Size of firm (total assets in millions of dollars)									
	1–10		10–50		50–250		Over 250		All sizes	
	First year[a]	Total[b]	First year[a]	Total[b]	First year[a]	Total[b]	First year[a]	Total[b]	First year[a]	Total[b]
A. Manufacturing, mining, contract construction										
Overpayment										
2.0 to 5.0	4.7	20.8	2.3	18.8	0.3	8.8	0.0	2.6	4.3	20.1
1.5 to 2.0	5.8	11.1	3.4	13.0	0.8	13.9	0.5	8.3	5.4	11.3
1.0 to 1.5	7.9	14.3	6.5	15.2	2.6	18.5	0.0	18.1	7.6	14.5
0.5 to 1.0	11.2	14.4	11.0	15.2	8.8	19.7	4.1	28.0	11.1	14.8
0.0 to 0.5	13.7	14.1	17.5	13.4	17.0	15.2	11.9	23.3	14.1	14.1
Underpayment										
−0.0 to −0.5	13.1	10.2	16.8	9.2	24.1	11.0	25.4	9.8	13.8	10.1
−0.5 to −1.0	11.5	6.1	14.0	5.5	19.4	6.0	30.8	4.7	12.1	6.0
−1.0 to −1.5	10.5	3.2	10.5	3.9	13.1	3.3	15.8	3.1	10.7	3.2
−1.5 to −2.0	7.4	1.7	6.7	2.5	6.4	1.7	7.0	1.8	7.3	1.8
−2.0 to −5.0	13.5	3.8	11.2	3.1	7.3	1.8	4.4	0.3	13.0	3.7
Less than −5.0	0.7	0.3	0.1	0.1	0.0	0.0	0.0	0.0	0.6	0.3
All firms	100.0	100.0	100.0	100.0	100.0	100.0	100.0	100.0	100.0	100.0
Weighted mean percentage of assets	−0.35	0.82	−0.42	0.78	−0.55	0.67	−0.61	0.49	−0.56	0.57
Addenda										
Number of firms	30,699		2,952		871		386		34,878	
Percentage of assets[c]	2.9		2.3		4.5		15.9		25.6	
Percentage of taxes[d]	7.7		6.2		10.9		38.9		63.7	

B. *Transportation, communication, electric and gas services*

Overpayment										
2.0 to 5.0	1.9	9.8	1.2	5.1	0.5	1.1	0.0	1.1	1.7	8.5
1.5 to 2.0	1.4	7.5	0.2	6.7	0.5	4.3	0.0	1.7	1.1	7.0
1.0 to 1.5	3.4	9.2	1.4	8.3	0.0	5.4	0.6	1.7	2.9	8.6
0.5 to 1.0	6.0	11.7	2.5	17.4	1.1	11.9	0.0	12.7	5.2	12.3
0.0 to 0.5	7.1	14.2	7.2	20.6	4.3	32.4	0.0	50.3	6.7	17.3
Underpayment										
−0.0 to −0.5	8.7	18.2	7.2	13.2	4.3	21.6	2.8	22.7	8.1	18.0
−0.5 to −1.0	9.7	13.9	10.0	11.3	10.8	11.4	3.9	6.1	9.5	13.1
−1.0 to −1.5	11.4	6.1	14.6	9.5	10.8	5.4	7.2	2.2	11.5	6.3
−1.5 to −2.0	12.4	4.0	21.1	3.2	17.8	4.3	16.6	1.1	13.7	3.8
−2.0 to −5.0	36.8	5.3	34.5	4.4	49.2	2.2	69.0	0.6	38.5	4.8
Less than −5.0	1.1	0.1	0.2	0.2	0.5	0.0	0.0	0.0	0.9	0.1
All firms	100.0	100.0	100.0	100.0	100.0	100.0	100.0	100.0	100.0	100.0
Weighted mean percentage of assets	−1.45	0.18	−1.68	0.02	−1.79	0.07	−2.02	0.27	−1.98	0.25
Addenda										
Number of firms		3,281		432		185		181		4,079
Percentage of assets[c]		0.3		0.4		1.0		9.8		11.5
Percentage of taxes[d]		0.6		0.7		1.3		8.5		11.0

Table 2-6 (continued)

Percentage of assets	Size of firm (total assets in millions of dollars)									
	1-10		10-50		50-250		Over 250		All sizes	
	First year[a]	Total[b]	First year[a]	Total[b]	First year[a]	Total[b]	First year[a]	Total[b]	First year[a]	Total[b]
C. Wholesale and retail trade, services										
Overpayment										
2.0 to 5.0	3.8	14.0	2.4	10.2	0.3	6.2	1.3	3.8	3.7	13.7
1.5 to 2.0	3.4	10.1	2.7	10.1	0.9	8.8	0.0	6.4	3.3	10.1
1.0 to 1.5	5.5	12.3	4.4	14.2	4.4	11.5	1.3	19.2	5.4	12.4
0.5 to 1.0	9.3	15.9	7.3	15.3	4.1	12.1	0.0	17.9	9.2	15.9
0.0 to 0.5	10.3	17.5	13.2	15.9	10.9	17.1	9.0	20.5	10.5	17.4
Underpayment										
−0.0 to −0.5	13.1	11.4	16.3	11.9	16.2	12.4	25.6	7.7	13.3	11.4
−0.5 to −1.0	14.0	5.8	14.5	8.5	17.6	15.9	25.6	11.5	14.1	6.1
−1.0 to −1.5	11.1	4.6	11.3	5.3	13.8	6.2	11.5	11.5	11.1	4.7
−1.5 to −2.0	9.2	3.4	9.9	4.1	10.3	6.2	9.0	1.3	9.2	3.5
−2.0 to −5.0	19.6	4.6	17.6	4.3	21.4	3.8	16.7	0.0	19.5	4.6
Less than −5.0	0.7	0.3	0.3	0.2	0.0	0.0	0.0	0.0	0.7	0.3
All firms	100.0	100.0	100.0	100.0	100.0	100.0	100.0	100.0	100.0	100.0
Weighted mean percentage of assets	−0.76	0.50	−0.75	0.40	−1.02	0.10	−0.56	0.56	−0.74	0.43
Addenda										
Number of firms	32,169		1,750		340		78		34,337	
Percentage of assets[c]	2.6		1.3		1.5		1.7		7.2	
Percentage of taxes[d]	5.3		2.4		1.9		3.0		12.6	

D. Finance, insurance, real estate

	Group 1 (a)	Group 1 (b)	Group 2 (a)	Group 2 (b)	Group 3 (a)	Group 3 (b)	Group 4 (a)	Group 4 (b)	All firms (a)	All firms (b)
Overpayment										
2.0 to 5.0	4.4	4.8	1.1	1.2	1.3	1.6	1.4	1.5	3.0	3.3
1.5 to 2.0	2.4	2.9	0.7	0.8	1.7	1.6	3.9	4.1	1.8	2.2
1.0 to 1.5	3.8	4.5	1.2	1.2	2.6	2.7	6.2	6.3	2.9	3.4
0.5 to 1.0	7.4	8.3	4.0	4.8	3.4	3.6	3.5	4.5	5.8	6.6
0.0 to 0.5	34.2	35.1	61.2	63.3	50.2	53.9	44.4	47.3	44.5	46.1
Underpayment										
−0.0 to −0.5	10.4	10.1	20.2	18.0	27.6	24.3	24.9	21.0	15.5	14.2
−0.5 to −1.0	4.8	5.7	3.8	3.7	6.5	6.2	9.7	10.0	4.8	5.2
−1.0 to −1.5	2.9	4.7	1.8	2.1	2.4	2.3	3.0	2.7	2.5	3.6
−1.5 to −2.0	3.2	5.8	1.2	1.7	1.7	1.8	1.0	1.2	2.4	4.0
−2.0 to −5.0	25.1	17.5	4.7	3.2	2.5	1.8	1.9	1.3	16.0	11.1
Less than −5.0	1.2	0.4	0.1	0.0	0.0	0.0	0.0	0.0	0.7	0.3
All firms	100.0	100.0	100.0	100.0	100.0	100.0	100.0	100.0	100.0	100.0
Weighted mean percentage of assets	−0.48	−0.17	−0.03	0.05	−0.00	0.05	0.24	0.27	0.14	0.19
Addenda										
Number of firms	15,877		8,880		2,507		772		28,036	
Percentage of assets[c]	2.2		6.9		9.9		36.8		55.7	
Percentage of taxes[d]	0.8		1.5		2.4		8.0		12.6	

Sources: U.S. Department of the Treasury, 1972 corporate tax model file. For method of derivation, see appendix text. Figures are rounded.
a. Percentage of firms for which the ratio of first-year overpayments to assets lies in the indicated range.
b. Percentage of firms for which the ratio of discounted total overpayments to assets lies in the indicated range; the overpayments caused in future years by one year's inflation are discounted at 5 percent.
c. Percentage of all business assets held by all firms covered in the sample that are accounted for by the firms in each column.
d. Percentage of all taxes paid by all firms covered in the sample that are accounted for by the firms in each column.

Table 2-7. Distribution of Nonfinancial Firms by Their Tax Overpayments in Every Year as Percentage of Assets, Assuming 10 Percent Steady-State Inflation, by Industry[a]

Percentage of assets	Size of firm (total assets in millions of dollars)				
	1–10	*10–50*	*50–250*	*Over 250*	*All sizes*
A. Manufacturing, mining, contract construction					
Overpayment					
2.0 to 5.0	22.7	21.8	12.4	3.9	22.2
1.5 to 2.0	12.0	14.0	14.4	11.7	12.2
1.0 to 1.5	14.3	14.9	19.9	21.8	14.5
0.5 to 1.0	14.4	15.1	18.0	25.9	14.7
0.0 to 0.5	13.9	11.9	14.8	19.4	13.9
Underpayment					
−0.0 to −0.5	9.2	8.7	8.5	8.8	9.1
−0.5 to −1.0	5.3	4.9	6.1	4.1	5.3
−1.0 to −1.5	2.8	3.6	2.9	2.3	2.9
−1.5 to −2.0	1.6	2.2	1.4	1.8	1.7
−2.0 to −5.0	3.4	2.8	1.7	0.3	3.3
Less than −5.0	0.3	0.1	0.0	0.0	0.3
All firms	100.0	100.0	100.0	100.0	100.0
Weighted mean percentage of assets	0.92	0.89	0.79	0.62	0.70
Addenda					
Number of firms	30,669	2,952	871	386	34,878
Percentage of assets[b]	2.9	2.3	4.5	15.9	25.6
Percentage of taxes[c]	7.7	6.2	10.9	38.9	63.7
B. Transportation, communication, electric and gas services					
Overpayment					
2.0 to 5.0	12.7	7.6	2.7	1.7	11.2
1.5 to 2.0	8.6	8.6	4.3	2.2	8.1
1.0 to 1.5	8.4	13.4	9.2	11.0	9.1
0.5 to 1.0	15.0	19.4	26.5	46.4	17.4
0.0 to 0.5	16.5	16.7	28.1	24.9	17.4
Underpayment					
−0.0 to −0.5	15.4	11.1	11.4	8.8	14.5
−0.5 to −1.0	11.4	11.6	9.7	1.7	10.9
−1.0 to −1.5	5.3	5.8	3.2	2.2	5.1
−1.5 to −2.0	1.9	2.1	3.2	0.6	1.9
−2.0 to −5.0	4.5	3.5	1.6	0.6	4.1
Less than −5.0	0.1	0.2	0.0	0.0	0.1
All firms	100.0	100.0	100.0	100.0	100.0
Weighted mean percentage of assets	0.40	0.27	0.38	0.67	0.63

Table 2-7 (*continued*)

Percentage of assets	Size of firm (total assets in millions of dollars)				
	1–10	*10–50*	*50–250*	*Over 250*	*All sizes*

B. Transportation, communication, electric and gas services (continued)

Addenda					
Number of firms	3,281	432	185	181	4,079
Percentage of assets[b]	0.3	0.4	1.0	9.8	11.5
Percentage of taxes[c]	0.6	0.7	1.3	8.5	11.0

C. Wholesale and retail trade, services

Overpayment					
2.0 to 5.0	15.4	12.1	6.5	5.1	15.1
1.5 to 2.0	10.3	10.7	11.2	5.1	10.3
1.0 to 1.5	13.1	14.6	12.1	23.1	13.2
0.5 to 1.0	16.5	15.3	10.6	17.9	16.3
0.0 to 0.5	17.6	15.6	19.7	19.2	17.5
Underpayment					
−0.0 to −0.5	10.7	12.5	11.5	7.7	10.8
−0.5 to −1.0	5.6	6.9	14.1	12.8	5.8
−1.0 to −1.5	4.5	5.0	5.3	7.7	4.6
−1.5 to −2.0	2.6	3.5	5.6	1.3	2.6
−2.0 to −5.0	3.5	3.7	3.5	0.0	3.5
Less than −5.0	0.3	0.1	0.0	0.0	0.3
All firms	100.0	100.0	100.0	100.0	100.0
Weighted mean percentage of assets	0.61	0.49	0.20	0.67	0.54
Addenda					
Number of firms	32,169	1,750	340	78	34,337
Percentage of assets[b]	2.6	1.3	1.5	1.7	7.2
Percentage of taxes[c]	5.3	2.4	1.9	3.0	12.6

D. Finance, insurance, real estate

Overpayment					
2.0 to 5.0	5.0	1.2	1.7	1.5	3.5
1.5 to 2.0	3.0	0.8	1.6	4.3	2.2
1.0 to 1.5	4.7	1.3	2.7	6.2	3.5
0.5 to 1.0	8.7	5.0	3.7	4.7	7.0
0.0 to 0.5	35.2	63.8	54.4	48.4	46.3
Underpayment					
−0.0 to −0.5	10.3	17.4	23.8	19.8	14.0
−0.5 to −1.0	6.2	3.8	6.2	10.0	5.6
−1.0 to −1.5	6.1	2.2	2.3	3.0	4.4
−1.5 to −2.0	7.9	1.8	1.7	0.9	5.2

Table 2-7 (*continued*)

Percentage of assets	Size of firm (total assets in millions of dollars)				
	1–10	*10–50*	*50–250*	*Over 250*	*All sizes*
D. Finance, insurance, real estate (*continued*)					
−2.0 to −5.0	12.2	2.6	1.6	1.1	7.9
Less than −5.0	0.4	0.0	0.0	0.0	0.2
All firms	100.0	100.0	100.0	100.0	100.0
Weighted mean percentage of assets	−0.10	0.07	0.06	0.28	0.20
Addenda					
Number of firms	15,877	8,880	2,507	772	28,036
Percentage of assets[b]	2.2	6.9	9.9	36.8	55.7
Percentage of taxes[c]	0.8	1.5	2.4	8.0	12.6

Sources: U.S. Department of the Treasury, 1972 corporate tax model file. For method of derivation, see appendix text. Figures are rounded.

a. Percentage of firms in each size class for which the ratio of yearly overpayments to assets lies in the indicated range.

b. Percentage of all business assets held by all firms covered in the sample that are accounted for by the firms in each column.

c. Percentage of all taxes paid by all firms covered in the sample that are accounted for by the firms in each column.

vestment assumed to have gone into equipment and into structures (property under sections 1245 and 1250 of the Internal Revenue Code) were based on 1971 proportions reported in an unpublished Treasury Department survey, with adjustments for earlier years based on year-to-year differences in these proportions reported in the *Annual Survey of Manufactures* of the Bureau of the Census and in the Commerce Department's investment series. Unpublished Treasury Department estimates were used for the proportion of capital depreciated by the straight-line method in each industry. Accelerated depreciation was computed by the 200 percent declining-balance method for equipment and by the 150 percent declining-balance method for structures, with allowance for additional first-year depreciation. The average tax accounting lives chosen for structures and equipment in each industry were those lives that made it possible to duplicate most closely the industry figures for capital, accumulated depreciation, and depreciation deductions reported in the 1972 *Statistics of Income.*

Tables 2-6 and 2-7 supplement tables 2-4 and 2-5 by reporting the variation across firms in the tax effects of inflation for four broad industry groups.

Comments by E. Cary Brown

The major tax-related inefficiency caused by inflation is the increase in the real rate of return required before investment appears worth undertaking. The other tax-related effects are less serious. The increased lock-in effect matters little for corporations and can be dealt with in other ways at the personal level. The increase in the debt-equity ratio is problematic and of little importance for efficiency. The increase in the required rate of return is greatest for long-lived assets and would cause a shift of investment from long- to short-lived assets. With the arithmetic underlying this conclusion of the paper by T. Nicolaus Tideman and Donald Tucker, I have no quarrel. I do question their basic assumptions, however. What should be compared with what? Should one tack inflation onto the existing corporation income tax structure? Or should one compare the existing system under inflation with a tax system that did not subsidize investment and did define income correctly? I think the latter comparison is most instructive. To hold otherwise comes close to claiming that distortions should also be adjusted for price changes.

Table 2-8 illustrates this point. It is based on depreciable assets that have useful lives of twelve and eight years. The assumptions are the same as those used by Tideman and Tucker. The real after-tax cost of capital to corporations is approximately 5.6 percent. The discount rate used in calculating the present value of depreciation deductions is the nominal market rate. The implicit rate of return is the cost of capital, calculated according to the Hall-Jorgenson formula, minus "true" depreciation, computed by the declining-balance method at one and one-half and two times the straight-line rate (as assumed by Tideman and Tucker). I also show the consequences of assuming tax depreciation life to be one-third shorter than economic life. Finally, the table shows both the implicit return for normal depreciation without a tax credit and the effects on the required rate of return of shortening tax lives.

If one starts with the existing tax treatment of corporations, as Tideman and Tucker do, the rate of return required from a twelve-year corporate investment is nearly 6 percent (see line 4, table 2-8); it rises to nearly 7 percent when inflation proceeds at 2 percent (line 6) and to about 8 percent when inflation is 7 percent (line 8). However, one might with equal validity start with a system that does not permit accelerated depreciation either explicitly or by shortened lives, and with no investment tax credit. In that case the required rate of return is 8 to 9 percent, depending on one's predilection regarding straight-line or double-declining-balance depreciation for tax purposes (line 2). The required rate of return is sensitive to assumptions regarding method of depreciation, investment tax credit, and depreciable lives. Even a 7 percent inflation with present tax adjustments does not require as high a return as when income is properly measured and prices are stable.

This exercise makes a simple point: if we are serious about defining corporate income correctly—by moving toward realistic depreciable lives, eliminating the investment tax credit, *and* adjusting depreciation for inflation—then corporate taxable income will increase, even if no account is taken of monetary gains and losses.

But let us suppose that we want to retain the existing set of investment incentives. Even then, Tideman and Tucker show, a substantial number of firms will face higher taxes as a result of inflation adjustments. More than half of all their firms experience such an increase in the first year after the onset of inflation, and 20 percent face an increase in the present value of the tax liabilities over the long run. I cannot imagine Congress legislating a tax system for the purpose of mitigating the impact of inflation that would increase the tax of one-fifth of all corporations during inflation. Congress might make the adjustments optional, but such an option would clearly worsen, not improve, the definition of income. Because such a retrograde step is quite possible, I would not favor serious discussion of indexing unless someone makes stronger arguments for its equity and efficiency than I have yet heard.

I would give more weight to the point that the tax-related effects of inflation are primarily distributional, affecting holders of existing assets. Considerations of efficiency relate primarily to new investment. Surely less cumbersome devices than those discussed in this paper exist to offset the effect of inflation. The investment tax credit, for example, could be made a function of the rate of inflation. It should not take much ingenuity to develop an investment tax credit that would neutralize the impact of inflation on asset durability. Perhaps I can summarize my views by restating Brown's law: "Any tax proposal that would increase AT&T's taxes by $1 billion is not going to fly."

Table 2-8. Real Rate of Return before Corporate Tax on New Investment Required to Earn a Real Market Rate of Interest of 5.6 Percent after a Corporate Tax on a Twelve-Year and an Eight-Year Depreciable Asset
Percent

Depreciation method and estimated life	Rate of return before tax assuming "true" depreciation as declining balance	
	At 1.5 times straight-line rate	At 2 times straight-line rate
No inflation,[a] *no tax credit*		
1. Straight line, 12 years	9.0	9.8
2. Sum of years' digits, 12 years	8.0	8.5
No inflation,[a] *7 percent tax credit*		
3. Straight line, 12 years	6.9	7.2
4. Sum of years' digits, 12 years	5.8	5.9
5. Sum of years' digits, 8 years	5.1	5.0
2 percent inflation,[b] *7 percent tax credit*		
6. Sum of years' digits, 12 years	6.6	6.8
7. Sum of years' digits, 8 years	5.7	5.7
7 percent inflation,[c] *7 percent tax credit*		
8. Sum of years' digits, 12 years	7.9	8.5
9. Sum of years' digits, 8 years	6.8	7.0

Source: This table uses the well-known Hall-Jorgenson formula for the rental cost of capital. (See Robert E. Hall and Dale W. Jorgenson, "Application of the Theory of Optimum Capital Accumulation," in Gary Fromm, ed., *Tax Incentives and Capital Spending* [Brookings Institution, 1971], pp. 14–18.) From the rental cost of capital is subtracted the "true" depreciation, calculated by the declining-balance method at 150 percent or 200 percent of straight-line rates in the table in order to find the required rate of return.

$$R = (\rho + \delta) \frac{1 - \kappa}{1 - \tau} - \frac{\tau Z}{1-\tau} - \delta,$$

where
R = rental cost of capital,
ρ = real rate of return after tax,
δ = rate of exponential decay (depreciation) of asset,
κ = rate of investment tax credit,
τ = rate of corporate tax,
Z = present value of tax depreciation, which for the straight-line case is

$$(1/12) \int_0^{12} e^{-(\rho + i)t} \, dt,$$

where ρ = real rate of return, and i = rate of inflation.
The real market rate of return after corporate tax is based on equation 2 in the Tideman-Tucker appendix A, using the following assumed values: $R = 0.12$, $f = 0.314$, $r_d = 0.0393$, and $r_e = 0.0926$. The tax rate on corporate profits is assumed to be 41 percent.
a. Real and nominal market rates after corporate tax are 5.6 percent; real and nominal market rates before tax are 8.9 percent.
b. Real market rate is 5.6 percent; nominal market rate, 7.6 percent (from Tideman and Tucker).
c. Real market rate is 5.6 percent; nominal market rate, 12.4 percent (from Tideman and Tucker).

Comments by George Tolley

The paper by T. Nicolaus Tideman and Donald Tucker provides empirical estimates of both the short- and long-run revenue impact of applying the proposals of the Financial Accounting Standards Board to the corporation income tax. The difference between the short- and long-run impact is quite illuminating and provides an interesting contrast with the other empirical estimates presented to the conference. Sidney Davidson and Roman Weil, in particular, focus on a single year, and they happen to have chosen a year that yields more dramatic results than almost any other in recent times. The results presented by Tideman and Tucker make clear that the picture is very different if one looks at the long run. I am pleased also that they have examined indexing the existing tax structure and have not tried to broaden their topic to include general tax reform.

I think that it is important to reconsider why we are interested in the effects of inflation on income tax burdens. A major reason is that our present tax system increases the instability associated with inflation and permits inflation to increase the inevitable uncertainty people must live with. The first effect is shown by the formula that relates the impact of a change in expected inflation, π, on the nominal rate of interest, r, if the real interest rate, i, stays constant. That formula is $r = i + \pi/(1 + t)$, where t is the marginal tax rate. The result of the present tax system is to increase the swings in nominal interest rates. This consequence adds to the windfall gains and losses that holders of existing assets and liabilities experience when the rate of inflation unexpectedly changes. Thus erratic inflation increases uncertainty, and when people begin to expect inflation, the tax system multiplies its effect on interest rates, inflicting additional windfall gains and losses.

If indexing becomes a serious proposal, its impact on Treasury revenues will become a prominent issue. I think that there has been some confusion on this subject. Let's suppose that we are going to treat issuers and holders of all private debt symmetrically. Then the revenue effect of debt adjustments will depend on the marginal tax rates of borrowers and lenders. On balance the marginal tax rates of borrowers are probably higher than those of lenders, primarily because of corporate borrowing and the double taxation of corporate-source income and because much lending is done by tax-exempt institutions. On balance the adjustment for private debt would probably increase revenues by $5 billion to $10 billion, but please do not hold me to these numbers. The story concerning debt issued by governments is quite different. The marginal tax rate of these "borrowers" is zero. Only the lenders would receive any adjustment; it would unambiguously reduce revenues, and by far more than the increase in revenues from private debt. For example, if holders of government debt face an average marginal tax rate of 30 percent (a modest estimate), then a 10 percent inflation could easily reduce revenues by $20 billion to $30 billion. The revenue loss from these two changes might constitute a powerful deterrent to support by a secretary of the treasury.

Discussion

Sidney Davidson initially expressed skepticism over the results reported by T. Nicolaus Tideman and Donald Tucker in tables 2-1 through 2-4, which seemed to indicate that firms in all industries on the average experienced an increase in taxation from indexing during the first year after the onset of inflation. This result contrasted markedly with the finding of Davidson and Roman Weil that some firms gained and some lost. E. Cary Brown pointed out that the Tideman-Tucker results were averages over industrial groups, while those of Davidson and Weil referred to individual firms. Frank Weston and Henry Aaron called attention to the fact that Tideman and Tucker's results deal with the consequences of one year's inflation following a long period of stable prices, while Davidson and Weil's results include the carry-over effects from the actual inflation before 1974. Davidson said he was satisfied that this difference between the two sets of estimates was sufficient to explain their somewhat dissimilar results.

Tideman challenged Brown's criticism that an indexed system should not be compared with the existing tax system but rather with one that was purged of investment incentives. He suggested that the investment tax credit was part of the Internal Revenue Code, not only (and perhaps not primarily) to offset inflation, but also to encourage investment in eligible assets rather than in real property. He also expressed doubt that the investment tax credit could easily be used to offset the effects of inflation, because one would need to know the future course of inflation and the result would be a very messy formula. Stanley Surrey suggested that supporters of the investment tax credit may well use any argument that is handy—that it offsets inflation when there is inflation, that it promotes investment when the goal is more investment. He supported Brown's alternative calculations as a desirable complement rather than as an alternative to those of Tideman and Tucker. Richard Goode challenged the contention that the introduction of the investment tax credit had anything to do with inflation. He recalled the various debates over the introduction of the investment tax credit and expressed the view that inflation had not come up during them.

Arthur Okun argued that the treatment of inventories in this paper and by the Financial Accounting Standards Board was inconsistent with the actual practice of many American businesses, particularly retail firms. Okun stated that firms often price items for sale at the time they enter the firm's inventory and do not reprice them despite subsequent increases in the cost of replacing them. Indeed, if that were not the case, retail prices would not lag behind wholesale prices. Similarly, manufacturing firms that take fixed price orders for future delivery do not earn inflation gains on their inventories. He acknowledged that these practices are less common than in the past but maintained that they remain widespread. For such cases FIFO accounting properly measures income. Davidson expressed doubt about Okun's characterization of firm behavior by recalling the *New Yorker* cartoon showing a woman with a shopping basket racing with a store clerk who is clutching a price overstamp to see who can reach the checkout counter first. Tideman and Tucker countered that the behavioral question was irrelevant, because the objective of the tax system is to measure income correctly, not to ascertain how it was earned. Tucker also held that Okun's position was inconsistent with the Haig-Simons definition of income, which requires that receipts and expenditures be recorded in real purchasing power units when received or incurred.

Martin Feldstein expressed doubt that the revenue consequences of adjusting interest income and debt for the consequences of inflation would be as important as George Tolley had suggested. Such adjustment could be limited to new debt so that the revenue effects would be small at first. Furthermore, if adjustments for inflation were made, lenders would require smaller interest premiums during inflation; as a result, the government could pay less interest on its debt. The net revenue and expenditure effect might be very small. John Bossons reinforced Feldstein's point by pointing out that indexing would reduce fluctuations in interest rates and the attendant oscillation in bond prices; the reduction in uncertainty facing bondholders would reduce the interest rate they would demand, further lowering the government's borrowing costs.

CHAPTER THREE

Inflation Accounting: Implications of the FASB Proposal

SIDNEY DAVIDSON *and* ROMAN L. WEIL

INFLATION has been a fact of economic life throughout the Western world for some time now, yet its effects have gone unrecognized in financial statements prepared in accordance with generally accepted accounting principles in the United States and most other countries where business annual reports are presented. In 1974, however, there was a rash of official proposals by the authoritative accounting bodies in the English-speaking nations that, if adopted, would require the publication of financial statement data adjusted for changes in the general price level (purchasing power of money) as supplements to the conventional financial statements.[1]

1. As far as we can determine, there are no official proposals by the established accounting bodies in the non-English-speaking nations of Western Europe that would require the publication of accounts adjusted for changes in the general price level. The countries we have surveyed include France, West Germany, Sweden, Italy, the Netherlands, and Belgium. In many of these countries (with the notable exception of the Netherlands) the organized accounting profession is relatively weak, and the state plays a much larger role in the accounting process. In the English-speaking nations the proposals for supplemental financial data, adjusted for changes in the general price level, have come without exception from organized professional groups that have held an established position for some time and have some measure of control over the actions of their members.

The United Kingdom acted first, perhaps because inflation has been a major problem for a longer time there than elsewhere. In May 1974 the Accounting Standards Steering Committee of the Institute of Chartered Accountants in England and Wales issued Provisional Statement of Standard Accounting Practice No. 7, which would require the publication of financial data adjusted for changes in the general price level along with the conventional statements. The implementation of this provisional statement was deferred, however, pending the report of a study group, known as the Sandilands Committee, appointed by the government to study the likely effects of publishing such data. In September 1975 the Sandilands Committee rendered its report, recommending that "current cost" data, rather than general-price-level-adjusted data, be provided as a supplementary disclosure in the financial statements.[2] The committee suggested that certain companies should adopt its proposals for accounting periods beginning not later than December 24, 1977.

In the United States, the Financial Accounting Standards Board (FASB) issued an exposure draft of proposed financial accounting standards on December 31, 1974, that would require financial statements issued in the United States to contain general price-level-adjusted data as supplements to the customary report.[3] The FASB accepted comments on the exposure draft until September 30, 1975. In the United States, as in the United Kingdom, the proposal for general price level adjustments had not been adopted as of mid-1976. In March 1976 the Securities and Exchange Commission issued Accounting Series Release 190, requiring large firms (those with over $100 million of inventories and gross plant and for which the amount of inventories and plant are at least 10 percent of total assets) to disclose replacement cost information about inventories, cost of goods sold, plant, and depreciation. The Securities and Exchange Commission requires, as it were, price level data based on *specific,* rather than general, price changes. In June 1976 the FASB announced that it was deferring action on its proposal.

In December 1974 the Canadian Institute of Chartered Accoun-

2. *Inflation Accounting,* Report of the Inflation Accounting Committee, F. E. P. Sandilands, Chairman (London: Her Majesty's Stationery Office, 1975), p. 159.

3. The FASB designates such statements "reporting in units of general purchasing power." See FASB, *Financial Reporting in Units of General Purchasing Power,* Proposed Statement of Financial Accounting Standards, Exposure Draft (Stamford, Conn.: FASB, December 31, 1974), p. 8.

tants (CICA) published a tentative guideline for the required reporting of general-price-level-adjusted data.[4] The CICA will probably reach a decision about issuing a formal "recommendation" (a Canadian euphemism for a requirement that certain accounting actions be taken) on this subject by the end of 1976. It seems likely that in Canada the final pronouncement will be one that calls for the presentation of current (replacement) cost data.

In each of these countries the proposals by the accounting organizations for inflation adjustments provide for restatement to reflect changes in the general purchasing power of money and do not call for the use of replacement costs, or current values. Put another way, the official accounting proposals call for a change in the measuring unit in which financial data are expressed. The unit would be changed from the historical dollar at the date transactions are entered into to a constant dollar representing a given quantity of purchasing power. The adjustments would be made by the use of a single general price index. This procedure is entirely different from one that seeks to state the current costs, or replacement costs, of individual items by using either specific item revaluations or a multitude of specific price indexes. In this latter approach, the valuation basis is changed from acquisition cost to current replacement cost. A major problem in this method is determining which index is appropriate for which items in financial statements. If the general price level were completely stable, there would be no adjustments under the first method, but adjustments would be required under the second method to record changes in relative prices.[5]

The FASB proposal, which is the "official" U.S. version of the constant measuring unit approach, designated the gross national product implicit price deflator as the index to be used in making the general price level adjustments. In the United Kingdom the designated index is the retail price index, a variant of the U.S. consumer price index. In Canada the index prescribed is the gross national expenditure implicit price index, which is roughly similar to the U.S. GNP deflator.

Although the official accounting proposals in all three countries called for the presentation of supplemental general-price-level-

4. See "Accounting for the Effects of Changes in the Purchasing Power of Money," *CICA Handbook,* Filing Instruction 13 (Toronto: CICA, December 1974).
5. See general discussion, chapter 9.

adjusted financial data, these countries have differed to some degree in their past approaches to the use of current values for individual assets in formal financial statements. In the United Kingdom revaluations of individual assets, especially land and commercial properties, have been made sporadically in the formal records and reflected in the regular financial statements. In the United States such revaluations have been barred since the issuance of an Accounting Principles Board opinion in 1965.[6] Not many such revaluations had occurred in the three decades before that date, but the 1920s had seen many such write-ups in the United States. In Canada individual assets were occasionally written up to replacement cost, or current value. A more far-reaching development occurred in Canada in 1975. Several companies published supplemental replacement-cost financial statements, with individual major asset and expense items restated in terms of their replacement costs, or current values.[7] We do not know of any published supplemental replacement-cost financial statements in the United States.[8] If the official proposals were adopted, however, all published financial statements in the three countries would contain supplemental restatements to reflect the effect of changing general price levels.

General Price Level Adjustments for Financial Reporting

In this section we explain the mechanics of the FASB's proposed general-price-level-adjusted accounting and illustrate them with an estimated general-price-level-adjusted income statement for the General Electric Company (GE) for 1974. We then present estimates of

6. American Institute of Certified Public Accountants, Accounting Principles Board, "Status of Accounting Research Bulletins," *Opinions of the Accounting Principles Board 6* (New York: AICPA, October 1965). But note the dissent by Sidney Davidson.

7. See, for example, the replacement-cost financial statements for Barber-Ellis in "How to Report Results in Real Dollars," *Business Week,* May 5, 1975, pp. 72–74.

8. In a statement dated August 21, 1975, the Securities and Exchange Commission (SEC) proposed requiring U.S. corporations to disclose some of the major items that would result from replacement-cost accounting in footnotes to the conventional statements. (See SEC, File no. 07F7-579.) The proposal suggested that the disclosures might be unaudited or might apply only to companies larger than a certain size, or both. The SEC invited comments on its proposal through January 31, 1976. Thus any requirements are unlikely to become effective before the end of 1976.

1974 general-price-level-adjusted financial income for the thirty companies in the Dow Jones industrial average and some observations on
the significance of those income estimates.

General-Price-Level-Adjusted Income Statements

General price level accounting adjusts the recorded historical cost
amount of each item disclosed in conventional financial statements
for changes in the general purchasing power of the dollar since the
item was first recorded in the accounts. The adjustments attempt to
show all financial statement items in terms of the purchasing power
of the dollar at the end of the year being reported by using the GNP
implicit price deflator as the index for restating all items in end-of-
year dollars.

General-price-level-adjusted income statements differ in essen-
tially five important respects from conventional income statements.
These differences, illustrated in table 3-1 with data estimated from
GE's 1974 annual report, are explained below.[9]

*Revenues and expenses occurring fairly evenly throughout the
year.* (See lines 1 and 5, table 3-1.) Sales and expenses, other than the
cost of goods sold and depreciation, usually occur fairly evenly
throughout the year. To restate them in terms of dollars of end-of-
year general purchasing power, they are adjusted for half a year of
general price change. Since the price increase in 1974 (as measured
by the GNP deflator) was about 11.8 percent, the price change for
half a year (geometric mean—see appendix A) was about 5.7 percent.

Sales and other income (except revenue recognized on the equity
method) as well as expenses (except cost of goods sold and depreciation) are increased by about 5.7 percent in the adjustment process.

Cost of goods sold. (Line 3, table 3-1.) With rising prices, the cost
of goods sold on a price-level-adjusted basis will be higher than that
reported in conventional financial statements. How much higher depends in large part on the cost-flow assumption—first-in-first-out
(FIFO), last-in-first-out (LIFO), etc.—used. During periods of rising prices and increasing inventory quantities, the inflation adjustment will be greatest for firms using a FIFO assumption.

---

9. The techniques for making these estimates are described in Sidney Davidson,
Clyde P. Stickney, and Roman L. Weil, *Inflation Accounting: A Guide for the Accountant and the Financial Analyst* (McGraw-Hill, 1976), chap. 8.

Table 3-1. General Electric Company Consolidated Income Statement, as Conventionally Reported and after General Price Level Adjustment, 1974
Dollar amounts in millions

Item	As con- ventionally reported (historical dollars)	After general price level adjustment (end-of-1974 dollars)	Change (percent)
Revenues			
1. Sales and other income	13,556	14,335	5.7
2. Equity method revenue	43	−24	−155.8
Total revenues	13,599	14,311	5.2
Expenses			
3. Cost of goods sold[a]	9,761	10,357	6.1
4. Depreciation[b]	376	545	44.9
5. All other expenses	2,853	3,017	5.7
Total expenses	12,990	13,919	7.2
6. Income before gain on monetary items (revenues minus expenses)	608	392	−35.5
7. Gain on monetary items[c]	...	177	...
8. Net income (including gain on monetary items)	608	569	−6.4

Source: Derived from *General Electric 1974 Annual Report*. See text for explanation of the methods used in deriving the estimates.

a. Eighty percent of inventories are valued by the LIFO cost-flow assumption; 20 percent by the FIFO assumption.

b. The depreciation method used is sum of the years' digits. The average life of depreciable assets is estimated to be 6.3 years; the price index increased by 44.9 percent during the 6.3 years preceding December 31, 1974.

c. The net gain on monetary items is computed as follows (in millions of dollars):

	December 31, 1974	December 31, 1973
Monetary liabilities		
Current liabilities and long-term (domestic) borrowings	5,068.3	4,401.3
Monetary assets		
Cash receivables (both long- and short-term), customer financing, recoverable costs, government securities, and advances to affiliates	3,430.5	3,031.7
Net monetary liabilities	1,637.8	1,369.6

The average of net domestic monetary liabilities for the year 1974 was $1,503.7 [0.5 × ($1,637.8 + $1,369.6)] million. The price change for the year was 11.8 percent. GE's gain from being a net debtor during 1974 when prices increased by 11.8 percent was thus about $177 million (0.118 × $1,503.7), the net gain shown in the table.

In calculating the cost of goods sold under all cost-flow assumptions, it is first necessary to determine the amount of purchases for the year. They can be calculated using the traditional accounting relationship:

$$\text{Beginning inventory} + \text{Purchases} - \text{Ending inventory} = \text{Cost of goods sold},$$

$$\text{Purchases} = \text{Cost of goods sold} + \text{Ending inventory} - \text{Beginning inventory}.$$

The cost-of-goods-sold amount is given on the income statement, and the amounts for beginning and ending inventories are given on the comparative balance sheet. Although the amount of purchases is unaffected by the cost-flow assumption used, the adjustment procedure differs depending on the flow assumption used.

GE reports in the footnotes to its financial statements that it uses a LIFO flow assumption for 80 percent of its inventory and a FIFO flow assumption for 20 percent. Our analysis indicates that this results in an average increase of a little over 6 percent in the cost of goods sold in the adjusted income statement.[10]

Depreciation. (Line 4, table 3-1.) General-price-level-adjusted depreciation is almost always much larger than conventionally reported depreciation. For most firms depreciable assets typically are acquired many years before the period being reported, and price levels have increased substantially since acquisition. The depreciation adjustment reflects a portion (equal to the depreciation rate) of the cumulative change in prices since the depreciable assets were acquired. Our analysis indicates that GE's depreciable assets were acquired, on the average, a little over six years before December 31, 1974. The cumulative price increase over that time has been about 45 percent; the depreciation expense is correspondingly increased.[11]

Gain or loss on monetary items. (Line 7, table 3-1.) Price-level-adjusted income statements explicitly show the gain for the period in purchasing power captured by a debtor (or the loss suffered by a creditor) during a period of rising general price levels. Since most industrial companies are typically net debtors, most will show purchasing power gains from this debt. The liabilities will be paid off, or discharged, with dollars of smaller general purchasing power than that of dollars originally borrowed. The difference between the purchasing power borrowed and that repaid is the gain on a monetary liability during the term of the loan. The gain from being in a net

10. Some of the companies reported on in table 3-2 use a FIFO assumption for all their inventories. Adjustments for some of these companies result in increases of the reported cost of goods sold by more than 10 percent.

11. Edward Gramlich points out that straight-line depreciation based on current prices during periods of moderate inflation increases depreciation relative to straight-line depreciation based on purchase prices about as much for moderate (5 percent) inflation as does accelerated (sum-of-the-years'-digits or double-declining-balance) depreciation. (See chapter 10.) In our calculations we assume that in switching over to current-price-level depreciation, firms would be permitted to continue using accelerated depreciation.

monetary liability position, although real in an economic sense, does not produce a current flow of cash.

The gain or loss from holding monetary items is in many ways the most meaningful of the general price level adjustments. The interest expense reported in the conventional income statements is the dollar cost of borrowing. It depends on the interest rate negotiated at the time of the loan. That interest rate, in turn, depends in part on the lender's and borrower's anticipations about the rate of inflation during the term of the loan. (Interest rates are increased when the lender expects inflation during the term of the loan. The borrower accepts the higher rate because he or she expects to repay "cheaper" dollars.) Thus the borrower's conventional income statement shows an interest expense that reflects the inflation expected by both the borrower and the lender. The gain from being in a net monetary liability position in a time of rising prices is in a real sense an offset to reported interest expense. It reflects a gain from being a debtor during a period of inflation that both parties to the loan expected. After the fact, whether the borrower or the lender benefited depends on whether the actual rate of price increase during the term of the loan differed from the rate anticipated by both parties at the time the loan was made. If the actual rate of price increase turns out to be less than the anticipated rate, then the lender benefits. If the actual rate turns out to be greater than the anticipated rate, then the borrower benefits.

The gain on monetary items might better be shown on the income statement as a deduction from reported interest expense. The net amount would represent the "real" interest expense after allowing for the inflation actually realized during the period. The FASB exposure draft, however, calls for the disclosure of monetary gains or losses as a separately reported component of adjusted income.[12]

Revenue recognized under the equity method. (Line 2, table 3-1.) Although the GE income statement is a consolidated statement, some subsidiaries (principally GE Credit Corporation) are not consolidated because the nature of their operations is so different from the main activities of the parent company; the practice of not consolidating credit companies, banks, and real estate companies is widespread. In presenting its conventional income statement, the parent company must recognize its share of the subsidiaries' net income. Thus the parent's share of the net income of the unconsolidated subsidiaries is

12. FASB, *Financial Reporting in Units of General Purchasing Power,* par. 54c.

shown as a separate item in the parent's income statement.[13] In preparing a price-level-adjusted income statement for the parent, the income statement of the subsidiary must be restated to reflect the adjustments in lines 1, 3, 4, 5, and 7 of the table. The GE Credit Corporation (100 percent owned by the parent) reported income of $42.7 million on a conventional basis; when restated on a general-price-level-adjusted basis, this would have been a *loss* of about $23.9 million. (For simplicity, the estimated restatement of the Credit Corporation is not presented here.) The large difference between conventional income and adjusted loss for GE Credit is caused almost entirely by its loss on holding net monetary assets during the period of general price increase. Conceptually, this loss probably should be subtracted from the gain on monetary items reported in line 7, but to do so would destroy the distinction between the reports of the parent and the unconsolidated subsidiary. This distinction is important in the later analysis of taxable income.

Summary of Results

The difference between income as conventionally reported and income adjusted for price level changes is equal to the sum of the five adjustments described in the previous section. We estimated income statement results for the other twenty-nine companies in the Dow industrials in a manner similar to that illustrated for GE in table 3-1. The results are summarized in table 3-2. Income before gain on net money items is decreased for all companies.[14] This reduction is caused by the substantial increase in depreciation charges and, except for LIFO companies, a more than half-year adjustment in the cost of goods sold.[15] The total of general-price-level adjusted net income before gain or loss on monetary items is a little over $10 billion, or 63.7 percent of the reported net income of almost $16 billion. For the in-

13. See AICPA, Accounting Principles Board, "The Equity Method of Accounting for Investments in Common Stock," *Opinions of the Accounting Principles Board 18* (New York: AICPA, March 1971).

14. Although Chrysler shows 577 percent in column 4 of the table, this means that its adjusted *loss* is almost six times its reported loss.

15. Since revenues are increased by an adjustment factor reflecting a half-year price increase (5.7 percent for 1974), the cost-of-goods-sold adjustment, if it is to reduce adjusted income, must be for more than a half year. GE uses FIFO for 20 percent of its inventories and has a 6.1 percent adjustment of the cost of goods sold, which represents about six and one-third months of price change (table 3-1, note b).

Table 3-2. Income as Conventionally Reported and as Estimated after General Price Level Adjustment, Thirty Dow Jones Industrials, 1974
Dollar amounts in millions

Company	Income as conventionally reported (historical dollars) (1)	Income after price level adjustment (end-of-1974 dollars)		Income after price level adjustment as a percentage of conventionally reported income	
		Before gain on monetary items (2)	Including gain on monetary items (3)	Before gain on monetary items (4)	Including gain on monetary items (5)
Allied Chemical	150.8	89.7	136.1	60	90
Aluminum Company of America	173.1	118.7	219.4	69	127
American Brands	136.6	76.0	150.2	56	110
American Can	95.1	59.6	99.7	63	105
American Telephone and Telegraph	3,169.9	2,397.5	5,997.0	76	189
Anaconda	247.1	231.6	270.6	94	110
Bethlehem Steel	342.1	220.2	283.0	64	83
Chrysler	−52.1	−300.6	−144.0	577[a]	276[a]
Du Pont	403.5	175.1	185.2	43	46
Eastman Kodak	629.5	536.2	467.2	85	74
Esmark	68.1	4.8	41.1	7	60
Exxon	3,142.2	2,678.0	2,752.6	85	88
General Electric	608.1	391.4	568.7	64	94
General Foods	99.4	20.2	66.7	20	67
General Motors	950.0	−185.3	1.0	−20[b]	*

Goodyear	157.4	1.2	147.7	1	94
International Harvester	124.1	−55.9	53.4	−45[b]	43
International Nickel	306.0	254.2	291.9	83	95
International Paper	262.6	168.1	212.7	64	81
Johns-Manville	72.0	60.3	75.8	84	105
Owens-Illinois	83.5	56.5	117.5	68	141
Procter & Gamble	316.7	262.8	310.6	83	98
Sears Roebuck	511.4	14.0	−16.7	3	−3[b]
Standard Oil of California	970.0	631.0	846.2	65	87
Texaco	1,586.5	1,527.2	1,673.9	96	106
Union Carbide	530.1	454.5	490.9	86	93
U.S. Steel	634.9	401.6	501.6	63	79
United Technologies (United Aircraft)	104.7	−4.4	26.5	−4[b]	25
Westinghouse Electric	28.1	−93.8	−46.8	−334[b]	−167[b]
Woolworth	64.8	−44.3	42.7	−63[b]	66
All companies	15,916.2	10,146.1	15,822.4	63.7	99.4
Median (percent)	...	...	...	64	89

Sources: Column 1 was derived from published income statements of the various companies and 10-K reports submitted by the companies to the U.S. Securities and Exchange Commission. Columns 2 and 3 were derived as were comparable items in table 3-1. Column 4 equals column 2 divided by column 1. Column 5 equals column 3 divided by column 1. Figures are rounded.

* Less than 0.5.

a. Estimated loss as a percentage of reported loss.

b. Loss equal to indicated percentage of positive net income.

dividual companies, the median of adjusted income before gain on net money items as a percentage of reported income is 64 percent.

The inclusion of gain or loss of money items increases adjusted net income in almost all cases because almost all corporations in the sample are net debtors, or borrowers. The exceptions are companies with relatively conservative financial policies, such as Eastman Kodak and Sears. The total of our estimates of general-price-level-adjusted net income for the thirty companies is $15.8 billion, or 99.4 percent of reported net income. The median of adjusted net income as a percentage of reported net income for the Dow industrials is 89 percent. The substantial difference between the two percentages is due to the large absolute size of AT&T, which shows the largest percentage increase in general-price-level-adjusted net income. These percentages are surprisingly high (to us and to most other observers, we believe). Eight of the Dow industrials showed adjusted incomes larger than reported income. Recognizing inflation effects, including gains from net debtor position, has only a moderate effect on adjusted net income on the average, and in a substantial minority of the cases income is increased by making the inflation adjustments.

The adjusted income amounts as percentages of reported income differ sharply among the Dow firms. The reported incomes of Sears and General Motors are converted into general-price-level-adjusted losses. At the other end of the scale, AT&T's adjusted income is nearly twice its reported income. When prices are rising, general-price-level-adjusted net income will tend to be relatively smaller when compared with conventional net income if a firm uses FIFO (Sears and General Motors), if it has large amounts of plant—much of it old (International Harvester)—or if it has an excess of monetary assets over monetary liabilities (Sears and Eastman Kodak). General price level net income will tend to be relatively large when compared with conventional net income when prices are rising if a firm uses LIFO, if it has relatively little plant—most of it new—or if it has an excess of monetary liabilities over monetary assets.

The gain or loss on monetary items has an especially strong effect when the rate of inflation accelerates, overwhelming the other factors for firms with substantial leverage. This is borne out by AT&T among the Dow industrials, and becomes even more apparent when the effect of general price level adjustments on the 1974 income of public utilities is considered. Table 3-3 compares reported and general-price-

Table 3-3. General-Price-Level-Adjusted Net Income as a Percentage of Reported
Net Income, Dow Jones and Standard & Poor's Utilities, 1974

	Adjusted income as a percentage of reported net income	
Utility company	Before gain on monetary items (1)	Including gain on monetary items (2)
Allegheny Power System	57	227
American Electric Power	66	277
Cincinnati Gas and Electric	64	214
Cleveland Electric Illuminating	74	208
Columbia Gas System	48	200
Commonwealth Edison	60	229
Consolidated Edison	71	239
Consolidated Natural Gas	56	183
Consumers Power	37	330
Dayton Power and Light	65	226
Detroit Edison	61	286
Houston Lighting and Power	78	214
Indianapolis Power and Light	57	236
Niagara Mohawk Power	67	225
Northern Natural Gas	69	138
Northern States Power	66	238
Pacific Gas and Electric	68	197
Panhandle Eastern Pipe Line	49	176
Peoples Gas (9/30 year end)	64	176
Philadelphia Electric	73	228
Public Service Electric and Gas	69	228
Southern California Edison	77	187
Southern Company	61	299
Entex (6/30 year end)[a]	78	154
Median	65.5	225.5

Source: Published income statements of the various companies and 10-K reports submitted by the
companies to the U.S. Securities and Exchange Commission. General-price-level-adjusted income was
calculated in the same way as for the comparable item in table 3-1.
   a. Formerly United Gas.

level-adjusted income for the twenty-four utilities in the Dow Jones
and Standard & Poor's averages. In every case again, adjusted income
before gain on monetary items is lower than net income. The median
of 65.5 percent is close to that of the Dow industrials of 64 percent.
For the utilities, general-price-level-adjusted net income (including
gains on monetary items) is sharply higher, reflecting the large
amount of debt in their capital structures. The median of adjusted net
income as a percentage of reported income, shown in column 2 of

table 3-3, is 225.5 percent. This is more than two and one-half times the corresponding figure for the Dow industrials shown in column 5 of table 3-2.

No service companies (brokerage firms or accounting firms) or banks are included in the two samples. Since they have relatively little inventory or plant, their adjusted income before monetary gains would probably be little affected by restatement into year-end dollars. The effect of restatement on adjusted net income for such firms would then largely depend on their holding of monetary assets and monetary liabilities. Most banks have a substantial excess of monetary assets over monetary liabilities. Thus their general-price-level-adjusted income would be sharply reduced.[16]

Based on other work, we surmise that general price level adjustments will affect the adjusted income of rapidly growing companies less than that of more slowly growing companies. Because on the average such companies have newer plants, the upward adjustment of depreciation expense is lower for them than for most slowly growing companies. This effect is compounded if, as is likely to be the case, the rapidly growing company has a higher portion of its capitalization made up of debt. In that case, it will have more monetary gains to report.

For believers in the desirability of economic growth, general price level adjustments to the financial statements may thus have a serendipitous effect. After general price level adjustments, the earnings of

16. See Sidney Davidson, James N. Kelly, and Roman L. Weil, "A Case Example of Effects of Proposed General Price-Level Adjustment Accounting Procedure," *Banking, Journal of American Bankers Association,* vol. 67 (July 1975), pp. 31–33, 90–91. Angela Falkenstein, in "Price Level Accounting: Bad News for Bank Earnings," Report R-17A-5 (Legg Mason Washington Service, September 1975), estimated the change in earnings of a sample of ten banks brought about by price level adjustments as follows:

	Percentage change
Bank America Corp.	−23.9
Chase Manhattan Corp.	−9.8
Detroitbank Corp.	−46.2
First International Bancshares, Inc.	−106.8
Girard Co.	−41.3
Harris Bankcorp	−81.6
Marine Midland Banks, Inc.	−11.9
Mellon National Corp.	−53.3
J. P. Morgan & Co.	9.4
Southeast Banking Corp.	−65.0

the more rapidly growing companies are likely to improve relative to those of the slower-growing companies. Whether one believes this will affect the cost of capital to them depends on whether one believes in the efficiency of capital markets. If general price level adjustments as proposed by the FASB were to be made available for measuring taxable income, this reporting advantage for rapidly growing firms would be more than offset by the relatively higher tax liabilities they would face.

General Price Level Adjustments for Tax Reporting

If general price level adjustments were permitted for tax reporting, what adjustments would be required? Is it possible to estimate the results of such a procedure?

The answer to the first question is relatively straightforward. The adjustment procedure would be virtually the same for tax reporting as for financial reporting, but the basic data upon which the procedures operate might be different because of differences between financial and tax reporting.

The answer to the second question is more complex. We derived our estimates of general-price-level-adjusted financial income from the published annual reports of the corporations. Because those reports disclosed the amount of net income determined on a conventional basis and also presented sufficient data about individual items, we were able to make the adjustments leading to our estimates of general-price-level-adjusted income. Thus in the tables in the previous section we compared conventional income as reported by the corporations with our estimates of general-price-level-adjusted income. The first number is stated by the corporation and cannot be questioned; it is what it is. We also have substantial confidence in our estimates of the second income number[17] and thus in the ratios between the two financial income numbers. But in attempting similar comparisons for adjusted and unadjusted taxable income, we lacked access to tax returns and therefore had to estimate both taxable income and its components for the corporations in our sample. Hence our estimates of adjusted income used for comparison with reported

17. Our confidence is largely based on the evidence presented in Davidson, Stickney, and Weil, *Inflation Accounting,* exhibit 8.7.

taxable income are subject to a much larger error than those in the preceding section.

Although the footnotes to the published annual reports of corporations are now rich with information about taxes and taxable income, one major bit of information is missing. We could estimate worldwide taxable income relatively satisfactorily, but we were unable to divide it into the portion representing U.S. taxable income and that representing taxable income reported to foreign governments. Thus we have compared estimated worldwide taxable income with our estimates of what that worldwide taxable income would be on a general-price-level-adjusted basis, using the measure of U.S. price increases for all adjustments. Of course, this caveat applies to the components of estimated taxable income as well as to the total.

Another problem in estimating taxable income lies in the area of consolidation. Since we do not know which subsidiaries are included in the consolidated tax return of the reporting corporation, we assumed for simplicity that all subsidiaries that are consolidated for financial reporting purposes are also consolidated for tax purposes and that those not consolidated in the financial reports are similarly not consolidated in the tax returns. In general, though, if we have included or excluded a subsidiary incorrectly, the error will merely affect the totals reported for taxable income and adjusted taxable income. The relationship between the two totals in most cases is not likely to be affected significantly.

General-Price-Level-Adjusted Taxable Income

Recognizing these two significant limitations, we then estimated the components of taxable income and the totals thereof using the procedures described in appendix B. We have illustrated the nature of the adjustments in estimating general-price-level-adjusted taxable income from these data by referring to an actual case, the General Electric Corporation, in table 3-4.

The adjustments to reflect our estimates of general-price-level-adjusted taxable income follow the same steps indicated in the previous section for estimating adjusted financial income, although the amounts shown for the components of income may differ. The adjustments for GE are as follows:

Sales and other income. (Line 1, table 3-4). These revenues are

Table 3-4. Alternative Estimates of Taxable Income, General Electric Company, 1974
Dollar amounts in millions

Item	As conventionally reported (historical dollars)	After general price level adjustment (end-of-1974 dollars)	Change (percent)
Revenues			
1. Sales and other income	13,556	14,335	5.7
2. Equity method revenue	0	0	...
Total	13,556	14,335	5.7
Expenses			
3. Cost of goods sold	9,761	10,357	6.1
4. Depreciation[a]	411	596	44.9
5. All other expenses[b]	2,633	2,784	5.7
Total	12,805	13,737	7.3
6. Taxable income before gain on monetary items (revenues minus expenses)	751	598	−20.4
7. Gain on monetary items	...	177[c]	...
8. Net income (including gain on monetary items)	751	775	3.2

Sources: Derived from *General Electric 1974 Annual Report.* See text and appendix B for explanation of the methods used in deriving the estimates.
   a. Average life of depreciable assets is estimated to be 6.3 years; price index increased by 44.9 percent during the 6.3 years preceding December 31, 1974.
   b. Income taxes, of course, are not included.
   c. See table 3-1, note c.

unchanged in amount from those shown in the published income report and are adjusted, as in table 3-1, for half a year to restate them in end-of-year dollars.

Cost of goods sold. (Line 3.) We estimate that the cost of goods sold is the same on the tax returns as in the financial statements, and the same 6 percent adjustment is appropriate.

Depreciation. (Line 4.) GE uses accelerated depreciation for most of its assets for both financial reporting and tax purposes, but with shorter estimates of useful lives (asset depreciation range lives) for the latter. Tax depreciation thus exceeds book depreciation. Our estimate of depreciation claimed on the tax return, as explained in appendix B, is thus raised to $411 million from the $376 million shown on the income statement. The average age of the depreciable assets is, of course, unchanged, at a little over six years. The cumulative price increase in that time has been about 45 percent and the depreciation claimed on the general-price-level-adjusted tax return is increased by the same percentage.[18]

All other expenses. (Line 5.) The amount of these expenses shown on the tax return is estimated to be $2,633 million, as explained in appendix B; $2,471 million—$2,853 million (see table 3-1) minus $382 million—is shown on the income statement for all other expenses, except income taxes. These items are again assumed to occur fairly evenly throughout the year and are adjusted for half a year of price change to restate them in end-of-year dollars.

Gain on monetary items. (Line 7.) This item would be the same as on the adjusted income statement. The $1,504 million of average net debt position (see table 3-1, note c) resulted in a gain on monetary items of $177 million because the general price level increased by 11.8 percent during the year.

Equity method revenue. (Line 2.) Since we assumed that subsidiaries that were not consolidated in the income statement were not consolidated in the tax returns, a zero appears on this line.

Following these procedures, table 3-4 shows that our estimate of general-price-level-adjusted taxable income for GE is, by coincidence, almost equal to our estimate of taxable income as shown on the tax return, running 3 percent higher.

Summary of Results

We estimated and compared reported taxable income and the general-price-level-adjusted taxable income for the other twenty-nine companies in the Dow industrials in a manner similar to that illustrated for GE in table 3-4. The results are summarized in table 3-5.

Analysis of our estimates of general-price-level-adjusted taxable income as a percentage of reported taxable income shows that they are closely similar to the estimates of general-price-level-adjusted financial income as a percentage of reported financial income. Al-

18. GE's use of shorter lives for tax purposes than for book purposes, and especially the use of accelerated methods for tax purposes and straight-line for book by other firms in the sample, indicates that charges for recent years should be weighted more heavily in the calculation of tax depreciation expense for some companies than our analysis indicates. The effect of this is to overstate general-price-level-adjusted tax depreciation charges as we report them and thus to understate general-price-level-adjusted taxable income. We believe the error is relatively modest and has the effect of understating our major conclusion that general-price-level-adjusted taxable income would be a high percentage of unadjusted taxable income. We wish to thank Emil Sunley for calling this discrepancy to our attention.

though differences between reported financial income and taxable income may be large in some cases, the procedure for general price level adjustment is the same for both types of income determination, and the similarity in the relationship between reported and adjusted figures would be expected. Thus most of the comments about the implications of general price level adjustments for financial reporting apply for tax reporting as well.

The median of 86.5 percent for the estimate of adjusted taxable income as a percentage of reported taxable income is close to the median of 89 percent for adjusted financial income as a percentage of reported financial income (table 3-2). Nine of the Dow thirty industrials show greater adjusted taxable income than reported taxable income, one more than for financial income, and seven of the companies appear on both lists.

Although the median of adjusted taxable income as a percentage of reported taxable income is 86.5 percent, the sum of the estimates of general-price-level-adjusted taxable income ($32,754.6 million) is almost exactly equal (100.6 percent) to the sum of the estimates of reported taxable income ($32,547.3 million).[19] This suggests it is the firms with the largest dollar-adjusted taxable income that lie above the median percentage of adjusted-to-reported taxable income. Table 3-5 bears this out: the four corporations with the largest dollar-adjusted taxable income are all above the median.

The highest ratio of adjusted to reported taxable income among the Dow companies is shown by AT&T, as was the case with financial income. This result emphasizes again the significance of gains on monetary items. Adjusted taxable income for public utilities would almost surely be substantially greater than reported taxable income.

Recognition of gains on monetary items in a price-level-adjusted tax system would diminish the tax-saving attribute of debt financing in a period of rising prices. As suggested in the previous section, the concept of gains on monetary items would probably be more easily understood if they were subtracted from interest expense.

Reference to the data for the Dow industrials in table 3-5 again emphasizes the diversity of results of general price level adjustments

19. The income figures for Exxon are so large that they swamp all the others. The Exxon amounts are 49.7 percent of estimated taxable income as reported and 50.2 percent of estimated adjusted taxable income. If the data for Exxon were deleted from the sample, the estimate of adjusted taxable income would be 99.7 percent of reported taxable income.

Table 3-5. Estimates of Taxable Income as Conventionally Reported and after General Price Level Adjustment, Thirty Dow Jones Industrials, 1974
Dollar amounts in millions

Company	Taxable income as conventionally reported (historical dollars) (1)	Taxable income after price level adjustment — Before gain on monetary items (end-of-1974 dollars) (2)	Taxable income after price level adjustment — Including gain on monetary items (end-of-1974 dollars) (3)	Taxable income after price level adjustment as percentage of conventionally reported taxable income — Before gain on monetary items (4)	Including gain on monetary items (5)
Allied Chemical	169.5	91.3	137.7	54	81
Aluminum Company of America	514.1	436.2	537.0	85	104
American Brands	298.0	249.0	323.2	84	108
American Can	155.0	117.1	157.2	76	101
American Telephone and Telegraph	2,489.8	1,039.2	4,638.7	42	186
Anaconda	150.9	127.0	166.0	84	110
Bethlehem Steel	502.5	356.4	419.2	71	83
Chrysler	−264.2	−525.2	−368.6	199[a]	140[a]
Du Pont	483.3	244.2	254.3	50	53
Eastman Kodak	992.5	920.0	851.0	93	86
Esmark	124.0	70.9	107.2	57	86
Exxon	16,168.8	16,357.2	16,431.8	101	102
General Electric	751.0	597.9	775.2	80	103
General Foods	235.8	152.3	198.8	65	84
General Motors	1,064.8	67.2	253.5	6	24

Goodyear	245.7	61.8	206.2	25	84
International Harvester	207.1	24.5	133.7	12	65
International Nickel	582.5	540.7	578.4	93	99
International Paper	387.3	285.5	330.2	74	85
Johns-Manville	66.7	45.8	61.4	69	92
Owens-Illinois	97.9	58.2	119.2	59	122
Procter & Gamble	528.0	462.9	510.8	88	97
Sears Roebuck	420.8	142.2	116.0	34	27
Standard Oil of California	1,635.2	1,334.3	1,549.5	82	95
Texaco	2,566.5	2,552.8	2,699.5	99	105
Union Carbide	684.0	557.9	594.4	82	87
U.S. Steel	788.8	542.1	642.2	69	81
United Technologies (United Aircraft)	197.5	95.4	126.3	48	64
Westinghouse Electric	202.3	76.0	123.0	38	61
Woolworth	101.2	-5.4	81.6	-5[b]	81
All companies	32,547.3	27,075.4	32,754.6	83.2	100.6
Median	...	...	...	70	86.5

Sources: Column 1 was derived from published income statements of the various companies and 10-K reports submitted by the companies to the U.S. Securities and Exchange Commission. Columns 2 and 3 were derived as were comparable items in table 3-4 and as explained in appendix B. Column 4 equals column 2 divided by column 1. Column 5 equals column 3 divided by column 1. Figures are rounded.

a. Estimated loss as a percentage of reported loss.
b. Loss equal to indicated percentage of positive net income.

among firms. This, coupled with the earlier data, suggests that the revenue loss to the Treasury from permitting FASB-type general price level adjustments for corporations would probably not be great, but some firms would pay less taxes.[20]

One person's borrowing must be another person's lending, however. We are relatively confident that, economy-wide, individual taxpayers through their holding of currency, government securities, and bank deposits as well as corporate debt are substantial net monetary asset holders. All taxpayers as a group, corporate and individual, are net monetary asset holders by an amount roughly equal to currency outstanding plus privately held government debt. If general price level adjustments were permitted for all taxpayers, then it is likely that income tax payments would be reduced and the Treasury would probably experience substantial revenue losses.

*Appendix A: Measuring Price Change for a Half Year**

Nearly all the general price level adjustments specified for the income statement in the FASB proposal are mechanical in nature once the dates of acquisition of revenue and expense items are determined. As a shortcut procedure, most firms will assume that sales and almost all expenses other than the cost of goods sold and depreciation occur evenly during the year and thus should be adjusted for a half year of price change. This adjuster is applied to the sales amount that for profitable firms is always larger than the "all other expenses" amount (total expenses less cost of goods sold and depreciation expense); since the difference between sales and all other expenses is usually quite large, relatively small differences in the estimate of price change for a half year can make relatively large differences in the amount of general-price-level-adjusted income. We think the FASB has illustrated this adjustment incorrectly, and if the FASB procedures are to be considered as a model for possible tax law revisions, it is important that this error be corrected.

---

* This appendix was adapted from a portion of chap. 6 in Davidson, Stickney, and Weil, *Inflation Accounting.*

20. For more comprehensive but less specific estimates of how the adoption of rules closely resembling the FASB proposals affect government revenues from the corporation income tax, see chapter 2.

The FASB illustrates the index for a half year by the result of the calculation

(1) $\dfrac{\text{4th quarter average GNP deflator}}{\text{Annual average GNP deflator}} - 1.$

There are two things wrong with this answer, the first procedural, the second conceptual. First, companies with fiscal years that end on a date other than December 31 cannot know what to do because there is no analogue of the annual average for them. Second, the fourth quarter deflator is an average for the period October 1 through December 31 and is more representative of November 15 prices than it is of December 31 prices, while the annual average represents June 30 prices, if any one day must be chosen. Thus the calculation of "one-half year of price change" suggested by the FASB is really the calculation of about four and one-half months of price change, from June 30 to November 15. As a substitute, we suggest a measure that represents a full six months of price change. The calculation begins with the measure of price change for a full year from the fourth quarter of last year to the fourth quarter of this one.[21]

(2) $\dfrac{\text{4th quarter average as of this year}}{\text{4th quarter average as of last year}} - 1.$

The rate of increase in prices over a six-month period is not one-half of the annual rate, but the square root of $(1 +$ the annual rate of change) minus 1. This procedure ignores changes in the rate of inflation within one year. If the annual rate is 12 percent, the increase during six months is 5.83 percent $(1.0583^2 = 1.1200)$ and 2.87 percent each quarter $(1.0287^4 = 1.1200)$. If the price index were

---

21. Even this undisputed calculation is not the best estimate of price change between January 1 and December 31 of a given year. Since the fourth quarter average represents prices as of November 15 and the first quarter average represents prices as of about February 15, the best estimate of price change between January 1, 1975, and December 31, 1975, is

$$\left(\frac{\text{4th quarter 1975} \times \text{1st quarter 1976}}{\text{4th quarter 1974} \times \text{1st quarter 1975}}\right)^{\frac{1}{2}} - 1.$$

The rate of price increase for 1974, measured by fourth quarter 1974 over fourth quarter 1973, mentioned in the text, is 11.8 percent; if we use the more exact method of this footnote, it is measured to be 11.3 percent. (These calculations are based on data in the 1975 *Economic Report of the President* for all numbers except the first quarter of 1975. Since that number is not available in the report, it is taken from the *Survey of Current Business,* April 1975.) This refinement probably involves more trouble than it is worth and cannot be used in practice because of the delay in getting the number for the first quarter of "next" year.

1.0 during the fourth quarter of a hypothetical year 19x0, the index in succeeding quarters would be 1.0287, 1.0583, 1.0887, and 1.1200. Using the FASB formula (equation 1), the half-year increase in prices would be calculated at $1.12 \div [(1.0287 + 1.0583 + 1.0887 + 1.1200)/4] = 1.0429$, indicating a 4.29 percent increase in prices, much below the actual six-month increase of 5.83 percent. For this reason we use equation 2 in constructing general-price-level-adjusted financial statements.[22] The formula for a geometric mean is approximately modified for companies whose years do not end on December 31. Using the arithmetic mean yields a satisfactory approximation for rates of inflation experienced in the United States, but not for very high rates of inflation. When inflation is 12 percent annually, the geometric mean is 5.83 percent and the arithmetic mean is 6 percent. If inflation were 100 percent, the geometric mean would be 41.4 percent, the arithmetic mean would be 50 percent.

Appendix B: Calculation of the Estimate of Taxable Income and Its Components

Since the income tax returns of the companies in the sample were not available to us, we had to employ a roundabout procedure to prepare our estimates of taxable income. Here, we explain that procedure, which requires only information presented in the financial statements and the notes thereto of the companies studied.

Determination of Total Taxable Income

Both limitations mentioned in the text apply here. That is, (1) we can measure only worldwide taxable income, and (2) we assume that those subsidiaries consolidated in the financial statements are also consolidated in the tax return and that those accounted for on the equity method in the financial statements are not consolidated in the tax return.

To net income we add the income tax expense shown on the income statement (net of any state and local income taxes) and the

22. This procedure for calculating a half year of price change is based on the assumption that it is *unit* purchases or sales that occur evenly throughout the year. If *dollar* amounts occur evenly throughout the year, then the best estimate of a half-year price change is based on a harmonic, not a geometric, mean.

minority interest in earnings of consolidated subsidiaries, if any, since that amount is not a tax deduction of the taxpaying entity. The resulting amount may be labeled "pre-federal income tax income" of the taxpaying entity as drawn from its financial records. From this amount we must deduct both "permanent differences" and "timing differences" between the financial records and the tax records to obtain the estimate of taxable income in historical dollars as shown on the tax return. (In principle, net permanent and timing differences could lead to additions to taxable income, but this would be unusual and we have not encountered such net additions in our sample companies.)

Timing differences between financial income and taxable income are defined by the Accounting Principles Board as

differences between the periods in which transactions affect taxable income and the periods in which they enter into the determination of pretax accounting income. Timing differences originate in one period and reverse or "turn around" in one or more subsequent periods. Some timing differences reduce income taxes that would otherwise be payable currently; others increase income taxes that would otherwise be payable currently.[23]

Probably the most conspicuous timing difference results from the use of accelerated depreciation for taxes and straight-line depreciation for financial reporting.

Permanent differences are defined as

differences between taxable income and pretax accounting income arising from transactions that, under applicable tax laws and regulations, will not be offset by corresponding differences or "turn around" in other periods.[24]

Examples of permanent differences are the excess of percentage depletion for tax purposes (where allowed) over cost depletion for financial reporting and premiums paid on officers' life insurance with the company as a beneficiary that are treated as an expense for financial reporting but are not deductible on the tax return.

The amount of individual timing differences can be calculated by reference to the footnotes to the financial statements or by determining the change for the year in the deferred tax account as shown in the comparative balance sheet. From either of these sources

23. See AICPA, Accounting Principles Board, "Accounting for Income Taxes," *Opinions of the Accounting Principles Board 11* (New York: AICPA, 1967), par. 13e.
24. Ibid., par. 13f.

(usually both are available), the amount of the net increase for the year in "postponed" tax liability can be determined. This amount divided by the marginal federal corporation income tax rate (assumed to be 48 percent throughout our calculations) equals the net amount of timing differences for the year. The federal income tax rate times the sum of taxable income plus timing differences equals the income tax expense shown on the income statement (net of state and local income taxes but plus the investment tax credit reduction of income tax expense for the year).[25] Since the tax rate, tax expense, and timing differences are known, taxable income can be calculated.

Determination of Components of Taxable Income

The data from the income statement and that used in determining total taxable income enabled us to determine the components of taxable income.

Sales and other income. These revenues are unchanged in amount from those shown in the published income statement.[26]

Cost of goods sold. We estimated that the cost of goods sold is the same on the tax return as on the income statement. Some companies under specialized circumstances may have differences between these two figures, but we believe such instances are rare.

Depreciation. To estimate the depreciation amount shown on the tax return, the portion of the timing difference caused by depreciation must be added to the depreciation amount shown on the income statement.

All other expenses. This component of taxable income requires the largest number of adjustments in going from the income statement to

25. The amount of investment credit to be added depends on whether the taxpayer accounts for the investment credit on a flow-through or deferral basis in its financial records. For flow-through companies the addition is the total amount of the investment credit claimed for the year. For deferral companies the addition is that amount of the investment credit of this and prior years that is used this year to reduce reported income tax expense.

26. Timing differences other than those relating to depreciation were all attributed to other expenses. In some cases this adjustment probably should be a decrease in revenues rather than an increase in other expenses. Since both of these components of income are adjusted by the same general price level change for half a year, the choice between these two components has no effect on general-price-level-adjusted taxable income.

the tax return. The amount shown for all other expenses on the income statement must be reduced by reported income tax expense (net of state and local income taxes) and minority interest in reported earnings of consolidated subsidiaries. To this must be added the permanent difference and that part of the timing difference not due to depreciation.

Appendix C: A Note on Definitions and Measures of Income

Discussions of adjustment of the income tax system to account for the effects of inflation can easily founder on confusion about the appropriate definitions of income. Here, we will illustrate how eight superficially plausible measures of income can result from the interaction of three factors: the cost basis used for depreciable assets, the measuring unit used, and the degree to which holding gains are recognized as income subject to current taxation. Cost can be measured either on an acquisition or replacement-cost basis. The measuring unit can be nominal (that is, historical) dollars or constant dollars. Holding gains can be ignored, recognized when realized, or recognized as they occur.

The conventional measure of income at this time uses acquisition costs measured in nominal dollars and recognizes holding gains as realized, although the realized holding gains on inventory (and plant) are not separately reported. Realized holding gains on debt are separately disclosed as extraordinary items.[27] General-price-level-adjusted accounting, as proposed by the FASB, uses acquisition cost measured in constant dollars and also recognizes holding gains as realized, although they are not separately reported for inventory (and plant).[28] Replacement-cost (or current value) accounting uses the replacement-cost basis of valuation, but there is no agreement among replacement cost proponents about which holding gains should be included in the income measure, if any. Finally, the general approach

---

27. FASB, *Reporting Gains and Losses from Extinguishment of Debt,* Statement of Financial Accounting Standards No. 4 (Stamford, Conn.: FASB, March 1975). Somewhat asymmetrically, accounting authorities do not require or even permit separate, extraordinary labeling of the gain or loss to the lender who is repaid before maturity.

28. FASB, *Financial Reporting in Units of General Purchasing Power.*

we favor combines the replacement-cost basis with a constant-dollar measuring unit.

Table 3-6 shows the data for our example. The example may appear too simplified because it contains neither plant assets nor, hence, depreciation charges. Plant assets and depreciation introduce no conceptual difficulties beyond those required in dealing with units of inventory. Once one understands the treatment of acquiring n units of inventory and selling one per year, one also understands the treatment of acquiring a plant asset with a depreciable life of n years depreciated on a straight-line basis.[29]

Table 3-7 shows the eight measures of income that we find useful to consider. Column 1 is the conventional measure that shows income determined on an acquisition-cost basis measured in nominal dollars. Column 2 shows acquisition cost measured in constant dollars, the method proposed by the Financial Accounting Standards Board. Columns 3, 4, and 5 reflect replacement-cost valuations in nominal dollars. Column 3 reports what we elsewhere call "sustainable" income, the amount of operating income we would expect in the future if activity levels remained the same but prices stopped changing.[30] Column 4 shows realized replacement-cost income that is exactly equal to conventional income (column 1) but with different components reported—operating income is separated from realized holding gains.

29. Analogous statements can be made for accelerated depreciation; sum-of-the-years'-digits depreciation, for example, is equivalent to acquiring $n(n + 1)/2$ units and selling n the first year, $(n - 1)$ the second, and so on.

The double-entry record keeping for plant is more complicated than for inventory because of the accounting convention of showing "original" cost and accumulated depreciation separately in the accounts. This leads to the problem called "revaloriza-tion," known in Britain as "backlog depreciation."

Assume a plant asset that costs $100 and is today 40 percent depreciated. Let the replacement cost of the asset increase by $10, 10 percent of original cost. The asset account is increased by $10 (debit), but there is a holding gain of only $6 (credit), and the accumulated depreciation account is increased (backlog depreciation) by $4 (credit). If we had acquired five units of inventory for $20 each and had sold two, and replacement cost increased by 10 percent of original cost, then the accounting is merely to increase the amount of the remaining units by $6 (debit) and to record a holding gain of $6 (credit). Whereas a holding gain on a unit of inventory is realized when the unit is sold, the holding gain on plant is realized when the depreciation charge becomes an expense (either directly or, for depreciation on manu-facturng equipment, when finished goods are sold).

30. See Sidney Davidson and Roman L. Weil, "Inflation Accounting: The SEC Proposal for Replacement Cost Disclosures," *Financial Analysts Journal*, vol. 32 (March–April 1976), pp. 58–59.

Table 3-6. Data for Illustrating Various Measures of Corporate Income

	Date		
Type of assumption	*January 1*	*June 30*	*December 31*
Conditions			
GNP deflator[a]	100.00	104.88	110.00
Replacement cost			
Item A	$10.00	$10.25	$10.50
Item B	$10.00	$12.00	$14.00
Selling price			
Item A	...	$13.00	$14.00
Item B	...	$15.00	$16.00
Perpetual annual payment of $1.60			
Market rate of interest	8.00%	10.23%	12.50%
Market price	$20.00	$15.64	$12.80
Events			
Purchases			
Item A: 3 units at $10	$30.00	...	...
Item B: 3 units at $10	$30.00	...	...
Borrowing (in perpetuity)			
Amount	$20.00	...	...
Rate	8.00%	...	...
Sales			
Item A: 1 unit at $13	...	$13.00	...
Item B: 1 unit at $15	...	$15.00	...
Dividend payment	...	$27.20[b]	...
Sales			
Item A: 1 unit at $14	...	...	$14.00
Item B: 1 unit at $16	...	...	$16.00
Debt retirement			
Amount of original borrowing			
(25 percent)	...	...	$ 5.00
Cost of retirement	...	...	$ 3.20
Realized gain	...	...	$ 1.80

a. If prices increase uniformly at a rate of 10 percent per year, then prices increase by 4.88 percent ($= \sqrt{1.10} - 1$) during half a year.

b. $0.80 is retained as a monetary asset to offset monetary liability for accrued interest payable. Net monetary liability position is thus maintained at $20.00.

Column 5 shows the nominal dollar amount of economic net income —the net increase in wealth (plus consumption, if any) of the entity. Columns 6, 7, and 8 are analogous to columns 3, 4, and 5 except that all amounts are reported in constant dollars.

Table 3-7. Illustration of Various Measures of Corporate Income before Taxes

Items used in deriving income	Income based on acquisition cost (holding gains included in income when realized, but gains on inventory not separately disclosed)		Income based on replacement cost					
			Nominal dollars			Constant dollars		
	Nominal dollars (1)	Constant dollars (2)	Holding gains excluded (3)	Holding gains included only when realized (4)	Holding gains included as they occur (5)	Holding gains excluded (6)	Holding gains included only when realized (7)	Holding gains included as they occur (8)
Revenue	58.00[a]	59.37[b]	58.00[a]	58.00[a]	58.00[a]	59.37[b]	59.37[b]	59.37[b]
Deductions								
Cost of goods sold	40.00[c]	44.00[d]	46.75[e]	46.75[e]	46.75[e]	47.84[f]	47.84[f]	47.84[f]
Interest	1.60[g]	1.68[h]	1.60[g]	1.60[g]	1.60[g]	1.68[h]	1.68[h]	1.68[h]
Holding gain								
Realized	...	...	...	6.75[i]	6.75[i]	...	3.84[j]	3.84[j]
Unrealized	...	...	...	...	4.50[k]	...	...	2.50[l]
Income on net monetary assets								
Gain (or loss) in purchasing power	...	2.00[m]	...	...	...	2.00[m]	2.00[m]	2.00[m]
Change in current market value								
Realized	1.80[n]	1.80[n]	...	1.80[n]	1.80[n]	...	1.80[n]	1.80[n]
Unrealized	...	...	...	...	5.40[o]	...	...	5.40[o]
Income before taxes	18.20[p]	17.49[p]	9.65	18.20[p]	28.10	11.85	17.49[p]	25.39

Source: Calculated from the data in table 3-6 as outlined in notes a through o below. Column 1 is the conventional accounting model; column 2 is the model proposed by the Financial Accounting Standards Board to take account of changes in the general price level.

a. $13 + $14 + $15 + $16.

b. ($28 × 1.0488) + $30.

c. 4 × $10.

d. $40 × 1.10.

e. $10.25 + $10.50 + $12.00 + $14.00.

f. [($10.25 + $12.00) × 1.0488] + $10.50 + $14.00.

g. 0.08 × $20.

h. 0.08 × $20 × 1.0488.

i. $10.25 + $10.50 + $12 + $14 − (4 × $10).

j. [$10.25 + $12 − (2 × $10 × 1.0488)] × 1.0488 + [$10.50 + $14.00 − (2 × 10 × 1.10)] = $1.34 + $2.50.

k. $10.50 + $14.00 − (2 × $10).

l. $10.50 + $14.00 − (2 × $10 × 1.10).

m. 0.10 × $20; might be only $0.50 in columns 6 and 7, but this is contrary to the FASB exposure draft and, as the text explains, to theory.

n. ¼ × ($20.00 − $12.80); shown in columns 1 and 2 as extraordinary item net of income tax effects in financial statements constructed in accord with generally accepted accounting principles.

o. ($20.00 − $12.80) × ¾.

p. The equality of income before taxes in columns 1 and 4 and in columns 2 and 7 is axiomatic, not coincidental.

The illustrative data in table 3-6 are entirely hypothetical but probably not too far removed from many actual situations in recent periods. With the assumed data, table 3-7 shows that income before taxes varies from $9.65 in column 3 to $28.10 in column 5, a spread of almost 300 percent. Compared with the income of $18.20 reported under the present conventional model (column 1), the lowest income is about 50 percent lower and the highest income is more than 50 percent higher.

The calculation of holding gains on inventory (and plant) is relatively straightforward, but some conceptual problems arise in connection with purchasing power gains and holding gains on debt. Whenever the measuring unit is constant dollars, as in columns 2, 6, 7, and 8, a purchasing power gain (in times of rising prices) or loss (in times of falling prices) accrues to those who have net monetary liabilities outstanding. (A symmetrically reverse statement applies to holders of net monetary assets.) The FASB did not propose deferring the recognition of this gain until the debt is retired. Thus columns 6 and 7 report the full purchasing power gain during the year, although these gains have not been converted to cash, but column 7 does not recognize the gain (or loss) on the change in the current market value until the debt is retired. This may appear inconsistent, but we think that just as reduced purchasing power of cash occurs as purchasing power declines, not as cash is spent, so the reduction in the purchasing power significance of the debt occurs as prices rise, not as debt is retired.

When debt is outstanding and interest rates change, there is a change in the current market value of the debt. (The debtor has a gain when interest rates rise and a loss when interest rates fall.) This change in the value of the debt leads to a holding gain or loss exactly analogous to the holding gain or loss on units of inventory. When both general price levels and interest rates are rising, there is both a purchasing power gain and a holding gain on debt. This situation occurred during 1974. In 1975, however, prices continued to rise, but interest rates fell, so debtors experienced purchasing power gains but holding losses.

Over the life of a loan that is outstanding until maturity, the sum of holding gains and losses plus amortization of those amounts must net out to zero. It is invalid to conclude, however, that holding gains and losses on debt need not be reported in financial statements as they occur. Such a conclusion would be analogous to saying that holding losses on inventory need not be reported as they occur because of an expectation that prices will return to former levels before the items are sold. On all long-term borrowing, one is speculating in money markets. If gains and losses on long-term borrowing need not be reported, then why should gains and losses on commodities speculation be reported?

In column 8, the measure of all economic income in constant dollars, we have both purchasing power gains (or losses) and holding gains (or losses) on debt. It is clear that over the life of a debt, the purchasing power gain plus the holding gain (if both interest rates and general price levels continue to rise) can exceed the amount borrowed. This may appear to be conceptually impossible, but we believe such a phenomenon is correct. Suppose, for example, that $100 is borrowed in perpetuity when the interest rate is 8 percent a year. Let the inflation rate for a year be 40 percent and the interest rate on the perpetuity rise to 50 percent as of the end of the year. Then there will be both a purchasing power gain of $40 (0.40 × $100) and a holding gain on the borrowing of $84 ($8/0.50 = $16; $100 − $16 = $84) during the year. Economic income on this borrowing for the year reported in end-of-year dollars is $124, $24 more than was borrowed in the first place. What these results are essentially saying is that in terms of end-of-year dollars, we borrowed $140. Of that $140 of end-of-year purchasing power borrowed, $40 has been "repaid" through lenders' losses in purchasing power and $84 has been forgiven by the market interest rate.

Conclusion

Compared with conventional accounting, measurements based on general price level adjustments (constant-dollar measuring unit) change the amounts but not the timing of revenues, expenses, gains, and losses. Replacement-cost measurements change the timing but not the amounts of income components in conventional accounting. The best measure of income in our opinion combines both general price level measuring units (constant dollars) with the replacement-cost basis. For financial reporting purposes, we would like to see holding gains recognized as they occur (column 8). Recognizing all the other features of current tax laws, we feel that for tax purposes, recognizing holding gains on income only as realized (column 7) may be more practicable and more equitable. The income reported in column 7 is identical with that in column 2—only the classification of components is changed. Thus we conclude that the FASB proposal (column 2) may be the best measure of income for tax purposes. Ideally, the income in column 6 would be taxed at higher rates than the remainder of the income in column 7; that is, realized holding gains would be taxed at lower rates than sustainable income.

Comments by Frank Weston

Sidney Davidson and Roman Weil treat a topic—procedures to identify and isolate the effects of inflation on financial data—that is of great interest to the financial community for several reasons. First, accounting procedures now are based on an assumption that the value of the measuring unit, the dollar, is stable over a period of years. That assumption is clearly false. Second, there is increasing interest in procedures to identify and to isolate unusual changes in cost and selling prices that occur independently of inflation, such as those experienced in the oil, sugar, and real estate industries in recent years. Third, there is growing interest in procedures to improve the accounting definition of income as an indicator of economic performance and financial position. It must also be noted that there is much confusion about each of these problems and about their solutions. This confusion is apparent in the comments addressed to the Financial Accounting Standards Board on the proposals to adjust financial statements for inflation.

Because data available in annual reports were insufficient to permit Davidson and Weil to follow the proposed steps in the FASB exposure draft in detail, they had to make a number of approximations in computing inflation-adjusted income. I think that they have used appropriate methods in light of the available information. In applying the FASB methods in detail, we are finding a great many additional problems. For example, the treatments of deferred income taxes and of the foreign operations of corporations are very difficult questions with which the accounting profession is now wrestling. Should foreign accounts be adjusted for foreign inflation or for U.S. inflation? Thus, in computing depreciation, should one translate the original investment to U.S. dollars at the exchange rate prevailing when the investment was made and then adjust the translated depreciation for U.S. inflation rates, or should one leave the investment in the foreign currency, adjust depreciation for foreign inflation, and then translate the resulting totals to U.S. dollars at the current rate? We also have problems with preferred stock that has mandatory redemption provisions and with a host of smaller mechanical problems.

We also need more information about the impact of inflation on individuals, institutions, pension funds, banks, insurance companies, investment trusts, and service companies. We need a lot more information, because we are talking about changes that may have an important effect on national income and the distribution of tax burdens.

Of the several adjustments carried out in the Davidson-Weil paper, the treatment of monetary gains and losses has provoked the most comment from industry representatives. Although most industry representatives agree that conceptually the monetary adjustment is an offset to interest expense or income, they argue that this adjustment should not be entered in income of the current year. (Some would reflect the gain or loss when the debt is paid; others would credit the amount directly to the capital accounts.) The resistance to this type of adjustment is enormous. Business spokesmen feel *something* should be done—that additional depreciation should be allowed—but because of their nervousness about adjustments for monetary gain or loss, the business community in general is opposed to any sort of broad overall adjustments. The FASB would have had to show great courage if it had required overall adjustments for inflation. In the past, the FASB (and the Accounting Principles Board before it) has been sensitive to the views of business because corporations might refuse to follow FASB rules and might appeal to the Securities and Exchange Commission and to Congress. On occasion Congress has sided with business. It is hoped that inflation-adjusted financial accounting and reporting will be instiuted in the near future.

Comments by George Tolley

Sidney Davidson and Roman Weil have shown in previous work that it is possible to adjust financial statements for inflation; in this paper they show that it is possible to adjust business tax returns for inflation. This is their broad accomplishment. I have three specific comments.

First, I would like to see aggregate estimates of the overall effect of inflation adjustments to compare with those of Davidson and Weil.[31] Second, I have not seen a satisfactory case made *against* replacement-cost depreciation. Isn't replacement-cost depreciation superior to adjustment of historical cost by the GNP deflator, the consumer price index, or any other single index applied to all goods? Suppose that all prices increase but that the prices of durable capital goods increase more than others. In that case, at the end of an accounting period, a firm has used up some of that capital but retains a stock of durable capital. Under replacement-cost depreciation, the firm is allowed a deduction of sufficient size to replace its capital at current market prices, but the firm is unable to do this if historical cost is adjusted by some price index. There is a logic to the use of replacement-cost depreciation. It makes any other changes in the treatment of income from business operations unnecessary since firms are already allowed to adopt LIFO, an option most have exercised.

Third, I now turn to adjustment in the treatment of income from financial assets. I am concerned that the list of assets on which adjustments are to be made be complete; that is, the sum of such assets, durable capital goods, and inventories should equal total assets. In some previous calculations, I attempted to follow the FASB rules, and it seemed that the total was smaller than the sum of all assets.

Discussion

John Shoven suggested that an important and necessary adjustment in business income had been omitted from the FASB exposure draft. When interest rates increase, the market value of outstanding debt declines. Because a firm has the option of repurchasing its debt at reduced prices, the change in the value of the firm's debt represents an accrued gain. Shoven found this gain impressive. The bonds and mortgages of nonfinancial corporations are now selling for $85 billion less than face value. During 1974 this discount rose $35 billion.

31. See John B. Shoven and Jeremy I. Bulow, "Inflation Accounting and Nonfinancial Corporate Profits: Physical Assets," *Brookings Papers on Economic Activity, 3:1975*, pp. 557–611.

While the gain has not been realized, it is nevertheless meaningful. Shoven suggested an example to illustrate this contention. Assume that all interest rates are 5 percent, that a family has $10,000 in the bank and that the family buys a $50,000 house, with no down payment and a $50,000 consol mortgage at the prevailing rate of 5 percent. Its annual mortgage interest is $2,500. Now, let inflation jump to 20 percent a year and interest rates to 25 percent. House prices are unaffected because the real rate of interest is unchanged. The family now withdraws its $10,000 from the bank and purchases a consol yielding $2,500. The family's net interest income is zero, as the interest income from the consol and the interest expenses from the mortgage exactly cancel one another. The family also holds title to a house worth $50,000. In effect the family has a net worth of $50,000 compared with a net worth of $10,000 before the increase in interest rates, a $40,000 profit.

Shoven pointed out that many institutions record the value of their bond holdings at market value—mutual funds, universities, foundations. But nonfinancial corporations do not. Shoven held that they should. In 1973 McCulloch Oil, for example, had a loss on regular operations, but it repurchased its bonds at 55 cents on the dollar and thereby maintained profits at levels close to those of previous years. Perhaps this profit should be averaged over several years, but it should not be ignored. When bonds decline in value because default risk increases, other accounting methods may be necessary. But even in this case the record profits Pan American Airways reported recently that were due to the repurchase of bonds at 30 cents on the dollar should not be ignored.

Shoven had other problems with the FASB exposure draft. He doubted whether accelerated depreciation, which was introduced in part as an alternative for replacement-cost depreciation, should be retained if historical-cost depreciation is inflated by the change in the price level. He had similar doubts about LIFO.

Frank Weston pointed out that in the case mentioned by Shoven, while the firm's debt became less valuable and therefore less burdensome, its oil properties and real estate might also have decreased in value. These losses might be large and unrecognized. Thus if current value measurements are to be used for one item, they should be used for all.

Alan Blinder pointed out that if Shoven's adjustment is applied to business, it should also be applied to households. Where businesses have a gain on their net debt, households will suffer a corresponding capital loss. Conversely, households will have a similar kind of gain on home mortgages that will be a capital loss for some bank. He raised the question of whether capital gains on mortgages should be taxed as accrued, along the lines Shoven suggested for businesses, or only when the house was sold; and he suggested that the indivisibilities might justify taxation only at realization in this case. Stanley Fischer suggested that the logic of Shoven's examples had not been carried far enough. If one wishes to recognize as current income any change in the command of a corporation over real wealth, then one should not bother with conventional measures of business income, depreciation, interest, and so on, but should directly tax the change in the value of the firm as measured by its stock market value. In that case the corporate income tax would become a capital gains tax levied directly on the corporation. Of course, the fact that the tax could be levied on the change in stock market value without having to calculate corporate income did not mean that accurate accounting was unimportant.

Martin Bailey argued that two of Shoven's positions were inconsistent. On the one hand, Shoven advocated the current taxation of changes in the market value of a firm's debt. But if this is done, the firm will incur offsetting losses as time passes and the bonds approach maturity. On the other hand, Shoven advocates averaging. If the averaging period is the life of the bond, these two effects will just cancel. Shoven replied that bonds had been selling at discount since 1945 and are further below par now than ever before. If averaging is permitted, substantial interest charges would have to be imposed on deferred taxes. Thus things would not cancel.

In reply to George Tolley, Sidney Davidson reiterated the distinction between inflation adjustment of depreciation and replacement-cost depreciation. The former deals only with changes in general price levels. The latter deals with changes in relative prices. He suggested that Shoven's treatment of the discount on bonds is really one aspect of replacement-cost accounting. If one holds that the consumption of real capital should be valued at the current market price of that capital, one should also hold that changes in the market value of debt should be included in income. He objected to the use of a single price level adjustment for real capital and to what amounts to the use of distinct price indexes for debt.

John Bossons pointed out that inflation increases the required rate of return on investments if historical-cost accounting is used. The FASB proposals must be interpreted as an effort to counteract that effect of inflation. He stressed the importance of applying the FASB rules to households as well as to businesses. Stanley Surrey raised the question of whether it would be desirable to adopt the FASB rules if they were applied only to businesses. Bossons said that he did not think so; moreover, he felt that monetary corrections for individuals should be taxed not at capital gains rates but at ordinary income tax rates.

In order to clarify the issues, Joseph Pechman asked Tolley whether he would favor replacement-cost depreciation even if prices were stable on the average. Tolley said that he would because that rule would exclude from taxation changes in the relative value of durable capital and (if LIFO were used) of inventories until the firm liquidated, was sold, or went into another type of activity and in the process depleted its stocks of goods. Richard Goode observed that the advantages claimed for replacement-cost depreciation had nothing to do with inflation adjustment and hence had very little to do with the subject of the conference.

Arthur Okun argued that to the extent that depreciable capital is financed by borrowing no adjustment for inflation is necessary. If the firm finances the purchase of a machine by issuing debt that matures at the same rate as the machine depreciates, then inflation reduces the value of the firm's debt at the same rate that it reduces the value of historical-cost depreciation. If the firm is viewed on an accrual basis, then the firm experiences a loss equal to the value of the capital good multiplied by the rate of inflation and a gain equal to the inflation rate multiplied by the value of outstanding debt. If the firm is viewed on a realization basis, then the firm enjoys a gain equal to the rate of inflation (cumulative over the life of the debt) multiplied by the debt retired during the current accounting period and a loss equal to the rate of inflation (cumulated over the life of the asset) multiplied by the amount of historical-cost depreciation claimed during the current accounting period. In either case the gains and losses just balance, and no adjustment for inflation is required. This equality led

Okun to suggest that one need not adopt the full set of FASB adjustments but could approximate them, as William Fellner and his col-
leagues had suggested in their American Enterprise Institute study,
by allowing replacement-cost depreciation (or inflated historical-
cost depreciation) only on that part of capital goods financed by
equity.[32] Fellner reiterated his support of this view.

32. See William Fellner, Kenneth W. Clarkson, and John H. Moore, *Correcting
Taxes for Inflation* (American Enterprise Institute for Public Policy Research,
1975).

CHAPTER FOUR

Inflation and the Definition of Taxable Personal Income

ROGER E. BRINNER

THIS CHAPTER focuses on a general definition of personal income and the implications of such a definition for federal income tax revenues. The central issues are:

—How should nominal wage, interest, dividend, and capital gain income be adjusted for tax purposes to reflect changes in the purchasing power of a dollar?

—Does the income tax on assets currently defined as "capital assets" under the Internal Revenue Code deserve any special adjustment in response to inflation?

—Would indexing the bracket rates of the personal income tax be a sufficient adjustment to remove all distortions caused by inflation?

—Given the theoretical conclusions, is it feasible to implement a desirable set of inflation adjustments to the income tax?

—What impact would such an adjustment have on total federal tax revenues in the aggregate and across income classes? What basic parameters would control this impact?

At the outset of the study, a basic definition of income is drawn

The author appreciates the advice and criticism of Henry Aaron, Otto Eckstein, Stanley Fisher, and Richard Musgrave.

from the writings of Henry Simons and Sir John Hicks, and the logical implications of this definition with respect to the first three issues are explored. Recent tax reform proposals pertaining to capital gains are also analyzed and found to be ill-conceived. Following this discussion, the practical challenges of implementation are explored and a theoretically appropriate set of inflation adjustments is argued to be quite feasible. Finally, estimates are presented of the impact of the proposed reform on aggregate revenues and the income tax burden of selected income classes.

The Basic Definition of Income

The study proceeds from the assumption that income rather than wealth or consumption is the object of the federal income tax.[1] The classic definitions of income are those of Henry Simons and Sir John Hicks. According to Simons, income is

(a) . . . the amount by which the value of a person's store of property rights would have increased, as between the beginning and end of the period, if he had consumed (destroyed) nothing, or (b) . . . the value of rights which he might have exercised in consumption without altering the value of his store of rights. In other words, it implies [an] estimate of consumption and accumulation.[2]

Hicks's "central criterion" is that

a person's income is what he can consume during the week and still expect to be as well off at the end of the week as he was at the beginning.[3]

Neither definition refers to price changes, but Simons notes elsewhere that "considerations of justice demand that changes in monetary conditions be taken into account."[4] The "value of a person's store of property rights" is thus properly interpreted as the command over *real* goods and services. In the absence of perfect money illusion, this is also a logical interpretation of Hicks.

1. The issue of the best potential target of federal taxation will not be debated. The narrow definition of the topic is intended to avoid certain unnecessary but practically inevitable disputes (such as the classic "double taxation of savings" argument) that concern the choice of a tax base rather than the definition of the components of a given base. It is the latter topic that is to be analyzed.

2. Henry C. Simons, *Personal Income Taxation* (University of Chicago Press, 1938), p. 49.

3. J. R. Hicks, *Value and Capital: An Inquiry into Some Fundamental Principles of Economic Theory* (2d ed., Oxford University Press, 1946), p. 176.

4. Simons, *Personal Income Taxation*, p. 155.

According to this definition, income is equal to the potential *quantity* of goods and services an individual could consume by spending his income; thus a price index must be chosen to convert nominal income into units of purchasing power. The emphasis on potential consumption suggests that the consumer price index (CPI) would be an appropriate choice. This index represents the cost of a fixed "market basket of goods" that officially represents the tastes of an urban worker. Equally important, the CPI is a highly visible statistic that is already familiar to the majority of citizens. Applying these principles, one discovers that income in current prices should be defined as the sum of two quantities. The first is the sum of wages, rents, interest, dividends, and other net business income, all measured in current dollars. The second is the difference between the end-of-period value of assets at current prices and the beginning-of-period value of assets multiplied by the ratio of the end-of-period value to the beginning-of-period value of the appropriate price index. Inflation-adjusted income, the sum of these two components, is in Simons's terms the amount by which "a person's store of property rights would have increased" in the absence of consumption.

This measure of real income is correct only if every asset and liability transaction takes place at the end of a period; but mid-period transactions are easily added. Instead of two periods, several must be dealt with, one appropriate for each time at which income is accrued. If the tax system is on a realization basis, changes in deflated asset values appear only when both the purchase and sale transactions have been recorded.[5]

The Scope of Inflation Adjustments

Tax equity requires the inflation adjustment of income from all assets and liabilities, not merely from the small class of transactions that give rise to capital gains and losses under current tax law. For example, a taxpayer may invest $1,000 in a savings account paying 5 percent interest or in a share of stock appreciating 5 percent during the year but paying no dividends. Assume that the investment is

5. Deferral can generate important tax savings, but this is a logically separate issue. For estimates of the combined impact of inflation losses and deferral benefits with respect to capital gains taxation, see Roger Brinner, "Inflation, Deferral and the Neutral Taxation of Capital Gains," *National Tax Journal,* vol. 26 (December 1973), pp. 565–73.

liquidated after one year and that the proceeds are consumed. Whatever the rate of inflation, the taxpayer's consumption opportunities are the same whichever asset he buys if tax consequences are disregarded. If there is no inflation, his potential consumption has increased by $50, and this is his true income. On the other hand, if prices rise 10 percent, the taxpayer's income in end-of-year prices is −$50.[6]

This example clearly indicates one way in which recent proposals to adjust narrowly defined capital gains for the effects of inflation do not go far enough. Inflation reduces the nominal returns to *all* assets; conversely, inflation reduces the burden of debt repayments, a gain that should be offset against interest costs. A comprehensive definition of income requires recognition of all these impacts of inflation on purchasing power. Just as inflation makes it more difficult for the stereotypical senior citizen, so also inflation enables a heavily mortgaged homeowner to repay his mortgage in dollars worth less than those borrowed. Both the losses and gains from inflation deserve the same response, whether they come from corporate securities, real estate, or savings accounts.

These gains and losses may be unanticipated—for example, if inflation (or its disappearance) is unexpected—but taxable income is, and theoretically should be, an ex post concept reflecting the actual events of the period. Unanticipated inflation creates windfall gains and losses that create or destroy taxable capacity in the same way other sources of windfall income do. If these income flows are substantial, the usual arguments for averaging apply. But no distinction should be drawn between expected and windfall income as long as taxable capacity is the measure of tax liability.

The inflation adjustment procedure just described does not negate the full impact of inflation on personal tax liabilities. It represents one of two logically separable steps—the aggregation of all types of income in current-dollar terms. Because this step produces a current-dollar measure of income, inflation would expand the tax base, and

6. Income on the savings account is the sum of $50 interest less the decline in the value of the asset. If the end-of-period price index is 1.00 (which is equivalent to using end-of-period prices), then the price index at the beginning of the period was 0.9090 . . . and the adjusted value of the asset was $1,100 ($1,000/0.9090). The asset is worth only $1,000 at the end of the period, however; hence a $100 capital loss must be added to the $50 income to yield a $50 loss. The computation for the stock is the same, except that a $50 nominal gain replaces the $50 interest payment.

under a progressive tax structure, the tax due would expand to be a larger fraction of income even in the absence of any growth in real income.

This type of automatic tax increase does dampen demand and therefore probably helps to stabilize the price level. The experience of the economy during 1969–71 and 1973–75, however, suggests that there may be an overabundance of demand-dampening responses to inflation. The recent combination of discretionary and automatic responses to inflation has twice produced an overkill of demand and has prematurely ended economic recoveries. Such "automatic stabilizers" are undesirable if the unemployment cost is too high relative to the deflation benefit. If this is the case and the income tax is to be deleted from the list of stabilizers, brackets, exemptions, and deduction levels could be price-level indexed. This second step would complete the insulation of personal income from inflation-induced changes in tax liabilities. But if the inflation adjustment of capital income and interest expenses is done on the current-dollar basis suggested in this study, the two steps are logically and administratively separable.

It is important to recognize that the taxes levied on wages are distorted by inflation only because the system of progressive tax rates and nonindexed exemptions, deductions, and rate brackets is progressive. In contrast, the measurement of capital income is currently distorted in two respects during inflation. First, capital income shares with wages the arbitrary inflation-induced increases associated with a progressive tax structure. Second, the contribution of capital to taxable capacity is overstated if a deduction is not allowed for that component of the return that merely maintains the purchasing power of initial net worth. The changes in income suggested in this study remove the second distortion. As a result, current-dollar wages and other nominal receipts are comparable to inflation-adjusted capital gains as elements of taxable capacity.

In view of the political difficulties probably inherent in a suggestion to adjust capital income but not labor income for inflation, this point perhaps deserves some additional comment. The classic definition of income has been shown to be the increase in potential consumption due to current-year activities and investments. Each household begins the year with a stock of assets and of labor resources. Income is the net return provided by these resources during the year. Because it is impractical if not impossible to estimate the increase or decrease in the market value of labor resources, wages less work-related expenses are the *net* income flow from labor. Net wages equal the increase in consumption that is possible due to the use of labor resources. Thus regardless of whether wages keep pace with, exceed, or fall behind inflation, nominal wages are a correct indication of the labor income contribution to taxable capacity.

The calculations of the equivalent net return—the increase in potential consumption due to current-year activities and investments—from nonlabor assets requires a subtraction from the gross return of the amount necessary to *maintain* the original purchasing power. This is achieved by writing up the original value by intervening inflation before calculating the net gain. This inflation-adjusted income is a current-dollar measure and thus, like wages, fully vulnerable to the inflation distortion due to a progressive tax structure.

Inflation Adjustment and Recent Tax Reform Proposals

A number of proposals intended to adjust capital gains for inflation have recently received serious consideration within the U.S. Congress. Most of these proposals would reduce the proportion of long-term capital gains subject to tax to below 50 percent, the proportion now included in taxable income. The adjustment procedure outlined above would also exclude part of nominal gains. Two important facts must be kept in mind, however. First, the proportion to be excluded is extremely sensitive to actual inflation between time of purchase and time of sale. Second, the adjustment should apply to a broader class of assets (and liabilities) than those now classified as capital assets.

In 1974, 1975, and 1976 the House Ways and Means Committee and the Senate Finance Committee have considered formulas that would permit taxpayers to exclude from taxation a larger proportion of each nominal capital gain the longer each asset had been held. On behalf of such a change, it was argued that the proportion of a gain due to inflation became larger the longer an asset was held. Unfortunately, this argument confuses *absolute* with *proportional* gains. The absolute gain due to inflation does increase with time (as long as consumer prices do not fall), but the inflation-related gain as a *pro-*

portion of the total gain actually is likely to decrease as the holding period increases.[7]

According to the definition of income presented at the start of this chapter, capital gains can add to purchasing power and therefore are properly subject to tax. If prices are rising, however, the full gain should not be taxed, because some of the apparent gain is lost to inflation. The properly excluded portion of the gain on an asset held one year equals the ratio of the inflation rate, π, to the appreciation rate, n. The present policy of excluding half of capital gains is the correct procedure only in a special case, when half the total gain is due to inflation. If capital gains were taxed on accrual, this policy would be correct if, and only if, the current rate of inflation equaled the rate of real growth in the value of the asset. With taxation of capital gains only when realized, the inclusion of half the gain is correct only if the rate of inflation exceeds the rate of real growth by ever larger amounts as the holding period lengthens.

Table 4-1 illustrates that the proportion of a capital gain properly subject to tax tends to increase with the length of the holding period and hence that inflation is an invalid justification for a declining schedule; on the contrary, the inflation argument generally supports an increasing schedule. The table also shows that no fixed schedule is appropriate. The volatility of inflation requires a flexible, responsive measure of income. Simple approximations will produce serious errors.

Implementing the Inflation Adjustment Principle

Fortunately, accurate adjustment of capital gains for inflation is a relatively straightforward matter. First, Schedule D, the income tax

7. This note contains proof of the text statement. Let k be the fraction of capital gains deemed to be properly subject to tax if prices are stable, n the rate of appreciation of nominal asset value, π the rate of increase in prices, and g the rate of growth in real asset values; $g = n - \pi$. Unless capital income is to be treated preferentially as an inducement to investment in capital assets, k is equal to one. Assume that the asset has a value of $1 at time of purchase. At the end of t periods the market value (in period t prices) is e^{nt}. The original purchase price, in period t prices, is $e^{\pi t}$. The properly defined capital gain is therefore $e^{nt} - e^{\pi t}$, and $k(e^{nt} - e^{\pi t})$ should be subject to tax. The nominal capital gain is $e^{nt} - 1$. The fraction of $e^{nt} - 1$ properly subject to tax is thus $k(e^{nt} - e^{\pi t})/(e^{nt} - 1) = F$. Dividing through top and bottom by e^{nt} yields $F = k(1 - e^{-gt})/(1 - e^{-nt})$. As t becomes larger, the numerator approaches k and the denominator approaches 1.

Table 4-1. Proportion of a Capital Gain Properly Subject to Tax, Selected Asset Holding Periods and Rates of Inflation[a]

	Percentage of capital gain properly subject to tax, by rate of inflation (π) and rate of nominal appreciation (n)			
Asset holding period (years)	$\pi = 0.01$ $n = 0.03$	$\pi = 0.03$ $n = 0.05$	$\pi = 0.05$ $n = 0.07$	$\pi = 0.07$ $n = 0.09$
1	67.0	40.6	29.3	23.0
5	68.3	43.0	32.2	26.3
10	69.9	46.1	36.0	30.5
25	74.6	55.1	47.6	44.0
50	81.4	68.9	65.2	63.9

Source: Calculated by author. See note 7 in the text.

a. The nominal rate of capital gain is assumed to be 2 percent higher than the rate of inflation, indicating that real growth is 2 percent. All rates of growth are instantaneous rates; thus 5 percent instantaneous growth leads to 5.127 percent growth after one year. The difference is equivalent to the additional interest paid on savings accounts when interest is compounded instantaneously.

form on which capital gains are reported, requires minor alterations. Second, a set of decisions must be made concerning the timing of the taxation of income from different assets and liabilities. In some cases accrual accounting is reasonable and in other cases realization accounting may be preferable.

Figure 4-1 presents a comparison of the present long-term capital gain tax form with the revised form required for inflation adjustment. The comparison includes the calculation of the taxable gain from a hypothetical purchase (in June 1963) and sale (in August 1974) of 100 shares of YBM Corporation stock and the purchase (in March 1971) and sale (in September 1974) of a $10,000 XT&T bond.

In each case, an inflation-adjusted gain is defined by the principle:

$$\begin{matrix} \text{inflation-} \\ \text{adjusted} \\ \text{gain} \end{matrix} = \begin{matrix} \text{net} \\ \text{sales} \\ \text{price} \end{matrix} - \begin{bmatrix} \text{historical-} & \text{inflation} \\ \text{cost} & \times \text{adjustment} \\ \text{basis} & \text{factor} \end{bmatrix}.$$

The form requires only minor changes in the column headings and the addition of a column that shows the result of multiplying the historical-cost basis by an inflation adjustment factor. Table 4-2 presents inflation adjustment factors similar to those the Internal Revenue Service (IRS) would publish each year. The inflation adjustment factor used in the multiplication is the sum of the basic inflation adjustment ratio from table 4-2, from set 1 (based on time of purchase), and the current year exact adjustment from set 2 (based on

Figure 4-1. Suggested Revision of Schedule D of the Federal Individual Income Tax Return

Current Schedule D

Part II   Long-term Capital Gains and Losses—Assets Held More Than 6 Months

a. Kind of property and description (Example, 100 shares of "Z" Co.)	b. Date acquired (Mo., day, yr.)	c. Date sold (Mo., day, yr.)	d. Gross sales price	e. Cost or other basis, as adjusted (see instruction Fᵃ) and expense of sale	f. Gain or (loss) (d less e)
100 shares, YBM Corp.	6/19/63	8/23/74	$ 2,000	$ 1,000	$1,000
Bond, XT&T	3/20/71	9/5/74	$10,100	$10,000	$ 100

Revised Schedule D

Part II   All Elements of Net Worth Involving Current-Year Closing Transactions

a. Kind of property and description (Example, 100 shares of "Z" Co.)	b. Date acquired (Mo., day, yr.)	c. Date sold (Mo., day, yr.)	d. Net sales price	e. Gross purchase price	f. Cost multiplied by inflation adjustment	g. Inflation-adjusted gain or (loss) (d less f)
100 shares, YBM Corp.	6/19/63	8/23/74	$ 2,000	$ 1,000	$ 1,595	$ 405
Bond, XT&T	3/20/71	9/5/74	$10,100	$10,000	$12,440	($2,340)

Source: Current Schedule D adapted from federal individual income tax form 1040; revised schedule prepared by author from data in table 4-2.
a. Cost of subsequent improvements [author's footnote].

Table 4-2. Inflation Adjustment Factors for Calculating Long-Term Capital Gains and Losses on Schedule D of the Income Tax Return, Taxable Year 1974

Set 1

Date of purchase	Basic inflation adjustment ratio	Date of purchase	Basic inflation adjustment ratio	Date of purchase	Basic inflation adjustment ratio	Date of purchase	Basic inflation adjustment ratio
1930	2.80	1950	1.94	January 1971	1.173	January 1973	1.095
1931	3.07	1951	1.80	February	1.172	February	1.089
1932	3.42	1952	1.76	March	1.169	March	1.079
1933	3.61	1953	1.75	April	1.166	April	1.071
1934	3.49	1954	1.74	May	1.160	May	1.065
1935	3.41	1955	1.75	June	1.154	June	1.059
1936	3.37	1956	1.72	July	1.151	July	1.057
1937	3.26	1957	1.66	August	1.148	August	1.039
1938	3.32	1958	1.62	September	1.147	September	1.035
1939	3.37	1959	1.61	October	1.146	October	1.027
1940	3.34	1960	1.58	November	1.143	November	1.019
1941	3.18	1961	1.56	December	1.138	December	1.012
1942	2.87	1962	1.55	January 1972	1.135	January 1974	1.000
1943	2.70	1963	1.53	February	1.131	February	0.989
1944	2.66	1964	1.51	March	1.129	March	0.979
1945	2.60	1965	1.48	April	1.127	April	0.973
1946	2.40	1966	1.44	May	1.124	May	0.962
1947	2.09	1967	1.40	June	1.122	June	0.954
1948	1.94	1968	1.34	July	1.117	July	0.947
1949	1.96	1969	1.28	August	1.115	August	9.935
		1970	1.20	September	1.111	September	0.925
				October	1.108	October	0.917
				November	1.104	November	0.909
				December	1.101	December	0.902

Set 2

Date of sale	Basic inflation adjustment ratio	Current inflation transaction adjustment
January 1974	1.095	0.000
February	1.089	0.011
March	1.079	0.021
April	1.071	0.027
May	1.065	0.038
June	1.059	0.046
July	1.057	0.053
August	1.039	0.065
September	1.035	0.075
October	1.027	0.083
November	1.019	0.091
December	1.012	0.098

Sources: The factors are derived from the official consumer price indexes (taken from the data bank of Data Resources, Inc.) by the methods given below. Set 1 is calculated by dividing the CPI for January of the tax year 1974 by the CPI for the respective dates of purchase, or 1 plus the percentage increase in the CPI from the date of purchase until January of the tax year. Set 2 is equal to 1 minus the ratio of the CPI in January to the CPI of the month of sale, an approximation of the rate of inflation for that part of the current year during which the asset was held. The sum thus approximately equals 1 plus the total inflation from date of purchase to date of sale and is the proper adjustment factor to convert the initial cost into current purchasing power. In a technical sense, the first number should be multiplied by the ratio of sale-date CPI to the January CPI, but because the second factor will typically differ from zero by less than 0.10, the benefits from the simplicity of addition would seem to outweigh the benefits from the precision of multiplication. The monthly differentials are necessary for assets held for short periods to remove incentives to change purchase and sale timing patterns so as to obtain unjustified inflation adjustments.

month of sale). This sum is then multiplied by the actual gross purchase price.

The inflation adjustments of the revised Schedule D in figure 4-1 are based on table 4-2. The inflation adjustment factor for the shares of YBM stock equals 1.595 (the sum of 1.53 from set 1 for 1963 and 0.065 from set 2 for August 1974). This changes the historical cost basis, $1,000, to an inflation-adjusted basis of $1,595. The resulting gain is $405 rather than $1,000. Similarly the inflation adjustment factor for the bond equals 1.244 (the sum of 1.169 from set 1 for March 1971 and 0.075 from set 2 for September 1974). The adjusted loss equals $2,340, versus the $100 gain indicated by the current form.[8]

This example illustrates a practical and administratively simple solution to the first problem in adjusting income for inflation, the alteration of Schedule D. It also embodies a possible response to the second problem, the timing of the recognition of tax liabilities on capital income, in that gains are taxed when realized. Taxation of gains upon realization is probably so well established that an inflation reform could not be usefully extended to encompass a switch to accrual-basis taxation, regardless of the theoretical justifications that exist for such a change.

On the other hand, current year recognition of inflation gains or losses may be preferred with respect to personal debt and savings because no administrative or political difficulties exist to counter the theoretical case. Lending and savings institutions could be required to issue a year-end statement to each borrower or depositor indicating (1) the nominal interest charges or payments (as they do now), (2) the inflation gain or loss on the *average* debt or deposit balance, and (3) the difference; that is, the net current-dollar, inflation-adjusted income.[9] Only the net interest income would be taxable. In a parallel

8. Note that in each case the taxpayer is better off paying tax on *all* his inflation-adjusted gain than he would be paying tax on *half* the nominal capital gains as now calculated. This result is an artifact of the numerical values chosen and should not be generalized without care.

9. Recognition of inflation losses from checking accounts has been excluded because the imputed income corresponding to the service provided is untaxed. Given that the taxpayer chooses to hold such a liquid asset rather than other assets whose yields rise with inflation, the "nominal convenience yield" on checking accounts must also rise with inflation. Basically, the reforms suggested in this study are limited to the inflation adjustment of net income streams currently covered by tax law.

fashion, taxpayers would report inflation-adjusted net interest payments rather than nominal interest payments as itemized deductions.[10]

The Impact of Inflation Adjustment

The reform suggested by this study would alter taxable income in two principal respects.

First, taxable income would be effectively reduced through the exclusion of that part of capital income that merely maintained the purchasing power of savings. For some assets and liabilities this offset would be readily calculated annually. For reasons of politics and practicality, however, the inflation offset for assets currently classified as capital assets would only be recognized at the time the asset was sold and the gain was realized.

Second, the reform fully recognizes the illusory nature of the inflation component of a capital gain and calls for its exclusion from the tax base. Given this recognition, a compelling argument in favor of excluding a fraction of capital gains is fully answered, and inflation-adjusted income from this source could logically be taxed on the same basis as other income. If less than half an individual's gain is illusory, he could thus end up with an increase in reported income. The exact result will critically depend on the yield and composition of his portfolio and the rate of inflation.

If all changes in asset values were taxed as accrued, the foregoing adjustments would yield a simple formula indicating whether a particular taxpayer would gain or lose from these reforms. The change in taxes would be $A_{-1}[(nq/2) - \pi]$, where A_{-1} is the taxpayer's net worth at the beginning of the taxable period; n is the rate of change in market value of the assets and liabilities included in A_{-1}; q is the proportion of those assets that previously would have received special treatment under the current tax law provisions for capital assets; and π is the rate of inflation of the CPI.[11]

---

10. Alternative treatments of debt that would delay the recognition of the inflation gains could be adopted to ease the impact on homeowners. One would be to recognize only the gain on debt that has been repaid during the tax year. This would be similar in spirit to the current practice of taxation of capital gains as realized rather than as accrued. It would lead to very small tax liabilities during the early years of ownership and substantial liabilities near the end of the mortgage term.

11. Under accrual taxation and without inflation adjustment, income would include $(B - B_{-1}) + \frac{1}{2}(C - C_{-1})$, where B refers to the market value of assets

This algebraic expression implicitly points out the complex tax equity issue presented by capital income and the inadequate recognition of this problem embodied in current tax law. Only if the expression $(nq/2 - \pi)$ were approximately equal to zero across income classes and across years would the current structure fortuitously be appropriate. Given the extreme variability of each of the key parameters—n, q, and π—the distortions in the current code are certain to be large.

There are systematic differences across and within income classes in the fraction (q) of net worth held in assets now classified by the Internal Revenue Code as capital assets and in the rate of appreciation of portfolios. For this reason it is important to attempt to estimate how the proposals advanced here would affect liabilities. As will be shown below, these changes would be likely to lower tax liabilities for all but the very highest brackets. But if inflation averaging over 5 percent a year should persist, the taxes on all brackets would decline, subject, of course, to offsetting changes in rates.

Before turning to these numbers, it is important to recall that the congressional debate on the reform of capital gain taxation has failed to consider the inflation losses corresponding to assets that do not primarily generate capital gains. There is no reason why savers purchasing such assets should be denied an inflation adjustment. Moreover, it cannot be fairly argued that all savers have the choice of investing more heavily in capital assets. The current interaction of the corporation income tax and the personal income tax generates a tax differential that encourages high-income individuals to seek corporate-source capital income and low-income taxpayers to seek other forms of investment.[12] Thus inflation adjustment of capital gains, but not of the income from other savings vehicles, would protect the

---

whose gains when sold are taxed in full, and C refers to the market value of assets generating long-term capital gains. With inflation adjustment, this quantity would become $[B - B_{-1} (1 + \pi)] + [C - C_{-1} (1 + \pi)]$, where π is the rate of inflation. The difference is $(B_{-1} + C_{-1})(- \pi) + \frac{1}{2}(C - C_{-1})$, or since $B_{-1} + C_{-1} = A_{-1}$, $- \pi A_{-1} + \frac{1}{2}(C - C_{-1})$. But $(C - C_{-1}) = nC_{-1} = nqA_{-1}$. Therefore, the change in taxable income is $A_{-1} [(nq/2) - \pi]$. These calculations abstract from the minimum tax on preference income or any other provision that makes the rates on long-term gains other than half the rate on ordinary income.

12. See Richard A. Musgrave and Peggy B. Musgrave, *Public Finance in Theory and Practice* (McGraw-Hill, 1973), pp. 277–85; or Martin J. Bailey, "Capital Gains and Income Taxation," in Arnold C. Harberger and Martin J. Bailey, eds., *The Taxation of Income from Capital* (Brookings Institution, 1969), p. 29.

affluent from inflation but leave most taxpayers fully exposed to its effects.

The Estimated Incidence of Inflation Adjustments

The discussion that follows presents numerical estimates of the impact on reported income of the adjustments for inflation suggested here. The estimates are based on wealth and income statistics for 1962. More recent estimates would be desirable, but reliable data are not yet available. The data on the composition of wealth by income class are those for 1962 provided by Dorothy Projector and Gertrude Weiss in *Survey of Financial Characteristics of Consumers.*[13] Data on purchases and sales of capital assets cross-tabulated by income class and length of holding period are drawn from a unique IRS study of capital asset sales in 1962.[14] It is fortunate that the two studies refer to the same year in that each is basically the only source of the required data for any year.

The IRS study provides the necessary information pertaining to transactions in four categories of capital assets: corporate stock; securities other than corporate stock, including U.S. government obligations, state and local securities, and other bonds, notes, and debentures; livestock; and real estate, including residences, nonbusiness real estate, real estate subdivided, and farmland. Data on residences as a separate category are also provided. For each asset category, selling price and cost totals are cross-tabulated by six adjusted gross income classes (all classes; total taxable returns; and taxable returns under $10,000, $10,000–$50,000, $50,000–$100,000, and $100,000 or more) and twenty holding periods (individual months up to twelve months, individual years up to five years, five–ten years, ten–fifteen years, fifteen–twenty years, and twenty years or more). This full detail is necessary to correctly calculate the estimated nominal gains, inflation-adjusted gains, and other pertinent information for each income class reported in table 4-3.

Table 4-3 reveals four prominent patterns. First, in the aggregate, exactly half of all nominal gains on taxable returns represented genuine increases in purchasing power. As a striking coincidence, the

13. Dorothy S. Projector and Gertrude S. Weiss, *Survey of Financial Characteristics of Consumers* (Board of Governors of the Federal Reserve System, 1966).

14. U.S. Internal Revenue Service, *Statistics of Income—1962, Supplemental Report: Sales of Capital Assets Reported on Individual Income Tax Returns* (Government Printing Office, 1966).

typical 50 percent inclusion rate embodied in current law for long-term gains was exactly right *on the average* in 1962. Second, this 50 percent average conceals major differences among income brackets. The under-$10,000 income bracket reported a gain of $885 million that turns into a $289 million real loss after adjustment for inflation. In contrast, fully 88 percent of the nominal gains reported by the highest income group represent true increases in the purchasing power of the underlying assets. Third, in 1962, securities other than stock yielded net capital losses on an inflation-adjusted basis for all income classes. This is to be expected for bonds and it does point out the need to recognize inflation losses on fixed-income assets such as savings accounts. Fourth, those in the income brackets of under $10,000 and over $100,000 had held the assets on which they realized gains and losses for more years than had members of the income brackets between $10,000 and $100,000. This pattern probably is explained by the age structure of the income classes, with older individuals decidedly concentrated at the extremes.[15]

Why did investors in the lowest income class do so poorly? First, both their residential and nonresidential real estate dealings were uniquely unprofitable after adjustment for inflation. Perhaps because of limited income and wealth, households in this class were unable to afford good information on investment opportunities. Also, causation may run the other way; low incomes may be due in part to poor investment experience for some households. Second, the realized gains on corporate stock were negative on both a nominal and an inflation-adjusted basis for taxpayers in the under-$10,000 bracket. While seeking an explanation for this, it is useful to note that the ratio of real gains to nominal gains rises steadily as income rises for the other three groups. The best explanation for these phenomena may be offered by a recent study of stockownership.[16] Investors in lower-income groups generally hold stocks with relatively higher dividend payout ratios and, hence, lower average rates of appreciation. The

15. Projector and Weiss indicate the following mean age distribution for heads of all households (not just those reporting capital asset transactions): 0–$3,000, 57 years of age; $3,000–$5,000, 47 years; $5,000–$10,000, 44 years; $10,000–$15,000, 47 years; $15,000–$25,000, 49 years; $25,000–$50,000, 52 years; $50,000–$100,000, 57 years; and $1,00,000 and over, 66 years. (See *Survey of Financial Characteristics of Consumers,* table A 33.)

16. Marshall E. Blume, Jean Crockett, and Irwin Friend, "Stockownership in the United States: Characteristics and Trends," *Survey of Current Business,* vol. 54 (November 1974), pp. 16–40.

Table 4-3. Nominal and Inflation-Adjusted Gains on Sales of Selected Capital Assets, and Holding Periods, by Income Class, 1962

Asset and adjusted gross income class	Nominal gain (millions of dollars) (1)	Inflation-adjusted gain (millions of dollars) (2)	Adjusted gain as a percentage of nominal gain (3)	Mean holding period (years) (4)
Corporate stock				
All income classes	3,148	1,905	61	3.6
Total taxable returns	3,216	2,096	65	3.7
Under $10,000	−91	−319	349	2.6
$10,000–$50,000	718	182	25	2.9
$50,000–$100,000	593	426	72	3.9
$100,000 or more	1,997	1,809	91	7.0
Other securities				
All income classes	−18	−165	917	2.6
Total taxable returns	34	−102	−300	2.7
Under $10,000	2	−9	−450	5.3
$10,000–$50,000	4	−47	−1,163	2.2
$50,000–$100,000	3	−27	−895	2.5
$100,000 or more	22	−24	−109	3.2
Real estate				
All income classes	2,256	296	13	9.8
Total taxable returns	2,005	463	23	9.7
Under $10,000	667	−259	−39	10.2
$10,000–$50,000	1,012	472	47	9.2
$50,000–$100,000	171	128	75	9.5
$100,000 or more	150	116	77	10.0
Residences[a]				
All income classes	487	−171	−35	10.0
Total taxable returns	427	−105	−25	9.9
Under $10,000	222	−133	−60	10.7
$10,000–$50,000	181	19	11	9.0
$50,000–$100,000	12	1	6	11.6
$100,000 or more	7	3	50	10.6
Livestock				
All income classes	622	599	96	4.5
Total taxable returns	403	388	96	4.5
Under $10,000	306	297	97	4.6
$10,000–$50,000	79	75	95	4.6
$50,000–$100,000	8	7	92	4.0
$100,000 or more	9	9	93	4.7

Table 4-3 (*continued*)

Asset and adjusted gross income class	Nominal gain (millions of dollars) (1)	Inflation-adjusted gain (millions of dollars) (2)	Adjusted gain as a percentage of nominal gain (3)	Mean holding period (years) (4)
Total: *Stock, securities,* *real estate, and livestock*				
All income classes	6,008	2,635	44	6.2
Total taxable returns	5,658	2,844	50	5.1
Under $10,000	885	−289	−32	6.3
$10,000–$50,000	1,813	683	38	4.2
$50,000–$100,000	775	534	69	4.2
$100,000 or more	2,178	1,910	88	6.7

Sources: U.S. Internal Revenue Service, *Statistics of Income–1962, Supplemental Report: Sales of Capital Assets Reported on Individual Income Tax Returns* (Government Printing Office, 1966). Column 1 is the difference between net sales revenue and initial purchase cost. Column 2 was calculated by writing up the purchase cost of the asset by the estimated inflation over the actual holding period. For assets held less than twelve months, 0.1 percent inflation was recognized per month. This equals the average monthly inflation during 1962. For longer-held assets, the inflation write-up factor equals the ratio of the December 1962 CPI to the CPI at the presumed average purchase date, the mid-point of the holding period interval. For example, assets held one to two years were granted an eighteen-month inflation adjustment. Assets held twenty years or more were credited with a twenty-five-year inflation loss. (See table 4-2 for the source of the CPI.) Column 3 equals column 2 divided by column 1 Column 4 is a weighted average of the individual holding periods by income and asset classes in which the weights are the sales prices as a proportion of total sales. Figures are rounded and, in columns 1 and 2, are summed across various holding periods; therefore, details may not add to totals. The numbers in column 3 were calculated from unrounded data.
   a. Also included in real estate.

total return offered by the sum of dividends and appreciation, however, was found not to differ significantly across income classes. These stock preference patterns probably reflect the relative importance to different income groups of the current preferential treatment of capital gains income.

The patterns of table 4-3 and all succeeding tables must be subject to an important caveat. The gains are not likely to be representative of the average portfolio performance of any group because only *realized* gains have been reported. There is no reason to presume a random sample has been sold. In fact, detailed evidence in the 1962 study that net short-term gains are close to zero or are negative suggests that a nonrandom, nonrepresentative sample of assets is sold each year.

An important corollary is that it is incorrect to assume that the same assets would have been sold had income in 1962 been defined on an inflation-adjusted basis. A different tax structure probably would have elicited a different set of sales. For example, if inflation-adjusted capital gains had been *fully* included in taxable income, capital gain tax liabilities of the $100,000-or-more group would have potentially doubled or tripled, while those in the under-$10,000 group would have been reduced by their losses.

In response to the alternative tax structure some high-income tax-payers could reduce sales to avoid or to defer taxes; others who need to raise a particular amount of cash after taxes might sell more. Conversely, members of the under-$10,000 group might realize larger gains under such a tax structure than they do now. Unfortunately, it is impossible to estimate alternative sale patterns with available data. Therefore the calculations of changes in tax liabilities presented in the remainder of this study abstract from changes in selling patterns as a consequence of the proposed redefinition of income and must be used with caution.

Table 4-3 necessarily excludes gains on the four major categories of assets not covered in the IRS capital gains study. These categories, representing 44 percent of total gains in 1962, are (1) assets used in trade or business, (2) the share of gain from partnerships and fiduciaries, (3) liquidation distributions, and (4) proceeds from prior-year installment sales. The excluded assets probably resemble corporate stock, other securities, and nonresidential real estate more closely than they do livestock and residential property. Therefore to estimate the corresponding inflation-adjusted gains, the excluded capital gains reported by each income class were written down by the ratio of inflation-adjusted gains to nominal gains on stock, securities, and nonresidential property. Table 4-4 shows the results of these adjustments for each income class in 1962. Column 3 shows total nominal gains and column 6 shows the total inflation-adjusted gains.

Table 4-5 indicates the changes in reported income, in the aggregate and per household, if suggested adjustments in capital gain taxation were adopted and if in addition gains and losses on savings accounts and net debt due to inflation were recognized. Columns 2 and 3 reflect the 1.2 percent inflation that occurred in 1962. The capital gain income effect reported in column 1 reflects the complex inflation adjustments used in calculating the entries for tables 4-3 and 4-4. The inclusion of $3.9 billion (table 4-4, column 6) in inflation-adjusted capital gains in place of $5.3 billion in gains reported in the IRS study and currently included in taxable income produces a total net reduction in reported income of $1.4 billion (column 1, table 4-5). The two lowest income classes substantially benefit, while the two

**Table 4-4. Nominal and Inflation-Adjusted Gains on Sales
of Total Capital Assets, by Income Class, 1962**
Millions of dollars

	Nominal gains			Inflation-adjusted gains		
Adjusted gross income class (dollars)	On assets included in IRS study (1)	On assets excluded from IRS study (2)	Total (3)	On assets included in IRS study (4)	On assets excluded from IRS study (5)	Total (6)
Under 10,000	885	830	1,715	−289	−1,046	−1,335
10,000–50,000	1,813	1,862	3,675	683	708	1,391
50,000–100,000	775	578	1,353	534	405	939
100,000 or more	2,178	1,124	3,302	1,910	989	2,899
Total	5,658	4,394	10,052	2,844	1,056	3,900

Sources: Internal Revenue Service, *Statistics of Income—1962, Supplemental Report: Sales of Capital Assets Reported on Individual Income Tax Returns* (Government Printing Office, 1966). Columns 1 and 4 are from table 4-3, columns 1 and 2. Column 2 was derived from IRS, *Sales of Capital Assets*, table B, p. 3. Column 5 equals column 2 multiplied by the ratio of inflation-adjusted to nominal gains on stock, securities, and nonresidential real estate. These ratios were derived from table 4-3 and equal −1.26, 0.38, 0.70, and 0.88 for the four income classes, from lowest to highest, respectively. Columns 1 and 4 do not add to totals because figures are summed across various holding periods.

highest classes must report increased capital gain income. The aggregate inflation loss on savings accounts produces a similar reduction in reported income, $1.3 billion. The primary beneficiaries as a group are again the two lowest income classes, although the upper income groups naturally enjoy larger reductions per household as a reflection of their larger accounts. The inflation gain on net debt significantly offsets the aggregate reductions of the preceding columns for all income classes.

The total change in reported income is only $0.3 billion, approximately $5 per household. However, an important redistribution of tax burdens among income brackets occurs. A large number of low-income households experience small average reductions in reported income. By contrast, a small number of high-income households experience very large increases in reported income, averaging $41,638 for households with incomes over $100,000 in 1962.

The substantially increased income of the two highest groups is primarily due to the large proportion of their nominal gains that represents true increases in purchasing power—69 percent for the $50,000–$100,000 group and 88 percent for the $100,000-or-more group. Statistics in the IRS special study reveal that these two groups included approximately 52.5 percent and 50.5 percent, respectively,

Table 4-5. Estimated Change in Reported Adjusted Gross Income in 1962 if Inflation-Adjusted Accounting Had Been Adopted

Income class (dollars)	Net change in capital gain income (1)	Inflation loss on savings accounts (2)	Inflation gain on net debt[a] (3)	Total change in reported income (4)
	All households (millions of dollars)			
Under 10,000	−2,299	−729	1,296	−1,732
10,000–50,000	−574	−562	1,115	−21
50,000–100,000	228	−36	15	207
100,000 or more	1,230	−7	26	1,249
Total[b]	−1,416	−1,334	2,452	−297
	Per household (dollars)			
Under 10,000	−49	−16	28	−37
10,000–50,000	−53	−52	102	−2
50,000–100,000	1,452	−229	96	1,318
100,000 or more	41,000	−233	871	41,638

Sources: *All households*: Column 1 equals column 6, table 4-4, minus nominal gains included in adjusted gross income in Internal Revenue Service, *Statistics of Income—1962, Supplemental Report: Sales of Capital Assets Reported on Individual Income Tax Returns* (Government Printing Office, 1966), table B, p. 3 (column 1 minus column 2). Column 2 equals −0.012, the negative of the price change in 1962, multiplied by aggregate savings account assets, which were derived from means in Dorothy S. Projector and Gertrude S. Weiss, *Survey of Financial Characteristics of Consumers* (Board of Governors of the Federal Reserve System, 1966), table A 10. Column 3 equals 0.012 multiplied by total debt minus mortgage assets minus nonmortgage loans to individuals (Projector and Weiss, ibid., tables A 9, A 10, A 14), weighted by consumer units in Dorothy S. Projector, *Survey of Changes in Family Finances* (Board of Governors of the Federal Reserve System, 1968), table S 22. Column 4 equals column 1 plus column 2 plus column 3.

Per household: Columns 1, 2, and 3 were derived from data for all households divided by the number of consumer units in each income class from Projector, ibid., table S 22. Column 4 equals column 1 plus column 2 plus column 3.

Figures are rounded.

a. Net debt is defined as the sum of outstanding mortgages on the household's home, personal loans, life insurance loans, and debts secured by investment assets minus loans extended by the household. It excludes holdings of corporate bonds, which were accounted for as "other securities" in table 4-3.

b. "Total" signifies total taxable units for column 1 but total population for columns 2 and 3, an unavoidable inconsistency, given the available data.

of capital gains in adjusted gross income.[17] The changes proposed in the present study would thus include an additional 16.5 percent (69.0 − 52.5) of the $50,000–$100,000 group's reported capital gains and an additional 37.5 percent (88.0 − 50.5) of the highest income group's gains.

Precise estimates of the impact on total tax liabilities in 1962 would require detailed information on the marginal tax rates. A rough estimate can be obtained by using the 1963 data in the

17. The IRS special study provided two modified estimates of adjusted gross income: one modified to exclude all capital gains, the other modified to include all gains. (*Sales of Capital Assets*, table B, p. 3.) By comparing these with the standard adjusted gross income totals, the inclusion proportions were derived.

Survey of Changes in Family Finances.[18] This survey, done as a follow-up to the *Survey of Financial Characteristics of Consumers,* estimated disposable income as a basis of an analysis of saving behavior. The difference between mean disposable income and mean gross income equals mean federal income tax payments by income class (column 2, table 4-6). The change in mean tax liabilities from a given income class to the next higher class divided by the change in mean income is an estimate of the marginal rate of the higher income class (column 3). An alternative estimate can be obtained by comparing the mean tax liability for each class with the tax liability ranges corresponding to each rate bracket applicable in 1962 for married taxpayers filing a joint return. The judgmental estimates in column 5 adopt the tax table rates except for the lowest and the two highest income classes. For the lowest an "average" marginal rate of 15 percent was selected in recognition of the possibility that the proposed reductions could be greater than taxable income for some units. Slightly lower values were adopted for the rates of the $50,000–$99,999 group in recognition of the significant difference between the column 3 and column 4 estimates. The aggregate rates of column 6 are averages based on income reported by each sub class.

Table 4-7 combines the data in tables 4-5 and 4-6 to produce estimates of the change in tax liabilities. All approximations inherent in the previous tables are compounded in this table, which suggests that the reform would have changed disposable income in the first two classes negligibly. Reform, however, would have reduced 1962 mean disposable income in the $50,000–$100,000 income classes by approximately 1 percent, and it would have reduced 1962 mean disposable income of the highest income group by nearly 20 percent. The aggregate increase in personal income tax liabilities of $0.7 billion equals approximately 1.5 percent of 1962 federal personal income tax revenue.

Summary

The conclusions of the study can be briefly summarized as follows:

1. Complete inflation adjustment of personal income can be logically separated into two components: the procedures necessary to

18. Dorothy S. Projector, *Survey of Changes in Family Finances* (Board of Governors of the Federal Reserve System, 1968).

Table 4-6. Estimated Mean Income and Marginal Tax Rates, by Income Class, 1962

				Alternative estimates of marginal tax rate (percent)		
			Change in tax divided by change in mean income	From standard	Judgmental	
Income class (dollars)	Mean income (dollars) (1)	Estimated mean income tax (dollars) (2)	(3)	1962 tax table (4)	By individual classes (5)	By major classes (6)
0–2,999	1,561	42	9.2	20	15	⎫
3,000–4,999	3,937	261	17.4	20	20	⎪ 20
5,000–7,499	6,155	647	15.4	20	20	⎬
7,500–9,999	8,694	1,039	18.6	22	22	⎭
10,000–14,999	11,894	1,635	21.8	22	22	⎫
15,000–24,999	18,064	2,981	31.3	30	30	⎬ 31
25,000–49,999	32,843	7,607	42.3	43	43	⎭
50,000–99,999	69,435	23,100	54.7	62	58	58
100,000 or more	157,683	71,389	...	78	75	75

Sources: Columns 1 and 2 derived from Dorothy S. Projector, *Survey of Changes in Family Finances* (Board of Governors of the Federal Reserve System, 1968), table S 17, p. 316. Rates in column 3 equal the ratio of the change in column 2 to the change in column 1 from the given income class to the next higher class. In column 4 each tax rate equals the marginal rate associated with the estimated tax in column 2 for a married couple filing a joint return in 1963. Columns 5 and 6 are author's approximations, explained in the text.

equitably measure the contributions to the taxable capacity of wages, interest, other receipts, and capital gains; and an adjustment necessary to respond to the progressive tax structure. This study focuses on the first step and demonstrates that at this stage only net income from assets and liabilities needs to be adjusted. This is achieved by writing up the price of each capital asset by the amount of consumer price inflation between the time of purchase and the time of sale, or equivalently, by reducing taxable interest receipts to recognize the net inflation loss on savings accounts, loans, and debt.

An asset price that has only kept pace with consumer prices has merely maintained the taxpayer's original purchasing power. No properly defined income has been generated. Inflation adjustments reflecting this principle should be applied to assets such as savings accounts as well as to the limited class currently defined as "capital assets." The loss in the purchasing power of the principal deposited should be recognized as an offset to the interest income paid on that principal. Moreover, just as inflation reduces the apparent gain from holding assets, inflation reduces the apparent cost of borrowing. In-

Table 4-7. Estimates of the Impact of Inflation-Adjusted Accounting on Tax Liabilities, 1962

Income class (dollars)	Change in tax liability		
	Per household (dollars) (1)	As percentage of mean income (2)	All households (millions of dollars) (3)
Under 10,000	−7	−0.2	−346
10,000–50,000	−1	−0.01	−7
50,000–100,000	764	1.2	120
100,000 or more	31,229	19.7	937
All classes	...	...	704

Sources: Column 1 equals column 6, table 4-6, times column 4, table 4-5. Column 2 equals column 1 divided by 1962 mean income reported in Dorothy S. Projector and Gertrude S. Weiss, *Survey of Financial Characteristics of Consumers* (Board of Governors of the Federal Reserve System, 1966), table A 33, pp. 148–49. Column 3 equals column 6, table 4-6, times column 4, table 4-5.

terest-paid deductions should be effectively limited to the excess of the interest charge over the inflation rate.

Once an equitable aggregation of wages, interest, and capital gains has been produced, the second inflation adjustment is readily achieved by indexing personal exemptions, standard deduction levels, and income levels defining rate brackets by an appropriate price index. Thus personal taxes would be prevented from rising as a percentage of income merely because prices rise. This second adjustment is discussed in other chapters in this volume.

2. Consistent, fair aggregation of income on an inflation-adjusted basis can be implemented by slightly changing the capital gains tax form, Schedule D, and by requiring modified reports from banks, savings banks, and finance companies. The Schedule D modification would call on the taxpayer to make a few additional calculations to write up the purchase price of each asset sold during the year. Most other calculations would be routinely left to the computers that currently process the annual bank and savings institution statements of interest paid or received from customers.

3. Current law permits the exclusion of one-half of each long-term capital gain from taxable income. This practice is frequently defended by the argument that approximately half the purchasing power of a typical gain is lost to inflation. If this is the primary rationale for the current practice, then the adoption of inflation adjustment procedures would argue for taxation of *adjusted* gains on the same basis as wages, that is, without any percentage exclusion. During periods of

moderate inflation the reform procedure proposed by this study would tend to reduce taxes for families with annual incomes below $50,000 and to increase taxes for families with incomes above $50,000.

The logic behind this conclusion is straightforward. All families would be granted a gross reduction in taxable income equal to their estimated inflation losses. Offsetting this reduction would be the taxation of the previously excluded share of each capital gain. The current portfolio preferences of different income classes imply that this offset would tend to be less than the inflation loss for low- and middle-income groups.

It is important to recognize several critical qualifications of these results. First, the magnitudes of the 1962 inflation adjustments are quite limited relative to the comparable adjustments that would be called for by the double-digit inflation rates of recent years. The Internal Revenue Service is currently completing a study of capital asset sales in 1973 that should provide an interesting contrast to the 1962 analysis. It is quite possible that all income classes will register capital losses on an inflation-adjusted basis. It is virtually impossible, however, to predict the results because gains are taxed on a realization basis rather than an accrual basis. The exodus of individual investors from the stock market during recent years implies substantial realization of long-held nominal gains, which may provide the basis for positive inflation-adjusted gains as well. The right to defer taxation until a gain is realized is thus a second qualification, and one that affects the interpretation of the 1962 data as well as the projection of future results. A third qualification is related to the second: any change in the tax structure relating to investment income is certain to change asset prices and choices as well as realization behavior. Therefore the shorthand expression A_{-1} $(nq/2 - \pi)$ presented earlier to analyze the change in taxable income can only be suggestive of the impact of a major redefinition of taxable income.

In the current environment of weak corporate security performance and high inflation, it is possible that the largest benefit of the proposed redefinition of income would accrue to the highest income groups. The inflation-adjusted components of gains accrued during the past five to ten years are probably less than 50 percent of nominal gains; hence the reform would provide for an exclusion of a greater fraction of gains than is currently allowed. Whatever course inflation may take, however, equitable taxation requires such an exclusion. Tables 4-6 and 4-7 do point out the pro-rich bias of the income definitions in 1962. A pro-poor bias may well exist today. Unless taxable income is redefined to reflect the eroded purchasing power of net worth during inflation, substantial horizontal and vertical equity problems will necessarily remain in the tax structure.

Comments by Stanley Fischer

Roger Brinner's paper is divided into two unequal parts. The first presents an appropriate definition of real income and also dismisses recent congressional proposals to adjust capital gains for inflation by reducing the proportion of gains subject to tax as the holding period increases. The second part of the paper discusses implementation of the changes in the tax system.

Brinner convincingly demonstrates that the congressional proposals are misconceived even for steady inflation; given a positive real rate of return and steady inflation, the taxation of real capital gains implies a declining exclusion proportion with time. But since inflation is not steady, the proper approach to the taxation of real gains is to measure real gains and tax them, rather than to make some arbitrary assumption about real rates of return and inflation rates likely to prevail in the future.

The argument that real capital gains should be taxed appears to lead Brinner to dispose of the capital gains exclusion entirely. But the capital gains exclusion is not part of the Internal Revenue Code as a rough-and-ready adjustment for inflation; it is there to encourage risk-taking and because the owners of capital are politically powerful. It would be unlikely to disappear if the tax system were to be indexed.

Brinner suggests that implementation of the changes is relatively straightforward. Certainly the Schedule D modifications he suggests are quite practicable. But there are three major issues that deserve further consideration and that suggest he is too sanguine about implementation. The first concerns the time at which capital gains should be taxed. The second concerns the scope of the adjustment of capital gains for inflation. The third concerns the timing of the introduction of the tax changes. Let me venture some remarks on the difficulties involved.

On the first issue Brinner recommends taxation of capital gains and losses associated with debt and personal savings accounts on an accrual basis; gains on all other assets would be taxed when realized. It is an open question whether a system in which some gains are taxed as accrued and some at realization is desirable. There are a number of options. One entails the use of accrual wherever possible. Since it is not administratively possible to tax all assets on an accrual basis (it would be necessary, for instance, to value houses and art on an annual basis), this method would produce some distortions. Under another, assets and liabilities would be matched—houses and home mortgages for instance—and gains within those matched categories would be taxed in the same way, on accrual or at realization, as the case may be. Such matching cannot in practice be done very neatly. The third option is to tax all gains only upon realization. This course leads to lock-in and seems inadvisable, even though it is essentially the current system. I doubt there are any general principles that can be invoked, but the problem is substantial and must be settled before reforms along the lines Brinner suggests are introduced.

The second issue concerns the scope of the inflation adjustment. Brinner proposes substantially widening the scope of taxation of capital gains and losses. The changes involved are the adjustments for capital losses and gains on savings accounts and debt—and there is no reason that the principle should not apply to checking accounts too. By using the accrual principle, the scope of capital gains taxation would also be widened; under current laws, for example, a capital gains tax is only infrequently paid on housing, and it is sometimes not paid on equity either. The magnitudes involved are large. Consider, for instance, homeowners. Their deduction for mortgage interest would be reduced by the decline in the real value of mortgage indebtedness, now about $450 billion, multiplied by the percentage change in prices. In 1974 such a provision would have wiped out the mortgage interest deduction and left homeowners with a net capital gain on their mortgages. The aggregate effect on the federal budget might be relatively small since the capital gains of mortgage-holders would be balanced, more or less, by the capital losses of deposit holders in the mortgage-financing institutions, but the distributional impact would remain. Consequent political pressures are obvious.

The third issue that needs to be addressed concerns how these reforms would be introduced. They would have to be introduced over a period of time and could be eased in gradually in at least three ways. First, legislation authorizing inflation adjustment might be enacted now but made effective only in, say, five or ten years. Second, taxable income might be a weighted average of income as now computed and income computed with adjustments for inflation. The weights could shift over time, ending with a fully indexed computation of income. Finally, the indexing law might have grandfather clauses, exempting assets and debts held before the reform of the tax system. The second approach is probably the most useful.

The last part of Brinner's paper contains empirical estimates of the impact of his adjustments on revenues. At 1.2 percent inflation in 1962, the reforms *increase* personal tax liabilities by 1.5 percent. This increase results from two factors: first, a change in tax base, and second, the indexing of taxes. The indexing component tends to reduce taxes relative to the current U.S. system as the inflation rate increases. Accordingly, at higher inflation rates, Brinner's reforms would have left personal tax liabilities in 1962 approximately unchanged. The results appear to indicate that losses and gains from rates of unanticipated inflation of the magnitude experienced recently would not produce major swings in tax revenues.

Comments by Arnold Harberger

I think I made a mistake when I agreed to let Stanley Fischer summarize Roger Brinner's paper and be the first critic—he took all the good points!

One of Brinner's main contentions is that once capital gains have been purged of illusory gains due to inflation, there is no further inflation-connected reason for the preferential treatment of capital gains. He makes a very good case that indexing is a better way to deal with this problem than is the exclusion from income of a proportion of gains. He proves the counterintuitive proposition that the proper exclusion fraction falls with the holding period. He also argues persuasively that savers who hold assets that do not generate capital gains deserve inflation adjustments as much as do savers who hold assets that do generate capital gains.

I like to think of the adjustment for inflation as a write-up of all assets and liabilities. This approach is simply Brinner's neat correction πA, where π is the rate of inflation, and A is net worth. The formula is neat and makes computations easy if used, but Brinner did not use it for subsequent calculations because its validity depends on taxation of all gains on accrual. I found his adjustments to Schedule D, which deal with individual assets, a practical solution. If Schedule D is revised to take account of inflation, it is unlikely that taxpayers will be required to make a full accounting of their net worth. Brinner also suggests an adjustment for savings account balances based on the average balance for the year, a satisfactory approximation. But he excludes demand deposits from the adjustment. His rationale for this exclusion, that imputed income from demand deposits is untaxed, makes no sense whatsoever. If inflation runs at 50 percent, the most one could say is that the first 2 or 3 percent of inflation loss just offsets the imputed income on demand deposits that is improperly excluded from income. On grounds of logical consistency, I would like to see Brinner's modification of Schedule D extended to include not only demand deposits but also mortgages and other assets and liabilities.

On grounds of political prudence, however, I do not think that it is desirable to index demand deposits. If demand deposits are indexed, then the full brunt of the "inflation tax" falls on currency. If neither is indexed, then the burden of the inflation tax is spread over demand deposits and currency. Indexing demand deposits is not inflationary in itself, but it does increase the amount of inflation that will result from a successful effort by a government to increase its command over real resources by a given amount without increasing taxes. Why do governments pursue monetary policies that cause inflation? They do so only because they are politically unable to impose the taxes necessary to pay for expenditures desired by the country and find resort to monetary expansion the lesser available evil. Although logical consistency requires that both demand deposits and currency be adjusted for inflation along with other assets, political prudence requires that neither be adjusted. Let us accept inflation as a safety valve. From time to time governments may resort to it, not because they want to, but because they are in dire straits.

When inflation rates are higher, however, taxation of income from time deposits must be indexed because, otherwise, prohibitively high interest rates would be necessary that would destroy long-term credit markets.

In one sense, indexing will reduce the instability of the economy. As pointed out by Martin Feldstein, Martin Bailey, Vito Tanzi and others, interest rates will fluctuate more widely during inflation if interest is not adjusted for inflation than it will if it is. The additional fluctuation is a function of the marginal tax rate. The exact formula is $r = i + \pi/(1 - t)$, where r is the market interest rate, i is the real interest rate, π is the expected rate of inflation, and t is the marginal tax rate of bondholders who are just compensated for inflation by the increase in the market interest rates. Much the same relationship governs the interest rate differential between taxable and tax exempt bonds. Those with lower marginal tax rates than a critical level will gain from the increase in nominal interest rates due to inflation; those with higher marginal tax rates will lose. With low rates of inflation, that added instability formerly seemed to me a small price to pay for the increase in economic stability that a tax system based on nominal income would provide. I now feel more comfortable with a tax system that is fully indexed, except for capital losses on currency and demand deposits. With such a regime one can be comfortable no matter what happens to inflation.

Discussion

Roger Brinner justified as a concession to political reality his assumption that gains on some assets would be taxed upon realization, while others would be taxed as accrued. He proposed taxing inflation gains and losses as accrued for those assets whose current income includes compensation for the loss of value from anticipated inflation, such as interest on bonds, and taxing inflation gains and losses at realization for those assets whose current income does not include compensation for the effects of anticipated inflation, such as stocks, real estate, and other capital assets in general. He justified not revising Schedule D to deal with liabilities on the grounds that financial institutions could do the adjustment quite simply by computer and could give taxpayers a report on the real interest income they had received during the year.

John Shoven proposed that the increase in the assessed values of houses be used not only for property taxes but also as a measure of capital gains, taxable to the owner as accrued. He pointed out that the importance of some kinds of accrual grew as inflation increased. Stanley Surrey observed that Brinner's adjustments would require a distinction between income from assets and income from other sources that would continue to trouble accountants and lawyers even if, as many urged, the distinction between capital assets and other assets now cluttering the Internal Revenue Code could be removed. Joseph Pechman agreed with Surrey, but doubted that the complications would be as serious as those resulting from the present distinctions. Brinner responded that he was not proposing that any changes should be made in the determination of whether an asset met the conditions for treatment as a "capital asset." Rather, he simply proposed a redefinition of the income from many assets.

Surrey underscored a theme he found common to many of the papers in the conference—that adjustments for inflation should not be taken one at a time. All of the changes in the computation of taxable income are linked and all of them should be enacted together, or none at all. Martin Feldstein raised a question regarding the impact on stock market prices of indexing bonds and suggested that these effects were possibly important but poorly understood.

Donald Tucker challenged Arnold Harberger's contention that the adjustment of taxable income for losses on demand deposits would aggravate inflation. He pointed out that such adjustment would reduce the cost of holding money balances in that form and would be likely to reduce the velocity of circulation. Peter Diamond pointed out that if households maximize utility and businesses maximize profits, then the imputed income from demand deposits must be precisely equal at the margin to the rate of interest on riskless assets. If that were so, then Harberger's statement that imputed income could offset no more than 2 or 3 percent of the loss due to inflation was incorrect, and Brinner's reason for excluding demand deposits from adjustment for inflation looked very good.

Arthur Okun restated Brinner's formula for adjusting the taxation of income from capital on an accrual basis. The difference between a tax base that defines property income and gains as the excess of returns over the amount necessary to keep *nominal* wealth intact and a tax base that defines property income and gains as the excess of returns over the amount necessary to keep *real* wealth intact is simply the rate of inflation times net worth. In other words, inflation is equivalent to a capital levy, where the tax rate equals the rate of inflation times the individual's marginal income tax rate. Okun suggested that looking at the problem in this light makes it clear that one need not bother adjusting matched assets and liabilities. If all income were taxed as accrued and historical costs were used for depreciation and inventories, the neutralizing adjustment to inflation would be a negative capital levy. Such a simple solution is not possible because of LIFO accounting, because some income is not taxed as accrued, and because some is not taxed at all. But we should keep our eye on this criterion. Edward Denison criticized Brinner for failing to recognize that as defined for tax purposes nominal income receipts include non-corporate inventory profits and the excess of noncorporate depreciation valued at replacement cost over noncorporate depreciation valued at original cost. They appear both in rents and in farm or entrepreneurial income. Their inclusion introduces an error into Brinner's definition of real income. To correct the definition, they must be eliminated from rents and from farm or entrepreneurial income so that nominal net income receipts will be uniformly based on current prices.

Okun then suggested that one reason for the present capital gains exclusion was to encourage holders of unrealized capital gains to realize them. If capital gains were taxed in full, so few gains might be realized that less capital gains tax might be collected than now. Thus Okun urged Brinner to take account of the impact on realization and on revenues of the proposals he advanced. He also urged that the question of constructive realization at death be linked with inflation adjustment because such a step, by discouraging retention of unrealized gains, might enable larger steps toward increasing the capital gains tax without unduly lowering realizations.

James Wetzler confirmed that members of the Ways and Means Committee were aware that an exclusion fraction for capital gains that increases with the holding period of the asset was not an inflation adjustment and were sensitive to the issue raised by Okun—how to increase realization of accrued gains and thereby to raise revenues. Wetzler also added a fourth possible method of phasing in inflation adjustment to the three proposed by Stanley Fischer: it is possible to adjust for inflation that occurs after the date of enactment, but not for inflation that occurred before. Such a method would make unnecessary any lengthy delay between enactment and implementation of inflation adjustment. He also pointed out that losses on assets under inflation adjustment would be subject to the limitation of deductions for capital losses against ordinary income to $1,000 a year. He suggested that losses from inflation adjustments be deductible against ordinary income without limit.

CHAPTER FIVE

Inflation Adjustment for the Individual Income Tax

EMIL M. SUNLEY, JR. *and* JOSEPH A. PECHMAN

INFLATION causes significant increases in the effective rates of the individual income tax on real incomes for two reasons. The first involves the effect of inflation on the measurement of particular items of income for tax purposes, principally capital gains, business income, and interest. These problems are treated in other papers in this volume. The second reason, which is the subject of this paper, is that fixed dollar amounts, such as the rate bracket boundaries and the per capita personal exemption and credit, enter into tax liability computations. These amounts do not increase automatically with inflation. When a family's money income increases just enough to offset inflation, its real income stays the same. But as its money income increases, the family is thrown into higher tax rate brackets and the fixed dollar deductions, exemptions, and credits eliminate a lesser fraction of income otherwise subject to tax. The result is that tax liabilities increase faster than inflation and take away an increasing percentage of the family's real income.

Research on the distributional effects of inflation under a nonindexed and an indexed individual income tax was supported by a grant from the RANN program of the National Science Foundation. The provisions of the tax code cited in this paper are those in effect in 1975.

153

The pros and cons of indexing the individual income tax to offset or moderate this effect are discussed in the papers by Martin J. Bailey and Edward M. Gramlich. In our paper, actual reductions in tax liabilities since 1960 are compared with the tax liabilities that would have applied under an indexed system, and the effect of inflation on tax liabilities under the Tax Reduction Act of 1975 are estimated for the years 1976 to 1981. We do not take into account the possibility that inflation may cause certain forms of income to increase more rapidly than others.

The Mechanics of Indexing Fixed Dollar Amounts

Although it would be feasible to index all fixed dollar amounts in the Internal Revenue Code, indexing the most important reference points—personal exemptions, the per capita credit, the low-income allowance, the standard deduction, the earned-income credit, and the rate brackets—would be simpler and would eliminate almost all the distortions caused by fixed dollar amounts.[1] This is essentially the system used in Canada, where a price index is applied annually to maintain those reference points at the same real values.[2] Assuming a 10 percent inflation, the personal exemption would be increased from $750 to $825; the per capita credit would be increased from $30 to $33; the low-income allowance would rise from $1,900 to $2,090 (from $1,600 to $1,760 for single persons); the standard deduction ceiling would increase from $2,600 to $2,860 (from $2,300 to $2,530 for single persons); and the maximum earned-income credit

1. Other dollar limitations include the $1,000 limit on capital losses, the $50,000 limit on capital gains at the 25 percent alternative tax rate, the $20,000 limit on the exclusion of capital gains on sales of principal residences by taxpayers aged sixty-five or over, the $150 limit on deductible health insurance premiums, the $35,000 income limit for child care and disabled dependent deductions, the $100 floor on deductions for casualty losses, the $100 ($200 if joint return) dividend exclusion, the $25,000 and $50,000 limits under the farm loss recapture provision, the various limits on sick pay, the $20,000 and $25,000 limits on excludable earned foreign income, the various limits on the retirement income credit, the $30,000 exemption under the minimum income tax, the $10,000 limit on the initial first-year allowance for depreciation, the $25,000 limit under the investment tax credit, and the $3,000 minimum for income averaging. These provisions would not be difficult to index, though some might argue that many of them are at unreasonably high levels and tax equity would be improved if inflation were permitted to erode their real values.
2. See chapter 8. Canada generally indexes only the personal exemptions and the rate brackets.

Table 5-1. Effect of 10 Percent Inflation on the Tax Liability of a Family of Four with an Annual Income of $8,000, 1975

Item	1975 level	No adjustment for inflation	After adjustment for inflation
		1975 level plus 10 percent inflation	
		Dollars	
Income	8,000	8,800	8,800
Less standard deduction	1,900	1,900	2,090
Less personal exemption	3,000	3,000	3,300
Taxable income	3,100	3,900	3,410
Tax before credit[a]	467	603	514
Personal exemption credit	120	120	132
Tax after credit	347	483	382
		Percent	
Effective tax rate[b]	4.3	5.5	4.3

Source: Calculated from provisions of the 1975 tax law.
a. The present law and inflation-adjusted rate schedules for the relevant brackets are:

Taxable income (dollars)

Present law	Inflation adjusted	Tax rate (percent)
Less than 1,000	Less than 1,100	14
1,000–2,000	1,100–2,200	15
2,000–3,000	2,200–3,300	16
3,000–4,000	3,300–4,400	17

b. Tax divided by income expressed as a percentage.

would be increased from $400 to $440.[3] The brackets in the tax tables would be adjusted similarly so that the $0–$1,000 bracket would become $0–$1,100, and so on.

The results of this type of indexing applied to a family of four with an $8,000 income at 1975 levels are shown in table 5-1. Before inflation the family would pay a tax of $347 on an $8,000 income for an effective tax rate of 4.3 percent. Inflation of 10 percent would increase the family income to $8,800. Unless there is an inflation adjustment, taxes would increase by 39 percent to $483. If the principal fixed-dollar parameters are indexed, taxes would increase only 10 percent to $382 and thus there would be no increase in the effective tax rate.

Table 5-2 gives the effect of a 10 percent inflation on the tax liabilities of a family of four at selected levels of income before infla-

3. The per capita credit, the earned-income credit, and the increases in the low-income allowance and the standard deduction have not been made permanent, but we assume that Congress will extend these provisions or make them permanent.

Table 5-2. Effect of 10 Percent Inflation on the Tax Liabilities of a Family of Four, Selected Income Levels, 1975

Income before inflation (dollars)	Tax before inflation		Tax after 10 percent inflation				Effect of not indexing[c]		
			No indexing[a]		With indexing[b]				
	Amount (dollars)	Effective rate (percent)	Amount (dollars)	Effective rate (percent)	Amount (dollars)	Effective rate (percent)	Percentage increase in tax	Percentage point increase in effective rate	Percentage reduction in income after tax
8,000	347	4.3	483	5.5	382	4.3	26.4	1.2	1.2
10,000	709	7.1	899	8.2	780	7.1	15.3	1.1	1.2
12,000	1,085	9.0	1,279	9.7	1,194	9.0	7.1	0.7	0.7
15,000	1,612	10.7	1,889	11.4	1,773	10.7	6.5	0.7	0.8
20,000	2,590	13.0	3,010	13.7	2,849	13.0	5.7	0.7	0.8
25,000	3,700	14.8	4,292	15.6	4,070	14.8	5.5	0.8	0.9
30,000	4,964	16.5	5,799	17.6	5,460	16.5	6.2	1.1	1.2
50,000	11,570	23.1	13,556	24.6	12,727	23.1	6.5	1.5	2.0
100,000	33,800	33.8	38,700	35.2	37,180	33.8	4.1	1.4	2.1
250,000	115,760	46.3	130,460	47.4	127,336	46.3	2.5	1.1	2.1
500,000	262,760	52.6	292,160	53.1	289,036	52.6	1.1	0.5	1.2
1,000,000	556,760	55.7	615,560	56.0	612,436	55.7	0.5	0.3	0.6

Source: Calculated from provisions of the 1975 tax law.

a. Assumes tax law applying in 1975. Tax liability computed on the assumption that the family deducts the low-income allowance of $1,900 or 16 percent of income, whichever is greater, and that the maximum tax rate on earned income does not apply.

b. The exemptions, the exemption credit, the low-income allowance, and the rate brackets of the 1975 law are increased by 10 percent. Assumes maximum tax rate on earned income does not apply.

c. Percentages computed from unrounded data.

tion.[4] Inflation has the greatest relative effect on tax liabilities at the lowest end of the income scale. However, the effect of inflation on effective rates and on income after tax (shown in the last two columns of table 5-2) is much more uniform by income classes. On the basis of these measures, the effect declines somewhat from the lowest income levels to about $25,000 of income, then rises to a maximum between $50,000 and $250,000, and declines again thereafter. The explanation for these irregular movements is that progression at the lowest end of the income scale is determined most by the low-income allowance and personal exemptions. This effect wears off as incomes rise and the graduation of the rate schedule becomes the determining factor. The maximum effect occurs at the point where the rate of graduation increases most rapidly.

Developments from 1960 to 1975

Although Congress has not provided for automatic adjustments to offset the impact of inflation on the effective rates of the individual income tax, it has reduced taxes periodically.[5] As a result of these changes in the tax law, effective tax rates have increased very little since 1960 and have generally fluctuated around 11 percent of adjusted personal income.[6] According to the data given in column 5 of table 5-3, the effective tax rate was 10.7 percent in 1960 and 11.3 percent in 1975. Because of the tax cuts in the Revenue Act of 1964, the effective tax rate fell to 10.1 percent in 1965. In 1969 the effective rate reached a high of 11.7 percent. The tax reductions provided in the Tax Reform Act of 1969 and the Revenue Act of 1971 reduced the effective rate again, but the rapid inflation in the last few years has increased it nearly to the historic high.

The reductions in taxes since 1960 have more than offset the in-

4. The table begins at $8,000 since tax liabilities below that income level are very low because of the personal exemptions, deductions, and the 10 percent refundable earned-income credit. The conclusion drawn from table 5-2, however, would not be altered if the table were extended below $8,000.

5. The major tax reductions were made in the Revenue Act of 1964, the Tax Reform Act of 1969, the Revenue Act of 1971, and the Tax Reduction Act of 1975. In 1968 Congress provided for a temporary surcharge. This surcharge is ignored in the discussion that follows.

6. This is the portion of personal income, as estimated in the national income accounts, that is subject to the individual income tax. For method of calculation, see table 5-3, note a.

crease in revenues caused by inflation. That is, if Congress had not cut taxes periodically but instead had indexed the individual income tax for inflation on the basis of the consumer price index (CPI), taxes would actually have been higher in 1975 than they were under the 1975 law.

Table 5-3 gives estimates of the income tax liabilities and the effective rates that would have applied to adjusted personal income if the income tax had been indexed for inflation since 1960.[7] The tax liabilities for 1975 would have been nearly $10 billion higher than the actual liabilities for that year, and the effective rate would have been 12.2 percent instead of the actual effective rate of 11.3 percent. Over the fifteen-year period, the effective rate would have increased from 10.7 to 12.2 percent if the tax system had been indexed for inflation and no other tax changes had been made. Because of the interaction between a progressive rate structure and growing per capita real incomes, per capita revenues tend to grow in real terms even if the tax system is completely indexed for inflation.

If there had been no periodic tax cuts and no automatic adjustments for inflation, the effective rate of the individual income tax would have increased since 1960 by over 50 percent—from 10.7 to 16.2 percent of adjusted personal income (table 5-3, column 7). The individual income tax liability would have increased from $39.5 billion in 1960 to $171.6 billion in 1975 (table 5-3, column 4). The periodic tax cuts provided since 1960 by Congress reduced 1975 tax liabilities by $51.9 billion. Indexing the rate structure alone would have reduced tax liabilities by $42.0 billion—19 percent less than the periodic adjustments have actually provided.

Simulations using the 1972 Brookings Tax File data identify the distributional effects of the actual adjustments in tax liabilities and permit comparisons with the adjustments that would have occurred if the individual income tax had been indexed for inflation.[8] The data in the file were projected to calendar year 1975 on the basis of actual changes in income for 1973 and 1974 and of projected changes

7. Table 5-3 was revised on the basis of comments by Richard Goode and others at the conference concerning the elasticity of income tax revenues to inflation.

8. The file consists of data from a stratified random statistical sample of federal individual income tax returns for 1972. For a description of the file and its uses, see Joseph A. Pechman, "A New Tax Model for Revenue Estimating," in Alan T. Peacock and Gerald Hauser, eds., *Government Finance and Economic Development,* Papers and Proceedings of the Third Study Conference, 1963 (Paris: Organisation for Economic Co-operation and Development, n.d.), Brookings Reprint 102.

Table 5-3. Individual Income Tax Liabilities, Actual, Assuming Automatic Inflation Adjustment, and Assuming No Tax Changes, 1960–75
Dollar amounts in billions; effective rates in percent

		Individual income tax liabilities			Effective tax rates		
Year (1)	Adjusted personal income[a] (1)	Actual[b] (2)	Assuming automatic inflation adjust- ments[c] (3)	Assuming no tax change[d] (4)	Actual[b] (5)	Assuming automatic inflation adjust- ments[c] (6)	Assuming no tax change[d] (7)
1960	370	39.5	39.5	39.5	10.7	10.7	10.7
1961	380	42.2	40.8	42.2	11.1	10.7	11.1
1962	404	44.9	44.3	45.3	11.1	11.0	11.2
1963	425	48.2	47.3	48.4	11.3	11.2	11.4
1964	455	47.2	51.4	54.0	10.4	11.3	11.9
1965	492	49.5	56.7	61.9	10.1	11.5	12.6
1966	538	56.1	62.9	69.6	10.4	11.7	12.9
1967	573	62.9	67.8	77.4	11.0	11.8	13.5
1968	623	71.5	74.5	87.2	11.5	12.0	14.0
1969	677	78.9	81.7	95.3	11.7	12.1	14.1
1970	717	81.9	86.5	100.4	11.4	12.1	14.0
1971	760	85.4	92.0	110.7	11.2	12.1	13.3
1972	831	93.6	101.8	126.5	11.3	12.3	15.2
1973	930	108.1	115.4	143.6	11.6	12.4	15.4
1974[e]	1,007	114.3[f]	124.2	161.0	11.4[f]	12.3	16.0
1975[e]	1,060	119.7[g]	129.6	171.6	11.3[g]	12.2	16.2

Sources: *Survey of Current Business*, vol. 56 (January 1976), pts. 1 and 2; and U.S. Internal Revenue Service, *Statistics of Income, Individual Income Tax Returns*, various issues.

a. Personal income less transfer payments and other labor income, plus employee contributions for social insurance.

b. As reported in *Statistics of Income*, less surcharge but including 1974 rebate.

c. Assumes that the elasticity of the individual income tax with respect to changes in real income is 1.4. See appendix, table 5-6, for the derivation of the tax liabilities.

d. See appendix, table 5-7, for the derivation of the tax liabilities.

e. Estimated.

f. After the rebate of 1974 taxes enacted in the Tax Reduction Act of 1975.

g. After enactment of the Tax Reduction Act of 1975.

based on the official economic forecast for 1975.[9] Income tax liabilities were first calculated for each return in the file on the basis of the 1975 law and then recalculated on the basis of the indexed limits of the rate brackets, the personal exemption, and the standard deduction in effect in 1960.[10] The difference between the two sets of tax

9. See *The Budget of the United States Government, Fiscal Year 1976*, p. 41.

10. The other fixed dollar limits in the tax law (see note 1) are of relatively minor significance when compared with the limits of the rate brackets, the exemptions, and the standard deduction and were therefore not indexed for these calculations. The indexed limits were based on the actual CPI up to 1974 and the estimate for 1975 shown in table 5-6.

Table 5-4. Comparison of Individual Income Taxes under the 1975 Law and under the 1960, 1965, and 1972 Laws, Indexed for Inflation, 1975

1975 adjusted gross income class (dollars)	Effective rates of tax (percent)				Percentage difference in effective rates			Percentage difference in tax[b]			Percentage difference in disposable income[b]		
	Actual 1975 law	Indexed 1960 law[a]	Indexed 1965 law[a]	Indexed 1972 law[a]	1975 minus indexed 1960 law	1975 minus indexed 1965 law	1975 minus indexed 1972 law	1975 minus indexed 1960 law	1975 minus indexed 1965 law	1975 minus indexed 1972 law	1975 minus indexed 1960 law	1975 minus indexed 1965 law	1975 minus indexed 1972 law
0–5,000	2.1	6.2	4.2	2.0	−4.1	−2.1	0.1	−67.1	−51.0	6.2	3.3	2.2	−0.1
5,000–10,000	7.4	10.0	7.9	7.1	−2.6	−0.5	0.3	−25.8	−6.2	4.2	2.4	0.5	−0.3
10,000–15,000	9.9	11.0	9.0	9.4	−1.1	0.9	0.5	−10.8	9.6	5.6	1.0	−1.0	−0.6
15,000–20,000	12.0	12.9	10.8	11.1	−0.9	1.2	0.9	−7.4	11.4	7.6	0.8	−1.4	−1.0
20,000–25,000	13.7	14.0	11.8	12.6	−0.3	1.9	1.1	−2.3	16.1	8.8	*	−2.2	−1.3
25,000–50,000	17.4	16.6	14.2	15.6	0.8	3.2	1.8	4.3	22.6	11.4	−1.2	−3.8	−2.1
50,000–100,000	26.7	23.7	20.5	23.7	3.0	6.2	3.0	12.7	30.0	12.4	−3.9	−7.7	−3.8
100,000–200,000	34.7	33.0	28.9	32.3	1.7	5.8	2.4	5.4	20.1	7.7	−2.1	−7.8	−3.3
200,000–500,000	40.4	41.0	35.9	38.7	−0.6	4.5	1.7	−0.6	13.3	4.9	1.8	−6.5	−2.1
500,000–1,000,000	42.2	44.7	38.5	41.5	−2.5	3.7	0.7	−4.6	10.4	2.5	5.7	−5.1	−0.3
1,000,000 and over	39.8	43.1	36.2	39.7	−3.3	3.6	0.1	−6.4	11.1	1.2	7.2	−4.7	−0.9
All classes	12.9[c]	13.7	11.4	11.9	−0.8	1.5	1.0	−6.4	12.7	8.2	0.6	−1.7	−1.1

Source: Brookings 1972 Tax File projected to 1975. Figures are rounded.

*Less than 0.05.

a. Under the indexed laws, the limits of the rate brackets, personal exemptions, and the standard deduction are adjusted for the change in the consumer price index to 1975.

b. Differences expressed as a percentage of tax liabilities or disposable income under the indexed laws.

c. Effective rate in this table differs from the effective rate in table 5-3 because incomes in the two tables are not the same. See note 11 in text.

liabilities are shown in table 5-4 by 1975 adjusted gross income classes.

As already indicated, in the aggregate the actual tax adjustments made since 1960 exceeded the adjustments that would have been made under indexing. For 1975 the average effective tax rate of all returns in the tax file is 12.9 percent; the indexed system would have produced an average effective rate of 13.7 percent.[11] Actual effective rates were lower than the indexed rates for all adjusted gross income classes under $25,000, higher between $25,000 and $200,000, and lower again above $200,000. The reductions at the bottom and the top of the income scale are due mainly to relatively large rate reductions under the Revenue Act of 1964. In the intermediate brackets, where progression is relatively steep, the reductions were not sufficient to offset the effect of inflation.

The same calculations for the 1965 and 1972 laws, which are also shown in table 5-4, indicate that in the aggregate the actual tax changes did not adjust tax liabilities fully for inflation. As in the case of the 1960 law, however, the lower income classes fared better under the 1975 law than they would have under the indexed 1965 law, whereas the higher income classes would have been better off under the indexed system. Again, effective tax rates increased the most in the adjusted gross income classes between $25,000 and $200,000. The tax liabilities in the top classes were greatly affected by the new tax on preference incomes and the increases in the capital gains tax that were enacted in 1969 and became fully effective in 1972. Nevertheless, the increases in the intermediate classes were relatively larger than those at the very top as a result of the effect of progression. All income classes would have been better off under the indexed 1972 law than under the 1975 law, with the intermediate classes gaining more than either the top or the bottom classes because of the effect of progression.

11. The effective rates in table 5-4 are somewhat higher than those in table 5-3 because the incomes in the two tables differ. (Table 5-4 excludes many low-income people not required to file income tax returns.) However, the difference in tax liabilities between the actual and the indexed systems are roughly the same. In table 5-4, it amounts to $8.2 billion, or 6.8 percent of the estimated 1975 tax liability of $120.8 billion calculated from the tax file. In table 5-3, the difference is $9.9 billion, or 8.3 percent of an estimated 1975 tax liability of $119.7 billion. Considering that the two sets of estimates are based on such different methods, the similarity of the results is remarkable.

Fiscal Effects of Inflation

The effect of inflation on individual income tax collections in future years may also be estimated with the Brookings Tax File. For illustrative purposes, we begin with estimates of income and tax liabilities for calendar year 1976 based on the official forecasts of income for that year, and a projection to the years 1977–81, assuming that the number of returns will increase 1 percent a year, that incomes on each return will rise 6 percent a year in real terms,[12] and that the 1975 tax law will be extended through 1981. Incomes were then increased another 2, 4, 6, 8, and 10 percent to simulate different rates of inflation. The resulting tax liabilities, which are shown in table 5-5, provide the basis for estimating the effect of inflation on individual incomes at various income classes.

In an earlier paper, Joseph A. Pechman found that the individual income tax responds to changes in money incomes (other than capital gains) in roughly the same way, whether the changes reflect only increases in real incomes or include substantial price effects as well, and that changes in the distribution of income of the type experienced during the past twenty-five years have little effect on the revenue estimates.[13] Hence the calculations in table 5-5 are good approximations of the effect of various rates of inflation if capital gains rise by roughly the same percentage as other income.

Even without inflation, both the amount and the effective rate of tax would increase as a result of the progressivity of the income tax. With a 6 percent growth in income per return and no inflation from 1976 to 1977, individual income tax liabilities would rise to $151 billion, or 13.8 percent of adjusted gross income. By 1981 tax liabilities would increase to $229 billion, and the effective rate to 16 percent. Liabilities in 1977 would be $4.7 billion higher with an inflation rate of 2 percent, $9.5 billion higher with an inflation rate of 4 percent, and so on until the additional yield amounted to a total of $23.9 bil-

12. This is higher than the normal rate of increase in real per capita income because 1976 continued to be a year of very high unemployment. Even with a 6 percent growth per year, unemployment would average about 5 percent in 1980.

13. See Joseph A. Pechman, "Responsiveness of the Federal Individual Income Tax to Changes in Income," *Brookings Papers on Economic Activity, 2:1973,* p. 413. For the other assumptions used in the calculations for table 5-5, see ibid., pp. 395–96.

Figure 5-1. Individual Income Tax Liabilities under the 1975 Law, at Various Inflation Rates, 1976-81[a]

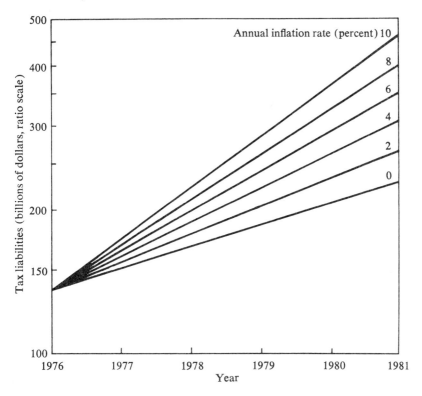

Source: Brookings 1972 Tax File projected to 1976–81.
a. Real growth of income per return per year is 6 percent.

lion for a 10 percent inflation. The increase is roughly $2.4 billion per point of inflation, with very little increase as inflation rises.

Over the longer period, the effect of inflation on income tax revenues is cumulative and becomes extremely large for high inflation rates. Figure 5-1 illustrates tax liabilities under the 1975 law for each year during the period 1976–81 for various rates of inflation. The bottom section of table 5-5 shows the situation for the terminal year, 1981. At the end of the five-year period, the additional tax due to inflation would amount to $18.3 billion per point for the first 2 percent of inflation, and to $29.0 billion per point for an increase in the inflation rate from 8 to 10 percent a year. At 2 percent inflation, the additional tax is 13.8 percent of the tax and 2.8 percent of disposable in-

Table 5-5. Effect of Inflation on the Yield of the Individual Income Tax, 1977 and 1981
Dollar amounts in billions

Percentage increase in income per return			Adjusted gross income[a]	Individual income tax liability	Effective rate of tax (percent)	Additional tax due to inflation		
Total	Real	Infla- tion				Cumula- tive amount	Per- centage of tax liability	Per- centage of dis- posable income
1977								
6	6	0	1,092.6	151.3	13.8	...	...	...
8	6	2	1,113.3	156.0	14.0	4.7	3.0	0.5
10	6	4	1,133.9	160.8	14.2	9.5	5.9	1.0
12	6	6	1,154.6	165.5	14.3	14.2	8.6	1.4
14	6	8	1,175.2	170.4	14.5	19.1	11.2	1.9
16	6	10	1,195.8	175.2	14.7	23.9	13.6	2.3
1981								
6	6	0	1,435.9	229.3	16.0	...	...	...
8	6	2	1,576.8	265.9	16.9	36.6	13.8	2.8
10	6	4	1,728.6	307.2	17.8	77.9	25.4	5.5
12	6	6	1,891.8	353.6	18.7	124.3	35.2	8.1
14	6	8	2,067.1	405.6	19.6	176.3	43.5	10.6
16	6	10	2,255.2	463.7	20.6	234.4	50.5	13.1

Sources: Brookings 1972 Tax File projected to 1977 and 1981. For assumptions used in the calculations, see Joseph A. Pechman, "Responsiveness of the Federal Individual Income Tax to Changes in Income," *Brookings Papers on Economic Activity*, 2:1973, pp. 395–96 and 413. Figures are rounded.

a. Assumes an increase of 1 percent a year from 1976 in the number of returns filed.

come; at 10 percent inflation, the additional tax is 50.5 percent of the tax and 13.1 percent of disposable income. These increases not only maintain but also raise real tax collections in the face of inflation. The real increase in income tax would be automatically eliminated by indexing the individual income tax. If Congress does not index, the additional revenues would be available for discretionary tax cuts or expenditure increases.

Conclusions

Any rise in income, whether from real growth or inflation, increases the effective rate of the individual income tax; inflation accentuates the rise. The impact is small when inflation is slow but large when inflation is fast or prolonged. For example, under the 1975 tax law and assuming real growth of 6 percent a year, an annual inflation rate of 2 percent would raise tax liabilities by about 3 percent in the first year and by 14 percent in the fifth year. By contrast, a 4 percent annual inflation rate would raise tax liabilities by 6 percent in the first year and by over 25 percent in the fifth year.

In the past, periodic reductions in tax rates have more than offset the inflation-induced increases in effective individual income tax rates in the aggregate. The distribution of the discretionary tax cuts, however, have been different from the distribution of reductions under an indexed system. In general the discretionary cuts have been larger for the low-income classes, while those in the higher-income classes just below the top of the income scale—say, between $25,000 and $200,000 where the rate of progression is steep—have not been compensated for inflation.

Appendix

Table 5-6. Derivation of Individual Income Tax under 1960 Law after Inflation Adjustment, 1960–75
Dollar amounts in billions

Year	Adjusted personal income (1)	Consumer price index (1967 = 100) (2)	Deflated adjusted personal income (3)	Deflated taxes[a] (4)	Tax under 1960 law after inflation adjustment (5)
1960	370	88.7	370	39.5	39.5
1961	380	89.6	376	40.4	40.8
1962	404	90.6	396	43.4	44.3
1963	425	91.7	411	45.8	47.3
1964	455	92.9	434	49.1	51.4
1965	492	94.5	462	53.2	56.7
1966	538	97.2	491	57.1	62.9
1967	573	100.0	508	60.4	67.8
1968	623	104.2	530	63.4	74.5
1969	677	109.8	547	66.0	81.7
1970	717	116.3	545	66.0	86.5
1971	760	121.3	556	67.3	92.0
1972	831	125.3	588	72.1	101.8
1973	930	133.1	620	76.9	115.4
1974[b]	1,007	147.7	605	74.6	124.2
1975[b]	1,060	161.2	583	71.3	129.6

Sources: For column 1, see table 5-3, column 1. For column 2, see *Economic Report of the President, January 1976*, table B-42, p. 220. Column 3 equals adjusted personal income in year *t* times the ratio of the CPI in 1960 to the CPI in year *t*. Column 4 equals the taxes from table 5-3, column 2, deflated by the formula in note a below. Column 5 equals column 4 in year *t* times the ratio of the CPI in year *t* to the CPI in 1960.

a. Deflated taxes in year $t = \left[\begin{array}{c}\text{taxes}\\ \text{in 1960}\end{array}\right] \times \left[1 + 1.4\left(\dfrac{API_t}{API_{1960}} - 1\right)\right],$

where API_t = deflated adjusted personal income in year t, and 1.4 = the elasticity of tax liabilities with respect to real adjusted personal income.

b. Estimated.

Table 5-7. Effect on Revenue of Changes in the Individual Income Tax, 1960–75
Billions of dollars

	Individual income tax liability had there been no tax changes since 1960 (1)	Tax changes since 1960							Actual individual income tax liability[a] (9)
Year		Depreciation guidelines (2)	Revenue Act of 1962 (3)	Revenue Act of 1964 (4)	Tax Reform Act of 1969 (5)	Revenue Act of 1971 plus introduction of asset depreciation range (6)	Tax Reduction Act of 1975 (7)	Total tax changes (8)	
1960	39.5	...	...	...	...	...	...	...	39.5
1961	42.2	...	...	...	...	...	...	...	42.2
1962	45.3	-0.2	-0.2	...	...	...	...	-0.4	44.9
1963	48.4	-0.2	...	...	...	...	...	-0.2	48.2
1964	54.0	-0.1	...	-6.7	...	...	...	-6.8	47.2
1965	61.9	-0.1	-0.1	-12.2	...	...	...	-12.4	49.5
1966	69.6	-0.1	-0.1	-13.3	...	...	...	-13.5	56.1
1967	77.4	-0.1	-0.1	-14.3	...	...	...	-14.5	62.9
1968	87.2	-0.1	-0.1	-15.5	...	...	...	-15.7[b]	71.5
1969	95.3	-0.1	-0.2	-16.5	0.4	...	...	-16.4[b]	78.9
1970	100.4	-0.1	-0.3	-17.3	-0.8[c]	...	...	-18.5[b]	81.9
1971	110.7	-0.1	-0.3	-18.6	-4.6	-1.7	...	-25.3	85.4
1972	126.5	-0.1	-0.4	-20.9	-7.4	-4.1	...	-32.9	93.6
1973	143.6	-0.1	-0.5	-22.9	-10.0	-2.0	...	-35.5	108.1
1974	161.0	-0.1	-0.5	-25.3	-10.6	-2.1	-8.1	-46.7	114.3
1975	171.6	-0.1	-0.5	-27.3	-11.4	-2.3	-10.3	-51.9	119.7

Sources: Column 1 equals column 9 minus column 8. Tabulation for columns 2–7 for the years 1960–74 provided by U.S. Department of the Treasury, Office of Tax Analysis, except for the figure for 1974 in column 7, which is from Department of the Treasury *News*, WS-264, March 29, 1975, p. 1; 1975 data are authors' estimates. Column 8 equals the sum of columns 2 through 7. Column 9 is from U.S. Internal Revenue Service, *Statistics of Income, Individual Income Tax Returns*, various issues, except for figures for 1974 and 1975, which are Department of the Treasury estimates.

a. Tax after credits, plus the minimum tax less surcharge in 1968–70 and including rebate of 1974 taxes.
b. Excluding Vietnam war surcharge.
c. Excluding extension of Vietnam war surcharge.

Comments by John Bossons

Emil Sunley and Joseph Pechman's paper is one of three (the others are by Roger Brinner and Martin Bailey) that explore the redistributive effects of indexing. None of these papers investigate such behavioral adjustments to inflation as changes in investment or in the realization of capital gains. Sunley and Pechman ignore any "shifting" of the changes in tax burdens occasioned by indexing. To a limited degree, Brinner and Bailey take such shifting into account. But none of the three concern themselves with market adjustments.

First, I should like to question the meaningfulness of comparisons of tax burdens under an indexed 1960 tax law with those under the actual 1975 law. Such a comparison seems to suggest that discretionary tax changes would not have occurred if the rate structure had been indexed. But there is no reason to make such an assumption. Furthermore, not all actual tax changes were motivated by a desire to offset the effects of inflation. The 1964 tax cut in particular was introduced for a variety of reasons, virtually none of which had anything to do with the rate of inflation, then less than 2 percent a year. In this context, the 1965–75 comparison is much more meaningful. But even here, the 1969 tax reduction did many things other than offset inflation. I do not think that it is meaningful to assume that the reforms and revisions in the tax base in the 1969 bill would not have been enacted if the income tax had been indexed. It would have been more reasonable to add the effects of these changes to those of indexing. For these reasons, I do not know what to make of the differences between tax burdens under the actual 1975 law and an indexed 1960 or 1965 law. Incidentally, I have no reason to think that in the future I will prefer the pattern of tax burdens that emerges from periodic discretionary tax changes to those that emerge from indexing.

Second, even if we remain within the context chosen by Sunley and Pechman of "impact incidence," that is, if we ignore all behavioral responses to tax changes that indexing might precipitate, I think we should compare changes in tax burdens not only among income brackets but also among age brackets. The latter comparison is important because within any income bracket older families generally derive a larger proportion of income from capital than do younger families. And inflation is likely to have effects on measured income from capital that are proportionately different from those on income from labor. Indexing the tax base would reduce the corporation income tax on equity capital. It would also reduce the tax on capital gains, at least if no other changes in taxation of capital gains were enacted. Furthermore, indexing would have some effects on interest income and expenses; the magnitudes and even the signs are unclear as they depend on rates of inflation and on the marginal tax rates of borrowers and lenders, but they cannot safely be ignored.

Comments by Richard Goode

The objectives of the paper by Emil Sunley and Joseph Pechman are quite limited, a fact that must be kept in mind in comparing it with Martin Bailey's paper. Despite its limited objectives, however, it is a very relevant exercise because the behavior of other countries makes clear that adjustment of bracket boundaries and of personal allowances is the most probable form of inflation adjustment.

Before turning to the paper, I want to express my concern with the tendency of much of the discussion here to link sweeping proposals for tax reform with the rather limited objective of automatically adjusting the tax system for inflation. I refer to comments about investment credits; accelerated depreciation; full taxation of capital gains, possibly on an accrual basis; cumulative averaging; and so on. They all have something to do with the subject of this conference, but they go far beyond the question of inflation adjustment. It would be a mistake to hinge recommendations regarding inflation adjustment on the resolution of these questions.

I do not share John Bossons' misgivings about the comparison of actual 1975 tax burdens with those under indexed 1960 or 1965 laws. To be sure, we might have had tax revision even if we had had indexing. Total tax reduction might have been greater than in fact it was. But I find it interesting and informative to compare what we actually did with what would have happened if we had indexed the rate structure of 1960 or 1965 and had done nothing else.

I was pleased to see the emphasis by Sunley and Pechman on the impact of inflation on the effective tax rate and on the change in disposable income. In a number of other countries there has been much discussion, some of it not very well-informed, about the percentage change in tax burdens due to inflation. It is true, of course, that a trivial increase in the tax burden of someone who had been paying very few dollars in tax might be a large percentage of previous liabilities. Sunley and Pechman show that such comparisons are largely misleading and irrelevant. The same thing can be said of discussions about the impact of inflation on the tax burdens of families of different sizes. One often hears that large families suffer disproportionately from inflation. This statement is true with respect to percentage changes in tax burdens but is not really applicable when it comes to effective tax rates and after-tax disposable income.

It is worth a footnote, incidentally, to point out that the effective tax rate as a percentage of personal income was exactly the same in 1974 as it had been in 1960—9.9 percent. This fact heightens the oddity that adjusted gross income is used in this paper, although many economists, notably Pechman, have stressed the shortcomings of this measure of income.

Whether the distribution of tax burdens that resulted from actual legislation is better or worse than that under an indexed 1960 law is a matter of taste. In my opinion the actual 1975 distribution is superior. The burden on both the lowest and the highest brackets is lower under the actual law.

I am somewhat concerned about the Sunley-Pechman projections for the future. The reliability of the projections is reduced both by the possibility that the composition of income might well change if inflation is prolonged and by uncertainty about the appropriate elasticity of income tax collections with respect to income. Sunley and Pechman state that this elasticity is the same whether income rises because of real growth or inflation. If it is not the same, however, projections based on elasticities estimated on data for periods when there was less inflation than now may be misleading. On balance I nevertheless find the projections interesting and useful, but I suspect the authors would agree that readers should view them with some skepticism.

Discussion

Alan Blinder suggested that the results presented by Emil Sunley and Joseph Pechman could simply be viewed as evidence of congressional intent to keep the ratio of personal income taxes to adjusted gross income approximately constant. Their results show how much of that job could be accomplished by indexing and how much would be discretionary changes in the tax code. Richard Musgrave pointed out that over the long run indexing would keep tax rates constant at given real incomes but not at given relative incomes. With economic growth, these tax rates would grow. If the objective is to keep constant the share of income collected through a progressive tax, then indexing on the price level is insufficient. Either additional discretionary tax reductions are necessary or the tax system must be indexed against the wage rate or per capita income rather than the price level.

Several discussants were uncomfortable about the assumption implicit in the Sunley-Pechman paper that inflation will increase adjusted gross incomes proportionately in all income classes. Arnold Harberger observed that when a 10 percent inflation causes a taxpayer whose income was $10,000 to move up to $11,000, his income, on the average, may have components different from the income of taxpayers who received $11,000 before the inflation. In general, he pointed out, labor income represents a declining proportion of total income as one moves up the income scale. Pechman replied that his calculations suggest that this effect is not distinguishable for the kinds of increases in money incomes experienced so far in the United States.

Martin Feldstein raised the question of what Sunley and Pechman implied about indexing the tax base. They claim to ignore that problem. But, Feldstein suggested, their results are best viewed as a calculation of the effects of indexing the rate structure if the tax base is already indexed. Only if this is the case might one assume that inflation would cause pre-inflation taxable incomes to rise proportionately, regardless of the amounts of those incomes derived from capital and labor. If the tax base is not indexed, one would expect inflation to increase capital and labor incomes by different amounts. In an extreme case, assume that the interest rate is 5 percent, that a taxpayer derives $50,000 of income from interest, and that initially the expected rate of inflation is zero. Then, suddenly, inflation comes to be expected at 5 percent, and the nominal rate of interest rises to 10 percent. The taxpayer's income doubles to $100,000. Sunley and Pechman would move that $50,000 income up by 5 percent to $52,500. But that is a very small part of the impact of inflation on this taxpayer. The point, Feldstein argued, is that Sunley and Pechman have not shown the impact of indexing the rate structure when the tax base is *not* indexed, the policy now followed in a number of other countries; rather they have come nearer to showing the impact of indexing the rate structure if the tax base *is* indexed. John Bossons agreed with this formulation of the Sunley-Pechman results.

Martin Bailey suggested that the Sunley-Pechman calculations could be interpreted as showing the consequences of indexing only the rate structure for those taxpayers whose income is entirely from labor. Pechman suggested that Feldstein's point was significant only for a minuscule fraction of all taxpayers, those with incomes in excess of $100,000 a year. In lower brackets the amount of income from capital, Pechman reported, is a very small part of total income.

George Tolley suggested that the composition of past discretionary tax changes would be a poor guide to their future composition should high rates of inflation persist. In the past he pointed out, Congress has adjusted exemptions, the low-income allowance, and the standard deductions, but has left the rate structure alone. In the future, however, Congress would not be able to avoid dealing with the rate structure. Stanley Surrey suggested that congressmen do not really care how taxpayers came to have the liabilities they now bear and hence would not necessarily wish to undo the effects of past inflation on the distribution of tax burdens but would be interested in indexing the present tax structure regardless of how it came into being.

CHAPTER SIX

The Implication
for Economic Stability
of Indexing the Individual
Income Tax

JAMES L. PIERCE *and* JARED J. ENZLER

INDEXING the federal income tax has great appeal because inflation causes unplanned and often undesirable changes in the tax structure. If the rate structure were indexed, individuals would no longer find their real disposable incomes reduced when inflation pushes them into higher tax brackets and reduces the real value of exemptions. Indexing might be undesirable, however, if it were to promote economic instability.

In this paper we assess the possible destabilizing effects of indexing the rate structure of the personal income tax system.[1] Indexing could be destabilizing because it would prevent real tax burdens from increasing as prices rise. Tax increases reduce disposable income and

1. Whether indexing other aspects of the tax base would materially affect economic stability is an important question but one we do not consider.

dampen aggregate demand. This dampening, other things being equal, reduces inflationary pressures. If the income tax system were indexed, this dampening effect would be removed and inflation, once started, might be harder to control. But before deciding not to index the rate structure on these grounds, one should determine how much indexing reduces economic stability.

We address this issue by obtaining simulations of a macroeconometric model to assess how, in both this world and a tax-indexed world, key economic variables respond to particular exogenous shocks or disturbances. Indexing the personal income tax system would be destabilizing if such shocks induced significantly larger movements in prices and real output when the rate structure is indexed than when it is not. But as it turns out, the estimated impact of indexing the rate structure on economic stability is negligible.

We are interested in the short-run effects of tax indexing on economic stability because problems might develop so quickly that discretionary policy could not cope with them adequately. Automatic stabilizers are most valuable in such situations since they require no discretionary action, but tax indexing reduces the power of automatic stabilizers.

The problem of analyzing tax indexing is complicated because it concerns a world that does not exist.[2] Consequently it is important that macroeconometric models used to simulate the response of the economy to shocks under the existing tax structure and under an indexed income tax system describe with reasonable accuracy the dynamic interconnection among tax receipts, aggregate demand, and the price level as they respond to different shocks. We use the Social Science Research Council-MIT-Penn (SMP) model because we are familiar with its properties and because we believe its dynamic structure is more carefuly specified and estimated than are those of most other models.

Some observers discount the importance of simulation results, which they claim simply "give back" the model's properties; if the model is severely misspecified or poorly estimated, its simulation results will not be useful. These fears have some merit, and we attempted to design the simulation experiments to minimize the risk of

2. To be sure, one can interpret the changes in rates and exemption levels in the postwar period as a form of indexing, but these efforts were infrequent and were not directly related to the inflation that was actually occurring at the time.

deceptive results. The major danger from a policy standpoint is that the model might imply that indexing would not significantly increase instability when, in fact, it would. The model is unlikely to understate the effects of indexing, but to reduce the risk of reaching policy conclusions that would have unfortunate consequences if adopted, we designed the simulations to "bias" the results in favor of showing significant instability. We consider the effects of large shocks in a world in which the personal income tax system is indexed by the *current* price level. Thus we assume that tax rates and exemption levels are adjusted immediately when the price level changes. This assumption maximizes the destabilizing effects of indexing the tax system. If the model fails to exhibit instability when indexing is instantaneous, it is even less likely to do so when indexing is lagged.

Setting Up the Simulation

To understand and evaluate the simulations, it is necessary to know how they were set up. The first step was to replace the equations in the SMP model for taxable income and for tax liabilities with ones that lend themselves better to the analysis of indexing.

The SMP model does not take capital gains into account in its equation for taxable income, and its equation for tax liabilities does not explicitly describe the movement of taxpayers into higher tax brackets with the rise in aggregate nominal taxable income. We eliminated these deficiencies by replacing the model's tax equations with equations recently developed by Pechman and by Gramlich and Ribe.[3]

The Pechman equation for taxable income is

$$\log (1 - Z/Y_a) = -0.7129 -0.2968 \log Y_a/N$$
$$+ 0.3816 \log E/N - 0.0289 \log (C/N)$$
$$+ 0.0252 \, D_{70-71},$$

where

Z = taxable income,

Y_a = personal income less transfer payments plus associated increases in personal contributions for social insurance,

3. See Joseph A. Pechman, "Responsiveness of the Federal Individual Income Tax to Changes in Income," *Brookings Papers on Economic Activity*, 2:1973, pp. 385–421; and Edward Gramlich and Frederick C. Ribe, "More on the Income Elasticity of Federal Personal Income Tax" (Brookings Institution, 1975; processed).

N = total population,

E = value of personal exemptions,

C = realized capital gains,

D_{70-71} = dummy variable for the years 1970–71 as a result of provisions in the Tax Reform Act of 1969.

The equation for tax liabilities is a version of a Pechman equation as modified by Gramlich and Ribe:[4]

$$\log T - \log R^* = 0.079 + 0.986 \log Z - 0.061 \, D_{54-63},$$

where

T = income tax liability,

R^* = a weighted average tax rate described below,

Z = taxable income,

D_{54-63} = dummy variable for the years before 1964.

The Gramlich-Ribe contribution lies in the construction of the weighted average tax rate, R^*, and in its introduction into an estimated equation for tax liabilities. The original Pechman specifications simply weighted the tax rates for each tax bracket by the ratio in 1967 of taxable income in that bracket to total taxable income. Gramlich and Ribe allowed the income distribution weights to change over time with taxable income by estimating a separate regression for each of the twenty-five marginal tax rate brackets in which the ratio of reported income in each bracket to total reported income for a given year was taken to be a linear function of taxable income. Each regression was estimated over the seven-year period 1964–70. The regressions were then used to predict the changes in each ratio (weight) in response to changes in taxable income. These predicted weights were used to construct the R^* variable. As taxable income grows, one would expect the bottom brackets to decline in importance and the higher brackets to increase in importance. Thus the effective tax rate should rise with taxable nominal income; Gramlich and Ribe show that in fact it does, and that it is important to allow for this effect. The simulation experiments with the SMP model use the Gramlich-Ribe system because it is precisely this kind of effect that indexing the rate structure eliminates.

The model required an additional adjustment because it does not generate a series for realized capital gains. It does, however, generate a series for actual capital gains—realized or not—for various

4. Pechman, ibid., p. 418; and Gramlich and Ribe, ibid., p. 4a.

assets. It was necessary, therefore, to relate changes in the value of assets generated by the model to realized capital gains of the Pechman equation. To link these series, we regressed Pechman's series of realized capital gains per capita[5] on a distributed lag of the change in the value of common stocks and on a distributed lag of the portion of the change in the value of the housing stock attributable to the change in the price of houses. The variables for both common stocks and the housing stock were deflated by current population.[6] The predictions of realized capital gains from the regression were used as inputs to the Pechman taxable income equation imbedded in the model.

The regression had the form

$$(1) \qquad (C/N)_t = a + \sum_{i=0}^{29} b_i (\Delta S_{t-i}/N_t)$$

$$+ \sum_{i=0}^{14} c_i (\Delta PH_{t-i} \cdot KH_{t-i-1}/N_t) + \epsilon_t,$$

where

C = realized capital gains,
N = total population,
ΔS = change in the value of common stock,
ΔPH = change in the price of houses,
KH = stock of houses.

The parameter estimates can be summarized as follows (figures in parentheses are t-statistics):

$$a = -0.122, \ \Sigma b_i = 0.972, \ \Sigma c_i = 0.584$$
$$(1.526) \qquad (6.190) \qquad (5.314)$$

$$R^2 = 0.705; \text{ standard error } = 10.35; \text{ mean } = 45.25.$$

Long distributed lags were required to relate changes in both the actual values of common stock and houses to realized capital gains. The lag for common stocks is longer than that for the housing stock, probably because the mobility of the population forces realization of gains on houses. The sum of the weights for both the gains on common stocks and on houses would appear at first glance to be unrea-

5. Pechman, "Responsiveness of the Federal Individual Income Tax," table A-1, pp. 416–17.

6. Because the realized capital gains variable is measured annually, but the SMP model generates quarterly observations, the realized capital gains variable was interpolated by distributing the realized gains equally over the four quarters of the year. Experiments with annual regressions of the same form yielded similar results.

sonably large. The estimates suggest that in the long run 97 percent of the gains on common stocks and 58 percent of the gains on houses are realized. These results, however, simply indicate that assets other than common stocks and houses contribute to realized gains, and they have not been included in the regression. Thus common stocks and houses have to carry the weight of all these excluded variables in explaining realized capital gains.

The next modification of the model involved the specification of economic conditions for the period over which the simulation experiments were conducted. Ideally one should measure the effects of indexing under a variety of conditions. Lacking space or resources for this, we decided instead to choose a "typical" historical period during which the economy was operating at about average levels of resource utilization (and had been doing so for some time) and was not subject to unusual influences such as price controls, oil price increases, devaluation, crop failure, or war. Unfortunately, no recent period has been typical. Consequently we had to rewrite history to create such a situation by modifying the model for the period 1964 through 1966. Each behavioral equation (including the Pechman and Gramlich-Ribe equations) was simulated separately for this period and the equation errors were recorded.[7] A simultaneous, dynamic simulation of the model, with these errors added to each equation, tracks history exactly. Then the model was resimulated with most of the effects of the Vietnam war removed. Real federal government expenditures (exogenous to the model) were made to grow at a steady 4 percent annual rate over the period, and the size of the armed forces was held constant at its 1963–64 level.[8] Monetary policy, defined in terms of M_1 (currency plus demand deposits), was left unchanged from historical levels. This simulation resulted in a fairly steady unemployment rate averaging just under 5 percent for the period. The results of this simulation were used as if they were actual historical data and served as the control simulation from which various experiments were conducted.

With the Pechman equation for taxable income, the Gramlich-

7. The choice of period caused one more complication. Several SMP model equations depend on nominal interest rates before 1965 and on real interest rates thereafter. We changed the model structure so that these equations depended on real interest rates at all times.

8. We are not interested in accurately removing the effects of the Vietnam war but in creating a "normal" period over which to conduct our experiments.

Ribe tax liability system and the special capital gains equation im-bedded in the model, and using our control simulation as a base, we examined how the model responded to various shocks that are de-scribed in the next section. For each shock, the model was simulated over the twelve quarters of the control simulation. Then the impact of the same shocks was calculated after the tax structure had been in-dexed. The results of these two simulations were compared to deter-mine the impact of indexing.

In order to index the personal tax system, we modified several equations. Under indexing, only that part of the increase in the value of household assets that does not arise from increases in the general price level are taxed as capital gains. The capital gains equation (as-suming population constant at unity) can be written

$$(2) \qquad C_t = \Sigma b_i \Delta S_{t-i} + \Sigma c_i (\Delta P H_i) K H_{t-i-1},$$

where the symbols are defined as in equation 1. We inflated the pur-chase price of assets on which gains are realized in this period by mod-ifying equation 2 as follows:

$$(3) \qquad C = \Sigma b_i P_t (\Delta s_{t-i}) + \Sigma c_i P_t (\Delta p h_{t-i}) K H_{t-i},$$

where
$$\Delta s_t = S_t / P_t - S_{t-1} / P_{t-1},$$
$$\Delta p h_t = P H_t / P_t - P H_{t-1} / P_{t-1},$$
$$P_t = \text{the consumer price index of period } t.$$

Thus capital gains include only the excess of today's value over what the asset would have cost at today's prices. If the prices of common stocks and houses rise at the same rate as P, no real capital gains occur.

The taxable income equation was adjusted by making exemptions proportionate to consumer prices. With this modification, if the price level (but not real income) rises, personal income and exemptions increase by the same amount and have offsetting effects on taxable income.[9]

Tax brackets were indexed by modifying the Gramlich-Ribe sys-

9. The adjustment provides only an approximation to true indexing and would be exactly correct only if the coefficients on exemptions and income were equal and of opposite sign. In the Pechman equation for taxable income, the coefficient on per-sonal income is negative and smaller in absolute value than the coefficient on exemp-tions. The relative sizes of these two coefficients imply that we slightly overindexed by making exemptions proportionate to consumer prices.

tem of equations. Taxable income was replaced by deflated taxable income in the regression equations determining the proportion of income in each tax bracket for given current dollar taxable income. Thus if real income remains constant but prices rise, the proportion of taxpayers in each bracket remains unchanged. Adjustment of exemptions and brackets reduces taxable income and taxes as prices rise, offsetting the increase in taxable income and in taxes due to the inflation-induced rise in personal income.

With these alterations, the model was used to estimate the response of the economy to shocks when the personal income tax is indexed. Each modified equation was simulated individually, using the data base from the control simulation, and the equation "errors" were recorded. The three altered equations obviously made rather large errors. The model was then resimulated simultaneously after each equation error was added in. This simulation simply reproduced the control solution in spite of the arbitrary nature of the equations that were adjusted for indexing. Finally, the system was subjected to the same external shocks as in the regime without indexing and new simulations were obtained. The difference between the results of these simulations and the control simulation provides a measure of the difference between the response of the economy to shocks in a world with an indexed personal income tax system and the response when the personal income tax is not indexed. Because both simulations used the same initial conditions, the exercise yields a direct measure of these differences.

The Exogenous Shocks

Three shocks were analyzed: to aggregate demand, to money demand, and to prices.[10] Each of these shocks has its own special effect and its own implications for stability. Each also has its own real-world counterpart.

Poole has shown that the impact on the economy of shocks to ag-

10. The first two correspond to the stochastic shifts in the IS and LM curves analyzed by Poole and the third to the kind of exogenous price shock we discussed in another paper. See William Poole, "Optimal Choice of Monetary Policy Instruments in a Simple Stochastic Macro Model," *Quarterly Journal of Economics*, vol. 84 (May 1970), pp. 197–216; and James L. Pierce and Jared J. Enzler, "The Effects of External Inflationary Shocks," *Brookings Papers on Economic Activity*, 1:1974, pp. 13–54.

gregate demand and to money demand depend on monetary policy. If the monetary authorities are pursuing an interest rate target, then shocks to aggregate demand will produce large effects on total aggregate demand. This result occurs because in pursuing an interest rate target the monetary authorities accommodate all income-induced changes in the demand for money. Because interest rates are not allowed to respond to the shock, its effects are magnified. In contrast, if the authorities pursue a money stock target, interest rates will change in the same direction as the shock and its economic impact will be reduced.

The results are reversed if the shock affects the monetary sector. A shock to money demand, for example, will affect the economy negligibly if the monetary authorities are pursuing an interest rate target because, in pursuing this target, they would accommodate the shift in money demand, leaving interest rates and the real sectors of the economy unaffected. If the authorities are pursuing a money stock target, then interest rates must adjust sufficiently to equate the changed money demand to the unchanged money supply. The movements in interest rates will affect aggregate demand and the real sectors of the economy.

Recent events have demonstrated that such external events as crop failures and price increases by the oil cartel directly affect domestic prices and the real economy. The response of the economy to such shocks depends on the response of monetary policy. An exogenous increase in prices reduces real money balances and real wealth and redistributes income. The public will attempt to increase its money holdings as the rise in prices increases the nominal value of transactions. If the monetary authorities adhere to a money supply target, the public will be unable to increase its money balances and interest rates will have to rise sufficiently to reduce the demand for real balances to the reduced real supply. The rise in interest rates will reduce real aggregate demand in the economy.

If the monetary authorities pursue an interest rate target, they will have to permit the nominal supply of money to rise sufficiently to meet the increased nominal demand at unchanged interest rates. In this case interest rates will be unaffected and real aggregate demand will expand unhindered by monetary restriction.

Whether the pursuit of an interest rate target is more or less destabilizing to the economy than a money supply target depends on what else is going on in the economy and on the weights society puts on losses in real output versus inflation.[11] If the economy is already experiencing substantial inflation and unemployment is low, an interest rate target may be undesirable. Whether it is better to suffer some of the loss of real output associated with a money supply target depends in part on how inflationary expectations are formed. If the exogenous price shock increases expected inflation, aggregate demand could rise, putting more pressure on prices. This effect would be magnified under an interest rate policy.[12]

The Simulation Results

We made the exogenous shocks large by historical standards in order to reveal any latent instability caused by indexing. The shocks simulated were a $10 billion exogenous increase in real exports (aggregate demand); a 6 percent reduction in the level of money demand (money demand); and a 3 percent exogenous increase, phased in over three quarters, in the nonfarm business deflator (price increase). The export and money demand shocks work to increase aggregate demand and hence to increase inflation. The price shock increases inflation directly but depresses aggregate demand. The effects of these shocks depend on monetary policy. It is assumed that no change occurs in discretionary federal spending programs, although such nondiscretionary expenditures as unemployment insurance do respond.

The results for the three different shocks are shown in tables 6-1, 6-2, and 6-3. In each case the simulated deviation from the control simulation due to a particular shock is shown for both a nonindexed and an indexed tax system. The differences between these responses, more than the absolute size of either, are relevant to the tax indexing question. The size and the composition of the responses to the three shocks differ widely, however, and depend sensitively on monetary policy.

The results in the three tables provide dramatic evidence on the

11. Poole did not have to face this dilemma because his model did not deal with price level determination.

12. It was this sort of consideration that earlier led us to favor a policy that would increase the money supply sufficiently to accommodate the increase in the demand for money associated with the initial shock to prices but would then pursue a target growth rate for the money supply from its expanded base. See Pierce and Enzler, "The Effects of External Inflationary Shocks," pp. 47–49.

vulnerability of the economy to shocks under different monetary policy regimes. The results demonstrate with equal force that this vulnerability is not significantly affected by indexing the rate structure of the personal income tax.

Table 6-1 summarizes the simulations of the response of the economy to a $10 billion increase in real exports. If the monetary authorities are pursuing an M_1 target and do not adjust the target in response to the shock (the assumption behind the results shown in the six columns on the left-hand side of the table), real output rises temporarily but the rise cannot be sustained. Interest rates must rise sufficiently to cause the velocity of money to increase and to support a higher value of nominal transactions with an unchanged money stock. The higher interest rates reduce the expansion in aggregate demand. After twelve quarters real GNP is only about $2 billion higher than it would have been in the absence of the increase in real exports, but nominal GNP is increased because higher aggregate demand caused a higher price level.[13]

In this case, indexing has little effect on nominal and real GNP. Both are only slightly higher in an indexed than in a nonindexed regime twelve quarters after the shock. Indexing does ease the burden of rising prices on taxpayers. Personal income is $1.4 billion higher, taxable income is $4.3 billion lower, and personal income tax receipts are $1.5 billion lower in the indexed case twelve quarters following the jump in exports. While indexing provides taxpayers some relief, it does not give enough to have any sizable impact on aggregate demand and inflation.

The right-hand side of table 6-1 shows the results of a much more expansive monetary policy. Here it is assumed that the monetary authorities expand the money supply sufficiently to hold the Treasury bill rate at its value for the control simulation despite the added demand for money caused by the rise in real exports. In the case where taxes are not indexed, nominal GNP rises almost $108 billion from the $10 billion increase in real exports. Once again, however, indexing makes little difference. Nominal GNP rises an added $10 billion to $118 billion in the indexing case after twelve quarters. The differences between the nonindexed and indexed cases for both nominal

13. If the control simulation had been generating higher unemployment, the increase in exports would have increased real output more and increased prices less than in the actual case.

Table 6-1. Response of the Economy to a $10 Billion Increase in Real Exports, with and without Indexing

	Deviations from control simulation											
	Exogenous currency and demand deposits (M₁), by quarter						Exogenous Treasury bill rates, by quarter					
Item	1st[a]	2d	3d	4th	6th	12th	1st[a]	2d	3d	4th	6th	12th
GNP (billions of current dollars)												
No indexing	11.7	15.5	19.3	22.1	26.5	30.0	12.0	16.4	21.4	26.3	39.0	107.7
Indexing	11.7	15.6	19.4	22.3	27.0	31.9	12.0	16.5	21.5	26.5	39.7	118.2
Real GNP (billions of 1958 dollars)												
No indexing	10.7	13.2	15.4	16.4	15.8	1.9	10.9	13.8	16.8	19.3	23.7	32.0
Indexing	10.7	13.3	15.5	16.6	16.1	2.6	11.0	14.1	17.2	19.9	24.9	36.7
Unemployment rate (percentage points)												
No indexing	-0.31	-0.68	-0.79	-0.85	-0.94	-0.52	-0.32	-0.71	-0.87	-1.0	-1.4	-2.4
Indexing	-0.32	-0.68	-0.79	-0.85	-0.96	-0.57	-0.32	-0.72	-0.87	-1.0	-1.4	-2.6
Consumption prices (index points)												
No indexing	0.20	0.43	0.69	0.98	1.8	4.8	0.16	0.36	0.61	0.92	2.0	10.1
Indexing	0.20	0.44	0.69	0.99	1.8	5.0	0.16	0.37	0.62	0.93	2.0	11.0
Personal income (billions of current dollars)												
No indexing	4.0	8.7	11.6	14.1	19.8	26.5	4.1	9.2	12.8	16.6	28.5	84.4
Indexing	4.0	8.8	11.7	14.3	20.2	27.9	4.1	9.2	12.9	16.7	29.0	93.0
Taxable income (billions of current dollars)												
No indexing	2.5	5.5	7.3	8.9	10.9	17.2	2.6	5.8	8.1	10.5	18.3	55.4
Indexing	2.3	5.1	6.7	8.1	11.0	12.9	2.5	5.5	7.5	9.7	16.5	48.9
Personal income taxes (billions of current dollars)												
No indexing	0.5	1.2	1.6	1.9	2.8	3.9	0.6	1.2	1.7	2.3	4.0	12.8
Indexing	0.5	1.0	1.4	1.7	2.3	2.4	0.5	1.1	1.6	2.0	3.4	9.9

Sources: Simulations from the SMP model. The basic data are official statistics from the model data bank.
a. Quarter in which the shock occurred.

Table 6-2. Response of the Economy to a 6 Percent Reduction in the Level of Money Demand, with and without Indexing

	Deviations from control simulation											
	Exogenous currency and demand deposits (M_1), by quarter						Exogenous Treasury bill rates, by quarter					
Item	1st[a]	2d	3d	4th	6th	12th	1st[a]	2d	3d	4th	6th	12th
GNP (billions of current dollars)												
No indexing	1.3	3.4	7.0	11.8	24.6	78.7	0.00	−0.03	−0.11	−0.23	−0.29	0.34
Indexing	1.3	3.4	6.9	11.8	24.9	81.4	0.00	−0.03	−0.11	−0.23	−0.29	0.33
Real GNP (billions of 1958 dollars)												
No indexing	1.2	3.0	5.6	9.7	18.0	31.5	0.00	−0.02	−0.10	−0.19	−0.21	0.35
Indexing	1.2	2.9	5.9	9.7	18.0	32.7	0.00	−0.02	−0.10	−0.20	−0.21	0.34
Unemployment rate (percentage points)												
No indexing	−0.04	−0.13	−0.27	−0.46	−0.95	−2.1	0.00	0.00	0.00	0.01	0.01	−0.02
Indexing	−0.04	−0.13	−0.27	−0.46	−0.95	−2.2	0.00	0.00	0.00	0.01	0.01	−0.02
Consumption prices (index points)												
No indexing	−0.19	−0.22	−0.09	0.03	0.53	6.1	0.00	0.00	0.00	−0.00	−0.01	−0.01
Indexing	−0.19	−0.22	−0.10	−0.02	0.53	6.3	0.00	0.00	0.00	0.01	0.01	−0.02
Personal income (billions of current dollars)												
No indexing	0.5	1.5	3.4	6.2	15.9	59.4	0.00	0.00	−0.4	−0.10	−0.19	0.18
Indexing	0.5	1.5	3.3	6.1	16.0	61.6	0.00	0.00	−0.4	−0.10	−0.19	0.17
Taxable income (billions of current dollars)												
No indexing	0.3	1.0	2.2	4.0	10.3	38.9	0.00	0.00	−0.02	−0.06	−0.12	0.11
Indexing	0.5	1.2	2.3	3.9	9.7	33.5	0.00	0.00	−0.02	−0.06	−0.11	0.12
Personal income taxes (billions of current dollars)												
No indexing	0.07	0.21	0.46	0.85	2.2	8.9	0.00	0.00	−0.00	−0.01	−0.03	0.02
Indexing	0.12	0.26	0.48	0.84	2.1	6.9	0.00	0.00	−0.00	−0.01	−0.02	0.03

Sources: Simulations from the SMP model. The basic data are official statistics from the model data bank.
a. Quarter in which the shock occurred.

Table 6-3. Response of the Economy to a 3 Percent Increase in Consumption Prices, with and without Indexing

	Deviations from control simulation											
	Exogenous currency and demand deposits (M₁), by quarter						Exogenous Treasury bill rates, by quarter					
Item	1st[a]	2d	3d	4th	6th	12th	1st[a]	2d	3d	4th	6th	12th
GNP (billions of current dollars)												
No indexing	2.0	2.9	4.0	5.3	8.7	15.4	2.1	3.2	4.7	6.8	13.1	42.6
Indexing	2.1	3.1	4.4	5.9	9.7	17.1	2.1	3.4	5.2	7.4	14.4	50.0
Real GNP (billions of 1958 dollars)												
No indexing	-2.3	-4.7	-6.2	-7.1	-8.1	-12.4	-2.2	-4.4	-5.6	-5.9	-4.7	5.3
Indexing	-2.2	-4.5	-5.8	-6.7	-7.4	-11.6	-2.2	-4.2	-5.2	-5.4	-3.7	8.2
Unemployment rate (percentage points)												
No indexing	0.10	0.22	0.32	0.38	0.46	0.81	0.08	0.21	0.30	0.32	0.30	-0.16
Indexing	0.08	0.21	0.30	0.35	0.42	0.75	0.08	0.20	0.28	0.30	0.24	-0.35
Consumption prices (index points)												
No indexing	0.9	1.6	2.1	2.5	3.3	5.1	0.9	1.6	2.1	2.5	3.3	5.8
Indexing	0.9	1.6	2.1	2.6	3.3	5.3	0.9	1.6	2.1	2.5	3.3	6.1
Personal income (billions of current dollars)												
No indexing	-1.0	-2.0	-2.3	-2.0	-0.7	3.4	-0.9	-1.8	-2.0	-1.3	1.6	19.8
Indexing	-0.9	-1.9	-2.1	-1.7	-0.1	4.7	-0.9	-1.7	-1.8	1.0	2.5	23.5
Taxable income (billions of current dollars)												
No indexing	-0.6	-1.1	-1.3	-1.1	-0.2	2.4	-0.5	-1.0	-1.1	0.6	1.3	13.2
Indexing	-1.4	-2.6	-3.2	-3.4	-3.1	-2.0	-1.3	-2.5	-3.0	-2.9	-1.4	9.3
Personal income taxes (billions of current dollars)												
No indexing	-0.12	-0.24	-0.29	-0.24	-0.05	-0.55	-0.11	-0.22	-0.24	-0.14	0.28	3.0
Indexing	-0.34	-0.63	-0.81	-0.87	-0.88	-0.85	-0.33	-0.61	-0.75	-0.76	-0.53	1.6

Sources: Simulations from the SMP model. The basic data are official statistics from the model data bank.
a. Quarter in which the shock occurred.

and real GNP are almost imperceptible for four quarters and become visible only at the end of three years. Indexing reduces taxable income and tax payments, but the reduction adds little to the inflation produced by a policy that holds the bill rate constant.

Table 6-2 presents results indicating that indexing negligibly alters the effects of a decline in the demand for money, whether the monetary authorities adopt an interest rate or a money supply target. With a money supply target, interest rates decline and both output and prices increase; but the results change very little when indexing is introduced. As can be seen in the right-hand side of the table, if money demand shifts down and the monetary authorities do not let the bill rate change from its values for the control simulation, aggregate output and prices are largely insulated from the shock and it makes no difference whether taxes are indexed or not.

The results of an exogenous price increase shown in table 6-3 are interesting because real output and prices move in opposite directions. If the monetary authorities do not increase M_1 in response to the price rise, aggregate real output falls and prices rise throughout the twelve quarters of simulation; but indexing affects the economy negligibly.

If the bill rate is prevented from responding to the initial rise in prices, nominal aggregate demand expands by much more than was the case for an exogenous M_1. Under this regime, the expansion of the money supply tends to maintain real money balances and thus avoids the rise in interest rates that results when M_1 is not allowed to respond to the jump in prices. When the bill rate is exogenous, real output has actually risen slightly relative to the control simulation after twelve quarters. While this policy maintains real output and employment, it would eventually cause an explosion in prices. Over the twelve quarters considered, however, its effect on prices is not very large relative to the exogenous M_1 regime. Whether or not the exogenous bill rate is a good policy choice, its effect coupled with the exogenous price increase is affected little by indexing.

Conclusion

The evidence presented in the three tables indicates that indexing the income tax system will not produce significantly greater economic instability than already exists. Even though the shocks are large and the economy responds rather strongly to them under some policy regimes, this response is altered negligibly by indexing. The results are particularly striking when one recalls that the indexing occurs instantaneously. There is no lag between the rise in the price level and adjustments to tax rates and exemptions. The elasticity of tax revenues with respect to prices is always equal to unity in the simulations. Use of a lagged rather than a contemporaneous deflator would reduce the marginal impact of indexing taxes.

Indexing matters so little in the simulations because the reduction in tax liabilities it causes are small relative to the shocks that induced the change in taxes. All three shocks produce the same results. There is simply no evidence that indexing the tax system would be harmful to economic stability.[14]

The small tax liability effect may seem unreasonable in light of the large capital gains associated with the inflation in some of the simulations. Not all gains would be realized, however, and when realized, they receive a weight of only 0.03 in Pechman's equation. Unless this parameter estimate is understated by a factor of ten or more, we can be fairly confident that inflationary shocks will not be significantly harder to cope with when taxes are indexed than when they are not.

While we did not analyze the effects of indexing the corporate income tax structure, it is unlikely that adding this complicated dimension would have changed our conclusions. But it is possible to devise indexing schemes that are destabilizing. For example, we experimented with a system in which all inflation-caused changes in household net worth were returned to taxpayers by a rebate. This scheme proved highly destabilizing.

Any conventional indexing scheme, however, seems to add little to economic instability. In light of the undesirable effects that inflation has on the tax system, it would appear from our results that indexing should be adopted.

Comments by George Perry

James Pierce and Jared Enzler did a careful and thorough job searching for the effects on economic stability of indexing the rate

14. A similar conclusion based on somewhat different techniques was reached for indexing the Canadian tax system. See John Bossons and Thomas A. Wilson, "Adjusting Tax Rates for Inflation," *Canadian Tax Journal*, vol. 21 (May–June 1973), pp. 185–99.

structure of the personal income tax. They went to considerable trouble to specify this type of indexing accurately in their large model, which is not an easy task, and their results seem entirely believable. Basically, indexing the rate structure of the personal income tax has a negligible effect on the cyclical stability of the economy.

This conclusion that indexing has little effect on stability, whatever the source of inflation, has some bearing on Alan Blinder's discussion of Edward Denison's paper.[15] Where inflation originates—whether on the demand side or the supply side or from excess domestic spending, crop shortages, oil cartels, or devaluation—is not crucial for deciding whether to index or not.

It is important to note that Pierce and Enzler do *not* say that the tax increases generated by inflation are unimportant or that their macroeconomic effects are negligible. What they show is that the macroeconomic effects of inflation will be much the same with an indexed or a nonindexed tax schedule.

Pierce and Enzler are not entirely at ease with their findings on capital gains, and neither am I. This is the one aspect of indexing the tax base, as opposed to the rate schedule, that they deal with. They note that assets other than stocks and houses are omitted from the capital gains equation and that the gains that are included thus have to do double duty. But I am not sure that significant capital gains are realized on any omitted asset. And I also wonder whether houses should play as large a role as they do in their estimates. People move a lot, but that is not the same thing as realizing a capital gain. The problem is very tricky, and I am not sure anyone else could have done better. The Treasury agonizes annually trying to estimate realized capital gains and annually fails to do so.

The more interesting issue regarding these gains is whether indexing would alter the pace at which capital gains are realized, by reducing the locked-in effect that now exists. Unfortunately, Pierce and Enzler do not address this issue.

Finally, we really are not sure about the impact of capital gains on consumption. Present estimates hinge on the historic relation between accrued and realized gains. If this were to change, it might require a change in our estimate of how consumption is affected.

Aside from their treatment of capital gains, Pierce and Enzler ignore indexing the tax base. I have no strong hunches about whether

15. See chapter 9.

indexing the base further would have much impact on economic stability. The most important effects would probably come from redefining the corporate tax base. Analysis of this case would be quite sensitive to the model of business investment being used, in contrast to the present exercise, whose conclusions would be much the same on any major econometric model of the economy.

Comments by Robert J. Gordon

The fact that James Pierce and Jared Enzler's paper concerns itself with only a part of indexing—the rate structure and some capital gains—is a serious shortcoming. The numbers that emerge from the paper are so small that it makes one wonder why people are concerned with indexing at all and why this conference needed to be held.

Pierce and Enzler attempt to adjust realized capital gains. But this is only a small part of the story, since losses on monetary assets and gains on monetary liabilities are being accrued. I think it is unreasonable to make the Pierce-Enzler kind of adjustment and not to make the adjustment for monetary assets and liabilities. If taxpayers receive a rebate equal to the rate of inflation times net worth, the authors tell us that the economy explodes. If so, then I would like to know how close to defensible principles of taxation we can get without suffering explosive instability in the economy.

I find nonsensical the simulations in which the monetary authorities try to keep the interest rate constant in the face of inflation. Who would want to do that? Such a policy would drive down real interest rates, induce huge multipliers, and produce the awful results in the right-hand columns of the Pierce-Enzler tables. I would prefer to have seen an exercise in which different forms of indexing were tested under sensible monetary policies. For example, I would like to see a simulation of the Canadian system for the United States. I would also like to see simulations that go beyond the twelve-quarter span shown in the tables.

In short, despite the authors' claim that they did everything to overstate the destabilizing effects of indexing, I find that they err in choosing an excessively partial kind of indexing that is almost guaranteed to have a meager impact on stability. We still do not know whether full-scale indexing of rate structure and base would be destabilizing or not.

Comments by Ray C. Fair

I have three comments on the paper by James Pierce and Jared Enzler. First, I doubt that their major conclusion, that indexing the tax system would add little to economic instability, is very model specific. For indexing to cause serious instability, the current price level would have to be sensitive to recent changes in aggregate demand, a relationship not apparent in most models. After receiving the Pierce-Enzler paper, I ran a similar set of experiments with my new econometric model and reached similar conclusions.

Second, in table 6-1 the impact on current dollar GNP of a $10 billion increase in real exports after twelve quarters (in the exogenous bill rate case) is $107.7 billion. This seems to me a bit excessive, even if the bill rate is pegged.

Third, Pierce and Enzler recommend that indexing be adopted because it does not cause serious instability and because the failure to index has undesirable effects on the tax system. What the results in tables 6-1, 6-2, and 6-3 really show, however, is that the failure to index does not have undesirable effects on the tax system in the short run. The largest difference between no-indexing and indexing regarding personal income taxes is only $2.9 billion after twelve quarters. Over a decade or so the revenue effects from not indexing are obviously greater. Given congressional willingness to change the tax laws periodically, however, I would conclude from the results in the Pierce-Enzler paper that the bad effects from not indexing are not serious, and I would recommend on grounds of simplicity that indexing not be adopted.

Discussion

James Pierce acknowledged some discomfort over the handling of capital gains in the paper that he and Jared Enzler prepared. Changes in the realization rate might be important, but he knew of no way to build such changes into the simulation. He defended the concentration of the simulations on rather short periods. Even three years was longer than the proper focus of concern about the impact of indexing on economic stability. Despite misguided monetary policies, monetary authorities can figure out what to do in three years if the economy gets out of hand, he maintained; the real concern should be over the impact of indexing one to four quarters after the economy receives an exogenous shock, the period during which people would be unsure of what was happening and before they could take remedial action. He also saw no point in searching for a particular form of indexing that would place the economy on the brink of instability. The purpose should be to test plans that have some reasonable prospect of adoption.

Edward Gramlich suggested and Pierce agreed that the SMP model was well suited to testing the effects of one widely discussed form of indexing not treated by Pierce and Enzler, namely replacement-cost depreciation.

A number of participants questioned the desirability of simulating accrual taxation of capital gains. Martin Feldstein expressed the view that such an exercise would be interesting, but that it has nothing to do with indexing the tax system for inflation. Roger Brinner, whose recommendations had been held up as a useful model for simulation, pointed out that he was urging accrual taxation only for monetary gains and losses due to inflation, not for gains on stocks or other assets.[16] John Bossons suggested that simulating such a scheme was not worth doing because Brinner's recommendations were undesirable (closely substitutable assets should not be taxed so differently) and because such a scheme was most unlikely to be adopted. Martin Bailey pointed out that all the problems created by capital gains could be resolved if the tax code provided for cumulative averaging with liabilities carried forward at a market rate of interest. Under such a system capital gains would be taxed at ordinary income rates when accrued, but taxes would not need to be paid until the taxpayer wished. Unpaid liabilities, however, would be accumulated at interest. Taxpayers could expense capital assets, obviating the need to index depreciation. During boom periods taxpayers would presumably choose to pay off their liabilities; in bad years they would defer payments. As a result, cumulative averaging would encourage taxpayers to act as automatic stabilizers.

George Tolley called for a comparison of results reported in this paper with those that would be obtained from other models. Arthur Okun, Roger Brinner, and Edward Gramlich all doubted that the results would differ, except possibly to show smaller effects from indexing.

16. See chapter 4.

Henry Aaron raised the possibility that more extensive indexing might reduce rather than increase instability. Pointing to the results obtained by T. Nicolaus Tideman and Donald Tucker,[17] he noted that the onset of inflation seems to raise rather than lower tax liabilities of firms in the aggregate. Under these circumstances, tax base adjustments would enhance the tendency of the tax system to prevent external shocks to the price level from propagating themselves. Bossons agreed with this view, but Tolley pointed out that if all gains and losses from inflation were indexed, all adjustments to private debts would generally cancel each other, except for differences in the average rates paid by borrowers and lenders. That would leave the adjustments for depreciation and for losses on money and government bonds that unambiguously would tend to reduce tax liabilities.

Vito Tanzi reminded the conference that in many countries the absence of indexing is regarded as inflationary because workers try to keep their disposable income constant. Robert Gordon referred to empirical work for the United States that suggests that wages rise by about 20 percent of any increase in personal income taxes.[18] Arnold Lovell said that he thought Gordon's estimates would have been roughly correct for the United Kingdom when inflation was modest, but that the fraction shifted forward had risen with the rate of inflation. Kenneth Messere reported that the process Tanzi described was one of the major reasons why Denmark indexed, but that Sweden preferred to retain flexibility. George Perry expressed strong a priori doubts about the process Tanzi described, because it implied that income tax increases are inflationary and that tax decreases are deflationary, a possibility he regarded as extremely remote.[19]

Pierce concluded the discussion by observing that on the basis of his and Enzler's results he felt that people would be better advised to worry about how monetary policy is formed when the economy is subjected to inflationary shocks than about the question of indexing. Monetary policy makes an enormous difference, but even if the effects of indexing are several times larger than shown in this paper, they are tiny by comparison.

17. See chapter 2.
18. See Robert J. Gordon, "Inflation in Recession and Recovery," *Brookings Papers on Economic Activity, 1:1971*, table 1, pp. 118–19.
19. For additional comments on the possibly inflationary impact of tax increases due to inflation, see the general discussion at the end of chapter 8.

CHAPTER SEVEN

Adjusting Taxable Profits for Inflation: The Foreign Experience

GEORGE E. LENT

THE United States is one of the few industrial countries of the world that has not provided for the revaluation of business accounts to reflect the worldwide inflation that has occurred since World War II. Others include Canada, the United Kingdom, and the Scandinavian countries. Austria, Belgium, France, West Germany, Italy, the Netherlands, and Spain have taken measures since 1945 to adjust for the effects of price increases on business income.[1] Ten Latin American countries beset by chronic inflation have also provided for revaluation of certain business assets, two of which included business liabilities as well. Indonesia, Israel, Japan, Korea, and several countries in Eastern Europe have recognized the effects of inflation on taxable earnings by authorizing the revaluation of various property accounts.

These revaluation plans have varied greatly as to their techniques, the accounts covered, the businesses affected, the frequency of adjust-

1. All but the Netherlands and Spain had instituted similar measures during the inflationary aftermath of World War I.

ment, and the treatment of revaluation gains (table 7-1).[2] Several countries have experimented with more than one approach over the years. Most of these countries limited the revaluation to depreciable assets, and few recognized the effect of inflation on inventories and other nonmonetary assets. Only two countries—Brazil and Chile— took account of the effects of inflation on monetary assets and liabilities.

Nature and Coverage of Plans

The great diversity in the coverage and other characteristics of revaluation schemes makes it difficult to evaluate them. It will be useful first to classify and describe them according to the scope of accounts covered.

Plans Limited to Capital Assets

Because the overriding concern was the adequacy of depreciation allowances to finance replacement under rising prices, all plans provided for the revaluation of depreciable assets or for depreciation allowances. A few covered other capital assets as well, including land and equity investments. The plans of Belgium and the Netherlands, which were similar, were intended to promote postwar reconstruction. The Belgian plan, enacted in 1947, provided for the reappraisal of industrial buildings and plant acquired before World War II but to not more than two and one-half times the value of assets on August 31, 1939, less physical depreciation.[3] In 1950 the Netherlands' plan limited the appraised values of assets acquired before 1942 to twice the 1949 depreciated book value. More recently Spain has authorized the revaluation of permanent investments.[4] Separate plans in 1961, 1964, and 1974 have covered not only fixed assets but also patent rights, shares, and fixed-interest securities as well as debts in foreign currency.

2. For a more detailed summary of these provisions, see George E. Lent, "Adjustment of Taxable Profits for Inflation," in International Monetary Fund, *Staff Papers*, vol. 22 (November 1975), pp. 641–79.

3. E. B. Nortcliffe, "Revaluation of Assets in Belgium," *Accountant*, April 23, 1949, pp. 323–26.

4. See Arthur Andersen and Co., *Tax and Trade Guide: Spain* (Arthur Andersen, 1965; 2d ed., 1972). See also Banco Central, *Boletin Informativo* (Madrid), no. 279 (November–December 1973), pp. 200 ff., and ibid., no. 280 (January–February 1974), pp. 27–31.

Table 7-1. Summary of Principal Revaluation Measures, Selected Countries, 1946–75

Country	Year	Accounts covered	Businesses included	Optional or compulsory	Method or measure
			A. Capital assets only		
Argentina	1959, 1967	Depreciable assets	All businesses	Optional	Index of nonagricultural prices
	1971–present	Depreciable assets	All businesses	Compulsory for large businesses	Index of nonagricultural prices
Belgium	1947	Prewar depreciable assets	Industrial companies	Optional	Appraisal, within specified limits
Bolivia	1972	Depreciable assets	All businesses	Optional	Depreciation of currency and building construction costs
Colombia	1960	Depreciation allowances	All businesses except proprietorships	Optional	15 percent of depreciation allowances
Indonesia	1971[a]	All fixed assets	Corporations	Optional	Depreciation of rupiah; land and buildings—indexes of prices
Israel	1958, 1964, 1969	Depreciation allowances	All businesses	Optional	Government coefficients based on depreciation of currency and building construction costs
Japan	1950–52, 1953	All fixed assets and shares	All businesses	Optional	Wholesale price index and real estate prices
	1954	All fixed assets	Large corporations	Compulsory	Wholesale price index and real estate prices
	1957	All fixed assets	Businesses excluded from 1954 act	Optional	Wholesale price index and real estate prices
Korea	1958	All fixed assets, equity investments, amortizable intangibles	Corporations (optional for others)	Compulsory	Wholesale price index
	1962	All fixed assets, equity investments, amortizable intangibles	All businesses	Optional	Wholesale price index

Table 7-1 (continued)

Country	Years	Accounts covered	Businesses included	Optional or compulsory	Method or measure
Mexico	1954	All fixed assets	All businesses in industry and agriculture	Optional	Appraisal, within specified limits
Netherlands	1950	Pre-1942 depreciable assets	All businesses	Optional	Appraisal, within specified limits
Peru	1967, 1971	All fixed assets	All businesses	Compulsory	Government coefficients; appraised value of land
Spain	1961, 1964, 1974	Fixed assets, patents, shares, and certain securities	All corporations	Optional	Government coefficients
B. Fixed assets, inventories, and other assets					
Austria	1948–53[b]	Depreciable assets and inventories	All businesses	Optional	Depreciable assets—government coefficients; inventories—adjustment of opening inventory to average price change for classes of goods
France	1948–58	Depreciable assets, inventories, investments	All businesses	Optional	Depreciable assets—index of construction costs; inventories—base-stock method
	1959	Depreciable assets, inventories, investments	Large businesses / Small businesses	Compulsory / Optional	Depreciable assets—index of construction costs; inventories —adjustment for price changes
West Germany	1949	All assets and liabilities[c]	All businesses	Compulsory	Fixed assets—appraisal; inventories—replacement cost; monetary accounts—10 percent of nominal value

Country	Year	Accounts/assets covered	Business coverage	Compulsory/optional	Method
Italy	1946, 1948	Depreciable assets, inventories, intangibles	All corporations	Compulsory	Depreciable assets—government coefficients; inventories—base-stock method
	1952	Depreciable assets, inventories, intangibles	All corporations	Optional	Depreciable assets—government coefficients; inventories—base-stock method
Uruguay	1961–present	All fixed assets and inventories	All businesses	Compulsory except for inventories	Fixed assets—separate coefficients for land and other assets; inventories—arbitrary adjustment of opening inventories
C. Comprehensive plans					
Brazil	1968–present	All accounts	All businesses	Compulsory except for working capital correction	Wholesale price index applied separately to depreciable assets and net working capital
Chile	1964–present[d]	All accounts	All businesses	Compulsory	Beginning net worth adjusted by consumer price index;[e] inventories revalued at replacement cost; net adjustment in value of certain monetary accounts and fixed investment charged to income

Source: George E. Lent, "Adjustment of Taxable Profits for Inflation," International Monetary Fund, *Staff Papers*, vol. 22 (November 1975), pp. 678–79.
a. Also 1953; details not available.
b. In 1954 monetary accounts were revalued to reflect currency reform.
c. The 1948 currency reform was applied to monetary accounts.
d. Chile has also periodically provided for voluntary revaluation of depreciable assets, subject to revaluation tax.
e. Before 1975 Chile provided for allocation of net worth adjustment, first, to capital assets, with balance to reduction of taxable income, not exceeding 20 percent of income.

Wartime inflation reduced the historical cost of Japan's industrial structure to a small fraction of its replacement cost, and in 1950 businesses were authorized to revalue depreciable assets, land, and other capital assets by the use of appropriate price indexes.[5] Because of limited response, Japan's law was extended in 1951; subsequent amendments in 1954 made revaluation compulsory for large businesses, and in 1957 businesses excluded from the 1954 act were given the option of revaluing. Korea adopted a revaluation plan in 1958 that covered certain intangible assets and investments in corporate stocks as well as depreciable assets.[6] This mandatory plan for corporations was followed in 1962 by an optional plan available to all businesses. Indonesia first introduced a revaluation plan in 1953; following the sharp inflation of the Sukarno regime, all corporations in Indonesia were authorized in 1971 to revalue their fixed assets acquired between 1960 and 1970.

Ten Latin American countries have provided for some form of revaluation of capital assets, usually by periodic legislation. Permanent plans have evolved in four of these countries; in two of them, inventories, monetary assets, and liabilities are also taken into account. In 1954 Mexico authorized all businesses engaged in industry and agriculture to increase the value of their fixed assets, but by not more than 40 percent over their 1954 book value.[7] In 1959 and 1967 Argentina enacted one-time plans for the revaluation of depreciable assets; permanent legislation in 1971 provided for annual revaluation of depreciable assets by all businesses.[8] Peru, in 1967 and 1971, required all businesses to revalue their fixed assets, including land as well as depreciable property.[9] More recently, in 1972, Bolivia permitted all businesses to revalue depreciable assets, and in 1973 it enacted legislation that authorizes the executive to provide for re-

5. For a detailed description and appraisal, see Sidney Davidson and Yasukichi Yasuba, "Asset Revaluation and Income Taxation in Japan," *National Tax Journal*, vol. 13 (March 1960), pp. 45–58.

6. See Samuel S. O. Lee, "Korean Accounting Revaluation Laws," *Accounting Review*, vol. 40 (July 1965), pp. 622–25.

7. Harvard Law School, World Tax Series, *Taxation in Mexico* (Chicago: Commerce Clearing House, 1965), sec. 6/5.1.

8. See Enrique J. Reig, *El Impuesto a los Reditos* (5th ed., Buenos Aires: Ediciones Contabilidad Moderna, 1970); and for the latest revaluation, see Law 19.742 (1971).

9. Law 18815, March 28, 1971.

valuation when the currency depreciates by more than 15 percent or prices increase by more than 15 percent.[10]

Rather than revaluing machinery, plant, and buildings, several countries have taken the simpler approach of adjusting depreciation allowances for price changes. In 1960 Colombia authorized depreciation allowances to be increased by 15 percent but by not more than 15 percent of taxable income. Israel's depreciation adjustments in 1958, 1964, and 1969 reflected the depreciation of the currency for imported goods and inflation in the price of domestic materials. Argentina introduced a similar provision in 1953.

Plans Covering Inventories and Other Nonmonetary Assets

Relatively few countries have provided for the adjustment of inventory profits arising from inflation. This is surprising since inventory gains may be no less important than historical-cost depreciation as a source of distortion in business profits. The last-in-first-out (LIFO) inventory method is available in only a few countries, including the United States, as a means of mitigating inventory profits.

France authorized annual revaluation of depreciable assets and inventories between 1945 and 1959.[11] Different provisions limiting the taxation of inventory profits have been in force in France since 1939. Between 1952 and 1959 the law exempted from tax inventory profits on a basic stock of goods—the "base-stock" method. The 1959 reform repealed the base-stock method but permitted an adjustment of taxable income for increases in the price of goods that exceeded 10 percent during the year.

For a few years in the late forties and early fifties, Austria granted firms the option of revaluing annual depreciation allowances or revaluing depreciable property on which they were based.[12] Its inventory adjustment conformed to price-level accounting. And in 1954 the revaluation of all balance sheet items accompanied a monetary reform.

10. Decree Law 11154, October 26, 1973.
11. Harvard Law School, World Tax Series, *Taxation in France* (Chicago: Commerce Clearing House, 1966), pp. 322–33; H. Peter Holzer and Hanns-Martin Schönfeld, "The French Approach to the Post-War Price Level Problem," *Accounting Review,* vol. 38 (April 1963), pp. 382–88.
12. Felix Kollaritsch, "Austria's Answer to Inflationary Profits and Taxation," *Accounting Review,* vol. 36 (July 1961), pp. 439–45.

West Germany undertook a mandatory revaluation in 1949 that covered all assets and liabilities.[13] Monetary assets and liabilities had to be written down to 10 percent of their book value to reflect the 1948 currency reform. Inventories and depreciable assets were restated at replacement cost. (Later legislation provided for deductible inventory reserves to take account of fluctuations in prices of basic raw materials.)

Italy enacted compulsory revaluation legislation in 1946, 1948, and 1951.[14] In 1952 these provisions were made optional. Depreciable assets were revalued in the conventional manner, and inventories by the base-stock method. Licenses and patents were also revalued.

In Latin America, Uruguay enacted a permanent revaluation plan in 1960 that required biennial revaluation of fixed assets by changes in the price level and permitted revaluation of opening inventories by government-determined ratios.[15] More recently, the LIFO inventory method has been authorized and revaluation has been put on an annual basis.

Comprehensive Revaluation Schemes

The schemes of Brazil and Chile are the most comprehensive of any country's in that they attempt to adjust taxable profits, not only for changes in the real values of nonmonetary accounts such as depreciable assets, but also of monetary accounts. The plan of neither country, however, conforms to the model for price-level adjustment of balance sheets proposed by the accounting profession in the United States and Great Britain.[16]

Brazil first authorized the revaluation of fixed assets in 1946 for financial reporting and then in 1956 for calculation of the excess profits tax as well; it was not until 1964, when revaluation was made mandatory, that firms were permitted to base depreciation allow-

13. H. Peter Holzer and Hanns-Martin Schönfeld, "The German Solution of the Post-War Price Level Problem," *Accounting Review,* vol. 38 (April 1963), pp. 377–81.

14. Arthur Andersen and Co., *Tax and Trade Guide: Italy* (Arthur Andersen, 1962); Harvard Law School, World Tax Series, *Taxation in Italy* (Commerce Clearing House, 1964).

15. Law 12804, November 30, 1960; Law 13420, December 2, 1965; and Law 13586, February 13, 1967.

16. The discussion of Brazil and Chile is based on a paper by Milka Casanegra de Jantscher, "Taxing Business Profits During Inflation: The Latin American Experience," *International Tax Journal,* vol. 2 (Winter 1976), pp. 128–46.

ances on revalued assets.[17] In 1968 Brazil also provided for the revaluation of so-called working capital;[18] it allowed the resulting adjustment, if negative, to be deducted from taxable profits. Because of its optional nature, the working capital adjustment has operated only to reduce taxable income.[19] This plan fails to tax net inflation gains arising from a reduction in the real value of monetary liabilities. All indexed transactions are treated in a special account. Until 1974 any excess of indexed payments over indexed receipts could be deducted from taxable income, but in 1975 net indexed gains were made taxable.[20]

Beginning in 1942 Chile enacted a succession of special provisions for the revaluation of fixed assets. In 1959, however, it adopted a unique plan for the correction of taxable income based on the adjustment of net worth at the beginning of the year for the increase in the consumer price index during the year. In 1964 this system was modified and made mandatory.

Until 1974 the amount of the adjustment had to be applied first to the revaluation of fixed assets; any remaining balance was deducted directly from taxable income but could not exceed 20 percent of such income. Beginning with 1975 sweeping changes were made in the scheme.[21] The entire net worth adjustment is now deductible from taxable income. Compensating adjustments to income, however, must be made for price-level changes in the following accounts: (1) beginning-of-year fixed assets, equity investment, patents, and copyrights; (2) inventory at replacement cost; (3) index-linked monetary accounts; and (4) monetary accounts in foreign currency. Operating results for the taxable year would reflect revalued accounts in accordance with accepted accounting principles, for example, depreciation and inventory accounting.

Chile has escaped the arbitrary limitations of its permanent system

17. Law 4357, July 16, 1964.

18. Working capital is defined as the difference between a firm's equity capital and the net book value of its fixed assets; if equity capital exceeds net fixed assets, working capital is positive; if the reverse, it is negative.

19. New legislation effective for 1975 required any revaluation gains on net working capital to be added to taxable income (Decree Law 1338, July 23, 1974), but the government later withdrew this requirement in the face of opposition (Portaria 544, October 21, 1974).

20. Before 1975 they were deducted from the gain on revaluation of working capital. See Decree Law 1338, July 23, 1974, for new provisions.

21. Decree Law 822, December 31, 1974.

by periodic provisions for the revaluation of assets. These generally permitted full price-level correction of fixed assets and inventories. Although a special tax was imposed on the resulting revaluation reserves, many taxpayers have taken advantage of these provisions. Indeed such a revaluation accompanied the new law and will greatly mitigate its effect of taxing unrealized gains as ordinary income.

Revaluation Techniques

Most countries limited revaluation to depreciable property; a few included land and such other permanent investments as licenses, patent rights, and equity interests. Different adjustment methods and various price indexes or other measures were used in these revaluations.

Depreciable Property

Revaluations in several countries immediately after World War II —in Belgium, Germany, Mexico, and the Netherlands—were based on company appraisals of the depreciated replacement cost of prewar assets. Most countries imposed overall ceilings or other limits. With the exception of Mexico, these one-time appraisals were closely tied in with postwar reconstruction plans and are not suitable to recurrent inflationary conditions.

The conventional revaluation method entails multiplication of the historical cost of less than fully depreciated assets by ratios of a current price index to that of the year of acquisition; depreciation reserves are adjusted by corresponding price changes. Bolivia, by contrast, provides for a uniform adjustment regardless of the age of the assets.

Several countries have avoided revaluation of assets and have simply adjusted depreciation allowances for yearly changes in prices. Austria and Argentina have given firms the option of revaluing assets or adjusting annual depreciation allowances for price changes. A committee on taxation and inflation appointed by the Australian government recommended in 1975 that depreciation allowances be adjusted by price coefficients based on the year of acquisition of the asset, without requiring the revaluation of assets.[22]

22. "Inflation and Taxation," Report of Committee of Inquiry into Inflation and Taxation (Canberra: Australian Government Publishing Service, 1975; processed), pp. 577–85.

To enable firms to recover for tax purposes their investment in depreciable property in money of the same purchasing power with which it was acquired, the index used in adjusting historical costs must be based on the prices of property of the same nature. Despite divergence in the prices of different classes of depreciable property, most countries use a single price index for industrial goods or the cost of construction. The government usually issues coefficients based on price (or cost) changes from previous years of acquisition. Some base such coefficients on construction cost (France), wholesale prices of nonagricultural commodities (Argentina), other general indexes of wholesale prices (Austria, Brazil, Japan, Korea, Uruguay), or exchange rates (for example, Bolivia, Indonesia, Mexico) when capital equipment is mostly imported. A few countries (Bolivia, Indonesia, Uruguay) have handled structures separately when building costs departed significantly from the general measures.

Chile has applied a general monetary correction based on an index of consumer prices. Brazil employs a wholesale price index not only for the adjustment of balance sheet accounts but also for its more general monetary correction system covering debt, rentals, and so forth.

Some countries have provided for flexibility in both the selection of assets for revaluation and the degree of adjustment within the limits of the announced official price coefficients. In France, for example, companies could postpone full application of the allowable increases, and until recently Uruguay issued maximum and minimum coefficients that could be elected.

Inventories

Relatively few countries have recognized the effects of inflation on profits from inventory investment. The LIFO inventory method is used in few countries other than the United States. France and the Netherlands employ the base-stock method; according to this method, only inventories in excess of a permanent investment level are taken into account in reckoning the cost of goods sold so that in an inflationary situation windfall profits on the base stock are not reflected. Austria and Uruguay have authorized arbitrary adjustment of opening inventories for yearly changes in the price level. Chile allows revaluation of opening inventories at current replacement cost. By 1951 Austria had developed a replacement-cost technique that also took into account inventory turnover: opening inventories for each category of goods were adjusted by 90 percent of the difference between unit values at the beginning and end of the period reduced by a factor that varied directly with the rate of turnover.[23] A similar technique, which does not adjust closing inventories, was recommended by the Australian Committee of Inquiry into Inflation and Taxation because of its simplicity.[24]

Monetary Assets and Liabilities

Several countries have recognized the effects of inflation in reducing the real value of debt used to finance capital assets, but none had fully provided for the correction of monetary accounts—either assets or liabilities—for inflation until Chile did so in 1975. The closest approximation had been Brazil's so-called working capital adjustment.

Brazil's working capital adjustment represented an attempt to revalue the net worth of a business at the beginning of the year for the increase in the general price level. But as fixed assets were revalued separately under Brazil's two-phase system, their unadjusted net book value was deducted from net worth. If the residual "net working capital" was positive (that is, if the net worth exceeded the net book value of fixed assets), the monetary correction could be deducted from net taxable income; if negative, the firm was not required to add the monetary correction to its taxable income. An attempt to correct this bias by a symmetrical application of the principle to negative as well as to positive "net working capital" was frustrated by business opposition.

For a decade, 1964–74, Chile provided for a mandatory price-level adjustment of net worth that reflected both nonmonetary and monetary assets. But as noted earlier, the monetary correction had to be applied first to the increase in the value of fixed assets, and the balance, if any, was used to reduce taxable income within a 20 percent limit. As in Brazil, the adjustment was asymmetrical, resulting only in a reduction of taxable income.

Chile's new legislation, effective with the taxable year 1975, represents a radical departure, not only from the previous system, but also from the model scheme supported by the American and British ac-

23. Kollaritsch, "Austria's Answer to Inflationary Profits and Taxation," pp. 443–44.

24. "Inflation and Taxation," pp. 569–76.

counting profession. By providing for a deduction from taxable income of the reduction in the real value of net worth at the beginning of the year due to price changes during the year, the government ensures that any reductions in the owners' equity capital will be restored from earnings before they are subject to taxation. This tax benefit is offset, however, by the taxation of any appreciation in the value of a firm's fixed assets and inventories at the end of the year, plus or minus the net change in the value of monetary assets and liabilities that are indexed or expressed in foreign currencies. Although the firm also has the benefit of higher operating costs for depreciation and inventories due to the price level adjustment, the tax on the nominal appreciation in value of fixed assets may offset tax reductions implicit in these factors and the monetary correction for net worth. It will be of interest to see how this new plan survives in a country that has experienced uncontrolled inflation.

Mandatory versus Elective Revaluation

Most revaluation provisions have extended to all businesses. Exceptions are found in Indonesia, where the 1971 plan was limited to corporations; in Belgium, where only industrial companies could elect the provisions; and in Mexico, where revaluation was restricted to industrial, agricultural, and fishing industries.

Policies differ among countries and over time on whether revaluation should be mandatory or optional. Most occasional revaluation plans have been optional, and in some countries discretion has extended even to the assets selected. In several countries voluntary plans have culminated in compulsory revaluation for large companies; for example, Japan's 1954 plan, France's 1959 legislation, and Argentina's 1972 provisions required all large companies to revalue their fixed assets. Smaller companies could generally elect. On the other hand, earlier compulsory provisions in Italy and Korea were followed by voluntary plans.

All Latin American annual revaluation plans are obligatory for all businesses, except in Argentina, but not necessarily for all accounts. Argentina's permanent legislation is limited to depreciable assets and is mandatory only for large companies. Uruguay requires annual revaluation of fixed assets but inventory revaluation is optional; Brazil's working capital correction has been discretionary.

Mandatory revaluation of assets, especially for large corporations, is usually dictated by financial accounting rather than tax purposes. When historical costs no longer reflect real values because of inflated price levels, it is believed necessary to disclose in financial statements the new values for financial analysis and regulatory purposes. While the same rule should be applicable in principle to all businesses, its restriction to large businesses may be explained both by the greater public interest in large enterprises and the difficulty of compliance by most small businesses.

Few small businesses have elected revaluation when they have had the option. In France, for example, only 10–12 percent of all businesses and about one-third of all corporations assessed on the basis of accounting income chose to revalue through 1960.[25] And in Japan only about 22 percent of the qualified juridical persons revalued under the 1950–51 legislation, although they accounted for about 72 percent of the potential revaluation that could be claimed.[26] The limited response in these countries may be ascribed in part to the special tax penalty on revaluation; this appears to have been true also in Indonesia, where no corporation availed itself of the revaluation privilege, and where there was a 10 percent tax on the revaluation gain. Widespread evasion of Korea's compulsory revaluation in 1958 is also reported, and the 1962 provision was made optional.[27] On the other hand, virtually all eligible companies in Belgium are reported to have taken advantage of the revaluation law.[28]

Taxation of Revaluation Gains

A number of countries have imposed a special tax on the reserve arising from the write-up in the value of assets; this tax has varied from a nominal rate of 0.5 percent to 10 percent as follows:[29]

25. *Foreign Tax Policies and Economic Growth,* A Conference Report of the National Bureau of Economic Research and the Brookings Institution (Columbia University Press for the National Bureau of Economic Research, 1966), p. 310.

26. Davidson and Yasuba, "Asset Revaluation and Income Taxation," pp. 50–51.

27. Lee, "Korean Accounting Revaluation Laws," p. 624.

28. Taxation and Research Committee, Association of Certified and Corporate Accountants, *Accounting for Inflation* (London: Gee and Company, 1952), p. 109.

29. Argentine rates were 3 to 10 percent on half of the increase in value. The French 5 percent rate applied only to debt-financed assets.

Country	Rate (percent)	Country	Rate (percent)
Korea	1 (later 0.5)	Bolivia	5
Spain	1.5	Japan	6 (later 3)
Argentina	1.5–5	Chile	10
France	3 (later 5)	Indonesia	10
		Peru	10

Increases in the book value of assets attributable to inflation do not reflect increases in real wealth. The taxation of revaluation gains is therefore inconsistent with the objectives of revaluation, and if the rate were high enough, the income tax benefits would be nullified. For example, Japan's 6 percent tax rate greatly narrowed the tax benefits on assets with a useful life of over fifty years.[30] The 10 percent rate applied in several countries greatly erodes the tax savings, depending on the rate of discount assumed on the depreciation allowances. The impact of the revaluation on liquidity was mitigated in some countries (for example, Indonesia and Japan) by extending payment of the tax over several years.

On the other hand, revaluation plans limited to depreciable assets give only partial recognition to the effects of inflation on real business income. Liabilities payable in depreciated money represent business gains that often offset the higher replacement costs of business assets. Failure to recognize this by adjusting the price level of liabilities correspondingly gives an undue tax advantage to firms that finance their assets by borrowing. Several countries (for example, France, Korea, and Spain) have justified a special revaluation tax on these grounds.

Annual versus Periodic Revaluations

Many of the revaluation measures were undertaken as part of a national stabilization program following the postwar disruption of the economy. Because of hyperinflation, financial statements based on historical costs departed significantly from real values, and their restatement at current values was believed necessary for both financial reporting and tax purposes. While in some countries (Belgium,

30. Davidson and Yasuba, "Asset Revaluation and Income Taxation," pp. 51, 53.

the Netherlands, and Germany) revaluation was a one-time measure to assist in the postwar rehabilitation of industrial facilities, in other countries the persistence of inflationary forces dictated annual price-level adjustments until the inflation abated (Austria, France, and Italy). Only in South America, where inflation has remained uncontrolled in several countries (Argentina, Brazil, Chile, and Uruguay), has revaluation been accepted as a permanent system.

Whether revaluation should be undertaken step by step in response to rising price trends or whether it should be accepted as a permanent accounting principle depends largely on the long-range economic outlook for the stabilization of prices. Policy in this respect has been rather pragmatic, depending on the exigencies of the economic situation. When prices have risen sharply because of national emergencies or a deteriorating economic situation, a one-time correction of asset values has been found essential to the reestablishment of realistic relationships between business costs and prices. The adoption of a permanent price-level accounting system in effect is a recognition of the uncontrollable nature of the inflationary process. One of the consequences is a built-in budget deficit, which further feeds inflation unless the revenue loss is offset from other sources.

Administrative Problems

Any major departure from conventional accounting principles is bound to increase the problem of compliance and the administration of an income tax. This is especially true of revaluation schemes that superimpose new techniques on existing accounting standards for the determination of taxable income and that sometimes require the observance of related rules governing the distribution and capitalization of revaluation gains. The effective use of revaluation provisions therefore rests largely on the quality of the accounts that are maintained in the country. Recognition of this fact is seen in the adoption of elective schemes in most countries and, where mandatory, their limitation to corporations or large businesses. While other considerations influenced the election of revaluation, the accounting requirements undoubtedly played a major role in the relatively low proportion of small businesses that opted for the provisions in France and Japan and the lack of compliance in Korea. On the other hand, it is reported that the 1947 revaluation in Belgium was carried out very smoothly.

Revaluation schemes have varied in their complexity, depending on the scope of the assets and other accounts covered, the frequency of revaluation, related provisions such as taxation of revaluation gains, and restrictions on their distribution. One-time plans limited to the revaluation of fixed assets pose fewer problems than continuing plans. The comprehensive revaluation schemes instituted by Brazil and Chile compound the problems of compliance as well as of administration. This is especially true with the introduction of refinements related to the nature of debt obligations (as in Brazil) and limitations on benefits (as in Chile). Periodic modifications of the law to meet changing conditions and the emergence of unforeseen technical problems have had a cumulative effect on the burden of compliance and administration.

The indexing of inventories presents special problems of enforcement because of the greater opportunities for manipulation. It is especially difficult to ascertain the various components of inventories and to be certain that the appropriate price index has been applied. The base-stock inventory method employed in European countries is relatively simple but does not lend itself to businesses with highly diversified goods and high turnover—department stores, for example. The LIFO inventory method substantially eliminates inventory profits and, once established, is not difficult to apply. Australia's Committee of Inquiry into Inflation and Taxation decided to revalue opening inventories by average unit book prices at the end of the year because this technique was considered to be simpler than the LIFO inventory method.

Summary and Conclusions

Because conventional accounting principles are based on historical costs, financial statements increasingly depart from reality during inflation. Unless adjusted for changes in the price level, taxable earnings are apt to be distorted. Since World War II more than twenty countries have provided for the revaluation of business accounts to reflect current prices, usually as part of an economic stabilization program. Some important industrial countries, however—including Canada, the Scandinavian countries, the United States, and the United Kingdom—have avoided such measures in favor of other provisions for income tax relief, such as accelerated depreciation, investment allowances, and special inventory measures.

The revaluation of plant and equipment to reflect current replacement costs increases depreciation allowances and reduces taxable income. Some countries also have adopted provisions for the elimination of inventory profits attributable to rising prices; these generally took the form of the base-stock inventory methods or revaluation of opening inventories rather than the LIFO inventory method adopted by the United States. Although two countries—Brazil and Chile—have recognized that inflation also affects the real value of monetary accounts and results in monetary gains from debt, none has fully implemented price-level accounting that taxes such gains. Several countries have imposed taxes on the revaluation gains reflected in financial statements that have partially offset the income tax benefits realized.

Revaluation systems have sometimes been selective in the eligibility of different forms and industrial classes of business. Some systems have been mandatory, especially for large corporations, but most have been optional. When they are optional, small businesses generally have chosen not to revalue.

In most countries revaluation has been introduced as a one-time measure to allow businesses to catch up with an inflationary episode; under persistent inflationary conditions the period has either been extended or the revaluation has been followed by successive revaluations. Several countries in Latin America have enacted permanent legislation requiring annual price level accounting, either limited to capital assets or including as well certain monetary accounts and inventories.

It is significant that these continuing plans have all succeeded periodic revaluation measures to keep in step with chronic inflation. Together with the indexing of wages, interest, rents, and personal income tax, they recognize inflation as a permanent feature of economic life to which a continuous adjustment has to be made. At what rate of inflation the introduction of permanent legislation for indexation can be justified is a decision that rests largely on the prospects for controlling it by restrictive monetary and fiscal policies. One-time revaluation measures may be dictated by the exigencies of rising prices without fully surrendering to inflationary forces, even recognizing that revaluation adds to inflationary pressures.

Despite the wide experience with revaluation, little analysis has been made of its effects on business investment, economic stability, allocation of resources, or indeed, revenue loss. The wide variation in the legislative provisions of foreign countries would make it difficult to arrive at any general conclusions as a guide to policy in the United States. Further consideration of price-level accounting would also have to take into account questions of equity as well as the administrative feasibility of alternative techniques for providing tax relief to business.

CHAPTER EIGHT

Adjusting Personal Income Taxes for Inflation: The Foreign Experience

VITO TANZI

THE INCREASE in an individual's personal income taxes due to inflation depends not only on the rates of inflation and the growth of real income but also on the taxpayer's initial income, his family status, the composition of his income, and the lags in tax collection. Empirical studies for Australia, Canada, the United Kingdom, and the United States have produced three similar findings regarding the effect of inflation on tax rates.[1] First, inflation increases the average income tax rate at all levels of real taxable income. Second, lower-income taxpayers and those with more dependents have generally

1. Taxation Review Committee, *Full Report, 31 January 1975* (Canberra: Australian Government Publishing Service, 1975), pp. 47–55; George Vukelich, "The Effect of Inflation on Real Tax Rates," *Canadian Tax Journal,* vol. 20 (July–August 1972), pp. 327–42; R. I. G. Allen and D. Savage, "Inflation and the Personal Income Tax," *National Institute Economic Review,* no. 70 (November 1974), pp. 61–74; and Charles J. Goetz and Warren E. Weber, "Intertemporal Changes in Real Federal Income Tax Rates, 1954–70," *National Tax Journal,* vol. 24 (March 1971), pp. 51–63.

experienced larger *percentage* increases in average tax than have high-income families or those with few dependents, both because inflation erodes the real value of exemptions and because the rate structures are progressive. But the percentage reduction in disposable income caused by inflation-induced tax increases, a more meaningful measure of the effect of inflation, has shown no simple pattern.[2] Third, discretionary tax changes frequently have not fully removed the effects of inflation.

Analytical Description of Adjustment Schemes

A well-designed adjustment scheme for inflation should be simple and should make the tax burden imposed on given real income independent of inflation regardless of the source of income and of the taxpayer's family situation.[3] Four different schemes have been proposed to index the tax system; only the last two described below, even in theory, could satisfy the conditions for a well-designed scheme.

Under the first, all statutory tax rates would be lowered proportionately to eliminate the increase in revenue due to inflation. This adjustment could prevent the growth in the average personal tax rate, but it would not prevent the unintended and undesired redistribution of tax burdens among taxpayers. For example, a relatively poor family that became subject to personal income taxation for the first time because of inflation would remain taxable even if statutory rates were reduced. By contrast, top-bracket taxpayers would benefit from progressively lower marginal tax rates. Several countries have cut rates during inflation, but none have based indexing on this method.

The second scheme would exempt the increase in income attributa-

2. See chapter 5 and discussion. It should also be pointed out that in these studies no attempt has been made to estimate the distorting effects of inflation among taxpayers who have different types (and not just levels) of income and who are subjected to different methods of tax assessment and collection. Thus the studies have dealt with only part of the problem.

3. For earlier descriptions of some adjustment schemes and their use in several countries, see Amalio H. Petrei, "Inflation Adjustment Schemes under the Personal Income Tax," in International Monetary Fund, *Staff Papers,* vol. 22 (July 1975), pp. 539–64; and David R. Morgan, "Inflation and Progressive Personal Taxation" (1974; processed). Some of the country data in this chapter comes from Petrei and Morgan and from Organisation for Economic Co-operation and Development, *The Adjustment of Personal Income Tax Systems for Inflation* (Paris: OECD, 1976).

ble to inflation, such as cost-of-living adjustments in wages and salaries. Alternatively, this inflation deduction could be calculated by multiplying the taxpayer's gross income in the previous year by the inflation rate for the taxable year.[4] This scheme is unsatisfactory because taxable income would remain constant in nominal terms but would decline in real terms. Consequently real tax payments and the average effective tax rate would also fall.

By 1975 only Israel had adopted such a scheme. Israel's plan, however, was neither automatic nor complete since it exempted only the cost-of-living adjustment component of wages and salaries at the discretion of the Ministry of Finance. Until March 1964 exemption was total; after that it was partial. In July 1975 a comprehensive tax reform abolished this system and replaced it with one similar to the fourth scheme discussed below.

The third scheme would deflate adjusted gross income to a base year; then taxable income would be calculated and the resulting tax liability would be multiplied by the ratio of the price index of the taxable year to the price index of the base year. The apparent complexity of this approach has so far prevented its adoption in any country.[5] However, one of the Swiss cantons, Basel-Land, does follow this approach and uses the cost-of-living index for January 1953 as the base.

The fourth scheme introduces price escalators into the income tax structure so that income tax rates apply to constant *real* incomes rather than to constant *nominal* incomes. The brackets, exemptions, and deductions expressed in fixed monetary values are increased annually at a rate equal to the rate of inflation. This scheme has received more support than any other and to varying degrees has been introduced and used in a number of countries, most recently in Canada in 1974.[6]

Some of these countries—Canada, for example—allow for full

4. See Douglas Adie and Svetozar Pejovich, "Inflation and Taxes: A Case for the Taxpayer" (Ohio University, March 1973; processed).

5. This scheme was suggested in Amotz Morag, *On Taxes and Inflation* (Random House, 1965), pp. 154–68.

6. In the United States this adjustment mechanism is usually associated with the name of Milton Friedman who backed it in his *Newsweek* column on March 3, 1969 (p. 76). A later elaboration is found in Milton Friedman, "Monetary Correction," in Herbert Giersch and others, *Essays on Inflation and Indexation* (American Enterprise Institute for Public Policy Research, 1974), pp. 25–61.

adjustment for inflation on an annual basis. Others, such as the Netherlands, make annual adjustments but only for part of the inflationary change. Still others adjust the tax structure only when inflation in a particular year has exceeded a stated rate—say, 5 percent (for example, France); under this variant, creeping inflation would not trigger any automatic adjustments regardless of the cumulative change in prices.[7] Finally, adjustment may occur automatically only when the cumulative increase in prices from a base year has reached a certain level, as in Luxembourg, for example.

Only the first alternative, properly applied, would maintain the structure of effective real tax rates. When inflation is rapid, however, the difference between the first alternative and the third and fourth disappears.

If inflation is accompanied by real growth in per capita income, the ratio of real taxes to gross national product increases and the distribution of collections among tax brackets changes. Only if the adjustment were made with an index based on per capita nominal income would the tax ratio remain constant. Indexing only for inflation is tantamount to accepting a rise in the ratio of personal income taxes to national income and the inevitable redistribution of the income tax burden when both are due to real growth but rejecting them if they are due to inflation. Iceland, since 1966, and Denmark, since 1974, have not accepted this conclusion and have indexed their income tax structure accordingly.[8]

Some Problems with Adjustment Schemes

The most important issues any indexing scheme must resolve are the choice of the index to be used for adjusting the rate structure; how to handle indirect taxes; the problem of lags; and the difficulties posed by such hard-to-index incomes as interest payments, capital gains, and profits.

Choosing the Index

The choice of the index depends to a large extent on the objective to be achieved through indexing.[9] The consumer price index (CPI)

7. This alternative is similar to that suggested by A. R. Prest in "Inflation and the Public Finances," *Three Banks Review,* no. 97 (March 1973), p. 26.

8. For a proposal and discussion of such a superindexing scheme, see Vito Tanzi, "A Proposal for a Dynamically Self-Adjusting Personal Income Tax," *Public Finance,* vol. 21, no. 4 (1966), pp. 507–19.

9. See chapter 9 and discussion.

has been used more often than any other because it is supposed to reflect changes in purchasing power. But several studies have shown that the basket of goods included in this index may not be, and in many cases almost certainly is not, representative of purchases by typical taxpayers, and possibly by any taxpayers.[10]

No country has tried to generate special indexes for different income classes. The Netherlands, however, has constructed a special "total population index" that is supposed to reflect the expenditure of the whole population better than the CPI does.[11]

Indirect Taxes

Should the index reflect changes in indirect taxes and perhaps in subsidies? If indirect taxes are raised, should the income tax structure be adjusted, causing an automatic decrease in income tax liability? The standard position has been that if the revenues from indirect taxes are reflected in higher government spending, which presumably increases the welfare of the taxpayers, the index should not reflect the change in indirect taxes. Others have held that taxpayers generally do not connect higher taxes with higher benefits from public spending and do not distinguish an increase in the consumer price due to an increase in taxes from one due to other factors. If this position is correct, no adjustment in the index ought to be made.

This issue is significant because most of the countries that now index their income taxes derive substantial revenues from excise and sales taxes. In the Netherlands, where the index is adjusted for changes in indirect taxes and subsidies, the differences between the

10. For example, see D. G. Tipping, "Price Changes and Income Distribution," *Applied Statistics,* vol. 19, no. 1 (1970), pp. 1–17; John Muellbauer, "Prices and Inequality: The United Kingdom Experience," *Economic Journal,* vol. 84 (March 1974), pp. 32–55; Ryotaro Iochi, *Measurement of Consumer Price Changes by Income Class* (Tokyo: Kinikuniyo Book Co., 1964); Y. Manzly, "Price Changes in the Consumption Baskets of Various Income Groups in Israel," Bank of Israel Research Department, *Economic Review,* no. 41 (April 1974), pp. 35–55; and Eleanor M. Snyder, "Cost of Living Indexes for Special Classes of Consumers," in National Bureau of Economic Research, Price Statistics Review Committee, *The Price Statistics of the Federal Government,* General Series 73 (NBER, 1961).

11. Because Dutch food prices have risen less rapidly than others in recent years, the increase of the total population index has been slightly more rapid than that of the CPI. For the 1972–74 period, annual increases in the CPI were 7.8, 8.0, and 9.6 percent, respectively, while for the total population index they were 8.0, 8.1, and 9.8 percent. The adjustments in the tax system were based on this total population index, but they were also affected by the changes in indirect taxes and the economic considerations discussed in the text.

corrected and uncorrected total population index have been significant. In 1972, for example, the total population index changed 5.7 percent with the correction for the change in indirect taxes and subsidies and 8 percent without it.[12] Under the Danish index "taxes and duties are, to the extent possible, deducted from the prices collected, whereas subsidies provided in order to achieve a general price reduction are added to the prices."[13] In contrast, Canada chose not to adjust the consumer price index on the ground that in a federal country, where various provincial governments can change sales taxes, adjustments for changes in taxes would be very difficult and perhaps inequitable.

The Problem of Lags

Two types of lags are relevant to the adjustment of taxation for inflation: the lag between the current inflation and the rate reflected in the adjustment index, and the lag between the earning of income and the collection of taxes. The first is more important, can be long, and can create difficulties, especially when inflation is rapid and changing.

Canada decided that, given the time needed to prepare the income tax forms, the adjustment in rates for each year should be based on the increase in the average price level between two twelve-month periods, one ending on September 30 in the preceding year, one ending on September 30 the year before that. Thus the index to be used in 1974 would reflect the average increase for the twelve-month period that ended September 30, 1973, over the twelve-month period that ended September 30, 1972. For the Netherlands the lag is even longer since the index for a given year reflects the change in prices for the twelve-month period ending in July of the previous year over the twelve-month period ending July of the year before that. Substantial lags exist in all the other countries that index their tax systems.

Hard-to-Index Incomes

Rules for indexing have generally been discussed and applied in foreign countries as if all types of incomes were equally affected by

12. In 1973 the difference was somewhat smaller: 7.8 and 8.1 percent, respectively. In 1974 no adjustment was made.

13. _Statistiske Efterretninger: Konjunkturoversigt_ (Statistical News: Economic Trends), no. 1 (Copenhagen: April 1975), p. 89. In 1973 the increase in the CPI in Denmark was 14.4 percent (January 1973–January 1974), while the increase in the wage-regulating price index was 12.9 percent. For January 1974–January 1975 the corresponding increases were 13.5 and 14.4 percent. (Ibid., p. 45.)

inflation. The truth is that different types of incomes are differently affected by inflation.[14]

Only a few foreign countries have worried much about indexing the personal income tax base. Perhaps as a crude adjustment for the impact of inflation on interest income, Canada, since 1974, the year when indexing was introduced, has permitted individuals to exclude annually up to $1,000 of interest income from Canadian sources.[15] Under Brazilian indexed loans, borrowers must return to lenders a principal amount, in addition to normal interest payments, adjusted for price change over the period of the loan. Only the interest payment is taxed. Before 1974 Colombian law required the borrower to pay not only the agreed upon interest but also a monetary correction at the end of each period as compensation for inflation; only the agreed upon interest was subject to the income tax.[16] Chilean and Israeli indexed loans carry similar provisions. Some other countries, including Finland, France, and recently the United Kingdom, have at times issued indexed loans that have carried particular tax advantages.

Few countries tax capital gains. In those that do, two adjustment mechanisms for illusory capital gains have been frequently suggested and in a few cases used. The first would reduce the proportion of the realized capital gain that would be taxed, or the tax payment itself, the longer the holding period. In Colombia the tax on capital gains from the sale of owner-occupied homes is reduced 10 percent for each year, beyond two, the house has been held.[17]

Under the more common method, the base value of the capital asset is increased in proportion to the rise in prices over the holding

14. See chapters 1, 4, and 11.

15. Canadian Tax Foundation, *The National Finances, 1974–1975* (Toronto: The Foundation, 1975), p. 36.

16. Colombia has not indexed its tax system and has now discontinued the use of indexed loans. For indexing in Colombia and Brazil, see Alexandre Kafka, "Indexing for Inflation in Brazil," in Giersch and others, *Essays on Inflation and Indexation,* pp. 90–91; and Albert Goltz and Desmond Lachman, "Monetary Correction and Colombia's Savings and Loan System," *Finance and Development,* vol. 11 (September 1974), pp. 24–26. For a more detailed discussion of these experiences and of the taxation of interest income under inflationary situations, see Vito Tanzi, "Inflation, Indexation and Interest Income Taxation," Banca Nazionale del Lavoro, *Quarterly Review,* no. 116 (March 1976), pp. 64–76.

17. See chapter 4 for a demonstration of the flaws in this approach. See also Taxation Review Committee, *Full Report,* chap. 23. The information on Colombia is from Alleeito Silva, *Manual de la Reforma Tributaria* (Bogota: Legislacion Economica Ltda, 1975), p. 43.

period as measured by the CPI or by some other suitable index. The taxable gain is the difference between the selling price and the adjusted base value. Both Argentina and Sweden apply this method to gains from the sale of real property held more than two years. Argentina uses a wholesale price index that excludes the agricultural sector to adjust the basis. In Sweden the National Tax Board annually fixes coefficients for the adjustment. Chile formerly used this method but discontinued it because, after the adjustment of the base, many gains became losses.

Practical Applications of Indexing in Foreign Countries

Countries that index their income tax rate structure fall into three groups on the basis of the type of adjustment made. For the first, the connection between the adjustment and the rate of inflation is direct and complete, apart from discrepancies introduced by the special problems mentioned in the previous section. In the second group, adjustments entail substantial discretion. The third group consists of countries whose inflationary adjustments are so partial that one is hesitant to label them as indexing for inflation.

Full, Annual, Automatic Inflationary Adjustments

Only two countries—Canada and Uruguay—fully, annually, and automatically increase exemptions, deductions in fixed amounts, and the rate brackets to reflect the change in a cost-of-living index.

The Canadian scheme has more relevance for the United States than any other. It went into effect on January 1, 1974, with a 6.6 percent adjustment of the whole nominal structure of the personal income tax. For 1975 the increase in exemption levels and in bracket limits due to indexing was 10.1 percent. The *absolute* tax reductions increase with income and became progressively larger between 1974 and 1975. The percentage reductions in tax liabilities are much greater for smaller incomes than for larger ones, but the ratio of tax reduction to before-tax incomes is similar at most income levels.[18] Indexing reduced income tax revenues about 400 million Canadian dollars in 1974 and $750 million in 1975.

18. This pattern is fairly common in the other countries that have indexed the personal income tax.

The Uruguayan scheme was almost identical to the Canadian one.[19] The income tax structure was adjusted fully, annually, and automatically for the change in the cost of living. Only the personal exemption and dependent allowance were adjusted, but since the brackets were expressed as multiples of the personal exemption, the whole structure was indirectly indexed.

Partial Indexing for Inflation

Partial systems of indexing are used by France, Luxembourg, the Netherlands, Israel, and Argentina.

The French have combined indexing with redistribution of the tax burden. Since 1968 the structure of the French personal income tax has been adjusted in any year during which inflation exceeds 5 percent. No adjustment is required if inflation remains below 5 percent. The authorities may adjust various brackets differently. For example, between 1968 and 1972, while the CPI rose by 25.5 percent, the maximum income subject to the lowest marginal rates rose by 31.6 percent, while maximum income subject to the highest rate rose 20.2 percent. At the same time, all rates were lowered three percentage points. In 1974 all brackets were raised by 12 percent.

The French plan demonstrates that adjustments need not be annual but may occur only when the rate of inflation exceeds a predetermined threshold. The shortcoming of this approach is its failure to deal with creeping inflation, which after several years could seriously distort the structure of the tax without triggering a correction.

Luxembourg provides that "if the average price index . . . for the first six months of a year varies by at least 5 per cent from its average level in the first six months of the previous year," the government will recommend a revision of the nominal tax structure in proportion to the variation in the CPI.[20] In this case it is not the increase in the index in a particular year but the cumulative increase from the time the nominal tax structure was last changed that sets the mechanism in motion. Since 1968 all the brackets have been adjusted strictly in line with the change in the price level.

19. The Uruguayan system prevailed between 1968 and 1973. On January 1, 1974, the government abolished the individual income tax, although it retained a schedular tax on incomes from industry and trade. Obviously, without a tax, there can be no indexing.

20. Luxembourg, Income Tax Act of December 4, 1967, article 125 (translation from OECD, *Adjustment of Personal Income Tax Systems*, p. 15).

In contrast with practices in France and Luxembourg, Dutch legislation enacted in 1971 provided for indexing regardless of the rate of inflation or the cumulative change in the price index but limited the adjustment to 80 percent of the rise in the relevant index if, in the view of responsible authorities, "financing difficulties" would result from full indexing. This discretion was used in 1972 and 1973 when the special index for tax adjustment rose by 5.7 percent and 7.8 percent, respectively. In those two years the nominal income tax structure was increased 4.56 and 6.24 percent, respectively. In 1974 the automatic inflation adjustment was not used at all. Once again, in 1975, the increase in the nominal tax structure was 6.64 percent, although the special index increased 8.3 percent. Partial indexing means that the government can allow inflation to increase real revenues somewhat. It also permits some of the distortions in the tax incidence due to inflation to occur.

The July 1975 Israeli tax reform abolished the system of indexing that had been in existence up to that time and replaced it by one somewhat akin to that of the Dutch. As a result, the nominal structure of the income tax is now linked to the cost-of-living index. However, while the escalation of the nominal values will be full and automatic for the tax credits (which in the new law have replaced some deductions) and for the remaining tax deductions, that for the tax brackets will be less than full if the minister of finance deems it desirable.

Since 1972 Argentina has automatically indexed exemptions and deductions but has adjusted the tax brackets on an ad hoc basis. This system keeps off the tax rolls those taxpayers who, because of their very low incomes, should not be subjected to any income taxation.

Indexing Mechanisms Not Directly Related to Inflation

Unlike the countries already discussed, Brazil, Chile, Denmark, and Iceland adjust their personal income tax structures, not with a price index, but by reference to other indexes based on the earnings of industrial workers, legal minimum wages, or per capita income. In these countries indexing reflects, in some degree, changes both in prices and in such other variables as productivity, economic conditions, or governmental willingness to adjust minimum wages or basic salaries.

The Brazilian indexing system has received considerable attention recently. It was introduced in 1961 with the decision to express the personal exemptions and the upper limits of the taxable income brackets as multiples of the largest monthly minimum wage for the country. After 1964 the new government, in its attempt to stabilize the economy, chose to increase the minimum wage by less than the rate of inflation. This policy would have increased tax burdens at all income levels, a result not desired by the government. Consequently in November 1964 the link to the minimum wage was cut. A new law combined the French approach with that of Luxembourg. Income tax brackets were to be adjusted whenever inflation exceeded 10 percent in one year or 15 percent in three consecutive years. In 1967 the minister of finance was given the option of adjusting the brackets by the increase in either prices or the minimum wage. The government of Brazil has taken full advantage of this discretionary power. For example, in 1973 and 1974 the upper limits of the highest brackets were raised by 15 percent and 12 percent, respectively, while the upper limits of the lowest brackets were increased 26 percent and 41 percent, respectively. In 1975 all brackets were increased 30 percent. In Brazil, as in France, indexing has been used to achieve an objective —the redistribution of the tax burden—not immediately related to distortions caused by inflation.

In 1954 the Chilean government decided to relate the exemptions for the schedular income taxes (applied at proportional rates to different types of income) and the brackets for the global complementary tax (applied at progressive rates to the total income of the taxpayer) to the minimum wage. The minimum wage was normally, but not always, adjusted on the basis of the change in the CPI of the previous year. The link to the minimum wage was cut on December 31, 1974. The income tax is now to be adjusted on the basis of a basic tax unit (*unidad tributaria basica*) that the government is to calculate annually. No details were given on how this basic tax unit would be calculated.

The Danes enacted a new income tax law in 1969 that became effective in 1970 and introduced two novelties. First, it established four basic income tax rates, ranging from 18 percent to 45 percent; each year Parliament was required to vote whether these rates should be applied in the coming year at their basic value, should be increased (up to 5 percent), or should be reduced. The law specified that the selected rates would be levied on income brackets adjusted annually, starting in 1971, on the basis of an index reflecting changes in the cost of living, excluding the effects of indirect taxes. Between 1971 and 1974 the income brackets were increased to reflect the changes in prices, and the basic rates were applied at 91 percent of their basic values.

In 1974 the Danish Parliament voted a new schedule for individual income taxes to be used in 1975 and changed the indexing scheme. The personal deduction and brackets are now related to changes in the index for the hourly earnings of an industrial worker. This index reflects changes not only in prices but also in real wages. Thus the Danish scheme has gone beyond inflation adjustment. The change was apparently motivated by the belief that indexing for price changes alone had not prevented sharp increases in tax burdens on the middle-income groups brought about by interaction between economic growth and a very progressive structure.[21]

Conclusion

The experience of various countries with indexing supports five major conclusions. First, indexing the rate structure does not present serious administrative problems. The tax authorities can easily produce new tax tables, and taxpayers can easily compute their tax liabilities with the new tables. Second, most countries that have indexed have done so without paying any particular attention to the tax base. Indexing the rate structure has failed to deal with vexing questions of equity. Third, indexing comes in many forms; simple increases in the nominal structure are most popular. Fourth, only about a dozen countries adjust their taxes at all, and only Canada now fully and automatically indexes its income tax structure. Finally, the search for an index, responsive to the actual rather than to past rates of inflation, continues in most countries. Lags in adjustment may significantly affect economic stability, particularly if the rate of inflation fluctuates widely.

21. It has been reported that Iceland adjusts its income tax on the basis of changes in the nominal per capita income of the country. Little specific information is available, however. Several Swiss cantons—including Aargau, Basel-Land, Basel-Stadt, Graubünden, and Solothurn—have been indexing their income taxes using various indexing schemes.

Discussion

The papers by George Lent and Vito Tanzi were not discussed at the conference. During a general discussion, however, participants from abroad described practices in their countries in somewhat greater detail than was possible in the survey papers presented by Lent and Tanzi, providing useful background information regarding indexing in several nations.

Kenneth Messere of the Organisation for Economic Co-operation and Development described a recently completed analysis of indexing based on the experience of OECD countries. He suggested that a considerable distance separates myth and reality about the effects of indexing the personal income tax rate structure. Countries that have indexed the rate structure, such as Canada, Denmark, and the Netherlands, have in practice continued to make ad hoc adjustments to their tax systems. The experience of these countries would thus suggest that indexing does not necessarily remove the need for discretionary tax changes but that such countries are likely to have both automatic and discretionary changes. He also pointed out that personal income tax receipts as a fraction of GNP have grown more rapidly in Denmark and Canada than in any other OECD country. This same fraction has risen least in Austria, Italy, and Japan, where tax systems are not indexed, and in France, where indexing is partial. One might draw the paradoxical conclusion that the more rigidly the income tax system is indexed the faster receipts seem to grow. But Messere warned that causation may well run the other way—those countries in which revenues are growing most rapidly are under the greatest pressure to index. Other independent factors (for example, method of tax collection, share of agriculture in GNP) are, however, more likely to explain the rapid growth in income tax revenues in some countries, but not in others.

Messere pointed to a second paradox. Income tax receipts rose more rapidly during the period from 1965 to 1967, when prices were relatively stable, than during the period 1969 to 1971, when inflation was more pronounced. It would be desirable, Messere suggested, to carry this comparison through more recent years in order to see whether the pattern persisted.

Messere drew the lesson from these comparisons that the debates about indexing may have more in common with theological disputations than with actual tax policy—that indexing the rate structure may not really matter very much. What matters is what policies the government really wants or feels obliged to follow in practice.

Joseph Gabbay of the Israeli Ministry of Finance described some of the provisions in the Israeli comprehensive tax reform, introduced in July 1975. Before that reform the tax schedule contained many quantities specified in nominal terms. About two-thirds of the increase in average marginal tax rates in the period 1973 to 1975 was due to inflation. Before the reform Israel excluded from tax the "cost of living adjustment," an increase in wages paid because of price increases on earnings up to the median income. As a result of this provision the effective tax rate on earnings below the median actually fell during inflation, while above that income marginal rates increased.

Under the reformed law, Gabbay reported, the minister of finance can decide to what extent brackets should be linked to the price index. He is now recommending that the brackets be widened by 70 percent of the increase in prices. Credits and allowances are automatically and fully indexed. Additional discussion brought out that depreciation is not adjusted for inflation, but Israel allows a two-year write-off period. Interest income is not explicitly indexed. The Israeli government, however, issues two kinds of bonds that are partially or fully indexed. In one class of bonds (the compulsory loans) the principal is indexed, but the interest is not. In the other class (voluntary saving) both principal and interest are indexed. The capital adjustment, due to inflation, is exempt from tax in either case, while the interest is free of tax in the former case and taxable in the latter.

Real capital gains are subject to tax at rates applicable to ordinary income up to a rate of 50 percent (the maximum marginal tax rate of ordinary income is 60 percent). In addition a 10 percent tax is imposed on nominal gains.[21]

Arnold Lovell of the British Treasury suggested that the administrative difficulties involved in operating a fully indexed fiscal system raised the question whether partial indexing was better or worse than none at all. The United Kingdom's experience was that a combination of discretionary adjustment and automatic indexing could produce

21. See chapter 4 for an explanation of the full indexing of capital gains.

anomalies and friction between government policies. In the United Kingdom most government social transfer payments were indexed, unemployment benefits and the state old age pension in particular. The income tax system was adjusted periodically to take account of inflation, but within the limits set by the current economic situation facing the government. In practice the need to curb the growth of government borrowing had inhibited full adjustment for inflation to the income tax and there was a collision between the tax and the social support system. In some circumstances, for example, unemployment pay could be higher than the post-tax earnings of a man on a low income.

Indexing the income tax system was resisted on the grounds that it would reduce the government's fiscal flexibility and that fiscal drag, through its effect on real incomes, could contribute toward the elimination of inflation. Some argued, however, that indexing might reduce cost-inflationary pressures because of its impact on labor negotiations. Unions concerned about after-tax incomes might reduce their demands if taxes were indexed.

On capital gains Lovell wondered whether it was justified to index gains on realization from the sale of assets if the interest payments on assets with fixed capital values were not also indexed. These assets included the bulk of small savings. There was also the question of the erosion of indebtedness, which benefited borrowers at the expense of lenders. He reported that some tax allowance for inflation effects had been introduced in respect of company inventories. The mandatory use of first-in-first-out accounting during inflation had resulted in sizable inventory profits which had led to a sharp rise in company taxable profits and had created difficult cash flow problems for many firms. To deal with this, firms were allowed to reduce inventory valuation by subtracting the excess of the value of final inventories at end-of-year prices over the value at beginning-of-year prices, provided that the increase exceeded a profits-related threshold reflecting increases in the volume of stock.

Lovell also briefly described the recommendations of the Inflation Accounting Committee. The committee recommended that all assets should be valued at current cost determined by a professional revaluation or by price indexes linked to particular commodities. It also confirmed the case for deferring taxation on inventory profits. The result of these changes would be to reduce the taxable return on capital to possibly very low levels. How monetary assets and liabilities should be treated is still being debated.

David Morgan of the London School of Economics reported that until the early 1970s the interaction of inflation and a fixed nominal tax schedule was held to be a desirable aspect of the Australian fiscal system. When inflation accelerated from 3 percent to 16 percent in the early 1970s, people began to wonder whether the stabilizing properties of the system were as useful as they had previously thought. The large increases in revenue were suspected of encouraging increases in government expenditures and were thought to increase wage demands by workers who seemed to be bargaining for after-tax income. Furthermore, stable nominal rates during inflation meant increasing real rates. These tax increases occurred despite discretionary tax reductions that appeared large.

A government committee was established in early 1975 to examine the question of indexing. The committee strongly favored indexing the personal income tax structure but was reluctant to recommend indexing the flawed tax schedule then in effect. It suggested that the government should introduce a new schedule and index it in the future. Morgan forecast action on the committee's recommendations in 1976. The committee also recommended indexing depreciation and inventories but made no recommendations regarding monetary gains and losses. The government took no immediate action but in the August budget gave an accelerated depreciation deduction as a temporary palliative.

Victor Halberstadt of the University of Leiden reported that the Netherlands has an indexing system, but that it is in something of a mess. Vito Tanzi has given a good description of its basic structure. As he mentioned, the government may increase the brackets and allowances by 80 to 100 percent of the change in the index. In practice the full range of this discretion has been used, and then some. In 1972 and 1973 the 80 percent option was used. In 1974 the automatic adjustment was suspended for one year, but basic exemptions were increased, a step of primary benefit for low-income groups. In 1975 everything was adjusted by 80 percent of complete adjustment, plus a temporary lowering of brackets and allowances by 1.5 percent of the rate of inflation. In 1976 rates will again be adjusted by 80 percent.

It should be apparent that this "automatic" system has been very "unautomatic." The reason is that budgetary and distributional considerations were always primary, not secondary. Political leaders have been unwilling to leave these considerations to one side while some impersonal formula offset the consequences of inflation. In this connection it is important to note that the Netherlands has used relatively regressive indirect taxes to replace the revenue loss from inflation adjustments in the income tax. This switch has helped to offset any increase in progressivity in the income tax from increases in basic exemptions.

On balance, the Dutch are not happy with the automatic adjustment scheme and feel that the whole tax system now needs to be reassessed, particularly in view of the continuing inflation. A small official committee is now studying this problem but will not report for at least two years. By then the Netherlands may well have a capital gains tax and may be forced to examine many issues it has been spared thus far.

CHAPTER NINE

Price Series for Indexing the Income Tax System

EDWARD F. DENISON

INFLATION impinges on income taxation in two distinct ways.[1] First, because of personal exemptions and a progressive rate structure, inflation raises income tax revenues by a percentage that exceeds the increase in prices. As a consequence, the greater the price rise has been since the tax structure was established, the higher the ratio of government revenue from income taxes to national income or product will be. This statement presumes that the method by which income in current prices is to be measured for tax purposes, the tax structure, and the size of real output are given.

Second, income in current prices as now measured for tax purposes becomes distorted when prices change or have changed in the past. Earnings from current production become distorted principally because traditional accounting practices cause business receipts and costs to be valued at prices prevailing at a variety of times; problems associated with depreciation and inventories are best known. As computed for purposes of income taxation, profits, rents, and income

1. Inflation also affects other taxes, and some provisions of these taxes—such as ceilings on payroll taxes, exemptions and brackets in the estate tax, and rates for specific excise taxes—could be indexed. In this paper I consider only income taxes.

from unincorporated businesses do not measure income in current prices; in fact, they do not measure income in prices of *any* date. Instead they are numbers that defy definition except by reference to the method of their calculation. Taxes levied on income so measured contain a random, irrational element. In addition to income earned in current production, tax measures of capital gains and other types of income that are taxed may be distorted by inflation.

The first effect of higher prices—the disproportionate increase in government revenue—can easily be avoided. The government need only instruct taxpayers to deflate their adjusted gross income (under the personal income tax) and taxable income (under the corporation income tax) by an appropriate price index, compute their tax liability (expressed in base-year prices) by using the usual tax schedules together with this deflated income, and then multiply this liability by the same price index to secure the actual tax liability expressed in current prices. Or, equivalently, the government can multiply the amounts of exemptions and the limits to the tax brackets by this index and provide these new figures on tax schedules that can be used with incomes in current prices.[2] The effect of either procedure is to tax on the basis of real income (income expressed in prices of a specified prior year) rather than of nominal income (income expressed in prices of the current year). In my examination of the proper price index to use, I shall refer only to these procedures. In this paper I shall consider whether different price indexes should be used for different taxpayers or one index for all taxpayers, and in either case what indexes or index should be selected.

The second effect of inflation is altogether different and requires a different cure. Distortions of measures of income in current prices cannot be eliminated by any price adjustment of net income as such. In the national accounts, for example, one cannot get from "corporate profits before tax" to "corporate profits and inventory valuation adjustment" by applying a price index to the former series.[3] To eliminate distortions, one must recalculate each type of net income so that all entries are measured in current prices. For business income the alterations include, but are not necessarily limited to, valuing de-

2. The two procedures are described in George Vukelich, "The Effect of Inflation on Real Tax Rates," *Canadian Tax Journal,* vol. 20 (July–August 1972), pp. 327–42. Some minor complications are ignored here.

3. Nor can one get from the change in the book value of inventories to the value of the change in the quantity of inventories by applying a price index to the former series.

preciation at replacement cost and measuring inventory change as the change in physical quantities times their current prices. The elimination of such distortions results in figures for business income in current prices that are comparable to those initially reported for other types of income earned in current production, such as wages and salaries. Capital gains and other types of income subject to tax may require adjustment to secure acceptable measures of income in current prices. When all types of income in current prices have been corrected, the increase in the government share of income that occurs because exemptions and tax brackets are expressed in current dollars will remain. The correction of errors in the way income is defined or the appropriate price index or indexes to be used in such adjustments will not be discussed further here.

A government's decision to eliminate either of the two types of inflation effect is logically independent of its decision with respect to the other. It may choose to index the tax system so as to tax income expressed in the prices of some former year instead of in current prices, however the latter may be measured; to eliminate distortions in the measurement of income in current prices; to do neither of these things; or to do both of them. In this paper it is assumed that whatever errors are present in current price income have been corrected or else that the government is content to have those errors remain when nominal values are adjusted to a real income basis by indexing.

To discuss indexing the income tax structure, it is necessary to write as if the government had in mind the price level of some particular and known date when it set exemptions, brackets, and rates. Although I would hesitate to specify any such date now for the present tax system, this requirement poses no bar to indexing. The adoption of indexing would require legislation, and Congress and the President would surely include the base date along with the corresponding tax structure in such legislation.

In this chapter I shall advance two propositions. First, if nominal quantities in the income tax system are to be indexed in order to prevent inflation from raising the government's share of income, the same price index should be used for all taxpayers. Second, an appropriate index would be the implicit deflator for national income.[4] The mea-

4. An official deflator for national income did not exist at the time of the conference, but the Bureau of Economic Analysis has since added this series to the national accounts. See *Survey of Current Business,* vol. 56 (January 1976), pt. 2, pp. 94–95.

surement of income in current prices when inflation occurs is unrelated to such indexing, and the conclusions just cited should not be extended to it.

Why One Index Should Be Used for All Taxpayers

If nominal values are indexed, should a single general index of prices be used for all taxpayers or should different taxpayers be assigned indexes representative of the particular bundles of goods and services they buy? The latter system would be more favorable than the former to taxpayers whose prices have risen more than average.

The idea of many indexes seems to stem from a particular way of describing the purpose of indexing. For example, former Canadian Minister of Finance John N. Turner introduced the subject in the following words from his Budget Speech in the House of Commons on February 19, 1973:

If a man gets a 5 per cent raise in salary, but the cost of living has also increased 5 per cent, he has the same real purchasing power he had before, and nothing more. Yet, the progressive tax system can leave him worse off than he was before because he has entered a higher tax bracket. What I want to do is eliminate that unfair and unintended result from our tax system.

This personalization of the problem is an effective device to promote the general idea of indexing, but if read literally it points to the use of a price index of the items bought by "a man" as the index appropriate for indexing his return in order to compute that man's real purchasing power. In other words, each taxpayer should have his own separate index. Yet the case for using the same price index for all taxpayers seems overwhelming.

Tax Law Ignores Differences in Prices

The first consideration is that tax law ignores differences between the prices that taxpayers pay at a point in time—and presumably would continue to do so if indexing, including specification of a base date, were enacted. Consider, for example, geographic differences. Taxpayers with the same dollar incomes pay the same tax throughout the United States regardless of differences in their living costs. Budget data from the Bureau of Labor Statistics (BLS) show these differences to be sizable. For example, in the autumn of 1974 the price of consumption included in an intermediate budget for a four-person family averaged 12 percent higher in metropolitan areas than in urban places with 2,500 to 50,000 population. Among forty metropolitan areas, it was lowest in Austin, Texas. Compared with Austin, the price was 27 percent higher in Boston and New York, 29 percent higher in Honolulu, and 45 percent higher in Anchorage.[5] If prices rise less in Anchorage or New York than in low-cost areas so that price differentials are narrowed—which is as likely as a contrary development—this surely will create no case for raising the share of taxes borne by the already overburdened taxpayers of these cities. Again, the Manpower Administration set the poverty level (as of April 30, 1975) 15 percent lower for farm than for nonfarm families and 15 percent higher in Hawaii and 25 percent higher in Alaska than in the other forty-eight states. The level for nonfarm families in Alaska is 47 percent above that for farm families in the forty-eight contiguous states.[6]

The differentials just noted reflect mainly geographic differences in prices of the same commodities, but it is also true that tax law ignores the relative prices of different commodities. It does not matter whether the ratio of one commodity price to others is high or low by reference to some other time or place at the time tax rates are set. This statement embraces the ratio of consumer goods prices as a group to capital goods prices as well as to relative prices of the components of each group. Where a condition—in this case relative prices—has no influence in setting the initial tax structure, there is no point in introducing automatic changes in the tax structure based on changes in that condition.

Differential Price Changes Not Usually Inflation Results

Suppose we disregard the preceding discussion. It still would be incorrect to use the prices of commodities purchased by each taxpayer in indexing. Since the objective of indexing is to tax as if the general price level were stable, then only those changes in relative prices that are consequences of inflation (a change in average prices) should be taken into account. Such changes do occur, mainly if not entirely because of leads and lags. For example, prices of goods tend on the

5. *Bureau of Labor Statistics News,* USDL 75-190, April 9, 1975, table 2.
6. Federal Statistics Users' Conference, *FSUC Newsletter,* vol. 16 (June 5, 1975), p. 10.

average to jump more than prices of services if there is a sudden burst of inflation. As the rate of inflation slackens, service prices rise faster than goods prices until they have caught up or until a new burst of inflation occurs. But it is not possible to determine accurately enough for use in taxation the detailed price structure that would have prevailed each year if the price level had remained unchanged from some base year. The choice is between actual current year and actual base-year relative prices.

Major changes in relative prices result from supply and demand conditions that are not the results of changes in the general price level. While the rate of inflation may have some effect on relative prices, it seems overwhelmingly probable that most of the change in relative prices is due to supply and demand factors that are independent of changes in the price level. If this is so, it would be more desirable to use a single price index for all taxpayers rather than indexes of actual prices paid by each, *even if* one wished to take account of the effects of inflation on relative prices.

Necessity of Using Indexes for Groups Rather Than for Individual Taxpayers

Suppose we disregard both preceding points. Even if it were deemed desirable for each taxpayer to use an index of actual prices weighted by the composition of his own purchases, such a system would be impractical. At most, a small number of indexes for large groups of taxpayers classified by a few characteristics would be feasible. The deviation of an index for the individual taxpayer from an index for the group in which he is placed may average little less than the deviation from a single general price index. If so, using a single index rather than any practicable set of multiple indexes would entail little loss even if a separate index for each taxpayer were appropriate. This seems likely because available evidence, some of it reviewed in the following paragraphs, suggests that differences between indexes representing purchases of various taxpayer groups usually are moderate. When this is so it does not matter greatly whether a single index or separate group indexes are used.

Other Considerations

Two other reasons to prefer a single index may be mentioned. First, the use of a single index is desirable from a social and political standpoint to avoid divisive debates over the choice of a base year for "parity"; with multiple indexes everyone would wish to choose the year most favorable to himself. Second, and perhaps unimportant, the use of a variety of indexes for prices paid by different taxpayers might to some degree offset the effect of changes in relative prices on relative incomes and thus weaken the effectiveness of relative prices in guiding the allocation of resources.[7]

Some Index Comparisons

In Canadian and U.S. experience, the use of multiple price indexes for different income classes, rather than one index for all, would have made little difference in the past. The Economic Council of Canada divided Canadian families of two or more persons among twelve income classes and computed a consumer price index for each.[8] With 1961 = 100, the highest of the twelve indexes was never more than 2.8 percent above the lowest in January of any of the years, 1969 through 1974, for which estimates were provided. That is, 2.8 percent represented the biggest divergence that developed during periods of eight to thirteen years. Much of even this difference is attributable to an exceptionally large rise (which occurred before 1969) in the index for one income class in the middle-income range; the maximum divergence among the other eleven income classes was 1.7 percent.

In the United States, since 1967 the BLS has compiled annual family consumption budgets for four-person urban families consisting of a husband thirty-eight years of age who is employed full time, his nonworking wife, a boy of thirteen, and a girl of eight.[9] The bud-

7. This will be so if increases in a product's price exert a favorable influence on the income of the producers (owners and workers together) and if the producers allocate less of their expenditure to that product than do others. The first is surely true; the second, at most, is likely to be a weak tendency.

8. For each commodity the same price index was used for each income class. Only the weights differed. See Economic Council of Canada, *Economic Targets and Social Indicators, 1974*, Eleventh Annual Review (Ottawa: Information Canada, 1974), pp. 170–74.

9. Jean C. Brackett, "New BLS Budgets Provide Yardsticks for Measuring Family Living Costs," reprint from *Monthly Labor Review*, vol. 92 (April 1969); *Bureau of Labor Statistics News*, USDL 72-240, April 27, 1972; ibid., USDL 74-304, June 16, 1974; ibid., USDL 75-190, April 9, 1975; and undated BLS tabulations on the annual costs of lower, intermediate, and higher budgets for autumn 1972. Data used here are for consumption, not for the total budget, which also includes gifts, occupational expenses, life insurance, and social security and personal income taxes.

gets are available for lower, intermediate, and higher levels of living, separately for metropolitan and nonmetropolitan urban areas.[10] As in the Canadian data, costs of the budgets move differently only because weights are different; the same price data are used.

With the budget cost in 1967 set at 100 for each group, indexes were computed for the years 1971 to 1974. The biggest difference among the indexes was 4.6 percent; it was the difference in 1972 between the index for the higher level of living in metropolitan areas and in the index for the higher level of living in nonmetropolitan areas. This difference developed over the five years from 1967 to 1972. After 1972 the indexes came together again; by 1974 the maximum difference among the six indexes (still with 1967 = 100) was only 2.0 percent, this time between the higher and the lower budget in nonmetropolitan areas. It thus appears that differences were due mainly to leads and lags, not to persistent differences in trend. Differences between indexes for the three levels of living within metropolitan and nonmetropolitan areas were generally smaller than those between metropolitan and nonmetropolitan areas. Within metropolitan areas the maximum difference among indexes for the three budget levels (1967 = 100) was 0.4 percent or less in three of the four years 1971–74 and 1.4 percent in the other (1972). Within nonmetropolitan areas the difference between the highest and lowest indexes for the three budgets ranged from 1.9 to 2.5 percent. Most of the latter dispersion arose from 1967 to 1971; starting with 1971 as 100, the maximum dispersion in 1972–74 was 0.9 percent.

The BLS also compiles price indexes for individual metropolitan areas. These are based on actual price data for each area, so differences among them include the effect of differences in actual price movements as well as of differences in weights.[11] They show bigger spreads than indexes compared previously. With 1967 = 100, the 1974 index for New York, N.Y.–Northeast New Jersey (154.7), the highest of the twenty-five area indexes, exceeded the 1974 index for Seattle (141.5), the lowest, by 9.3 percent.[12] The New York in-

---

10. Data for metropolitan areas, for nonmetropolitan areas by region, and for all areas combined are also presented. In addition, estimates are provided for families of other sizes and ages, but they are obtained as constant multiples of the series described in the text and thus provide no evidence as to similarity of movement.

11. Data used here are from the U.S. Bureau of the Census, *Statistical Abstract of the United States, 1975* (Government Printing Office, 1975), p. 424.

12. Note that the extremes are both high-price cities.

dex is considerably above all the others. Exclusive of the extremes (New York and Seattle) the spread is 7.2 percent. Indexes for twenty-one areas are available for the longer period since 1960. If 1960 is taken as 100, the biggest spread among the indexes in any of the four years from 1971 through 1974 is 10.5 percent in 1972, the percentage by which the New York, N.Y.–Northeast New Jersey index (150.5) exceeds the index for Seattle (136.2). Exclusive of the extremes (New York and Seattle), the range was 7.2 percent. Lengthening the period from seven years to eleven-to-fourteen years thus increased the spreads only a little.

The biggest divergences between area indexes are sufficiently large over a period of a few years for it to make some difference in the distribution of the tax burden whether or not separate geographic indexes are used in indexing. The use of separate indexes for different income classes would not have much effect. At least this would be so if the indexes differed only because of weighting, and I surmise that this would also be so if actual price data were available for different income groups, except as a result of the correlation between income size and geographic area.

The indexes compared so far are representative only of the taxpayer's personal consumption. I defer discussion of what an appropriate index should cover but note that it is arguable (and I shall in fact argue) that the index should include investment goods. In that case, if a separate price index were to be used for each payer of individual income tax or for a category of such taxpayers, the index should include investment goods with a weight presumably equal to the taxpayer's net saving or perhaps his net investment in real assets. Price indexes for individual corporations under that system might be weighted averages of prices of consumer goods, given the weight of dividends, and prices of investment goods, given the weight of the corporation's net saving or net investment. No such indexes exist, but consumption and certain investment goods price indexes can be compared.[13] Over the seventeen years from 1957 through 1973 the ratio of the implicit price deflator for nonresidential fixed investment to that for personal consumption expenditures fluctuated within a range of only 3.0 percent, and the difference between the ratios in the first and last years was less than 1 percent. Over these years, the weighted

13. Data used are from the *Survey of Current Business*, vol. 55 (May 1975), and earlier issues. Data are in 1958 prices.

averages of prices of consumer goods and these investment goods would not differ much even if the weights were very different. In 1974 the ratio fell below its 1957–73 low and in the first quarter of 1975 rose above the 1957–73 high; with these dates included, the nineteen-year range (1957 through 1975) is 4.5 percent. Earlier, from 1947 to 1957, the prices of fixed nonresidential business investment had persistently risen much more than the prices of personal consumption expenditures.

Even in the 1957–73 period when this ratio was fairly stable, the prices of nonresidential structures rose far more and the prices of producers' durable equipment far less than consumer goods prices. The prices of residential structures also rose sharply, though less than nonresidential construction. There was also wide dispersion of prices for individual producers' durables. Since purchases of investment goods by individual firms and even by whole industries are concentrated in particular items, the price indexes for investment goods bought by individual business taxpayers can be expected to deviate widely from the average for all investment goods.

If the appropriate price index for all taxpayers combined is a comprehensive one covering all of the nation's output—whether measured by gross or net national product or national income—the price indexes for individual taxpayers or groups would need to include prices paid by government.[14] These prices have risen by much above average amounts.

One Index Used in Foreign Countries

Insofar as I can learn, all countries that have indexed nominal quantities in their income tax systems have chosen to use a single price index, and it appears that this choice has reflected not only administrative convenience but also a conclusion that this choice was theoretically correct.[15]

14. Some expedient, such as a proportional adjustment of indexes covering consumption and investment, would almost surely be required. Otherwise it would be necessary to allocate the benefits of government purchases among taxpayers (to secure weights) and to do so in considerable detail (to permit calculation of a government price index specific to the services benefiting each taxpayer or taxpayer group and thus comprising part of his, or its, real income).

15. Only individual income taxes have been indexed, so countries have not had to decide whether to use different indexes for individuals and corporations, or for different corporations.

Unequal Burden of Inflation Not Rectified by Indexing

The indexing of nominal values for tax purposes is sometimes supported in the belief that it will give the greatest relief to those suffering from inflation and reduce the adverse effects of inflation in this way. It is obvious that this cannot be so, except by coincidence, if a single price index is adopted.[16]

The Selection of an Appropriate Index

If it is agreed that indexing nominal values for income taxation calls for the use of a single price index, what should the characteristics of that index be?

In the following discussion the indexing of both the corporate and the individual income tax is envisaged. In the case of the corporate tax only the $25,000 and $50,000 dividing lines separating the three rates in the tax schedule need be indexed. I assume that only the main reference points in the individual income tax—at least personal exemptions and the rate bracket boundaries but perhaps also the per capita credit, the low-income allowance, the standard deduction, and the earned income credit—would be indexed.[17]

Use of Prices or Incomes?

The first question is whether the desired index is a price index at all; should it, instead, be an index of income? The answer depends on the purpose of indexing.

With exemptions and progressive rates, a rise in per capita income raises government revenues from the income tax as a percentage of total income whether the income rise is real or stems from higher

16. Actually, the argument in any case uses "inflation" too loosely to bear analysis. A common example is the jump in food prices that raised the income of farmers in 1973 and was particularly adverse to low-income urban families because they spend much of their income on food. But it was conditions specific to foods, the combination of international crop failures and soaring demand, that raised food relative to other prices. These conditions also raised food prices absolutely, and this was part of the general inflation. But the relative positions of farmers and urban low-income earners would have been the same if inflation—a rise in average prices —had been prevented (without altering the year's output) by some splendidly successful aggregate demand policy.

17. The latter coverage is assumed by Emil Sunley and Joseph Pechman in chapter 5.

prices.[18] A country may wish to prevent an automatic rise in the government share from either cause rather than from inflation only. In that case it would index by a measure of average money income rather than of prices. Unlike indexing by a price index, this method would save taxpayers whose real incomes grew at the average rate from being pushed up the rate structure when real income rises. In 1966 Vito Tanzi proposed such a system, with indexing based on per capita income.[19] Denmark actually adopted a similar system in September 1974, switching from a consumer price index to the average hourly earnings of industrial workers. The change seems to have been based in part on a conscious selection between the two goals I have stated, though partly also on more ad hoc considerations.

Timing of the Price Index

The choice of the period to which the change in the selected index refers is perhaps more important than the selection of the index itself. Suppose that 1974 is the base year for indexing and that the tax on 1975 income is to be adjusted for calendar year taxpayers. It seems natural to use the change in the chosen index from its January–December 1974 average to its January–December 1975 average. But this is not at all what foreign countries do. As the 1974–75 change, Canada would use the change from the average for October 1972–September 1973 to the average for October 1973–September 1974, Denmark the change from March 1973 to March 1974, and the Netherlands the change from the average for July 1972–June 1973 to the average for July 1973–June 1974.

Such timing discrepancies often introduce big differences between the price change used in indexing and the actual change in the selected price index over the pertinent period. These differences between price changes displayed by the same index in different periods are likely to dwarf differences in price changes displayed by alternative indexes over the same time period. The importance of the error introduced by lags makes close consideration of the selection of an index seem a superfluous refinement. But lags appear to be unnecessary.

18. "Per capita" income is used as an approximation for a complex phenomenon, made more so by the differences between corporation and individual taxes. Income per family or per taxpayer might come closer.

19. Vito Tanzi, "A Proposal for a Dynamically Self-Adjusting Personal Income Tax," *Public Finance*, vol. 21, no. 4 (1966), pp. 507–19.

Canada selected the period it did because the index value for September 1974 is the last observation obtained in time to prepare and print forms for withholding tax during 1975, and the use of twelve-month averages was regarded as necessary to eliminate seasonal and erratic changes.[20] Considerations in the other countries presumably were similar. But the long lag seems to me unnecessary, at least in the United States. First, if the use of the index for withholding and declaring estimated tax can be dispensed with, this in itself will save a year. This should be possible. For any taxpayer the amount withheld or declared is simply an estimate that is corrected later. Even without indexing, the amounts withheld from wages and current payments based on declarations of estimated tax are only crude estimates of the final tax liability. The range of errors need be little greater if, with indexing, a forecast or assumed price change is used to set the schedule. As has been done when tax rates were altered, withholding rates could even be changed during the year if amounts withheld appeared to be seriously in error. Final payments or refunds would continue to be made when the taxpayer filed his return after the tax year was over. Second, the need to allow time after the index has been determined for the printing and distribution of income tax forms can be avoided by adopting the method of using deflated income in filling out the tax form, rather than the method of changing the form itself. It would be necessary to announce the index publicly only in time for its use by taxpayers. A February release of the index should permit retention of the April 15 filing deadline for calendar year taxpayers. For any of the principal price indexes or variants of them, this would allow the use of annual averages of at least the degree of finality of those contained in the *Economic Report of the President*. If only personal exemptions and rate bracket boundaries are indexed, this procedure is extremely simple. To index the optional standard deduction would require a more complicated adjustment of the tax form, especially if the taxpayer is to be sure he decides correctly whether to itemize.

20. It has sometimes been argued that the use of the wrong time period is a virtue; a time lag is advantageous because it would "minimize the effect of such an automatic adjustment on the built-in macroeconomic stabilizing properties of the system." (Vukelich, "The Effect of Inflation on Real Tax Rates," p. 328.) But in the absence of a regular and predictable correlation between the lagged change in prices and the employment rate, it would seem that only random error in stabilization policy is introduced by a time lag.

246 *Inflation and the Income Tax*

The use of the announcement method would also permit the correct treatment of fiscal year taxpayers. In my example, where calendar 1974 is the base date, a taxpayer filing for the fiscal year ending June 30, 1976 (using a 1975 tax form) should be entitled to indexing based on the change in prices from January–December 1974 to July 1975–June 1976. Announcement of the index for taxpayers filing within each monthly or quarterly period (depending on the frequency with which the desired index is available) could be made routinely.

Main Questions Governing the Choice of a Price Index

To select an appropriate price index, three main questions of principle must be settled. What should the index cover—only consumption or all output and, if the latter, gross or net output? Should it be an index of market prices or of factor-cost prices? What formula should be used to compute the index?

The indexes actually used in Canada and the Netherlands, and that formerly used in Denmark, cover only private consumption. These countries index only the individual income tax, and this may have made the decision to use a price index for consumption seem natural. Failure to index the corporate tax, however, may imply only that indexing was unnecessary, not that it was inappropriate. Because of almost flat rates and no exemptions, the indexing of the corporate tax, where present at all, would have little effect.[21] Even if adjustment is confined to the rate structure of the personal income tax, I shall argue, foreign countries are wrong to confine the price index to personal consumption; it is where income comes from, not how it is spent, that matters. Because they selected consumption rather than output prices, the question of gross or net output did not arise.

The Netherlands measures prices at factor cost. So did Denmark when that country used a price index. The Economic Council of Canada seems to indicate that factor-cost prices would be correct, although market prices are used in practice in Canada.[22] All these

21. As John Bossons and Thomas A. Wilson said of Canada, "Except for small private corporations, the corporation income tax exhibits no progression in tax rates and hence is immune from inflationary increases in effective real tax rates." ("Adjusting Tax Rates for Inflation," *Canadian Tax Journal*, vol. 21 [May–June 1973], p. 189.)

22. According to the Economic Council of Canada, "The existing scheme, *apart from the problem caused by the inclusion of indirect taxes in the consumer price*

countries use degenerate Laspeyres indexes similar to the consumer price index in the United States; that is, fixed weights are used that refer to a date before the earlier of any pair of years compared.[23] The countries doubtless would have preferred a true Laspeyres index, with the base year the same as the base year for indexing, if such indexes had been available.

I shall argue that the countries are conceptually correct in using, or wishing to use, factor-cost prices, but that it is not desirable to use the fixed-weight Laspeyres formula.

To index the structure of rates (including exemptions), I shall recommend the implicit deflator for national income (also called net national product at factor cost). The recommended series covers not only private consumption but also net private capital formation, government purchases, and exports less imports. It measures prices at factor cost. Viewed as a continuous time series it has shifting weights. If, as would be desirable, it were calculated with the base year the same as the base year for indexing, it would be a Paasche index. The rest of this paper explains why the national income deflator is my choice.

Criteria for Selecting an Output Measure

The purpose of indexing the rate structure is to prevent a change in the general price level from changing the ratio of income taxes to the value of the nation's output or—a synonymous word in the context—its income. Given real output, the ratio of income tax revenues to output measured in current prices is to be the same whatever the price level.[24]

Expressed another way, the purpose of indexing the rate structure

---

index, enjoys the advantages of simplicity, widespread acceptance, and independence from direct government intervention." (*Economic Targets and Social Indicators, 1974,* p. 171. Emphasis added.)

23. The Laspeyres formula for the comparison of prices in year 0 and year 1 is $\Sigma p_1 q_0 / \Sigma p_0 q_0$, where p is price and q is quantity. The Paasche formula is $\Sigma p_1 q_1 / \Sigma p_0 q_1$. Actual indexes use $\Sigma p_1 q_{-x} / \Sigma p_0 q_{-x}$, where $-x$ is some year before year 0.

24. The Economic Council of Canada put it this way: "Without indexation, the proportion of income represented by income taxes will increase during a period of inflation without any change in real income or in statutory tax rates. This is a source of hidden gains to governments at the expense of all taxpayers, but especially at the expense of taxpayers whose incomes are subject to the steepest progressivity. Indexation of exemption levels and tax brackets may ideally eliminate these gains." (*Economic Targets and Social Indicators, 1974,* p. 174.)

is to make the real tax on a given real income invariant to the price level. If it is agreed that a single price index is to be used for everyone, the two ways of stating the objective are interchangeable.[25] "Real income" should then refer to the *nation's* real income—which is synonymous with its output. For the nation, obviously, the real tax on a given real income must be invariant to the price level if the ratio of nominal taxes to nominal income is invariant to the price level, because the price index used to convert nominal income to real income is the same as the price index used to convert nominal taxes to real taxes. At least I have not heard advocates of the criterion of making the real tax on real income invariant to the price level espouse the use of different indexes.

The first way of expressing the purpose of indexing is more convenient for testing different indexes and is the one I shall stress.

Some measure of the nation's output must be specified if the index is to be chosen that will best assure that the ratio of income tax revenues to given real output, measured in current prices, is the same whatever the price level. The three principal comprehensive output measures are gross national product at market prices (GNP), net national product at market prices (NNP), and national income or net national product at factor cost (NI). It turns out that the main question for selecting a measure for the purpose of indexing is not which of the indexes is the best measure of output—granted that all are fairly satisfactory.[26] Rather, it is which corresponds most closely to the definition of income that is subject to the personal and corporate income taxes.

25. On the other hand, if one assigns each taxpayer his own price index, the criterion of making the real tax on a given real income invariant to prices would provide hardly any guidance in selecting the index. The criterion is met by any index accepted as appropriate to deflate nominal income and taxes to secure real income and taxes; and "a given real income" is a very imprecise term unless it is a synonym for a given package of output—for example, a nation's real income or product or the national income or product originating (produced) in a certain sector. When real income does not represent a package of output—for example, in the case of real disposable personal income or of real corporate profits—one is dealing with a vague concept that can be implemented statistically only by adopting some convention, such as deflating by the consumer price index or by the GNP deflator.

26. As an output measure I prefer either NNP or NI (which include identical bundles of goods and services but value them differently) to GNP because they are unduplicated. (This preference assumes that they are constructed with capital consumption measured by a consistent and reasonable method.) I have little preference between NNP and NI; NNP is usually regarded as suitable for welfare analysis, NI for resource allocation and productivity analysis, but in the past these two measures of real output have moved much alike and either is satisfactory.

The way to approach the choice of a price index is to compare income that is taxable with the content of each of the three output measures under consideration and, because foreign countries have used indexes of consumer prices, with income earned in producing for consumption. The comparison with consumption will be made first.

Prices of Output or Consumption?

Should all output or only personal consumption be included? The question cannot be answered by asking how income recipients spend their money; one should ask how they derive their income. Income subject to income tax is earned in the production of goods and services for all final purchasers—private consumers, business (with respect to purchases on capital account), governments, and foreigners. An increase in prices paid by *any* of these groups will raise someone's earnings and hence the effective tax rate—unless the price increase is matched instead by an increase in the prices paid for imports. Therefore output must include purchases by all the specified groups, minus imports, and the desired price index must have the same coverage. Gross and net national product both qualify in this respect, and they do so whether output is valued at market prices or at factor cost. Consumption, or anything narrower in scope than the national product, will not do so.[27]

Gross Output or Net?

Should output be measured gross or net of depreciation? Income subject to taxation is measured after deduction of depreciation charges. The output measure should therefore also be measured net of depreciation, and the price index should be one appropriate for deflation of a net national product series (NNP or NI). If GNP is used instead, the prices of components of fixed investment will be greatly overweighted in the price index; they will erroneously receive the weight of gross investment instead of net investment.

Market Prices or Factor Costs?

Should net national product be valued at market prices (NNP) or at factor cost (NI)? NI equals NNP minus indirect business taxes minus private transfer payments minus the current surplus of government enterprises plus subsidies. In all these respects the definition of

27. This issue was discussed extensively at the conference. See pp. 264–67.

income for taxation corresponds to NI rather than NNP. Indirect business taxes, including property taxes, are not themselves income to any individual or corporation, and since they are deducted in computing the income of business taxpayers they are not part of corporate or noncorporate profits. Business transfer payments consist of auto liability payments for personal injury from business to individuals, write-offs of bad debts owed by individuals to business, corporate contributions to nonprofit organizations, and a small amount of unrecoverable cash thefts by individuals from business. All are deductions from business income without (as a practical matter) becoming taxable individual income. The current surplus of government enterprises is not income to any taxpayer. And subsidies, included in NI but not NNP, normally result in taxable income just as do receipts from the sale of a product.

Price Index Formula

What formula should be used to compute a price index? The governing consideration is to devise a price series, not for its own sake, but because its characteristics are such that when it is divided into the value of output it will yield the desired quantity series for output, a series that is the same as if prices had not changed.[28] This considera-

28. This consideration is significant because the Laspeyres formula is generally considered preferable, but it cannot be used for both quantity and price indexes if their product is to equal the index of value. In comparisons of a base year and a later year, if one of the two is Laspeyres, the other must be Paasche. Considered over a series of years, if one index has fixed weights the other must have variable weights.

Fixed-weight indexes are clearly preferable for a series that is of interest in itself; the general preference seems also to be for the Laspeyres formula. Hence it is not surprising that in dividing changes in GNP between quantity and price the Bureau of Economic Analysis (BEA), which has been primarily interested in quantity (real output), has used fixed weights and (for comparisons of the base year and later years) the Laspeyres formula for quantities, relegating shifting weights and the Paasche formula to the corresponding price index, the implicit deflator. Because of the growing general interest in price movements in recent years, supplementary fixed-weight and chain price series have also been made available, however. Similarly, the BLS, which is primarily responsible for price data, has used fixed weights and a variant of the Laspeyres formula for price indexes; this relegates the use of shifting weights and the Paasche formula to real consumption, real wages, or real income when they are obtained by dividing current values by the price index. In the indexing of taxes, the object is to secure a quantity series whose movement is unaffected by price changes; thus it is desirable to follow the BEA practice. The implicit deflator for national income, obtained by dividing NI in current prices by NI in constant prices, provides the desired index. If possible, it should be computed with the same base year as that for the indexing scheme so that in comparing the latter year with any subsequent year a true Laspeyres price index will be used.

tion dictates the use of a Paasche index of the form $\Sigma p_1 q_1 / \Sigma p_0 q_1$, where p is price, q is quantity, the subscript 0 refers to the year to which the rate structure is to be indexed, and 1 refers to the current year. If this index is divided into national income in current-year prices, $\Sigma p_1 q_1$, it yields $\Sigma p_0 q_1$, a measure of current quantities valued in prices of year 0, the year to which the rate structure is indexed.

Arithmetic Example of Alternative Indexes

Table 9-1 illustrates the use of alternative indexes as simply as I can do so. The economy consists of a manufacturer of shoes who sells to consumers, a manufacturer of shoe machinery who sells to the shoe manufacturer, and a government whose only activity is to collect a sales tax on shoes. The only capital is the shoe manufacturer's machinery, on which depreciation is valued at replacement cost.[29] Lines 1 to 14 provide assumed data.

From year 0 to year 1 no physical quantity changes, so output is unambiguously unchanged. In the second part of the table (lines 16, 19, and 22), constant price data for GNP, NNP, and NI all show this. The prices of shoes and shoe machines do change, and by different amounts, and the sales tax on shoes is raised from 2 percent to 5 percent. Consequently the implicit deflators for the three series differ.[30]

The point of the example is so simple that, once grasped, the example itself may seem superfluous. Suppose that in addition to the transactions shown a progressive income tax existed in this economy and that the tax system was to be indexed. Make the crucial assumption that income in current prices is defined for tax purposes as it is in national income measurement. Because real transactions are unchanged between year 0 and year 1, the ratio of income tax revenue to output should be unchanged after indexing. Accordingly, income subject to tax, when deflated by the price index selected, must be unchanged.[31]

This condition is met *only* if the national income deflator is used because it is national income that is taxed. Although output as

29. The machines have five-year service lives, and the straight-line depreciation formula is used. There are five machines in the stock, so depreciation (one-fifth of the value of each machine) is the equivalent of one entire machine.

30. The deflator for NI differs from that for NNP for two reasons: shoes are weighted less heavily, and their factor-cost price rises less than their market price.

31. Even then the distribution of income with respect to anything affecting taxes must also be unchanged.

measured by deflated GNP is unchanged, income subject to tax (which is the same as NI) deflated by the GNP deflator is changed; its index is 98.76 (147.73 ÷ 149.59). Similarly, output as measured by deflated NNP is unchanged, but taxable income deflated by the NNP deflator is changed; its index in the example is 97.33 (147.73 ÷ 151.79). When output as measured by deflated NI is unchanged, however, taxable income deflated by the NI deflator *is* unchanged; its index is 100.00 (147.73 ÷ 147.73).[32]

Inasmuch as a consumption price index is so widely used, I may add that if income subject to tax is deflated by a consumption price index at either market prices (154.41, the index of the market price of shoes in the example) or factor cost (150.00), deflated income subject to tax will be changed, although the three deflated output measures and deflated consumption itself are all unchanged.

The finding that national income yields a precisely consistent solution in the example results from the assumption that income subject to income taxation and national income are identical. In fact, of course, there are differences, but these differences are also present between income subject to tax and the other output measures. As shown above, where the output measures differ it is national income that corresponds more closely to income subject to taxation than do other measures of output. Hence use of the national income deflator yields the most nearly unchanged ratio of tax revenue to output in the presence of inflation.

Possibility of Adjusting National Income

Should an attempt be made to improve consistency by adjusting the national income figures to correspond more closely to tax law before they are used to index the rate structure? Imputed rent on owner-occupied homes might be excluded from the scope of national income, as it was before 1947.[33] Interest paid by government and

32. In this example the Laspeyres and Paasche price indexes are the same because quantities are the same in both years. Hence the example cannot illustrate the choice of formula. If quantities changed, the indexes would differ, and division of value by the Laspeyres price index would not yield the Laspeyres movement of quantities.

33. The deletion also has numerous other consequences. It turns mortgage interest into consumer interest (a transfer payment), property taxes into personal taxes, and maintenance and net purchases of dwellings by owner-occupants into personal consumption expenditures. It also eliminates the deduction of depreciation on owner-occupied dwellings. Rent would get much less weight in the price index and residential construction much more, while maintenance would need to be introduced.

Table 9-1. Arithmetic Example of the Use of Alternative Indexes

Item	Year 0	Year 1	Index
Assumed data			
Shoe manufacturer			
1. Pairs of shoes made and sold to consumers	100	100	...
2. Market price of shoes per pair	$20.40	$31.50	...
3. Shoes sold to consumers, market price value	$2,040	$3,150	...
4. Sales tax [2 percent in year 0, 5 percent in year 1]	$ 40	$ 150	...
5. Shoes sold to consumers, factor-cost value [3 − 4]	$2,000	$3,000	...
6. Factor cost of shoes per pair [5 ÷ 1]	$ 20	$ 30	...
7. Depreciation, number of shoe machine equivalents	1	1	...
8. Price of shoe machines [from 12]	$ 200	$ 250	...
9. Value of depreciation on shoe machines [7 × 8]	$ 200	$ 250	...
10. Wages and profits [5 − 9]	$1,800	$2,750	...
Shoe machinery manufacturer			
11. Number of machines made and sold to shoe manufacturer	2	2	...
12. Market price and factor cost of machines, per unit	$ 200	$ 250	...
13. Sales of machines to shoe manufacturer, market price and factor-cost value [11 × 12]	$ 400	$ 500	...
14. Wages and profits [from 13]	$ 400	$ 500	...
Derived series			
Gross national product			
15. Current prices [3 + 13]	$2,440	$3,650	149.59
16. Constant prices [16a + 16b]	$2,440	$2,440	100.00
a. Shoes [1 × 2, year 0]	$2,040	$2,040	100.00
b. Shoe machines [11 × 12, year 0]	$ 400	$ 400	100.00
17. Implicit deflator [15 ÷ 16]	...	...	149.59
Net national product			
18. Current prices [3 + 13 − 9]	$2,240	$3,400	151.79
19. Constant prices [19a + 19b]	$2,240	$2,240	100.00
a. Shoes [1 × 2, year 0]	$2,040	$2,040	100.00
b. Shoe machines [(11 − 7) × 12, year 0]	$ 200	$ 200	100.00
20. Implicit deflator [18 ÷ 19]	...	...	151.79
National income			
21. Current prices [10 + 14]	$2,200	$3,250	147.73
22. Constant prices [22a + 22b]	$2,200	$2,200	100.00
a. Shoes [1 × 6, year 0]	$2,000	$2,000	100.00
b. Shoe machines [(11 − 7) × 12, year 0]	$ 200	$ 200	100.00
23. Implicit deflator [21 ÷ 22]	...	...	147.73

consumers (which would include mortgage interest if owner-occupied homes were eliminated) might be added to NI, also as before 1947; sensible deflation of such interest would raise problems, however, as it did before 1947. Payroll taxes levied on employers are part of NI but are not taxed as income. They might be eliminated from NI for use in indexing and handled like indirect business taxes in order to bring the NI series closer to the income tax concept. Such changes would tend to transform NI from a sensible output measure to an ill-defined aggregate, destroying the independent meaning of the corresponding price series. My preference would be not to adjust NI for use in indexing, but I could not argue strongly against some of the adjustments.

Most differences between income subject to tax and NI could not be handled by adjusting NI, because they neither consist of product values that can be resolved into quantity and price nor can they (like indirect business taxes) be construed as representing differences between alternative values of commodities included in NI.[34] Among them are items, such as capital gains and gambling profits, that are taxable but are not earnings from current production; special deductions, such as percentage depletion, which are allowed in computation of incomes from business; and corporate dividends, which are taxed again after corporate profits have already been taxed. Tax credits, such as the investment credit, and such personal deductions as that for medical care may introduce wedges between movements of income and taxes.

Comparison of Price Indexes

What difference would the choice of price index have made in past periods? In an earlier study I prepared statistically comparable annual estimates of GNP, NNP, and NI in current and constant (1958) prices for the entire 1947–69 period and the individual years 1929, 1940, and 1941.[35] Implicit deflators can be computed by division.

34. I would have included government and consumer interest in the former category had not the official national income series at one time considered them to be a payment for a service and included them in national income and product.

35. Edward F. Denison, *Accounting for United States Economic Growth, 1929–1969* (Brookings Institution, 1974), table A-1, p. 153. The basic data were from the BEA. My implicit deflator for GNP differs slightly from that published by BEA because BEA's "price series 2" rather than its "price series 1" was used to deflate private nonresidential construction and its estimates of institutional depreciation were adjusted to current prices.

Table 9-2 compares those series, as well as the implicit deflator for personal consumption expenditures (PCE) of the Bureau of Economic Analysis and the CPI of the Bureau of Labor Statistics for the same dates.[36]

The effect of deducting depreciation can be judged by comparing the implicit deflators for GNP and NNP.[37] The ratio of the deflator for NNP to that for GNP (table 9-2, column 6) varied within a range of 2.9 percent. Over the 1947–69 postwar period the range was 0.9 percent; for 1952–69 it was only 0.5 percent.

The effect of using factor-cost prices can be judged by comparing the implicit deflators for NNP and NI. The ratio of the deflator for NI to that for NNP (column 7) varied within a range of 2.7 percent when all available years were considered. Over the 1947–69 postwar period the range was 1.7 percent and during 1952–69, 1.1 percent. In the postwar years most of this range stemmed from changes in indirect taxes. Little stemmed from the difference between factor cost and market price weights for output components. I infer this from the similarity of movement of real net product at factor cost and at market price. The ratio of the former to the latter varied within a range of only 0.3 percent in 1947–69 and 1952–69. The range of variation was 1.2 percent with 1929 included, but most of this range resulted from the big increase in the quantity of alcoholic beverages after the repeal of prohibition combined with the heavy tax on them in the base year, which gave them a much bigger weight at market price than at factor cost.

The combined importance of using prices of net rather than gross output and of factor cost rather than market prices—and consequently of using the conceptually preferable measure rather than the nearest currently available official index—can be judged by com-

36. During the five years 1970 through 1974 the ratio of the implicit deflator for personal consumption expenditures to that for GNP fluctuated within a 1.1 percent range, and the ratio of the CPI to the implicit deflator for GNP within a 1.6 percent range. In 1969–74 the range of the former ratio was 2.0 percent and that of the latter ratio was still 1.6 percent. Implicit deflators for NNP and NI were not estimated after 1969.

37. Depreciation estimates used were computed by the straight-line formula with the Winfrey distribution, based on Bulletin F service lives, and measured at reproduction cost based on price series 2. See Denison, *Accounting for United States Economic Growth,* app. A; and U.S. Treasury Department, *Bulletin "F" (Revised January 1942): Income Tax Depreciation and Obsolescence, Estimated Useful Lives and Depreciation Rates* (Government Printing Office, 1942).

Table 9-2. Implicit Deflators for Gross National Product, Net National Product, National Income, Personal Consumption Expenditures, and Consumer Price Index, with Ratios, Selected Years, 1929-69
1958 = 100

						Ratios of implicit deflators and price indexes				
	Implicit deflator or price index					NNP to GNP	NI to NNP	NI to GNP	PCE to NI	CPI to NI
Year	GNP (1)	NNP (2)	NI (3)	PCE (4)	CPI (5)	(6)	(7)	(8)	(9)	(10)
1929	50.9	52.3	52.5	55.3	59.2	1.028	1.004	1.031	1.053	1.128
1940	43.9	44.5	43.7	45.5	48.5	1.014	0.982	0.995	1.041	1.110
1941	47.3	47.9	47.3	48.7	50.9	1.013	0.987	1.000	1.030	1.076
1947	74.9	75.5	76.1	77.9	77.3	1.008	1.008	1.016	1.024	1.016
1948	79.7	80.3	80.9	82.3	83.3	1.008	1.007	1.015	1.017	1.030
1949	79.3	79.7	79.9	81.7	82.4	1.005	1.003	1.008	1.023	1.031
1950	80.3	80.6	80.9	82.9	83.3	1.004	1.004	1.007	1.025	1.030
1951	85.8	86.0	86.8	88.6	89.8	1.002	1.009	1.012	1.021	1.035
1952	87.6	87.8	88.1	90.5	91.8	1.002	1.003	1.006	1.027	1.042
1953	88.5	88.6	88.7	91.7	92.5	1.001	1.001	1.002	1.034	1.043
1954	89.8	90.1	90.3	92.5	93.0	1.003	1.002	1.006	1.024	1.030
1955	90.9	91.2	91.5	92.8	92.6	1.003	1.003	1.007	1.014	1.012
1956	94.1	94.1	94.3	94.8	94.0	1.000	1.002	1.002	1.005	0.997
1957	97.5	97.5	97.5	97.7	97.3	1.000	1.000	1.000	1.002	0.998
1958	100.0	100.0	100.0	100.0	100.0	1.000	1.000	1.000	1.000	1.000
1959	101.6	101.5	101.3	101.3	100.8	0.999	0.998	0.997	1.000	0.995
1960	103.2	103.2	102.6	102.9	102.4	1.000	0.994	0.994	1.003	0.998
1961	104.4	104.6	104.0	103.9	103.5	1.002	0.994	0.996	0.999	0.995
1962	105.6	105.8	105.1	104.9	104.6	1.002	0.993	0.995	0.998	0.995
1963	107.0	107.2	106.3	106.1	105.9	1.002	0.992	0.993	0.998	0.996
1964	108.6	108.9	108.2	107.4	107.3	1.003	0.994	0.996	0.993	0.992
1965	110.6	111.0	110.4	108.8	109.1	1.004	0.995	0.998	0.986	0.988
1966	113.7	114.1	114.1	111.5	112.2	1.004	1.000	1.004	0.977	0.983
1967	117.3	117.8	117.4	114.4	115.5	1.004	0.997	1.001	0.974	0.984
1968	122.0	122.5	121.7	118.4	120.3	1.004	0.993	0.998	0.973	0.988
1969	127.9	128.4	127.4	123.5	126.8	1.004	0.992	0.996	0.969	0.995

Sources: Columns 1–3 derived from Edward F. Denison, *Accounting for United States Economic Growth, 1929–1969* (Brookings Institution, 1975), p. 153; column 4, data from U.S. Bureau of Economic Analysis; and column 5, data from U.S. Bureau of Labor Statistics. Columns 6–10 computed from columns 1–5.

paring the implicit deflators for NI and GNP. With all years shown in table 9-2 considered, the ratio of the deflator for NI to that for GNP (column 8) varied within a range of 3.8 percent. Over the 1947–69 postwar period the range was 2.3 percent and over the

1952–69 period it was 1.4 percent (with the highest ratio in 1955 and the lowest in 1963). Year-to-year changes in the GNP and NI deflators differed as much as 0.5 percent in five postwar years.

The implicit deflator for personal consumption expenditures differs from the deflators for the production series much more than the latter differ among themselves, and it rises less over extended periods. The ratio of the implicit deflator for PCE to the deflator for NI (column 9) varied within a range of 8.7 percent in the years examined and 6.7 percent in both 1947–69 and 1952–69. The Bureau of Labor Statistics CPI differed from the implicit deflator for NI even more when all the years examined were considered.[38] The ratio of the CPI to the NI deflator (column 10) varied within a range of 14.8 percent. When consideration is confined to 1947–69 or 1952–69, however, the range is 6.1 percent.

There is no fixed-weight index for national income that could be compared with the implicit deflator for NI to ascertain the effects of weighting. The nearest one can come to such a comparison is to compare the implicit deflator for GNP based on 1958 weights with a fixed-weight price index for GNP based on 1967 weights, and this comparison must be limited to the years 1958 and 1967–74.[39] The range of variation is 2.4 percent. It is also 2.4 percent for the 1967–74 period alone. The fixed-weight index rose more than the implicit deflator after 1967 and especially after 1970. The divergence probably is due partly, and perhaps wholly, to the use of a later base year rather than to the use of a different formula.

In summary, differences among annual series for the implicit deflators for GNP, NNP, and NI are not very big if the postwar period alone is considered, and the limited evidence available suggests that the results also are not sensitive to the choice of formula.[40] If there is agreement that a comprehensive series is appropriate for indexing, the necessity of choosing a particular series should impose no great difficulty. All the comprehensive price series differ from the implicit

38. The CPI is a fixed-weight index, whose weights have been changed periodically. Currently it is weighted by expenditures of urban workers, but a more comprehensive index is expected to be started. There are a number of conceptual differences, particularly important in the housing area, between the CPI and the implicit deflator for PCE.

39. Data are from the *Economic Report of the President, February 1975*, p. 254; and U.S. Bureau of Economic Analysis release, BEA 75-26, April 17, 1975.

40. The formula seems to have a greater effect, at least occasionally, on quarterly changes.

deflator for PCE and the CPI by much bigger amounts than they differ among themselves. The major choice to be made is between a comprehensive series and one restricted to consumption.

Some Points of Detail

My answers to the questions this paper set out to explore have now been provided, but a few points of detail still need to be considered from a different standpoint and against the background of previous literature on the subject.

Imports and Exports

When indexing the rate structure was introduced in the Netherlands, it was perceived that a change in the terms of trade creates a problem if an index of consumption prices is used. If import prices rise, the extra income goes to foreigners. The money income of residents is unchanged, the prices that consumers and other buyers of end products pay rise to cover the higher import costs, and the real output that will be available for domestic use declines. With money income subject to tax unchanged, indexing the rate structure based on consumer or other end-product prices pushes taxpayers into lower brackets and causes income tax revenues to decline. To the extent of their marginal tax rates, taxpayers are protected against bearing their share of the decline in real incomes. Correspondingly, government income tax revenues bear a disproportionately large share of the burden. To prevent this, Dutch analysts suggested, the effect of import prices on consumption prices should be eliminated. This was not done, because of the difficulty of allocating changes in import prices between the prices of consumption goods and of other end products. This difficulty disappears if all end products are in the price index used. The problem is not present at all if the implicit deflator for NI (or GNP or NNP) is used for indexing, because imports are deducted in calculating current and constant price NI. The rise in import prices leaves NI unchanged in current and constant prices, hence the implicit deflator and consequently taxes paid are also unchanged. Taxpayers bear their "proper share" of the burden of higher import prices; that is, they retain an unchanged percentage of current-dollar income. (Relative prices paid by the private sector and government are likely to change when import prices change.)

When prices of consumer goods or of a broader range of end products other than exports are used for indexing, a similar difficulty arises, but in the opposite direction, if export prices change. If export prices increase while other prices are unchanged, money income subject to tax will rise, but there will be no change in the price index used. Taxes paid will therefore go up. To the extent of their marginal tax rates, taxpayers will be denied their full share of the rise in real income made possible by higher export prices, and the government will receive a disproportionately large share. Use of the implicit deflator for NI (or for GNP or NNP) automatically eliminates the difficulty because it includes export prices. Use of the NI, NNP, or GNP deflator therefore correctly handles changes in the terms of trade stemming from either exports or imports.

Compensation of Government Employees

The compensation of employees of general government, households, and nonprofit organizations serving individuals makes up an appreciable part of national income and product. The components of such compensation are deflated by the use of a price index of employee compensation. I suspect some would argue that this method is so unsatisfactory that it would be better to omit the output of these employees from the price index. The omission of the compensation of these employees would reduce the long-term rise in the price index and consequently the amount by which indexing the rate structure would cut into tax revenues. It would be equivalent to deflating the compensation of government employees by the price of all other goods and services.

My preference is to retain this compensation in the NI measures, but there is little to discuss. The omission of the services of the employees under consideration would imply that the true price for them moves less like their compensation than like the price of all goods and services sold by business. Unfortunately, no one knows what a true price series for the services of these employees would be. How can one show which of two known indexes is more similar to an unknown third index, which is undefined, unmeasured, and unmeasurable?

Indirect Business Taxes

The chief advantage of a price index based on factor cost rather than on market prices is, as stated earlier, that factor cost corresponds more closely to income subject to income taxation. The Dutch, the Danes, and the Economic Council of Canada also favor factor-cost prices.

Bossons and Wilson, however, in discussing the Turner proposal for indexing in Canada, registered only qualified agreement. They distinguished between unitary and federal government structures. They argued that there is little reason to eliminate indirect taxes in a unitary state such as the Netherlands because "the inflationary effects of an increase in sales tax rates are no less inflationary for being the result of government policy."[41] Though true enough, this observation does not deal with the real issue: what is taxable? Bossons and Wilson believed the case for eliminating indirect taxes to be stronger in a federal state such as Canada than in a unitary state. The inclusion of indirect taxes would create incentives (which they regard as weak) for provincial governments to raise sales taxes:

Such incentives arise from the partial shifting of the burden of the sales tax to other jurisdictions through the reduction in provincial and federal personal income tax revenues that would result from the price increases generated by the imposition of increase in sales tax rates by any one government.[42]

This consideration might give some additional reason to prefer factor-cost prices, but it is slight and really unnecessary.

A report by one international group seems to lean toward factor cost even though the criterion of matching income subject to taxation is omitted. It notes that if indirect taxes are raised as part of a restrictive fiscal policy, it could be considered as counterproductive to compensate taxpayers via indexing for the resulting price increases.[43] The pertinence of other considerations that are mentioned largely eludes me; I repeat them without discussion. It is suggested that if increases in indirect taxes finance public expenditure of a social character that benefit taxpayers, the loss of real income from the higher indirect taxes "is compensated for by the increased availability of 'public' goods." If so, the increase in prices from the increased tax should be eliminated, whereas it should not be if one accepts the view that the link between the increase in taxes and in government expenditure is

41. Bossons and Wilson, "Adjusting Tax Rates for Inflation," p. 197.
42. Ibid.
43. Organisation for Economic Co-operation and Development, *The Adjustment of Personal Income Tax Systems for Inflation* (Paris: OECD, 1976), p. 29. This publication is a rich source of information on practices abroad.

too tenuous to consider. Again, the report suggests that where an increase in a subsidy prevented the cost-of-living index from rising as much as otherwise, it would be paradoxical to claim that this should be disregarded (as it would be in a market price index) in calculating the index compensation due through the tax system.

Conclusions Confined to Indexing

At the outset of this paper I cautioned that it deals only with indexing, not with the measurement of income in current prices. In this concluding paragraph I stress that my conclusion that only one price index should be used in indexing has no application to the adjustment of income in current prices, including business profits, to take account of inflation. That subject has not been considered here.

Comments by Alan Blinder

Edward Denison has provided a blueprint for rewriting our personal income tax code to allow for indexing the rate structure. Since I find myself satisfied with his overall floor plan, I will only suggest a few minor revisions in the furnishings and the placement of the doors and windows.

First, although policymakers certainly *can* index the tax form without fixing up the definition of income, I think it would be a mistake to do so. Inflation creates two kinds of distortions, not one. Applying an appropriately adjusted tax form to inappropriately defined income is a halfway house in which legislators might take refuge. But the problem of indexing the tax system would not really have been solved.

I make this point because I think it is important, not because I think Denison disagrees with it. For there is a major reason for favoring indexing other than those Denison mentions, namely macroeconomic stability. When both inflation and unemployment are too high, a situation that has prevailed since 1973, it is undesirable for real tax receipts to rise. But real tax receipts rise with inflation in an unindexed tax system. And it does not matter whether inflation fills the government's coffers because bracket rates and exemptions are not adjusted or because capital gains are overstated and depreciation is understated. The net effect is the same. And since plenty of business income is reported on individual income tax returns, even indexing the individual income tax requires more than merely an adjustment of the rate structure.

Second, I agree with Denison that the same price index must be used for all taxpayers, though I would base my rationale on more mundane reasons. The introduction of different indexes for different groups of taxpayers would open a mare's nest of endless haggling over which groups were being treated preferentially. Given the insolubility of the index number problem, no number of economists, lawyers, and accountants could really prove to any group that its claims were invalid. In principle it might be "fairer" to give more indexing to those groups whose costs of living have risen most. But in this case, the appearance of equity is more important and more attainable than the reality.

Third, I agree with Denison's argument for using a national income deflator to adjust the tax system but would be much more eager than he to devise a deflator that came even closer to the base of the personal income tax, *if* possible. "If" is the biggest word in this sentence. To reach taxable income from national income, one must subtract employer contributions for social insurance, imputed income, other labor income, corporate profits, and income tax deductions and exemptions; and one must add capital gains, dividends, and interest paid by government and consumers. On reflection, I must admit that it is not obvious how these categories should be deflated. But if anyone can do it, Denison can; and it is worth a try.

Denison's choice of a deflator for national income at factor cost is appropriate, not only for the reasons he suggests, but also from the standpoint of stabilization. Suppose, for example, that indirect business taxes were included in the index. Then a rise in excise taxes would automatically call forth a cut in income taxes, thus reducing, and perhaps completely eliminating, the usefulness of federal excise taxes as stabilization instruments. This would be particularly unfortunate if the "stagflation" problem stays with us because, for a given stimulus to aggregate demand, cuts in excise taxes probably have a more favorable effect on the price level than any other weapon in the fiscal arsenal. Our failure to have used this weapon to date should not prevent us from considering its use in the future. It would be a shame to undermine the usefulness of such a potentially effective instrument before it has ever been tried.

Eliminating import prices, export prices, or both from the index would lead to analogous difficulties. Suppose that the prices of imported goods go up because of inflation abroad. Since the price of imports appears both in consumption (or investment) and in imports, the GNP deflator is unaffected. A proper deflator for national income would also remain unchanged. If import prices were excluded, however, the index would rise, causing a cut in income taxes, stimulating the economy, and possibly adding to inflation. This is surely one mechanism for the international transmission of inflation that we would not want to create.

My only major disagreement with Denison concerns timing, and here I object on both practical and conceptual grounds. On the practical level, Denison is correct that the Internal Revenue Service has two ways to index the rate structure and that the two procedures are perfect substitutes in principle. But the practical advantage of giving taxpayers forms with brackets, exemptions, and so on, already properly adjusted for inflation, rather than requiring them to use an index to adjust old brackets, exemptions, and so on, is enormous. Even in the era of the Bowmar Brain, administrative considerations dictate that the Internal Revenue Service do the deflating.

The conceptual issue is over how current the index should be. While the decision is crucial for macroeconomic stability, the "right" answer is unclear. Let me explain the choices.

Indexing reduces the response of real aggregate demand to the price level. Lagged indexing is incomplete indexing in that it allows the depressing effects of inflation on aggregate demand through the tax system to persist longer. Is prompt or delayed indexing preferable? My answer depends on the source of inflation.

Suppose inflation is demand-induced, as it used to be in the good old days. Then delayed indexing allows the progressivity of the tax system more time to operate to puncture the inflationary bubble. From the standpoint of stabilization, the longer the lag the better. Better still, indexing could be skipped altogether.

But things are very different if inflation comes from the supply side, as seems to be the case in the bad new days. As prices rise and output falls, an indexed tax system will offset the tendency of inflation to enlarge tax receipts, cushioning the decline in demand, although increasing the vulnerability of the economy to inflation.

Lagging the index helps in one case and hurts in the other. There is clearly room for debate over which risk is more serious. In my opinion, preventing external inflationary shocks from causing recessions is much the more important goal. For this reason I favor making the index as current as is feasible. If possible I would apply indexing to the tax system only when inflation is supply-induced, not when inflation is demand-induced. We might be able to devise a trigger for the introduction of indexing—for example, index for inflation only if real GNP is falling. Clearly, there are likely to be serious problems with this, or perhaps with any other, triggering device. Nevertheless, I want to suggest a principle: that indexing be applied only, or mostly, for supply-induced inflations if a suitable triggering device can be found.

Comments by Robert J. Gordon

I agree with Edward Denison on most of the minor issues, but I disagree with him on one of his major points—his recommendation that an income-based index be used rather than a consumption-based price index.

Let's go back to basics. Why do we have exemptions and a progressive rate structure? Why is no tax imposed on households whose incomes are less than the sum of their exemptions and deductions? Why does exempted income rise with family size? Surely, the answers are that we wish to allow each household a minimum amount of consumption and that only income above this level should be taxed, that consumption consists increasingly of discretionary items as income rises above that level and hence more of it can be taxed, and that each household should be allowed a minimum subsistence level of consumption, including enough for children, before taxes are collected. Leaving aside loopholes, the present progressive tax system represents a political judgment that two households with the same consumption opportunities should pay the same tax rate.

The crucial point for an evaluation of Denison's paper is an acceptance of the idea that in a no-inflation world there are good reasons for graduated tax brackets based on differences in real consumption opportunities. I want to apply the principle on which our progressive tax system is based—that any change in real income, defined as a change in real consumption opportunities, should change taxable income and tax brackets.

I shall illustrate this argument with Denison's own example. I want to simplify the example by eliminating the sales tax increase and keeping the price of consumption goods constant. The price of investment goods rises 25, as in Denison's example. Given these facts, the consumption deflator is fixed, because the price of shoes is unchanged; but the national income deflator rises by 2.5 percent. Using the national income deflator, real taxable income is constant. But, in fact, people are really better off. The real consumption opportunities of the recipients of wages and profits in the whole economy have increased by 50 units. This increase in welfare is no different from the increase due to economic growth that pushes people into higher tax brackets under our present tax system.

Take another example. Suppose that all investment is in structures, investment is 10 percent of GNP, and structures are made entirely with labor. Now, assume that the price of structures doubles, but the price of consumption is unchanged. Given these facts, the real consumption opportunities of construction workers have doubled. They should be pushed into the same bracket that was occupied by people who in the base year were paid twice the income construction workers received in the base year. In Denison's case the national income deflator would go up by 10 percent and trigger an adjustment in bracket widths, exemptions, and so on, that would reduce the extra taxes of construction workers and actually cut the taxes of workers in consumption goods industries whose wages and consumption opportunities are unchanged.

Now, consider changes in export and import prices. Assume that there is no investment. In the base year imports equal 10 percent of GNP. The price of imports doubles. Denison correctly observes that indexing based on a consumption deflator would push workers into lower tax brackets, but then he goes astray by objecting to this tax cut. He should not object. Brackets and exemptions are based on real consumption opportunities. Just as the government shares disproportionately when these opportunities increase, it should share disproportionately when they decrease. An adverse movement in the terms of trade is equivalent to negative economic growth.

Turning now to the impact of indexing on stabilization, a topic Alan Blinder stressed, a consumption price index is as good as a national income deflator for demand-induced inflations and better for supply-induced inflations. In 1974, for example, indexing with a consumption deflator would have been desirable. We would have re-

duced taxes more if a consumption deflator had been used for indexing than if a national income deflator had been used. If there had been
a demand-induced increase in the price of imports, there would have
been little or no difference between the two. In that case, the prices of
all tradable goods would have been likely to increase. If there is a
demand-caused price increase in the rest of the world, we will observe
not just an increase in import prices but also a simultaneous increase
in export prices, and the increase should be the same if the product
mix is the same.

In short, given a demand shock, a consumption deflator and a national income deflator work equally well; but with a supply shock,
the goals of stabilization are achieved better by a consumption deflator than by a national income deflator.

Finally, consider an increase in the relative price of government
services; for example, because we shift over to a volunteer army and
increase the pay of soldiers. If all other wages and prices are unchanged, no change occurs in average real consumption opportunities in the economy as a whole. The gains of soldiers are exactly offset by the higher taxes others must pay. Denison would deflate away
part of the real income gain of soldiers; I would treat this as a gain in
real income.

One final point about the recommendation that a single index be
used for all taxpayers. The logic of my position suggests that geographic and other differences in the cost of living should be used to
deflate the present system in order to impose the same real tax burden on two households with identical real consumption opportunities.
I must acknowledge, however, that the administrative complexities
of such a system would be insupportable, particularly in view of the
sizable degree of geographic mobility. I agree that in selecting an index only one must be chosen, but I would urge that the consumption
deflator be given very serious consideration.

Discussion

Whether a consumption price index or a national income index
should be used for nominal indexing was the major topic of discussion. In reply to the discussants, Edward Denison maintained that
since we have chosen to tax income (that is, consumption plus savings) rather than consumption alone, it is natural to choose an index

that will make the ratio of revenues to income invariant to the price level. John Shoven, concurring with Denison, returned to Robert Gordon's example involving an increase in the pay of soldiers, other prices held constant. In such a case, Shoven held, prices and nominal income have gone up, but real income has not. A national income deflator would yield such a result; a consumer price index would not.

William Fellner asserted that Gordon's view that consumption opportunities are the object of income tax receives no support from the Internal Revenue Code. Joseph Pechman pointed out that Gordon had been careful to speak of consumption opportunities, not of consumption. The point that some people save as well as consume is therefore not crucial. Pechman argued that the term "real income" cannot be understood except as a measure of consumption opportunities, though in his opinion this did not justify the substitution of a consumption tax for the income tax. Richard Musgrave countered that the choice of a base for taxation largely dictates the appropriate index to be used. If one has a consumption tax, a consumer price deflator should be used. If one feels that income is the correct tax base, then a national income deflator should be used. Eytan Sheshinski pointed out that the choice of an index may have distributional consequences. Since consumption is a larger fraction of the incomes of those with relatively low incomes than of those with relatively high incomes, indexing by a consumption price index would have an insurance aspect that is of particular importance for those who are relatively poor.

Martin Feldstein asked why the criterion for indexing should not be to keep the real purchasing power of the federal government invariant to the price level. Denison replied that this issue concerned resource allocation and changes in relative prices. If the prices of things the government buys increase relative to the prices of other commodities, the government ought to have to buy less, unless a political decision is made to increase revenues. Indexing should not short-circuit such a decision.

Arthur Okun returned to Gordon's example in which the pay for soldiers went up, while all other prices remained unchanged. The use of a national income deflator would hold revenues as a fraction of national income constant, the desired result if the price elasticity of demand for publicly provided goods is unitary. A consumption deflator, by contrast, would lead to an increase in the ratio of revenues to national income, the desired result if the price elasticity of demand to publicly provided goods is less than one. Which solution is better depends on the assumed price elasticity of demand for publicly provided goods and services. George Perry suggested that indexing is meant to handle changes in the price level, and that asking it to deal also with changes in relative prices was asking too much. Differences between the rates of change in the prices of government commodities and other commodities is a fact of life, whatever the normal rate of inflation. Denison's solution is as good in an inflationary world as the present situation is for a noninflationary world. Richard Goode said that he felt the foregoing discussion suggests that economists like to talk about second-order problems instead of first-order problems. He expressed the view that the advantages of congruity between the deflator used for indexing and the tax base had been exaggerated, that major differences between taxable income and national income were inevitable (for example, capital gains), that public familiarity with and acceptance of the index were of primary importance, and that the gross national product deflator therefore had considerable appeal.

Feldstein then raised an issue that Denison had expressly omitted from his paper: what index or indexes should be used to index the tax base? He stated that indexes other than the one used for nominal indexing might be preferable for indexing the tax base. In thinking about capital gains, for example, Feldstein said that a consumption index seemed the natural one. Denison refused to take any firm position on this question but agreed that a general price index should not be used to handle depreciation and inventories.

Henry Aaron suggested that replacement cost is not used now when prices are stable and that an effort to index the tax base could safely ignore it as well. Sidney Davidson replied that the introduction of indexing could be used as the occasion to introduce replacement-cost accounting for inventories and depreciation, thus solving two problems rather than one. George Tolley stated his preference for using as detailed a set of indexes for the tax base as is feasible. This objective can be achieved by using replacement-cost accounting for inventories and depreciation, thus avoiding the need for choosing among general deflators. With respect to gains and losses on monetary assets, some general deflator must be chosen. He agreed that a single general deflator should be used for nominal indexing. Fellner suggested that a general deflator might be appropriate even for inventories and depreciation if one wished to tax increases and decreases in the value of stocks of goods relative to the general price level at the time they occur rather than to tax them only when such goods were sold. John Bossons countered that such a procedure would be equivalent to accrual taxation of capital gains and losses. In contrast to Tolley, Bossons also raised the possibility of using several indexes for the indexing of gains and losses on monetary assets and liabilities. Aaron held that the use of a single aggregate index for depreciation and inventories really implied nothing about accrual taxation of capital gains; the question, rather, concerns the circumstances under which realization is deemed to have occurred. Does realization occur when inventories and equipment are replaced, or only when the firm depletes its stocks—an event that may not occur, under current accounting standards, until the firm liquidates. Fellner asserted that the FIFO option and actual depreciation practices imply that "realization" occurs when there is a turnover of real capital.

Some discussion dealt with the lags in indexing and the implication of such lags for the choice of an index. Denison stated that if for any reason a substantial lag was required, the choice of an index became a trivial and silly question because all indexes are apt to behave much more like one another than like the change in the price level in some previous year. Alan Blinder pointed to the mechanical problems created by the need to print tax forms before the end of the tax year. Stanley Surrey felt that this problem could be solved in any number of ways—for example, the government could adjust refunds or send out bills for balances due in light of price changes in the last months of the tax year reported after forms had been printed. Emil Sunley argued that the problem was not very serious unless the rate of inflation was highly uneven. But in that case, one is interested in average prices for the tax year, and these will be approximated by prices in June or July. Such prices are readily available in adequate time for forms to be printed. Small adjustments could be accomplished as Surrey had suggested.

Martin Bailey observed that most of the problems vanished if one allowed firms to expense capital goods and included in individual incomes only the excess of proceeds from the sale of assets over expenditures for the purchases of new assets. But, he acknowledged, those rules would amount to the adoption of a consumption tax, a topic the chairman had ruled out of order.

CHAPTER TEN

The Economic and Budgetary Effects of Indexing the Tax System

EDWARD M. GRAMLICH

DISCUSSIONS of whether or not to index the federal tax system against inflation usually proceed as if the tax system were not now indexed and as if the economic consequences of indexing were clear. Actually neither proposition is true. Important parts of the federal tax system are already automatically indexed against inflation. Other formally nonindexed taxes usually are revised legislatively soon after the fact. Still other nonindexed taxes in some cases show rising, sometimes falling, real tax yields as prices change. When combined with the fact that many budget expenditures are also indexed, and some are *overindexed*, the budgetary implications of indexing income taxes and expenditures become a good deal more complex than would at first be apparent.

This chapter addresses these issues. I first describe the present federal budget, indicating where it is or is not properly indexed, how much the deviations from indexing affect the budget during inflation, and whether the indexing is accomplished automatically or

271

by discretionary legislative action. I then examine the impact of deviations from an indexed tax system on the economy, the federal budget, and the distribution of income and tax burdens. In the process, the egregious sins of a nonindexed tax system are compared with the many other egregious sins of the present-day tax system. Key issues that must be dealt with in any discussion of whether or not to index federal taxes are highlighted.

The Present Mixed System

A budget item is indexed if the real revenue yield or real expenditure is unaffected by the rate of inflation. A proportional income tax is indexed because revenues increase at the same rate as prices, leaving real revenues unchanged. If tax rates are proportional, but the tax allows deductions or exemptions fixed in dollar terms, inflation increases real revenues by eroding the real value of exemptions or deductions. If rates are proportional but apply only to income below a fixed dollar ceiling, inflation reduces real revenue because the real maximum taxable income falls. Inflation also reduces revenues from specific excise taxes. Expenditures are indexed when they are adjusted automatically for changes in prices so that they remain constant in real terms.

Table 10-1 divides federal taxes and expenditures for 1973 into three categories: underindexed, indexed, and overindexed. The table also shows the inflation elasticity for each item; that is, the ratio of the percentage increase in the current dollar value of the item to the percentage increase in prices. When this inflation elasticity is unity, the item is unaffected in real terms by inflation and is therefore indexed. The elasticity can be greater or less than unity depending on whether the item is underindexed or overindexed in a way that raises the item more or less than proportionately as prices change.

Sixty-eight percent of total spending—$179.9 billion—is now automatically indexed or overindexed for inflation. The average elasticity of all expenditures over a one- or two-year period is about 0.68. The overindexing of social security grows with time, however; as a result, this elasticity would look much different if it were computed over many years. The difference arises because social security benefits, though properly indexed for those currently retired, are very much overindexed for those not yet retired. To take an extreme case,

Table 10-1. Degree of Indexing of Expenditures and Receipts of the Federal Budget, National Income Accounts Concept, 1973, and Inflation Elasticities

Budget item and degree of indexing	Amount (billions of dollars)	Inflation elasticity[a] (percent)
Total expenditures	264.2	0.68
Total underindexed expenditures	84.2	0.00
Nonwage purchases	53.7	0.00
Grants-in-aid to state and local governments	27.9[b]	0.00
Transfers to foreigners	2.6	0.00
Total approximately indexed expenditures	119.9	0.98
Compensation of employees	52.8	1.00
Nonpension transfers to persons	45.5[b]	0.95[c]
Net interest	16.3	1.00[d]
Subsidies to government enterprises	5.3	1.00
Total overindexed expenditures	60.0	1.05
Social security	50.7	1.00[e]
Civil service and military retirement	9.3	1.33
Total receipts	258.5	1.17
Total underindexed receipts	137.0	1.32
Individual income taxes	108.9	1.55[f]
Estate and gift taxes	5.2	1.70[g]
Excise taxes	17.8[h]	0.10[g]
Unemployment insurance tax	5.1	0.20[g]
Total approximately indexed receipts	121.5	1.00
Corporate profits taxes	43.7	1.00[i]
Nonunemployment payroll taxes	74.4	1.00
Customs duties	3.4	1.00

Sources: Federal budget amounts are from *Survey of Current Business*, vol. 54 (July 1974), tables 3.1, 3.8, 3.9, 3.10. Elasticities are author's estimates, qualified as shown in notes f and g.

a. Percentage increase in the budget item per 1 percent increase in prices.

b. Public assistance payments have been reclassified as transfers to individuals, not as grants-in-aid to state and local governments. The transfer figure includes payments of $6.5 billion for veterans and miscellaneous federal civilian pensions.

c. Using 1.0 as elasticity for all transfers except public assistance and 0.8 (an estimate obtained from U.S. Department of Health, Education, and Welfare, "The Impacts of Inflation and Higher Unemployment: With Emphasis on the Lower Income Population," Technical Analysis Paper 2 [Office of Income Security Policy, 1974; processed]) for public assistance.

d. Set at unity because interest payments are approximately indexed, even though the actual inflation elasticity of payments is well above unity. See text discussion.

e. This elasticity applies to a one-year period only. If the elasticity were computed over a longer horizon, it would be much higher. See text discussion.

f. This elasticity is from Joseph A. Pechman, "Responsiveness of the Federal Individual Income Tax to Changes in Income," *Brookings Papers on Economic Activity*, 2:1973, p. 408. A similar estimate (1.6) is given by the President's Council of Economic Advisers in *Economic Report of the President, February 1975*, p. 143.

g. Based on information given in William Fellner, Kenneth W. Clarkson, and John H. Moore, *Correcting Taxes for Inflation* (American Enterprise Institute for Public Policy Research, 1975). The unemployment insurance tax calculation assumes that only 20 percent of wages are now below the ceiling level.

h. Includes nontax receipts of $1.2 billion.

i. Since corporate tax rates are roughly proportional and the corporate share of national income is not regularly related to the rate of inflation, this tax is considered approximately indexed. While inflation does affect the tax base, the impact is fairly small after a few years. See chapter 2 for a discussion.

the elasticity is 18 over a seventy-year horizon; that is, for every 1 percent increase in prices, money benefits payable seventy years hence increase 18 percent, and real benefits rise 17 percent.[1]

Forty-seven percent of tax revenues—$121.5 billion in 1973—are indexed. The average revenue elasticity is 1.17 because the under-indexed but progressive personal income tax much outweighs the underindexed but regressive excise and unemployment taxes. A 10 percent rise in prices would then raise the budget surplus by 4.9 percent (11.7 percent minus 6.8 percent) of revenues or expenditures, or $13 billion at 1973 levels.

Approximately Indexed Items

The main expenditures that are approximately indexed are wages and salaries and transfer payments. Since 1962 the salary schedules for federal employees have been based on a survey of wages paid for "comparable" jobs in private industry. As private wages rise, federal pay is proportionately adjusted.[2] Most federal transfers are also auto-matically adjusted for price changes. The major in-kind programs—Medicare, Medicaid, and food stamps—are automatically increased either because benefits are a constant fraction of the cost of services (Medicare, Medicaid) or because payment levels are automatically adjusted for inflation (food stamps). State unemployment insurance benefits usually equal a proportion of previous wages up to a maxi-mum. The benefits of a worker who does not receive the maximum automatically rise with earnings, and twenty-eight states now auto-matically adjust the maximum levels. Only three states automatically adjust benefits under the Aid to Families with Dependent Children program, but the benefits have nearly kept pace with price changes in recent years. Benefits under the new supplemental security income program rise automatically when prices increase. Congress has also raised veterans' benefits whenever indexed social security benefits have risen, and bills have been introduced to make this adjustment automatic.[3]

1. This calculation is based on information in Barry M. Blechman, Edward M. Gramlich, and Robert W. Hartman, *Setting National Priorities: The 1976 Budget* (Brookings Institution, 1975), table 6-2, p. 180.

2. The recent congressional decision to hold pay increases to 5 percent in fiscal 1976 can be considered the exception that proves this rule.

3. See U.S. Department of Health, Education, and Welfare, Office of Income Se-curity Policy, "The Impacts of Inflation and Higher Unemployment: With Em-

Government interest payments and subsidies of government enterprises in effect are automatically indexed. The deficits of government enterprises tend to increase when prices rise, necessitating increased subsidies. Federal interest payments rise automatically with inflation because interest rates tend to rise roughly by the increase in the rate of inflation, although the actual relationship between the market interest rate and inflation is quite complex.[4]

On the tax side, the most important approximately indexed tax is the corporate profits tax. This tax behaves as if it is approximately indexed because rates are roughly proportional, the corporate share of total income is not greatly affected by inflation, and the deviations from approximate indexing are not substantial over a period of a few years.[5] Yet there are three ways in which the tax base is not indexed in the strictest sense. First, firms not opting for the last-in-first-out (LIFO) method of valuing inventories suffer taxes on inventory capital gains.[6] Second, depreciation of fixed capital is based on historical, not replacement, costs. In effect, businesses are prevented from using LIFO, or even inflated first-in-first-out (FIFO), accounting on their

phasis on the Lower Income Population," Technical Analysis Paper 2 (Office of Income Security Policy, 1974; processed), especially pp. 34–36, for further discussion of the response to inflation of all of these programs.

4. For example, if a 2 percent increase in the current rate of inflation led to an increase in the expected rate of inflation by 2 percent and to a rise in the nominal interest rate from 5 to 7 percent, and if all Treasury debt were in one-year securities, the 2 percent increase in prices would lead to a 40 percent increase in interest payments. The rise in nominal interest rates might be even greater because of income taxes. If so, government interest payments would increase more than 40 percent. On the other hand, much long-term debt would have been floated a long time ago, and interest payments would increase on this debt only as it is retired. In this case interest payments would be apt to increase less. And so it goes.

5. See chapter 2.

6. When all prices are rising at the same rate, LIFO is tantamount to complete, if optional, indexing when inventory stocks are not declining. When prices are rising at different rates, LIFO excludes from tax all capital gains and losses on inventories, whether due to changes in the average price level or to deviations of particular prices around the average. Alternatively, original inventory costs could be inflated by the rate of general price inflation over the inventory holding period. This inflated FIFO option would exclude from tax the capital gains on inventory consumption resulting from general inflation. But it would add relative capital gains when the prices of goods in inventories rose more than average and subtract capital losses when the prices rose less than average. Whether these relative capital gains and losses should be taxable or not depends on whether one views the firm as being forced to buy these particular goods (in which case it is no better off, even with relative capital gains) or as being able to buy a general market basket of goods (in which case it is better off).

fixed investments. Third, the corporation tax, like the personal income tax, allows the deduction of interest costs in computing taxable income but does not tax gains from the decline in value of the firms' liabilities that are fixed in nominal terms.

As for the other taxes, both customs duties and payroll taxes are now essentially indexed for inflation. Until 1972 social security payroll taxes were assessed at a flat rate on earnings below a fixed maximum that was changed periodically by Congress as benefits were increased. Since then this ceiling on taxable earnings has been adjusted automatically as average earnings increase. Payroll taxes on federal civilian employees are a constant proportion of federal wages, which are also indexed.

Overindexed Items

Among the more dramatic examples of congressional ineptitude are the methods adopted to adjust social security and federal retirement benefits for inflation. Congress presumably wished to index these benefits, but through ignorance or conceivably by buckling to the power of lobbyists, it went much too far.

The overindexing of social security benefits has received considerable attention lately.[7] The problem arises because active workers receive a double adjustment for inflation; not only are the earnings increased upon which benefits are calculated, but so also is the formula used in computing benefits. Thus under present law, the higher the rate of inflation, the higher the replacement rates are. The seriousness of the problem is indicated by the fact that payroll taxes will have to rise from their present 10 percent to 21 percent by the middle of the twenty-first century if inflation averages 4 percent and to 41 percent if inflation averages 10 percent. The problem can be solved in various ways, however, and if it is, payroll taxes need rise only slightly.[8] Surely Congress does not intend to subject our grandchildren to such a capricious lottery.

The overindexing of federal civilian and military retirement benefits constitutes possibly an even more blatant giveaway. Whenever the consumer price index (CPI) rises by 3 percent or more since the

7. See, for example, Blechman, Gramlich, and Hartman, *Setting National Priorities,* pp. 175–84. More detailed reviews are given in the many official and nonofficial references cited there.

8. See *Reports of the Quadrennial Advisory Council on Social Security,* H. Doc. 94-75, 94:1 (Government Printing Office, 1975), for a number of proposals.

last adjustment and remains at that level for a three-month period, the benefits of civil service retirees rise by the percentage increase of the CPI plus 1 percent. Thus if the CPI rises by 3 percent a year, retirement benefits rise by 4 percent a year; if the CPI rises by 3 percent a quarter (12.6 percent a year), retirement benefits rise by 4 percent a quarter (17 percent a year). If measures to index income and corporate taxes cannot be designed any better than the automatic adjustment of social security and civil service pensions was, it would be far better to not even attempt to make adjustments on the tax side.

Underindexed Items

The major tax that is not indexed for inflation is the personal income tax. Because rates are progressive and bracket widths, exemptions, and other provisions are fixed in nominal dollars, real tax burdens rise during inflation. Since World War II, however, Congress has periodically adjusted income tax rates so as to prevent average effective tax rates from rising in response either to inflation or economic growth.[9] Thus although the personal income tax rate structure is not formally indexed, it has changed much as it would have if indexed.

Inflation has also distorted the base of the personal income tax, however, and Congress has not done anything directly about this problem. The most serious distortions relate to net income from capital. Households must report their entire interest income, although part of such income merely replaces the decline in the real value of assets with fixed nominal value. Not all capital gains are taxed, but households are prevented from deducting that part of capital appreciation that simply maintains the real value of the property. Finally, as with the corporate tax, households may deduct the full cost of interest expense from taxable income but are not required to report as a gain the decline in the value of liabilities with fixed nominal value. These conventions unfairly distort tax burdens among households in the short run and may lead to unintended and possibly adverse changes in the rates of return on assets and liabilities in the long run.

Other underindexed taxes include estate and gift taxes, excise taxes, and the payroll tax for unemployment insurance. The fact that exemptions and the bracket limits under the estate and gift taxes are not adjusted for inflation implies that effective tax rates are increased

9. See chapters 5 and 11.

in inflationary times. The fact that the dollar levy is set in nominal terms on a fixed real quantity (excise taxes) or that a proportional rate is assessed up to a maximum ceiling (unemployment insurance) implies that effective tax rates fall in inflationary times.

The Effect of Underindexing the Tax System

It is impossible to make a forceful case on principle for not indexing the tax system. Nobody wants tax liabilities and incentives unpredictably influenced by inflation. At the same time, few would defend the present tax system as ideal or argue that it should be preserved in detail. The absence of indexing may cause inflation to mitigate certain problems with the system or may necessitate a periodic review of the tax system during which some of the problems could be resolved. Consequently it is helpful to determine whether the failure to index taxes aggravates or ameliorates present shortcomings in the personal and corporation income taxes before deciding whether to support indexing and in what form.

Rate Progressivity

The automatic rise of real revenues from the personal income tax during inflation has been widely discussed. But Congress has demonstrated the capacity to hold real income tax revenues constant through periodic legislation. The real question, then, is whether automatic adjustment by formula is better than discretionary adjustments by Congress. The issue closely resembles the choice between rules and discretion in the setting of monetary policy that economists have debated for the past two decades.

The issue is a difficult one. A possible argument against automatic indexing rests on the stabilizing effect of automatic increases in real tax revenues during inflation. There may be something to this argument, but it has two important flaws. First, the argument confuses levels with rates of change. Real tax levels are raised permanently by an increase in prices. The added revenues help stabilize the economy as inflation occurs but continue to flow into the federal coffers even after prices have stabilized at a higher level and when inflation fighting may no longer be necessary. The second and more serious flaw in the argument becomes apparent in light of recent economic history. When devaluations of the dollar, price increases by raw materials cartels, and world food shortages cause sharp bursts of inflation unrelated to excessive domestic demand, it may be inappropriate to let real tax levels rise and the budget become more restrictive. If anything, the events of 1974 suggest that higher prices, accompanied by a drain of spending power, should have occasioned a less, not more, restrictive budget.

But the automatic stabilization argument against indexing should not be totally discounted. Congress finds raising taxes harder than cutting them, and hence finds it harder to deal with demand-pull inflation than with recessions. In such cases political economists may be willing to exchange small delays in the enactment of tax cuts necessitated by externally generated inflation in return for automatic and desirable tax increases caused by domestically generated inflation and not dependent on current congressional action.

A second argument, this one in favor of indexing, points to the fact that a nonindexed tax system raises taxes more than proportionately for low-income households and thus appears to be a regressive force. If the impact of inflation on the tax base is ignored, the first part of the allegation is true but not the second.[10] Taxes do increase disproportionately for low-income households, but because average tax rates are lowest for households with low incomes, the percentage reduction in after-tax income caused by inflation varies little for all households with incomes under $50,000 and then rises for all but the superrich. The effect of a nonindexed rate structure on the distribution of income is therefore basically neutral, with slight progressivity at the very highest levels. Moreover, discretionary adjustments have reduced taxes more for low-income households than for high-income households.[11] The promotion of equality in the distribution of after-tax incomes is, then, not a good argument for indexing.

The central issue in the debate about indexing the rate structure is really a matter of politics—would Congress make more sensible tax and expenditure policies if it constrained itself by automatic rules, or if it made periodic reappraisals? A nonindexed system of expenditures moves in the direction of "zero-base" budgeting—the requirement that all expenditures be justified anew each year. Every year that prices rise, expenditures that are not indexed decline in real

10. The effect of inflation on the tax base is considered below. See also chapters 2, 4, 5, and 11.
11. See table 5-4, chapter 5.

terms. By contrast, taxes that are not indexed rise in real terms on the average. The "fiscal dividend" increases because inflation revokes a portion of past expenditure increases and increases taxes. Congress may do nothing in response, or it may cut taxes, or it may raise expenditures. Farsighted liberals who are worried about the difficulty of budgetary planning may be cheered by the automatic repeal of a portion of past expenditures or troubled by the decline in real expenditures. Farsighted conservatives, concerned about the long-term growth of government, may be either cheered by the automatic decline in real expenditures or worried by the automatic rise in real revenues. Thus whether a partially nonindexed budget will lead to more or less government, a more or less responsible budget policy, more or less redistribution of income, or anything else becomes very difficult to forecast. Any assertion can be met with an equally persuasive counterassertion.

The ambivalence I impute to both liberals and conservatives does depend on the fact that some expenditures are not now indexed, however. If all were, conservatives would have more reason to fear that inflation-induced increases in real tax payments would permit the future growth of real expenditures and would be more strongly in favor of indexing taxes. Liberals might worry more that indexing would erase fiscal dividends and might oppose indexing more strongly.

Whatever conclusion one reaches on indexing the tax structure, failure to correct the overindexing of social security can have serious consequences. The longer transfer programs remain indexed or overindexed while other expenditures are not, the longer the indexed portion of the budget will be apt to grow more rapidly than the nonindexed portion. If this should happen, the weighted average inflation elasticity of expenditures would increase and eventually might even surpass that of taxes. The budget would become more "uncontrollable," and the political debate over indexing the tax system would sharpen.

Distortions in the Tax Base

Tax laws define property income as all receipts from property in excess of those required to maintain nominal capital intact. When prices rise, the receipts required to maintain *nominal* capital intact are different from those required to maintain *real* capital intact. Hence wealthholders collectively suffer losses from inflation at the hands of the tax system. Holders of dollar-denominated assets are taxed on nominal and not real interest. Sellers of equities are taxed on gains, part of which may simply preserve the real value of the stock. Businesses may deduct only depreciation based on historical cost when computing profits.

If all returns from wealth were taxable as accrued and all associated costs were deductible, the effect of inflation could be offset by allowing each taxpayer to deduct from taxable income an amount equal to the inflation rate times his wealth. But if not all returns are taxable, such a simple remedy loses its appeal. For example, it would be hard to justify such treatment for the holders of common stock whose long-term gains are taxed at half the normal rates and whose taxes are deferred until gains are realized or are forgiven altogether if the asset is held until death.

Given the extremely uneven treatment accorded property income by the present system, it would be preferable not to make a uniform wealth adjustment for inflation but to correct the inflation-induced distortions in taxable incomes and payments as they arise. The items most obviously in need of attention are historical-cost depreciation, capital gains, and interest payments and receipts.

Most discussions of tax base indexing refer to a situation in which the rate of inflation was improperly anticipated. Unanticipated inflation causes random shifts in the income distribution. The size of these shifts depends on whether inflation was generally underestimated or overestimated, the variance in expected rates of inflation, the composition of private portfolios, and the tax treatment of various returns. The larger such shifts are, the better the case is for indexing tax bases on simple grounds of equity. As inflation becomes more generally anticipated, however, and as disagreement about expected rates diminishes, this rationale becomes less important. Over this longer run, borrowers, lenders, savers, and investors can all protect themselves from inflation as long as they know what the rate will be and how the Internal Revenue Service will deal with inflation-induced gains and losses. Thus the decision to index the tax base should hinge not so much on short-term equity considerations as on the economic forces set up as various groups move to protect themselves against inflation. The following sections are appraisals of both historical-cost depreciation and the tax treatment of interest incomes and costs from this longer-term perspective.

HISTORICAL-COST DEPRECIATION. What historical-cost basis should firms be allowed to use in computing depreciation? Since inflation prevents firms from replacing their capital at historical cost, the failure of existing tax rules to recognize this fact understates true capital costs. As with the FIFO inventory correction, the firm in effect is taxed on all nominal and relative capital gains on the taxable capital it consumes in production. Once prospective investors come to anticipate inflation, they will require higher expected rates of return than would otherwise be the case to cover anticipated losses through understatement of depreciation. Thus inflation reduces the value to the firm of historical-cost depreciation and impedes capital investment and growth.

The size of the impediment depends on the expected rate of inflation and may be large. If firms invest as long as the net yield on productive capital exceeds the rate of interest (appropriately discounting for risk, taxes, inflation, and other factors), the standard equilibrium cost-of-capital expression developed by Hall and Jorgenson may be used to estimate the size of the impediment. Let

(1) $$c/q = (r+d)(1-k-uz)/(1-u),$$

where

c = the average return earned by a new investment;
q = the price of the investment good;
r = an appropriate risk-corrected, after-tax, real interest rate;
d = the true exponential rate of depreciation of the investment;
k = the rate of investment tax credit;
u = the corporate tax rate;
z = the present value of the depreciation deduction for an investment initially costing one dollar.[12]

Table 10-2 shows present values of the depreciation deduction for various asset lives, depreciation conventions, and anticipated rates of

12. See Robert E. Hall and Dale W. Jorgenson, "Application of the Theory of Optimum Capital Accumulation," and Charles W. Bischoff, "The Effect of Alternative Lag Distributions," both in Gary Fromm, ed., *Tax Incentives and Capital Spending* (Brookings Institution, 1971), pp. 9–60 and 61–125.

Table 10-2. Present Value of Depreciation Deduction (z) as a Percentage of Instantaneous Depreciation (Expensing = 100) of an Asset, by Selected Asset Lives, Anticipated Rates of Inflation (g), and Depreciation Methods, Assuming an After-Tax Real Interest Rate (r) of 5 Percent
Percent

		Method of depreciation		
Asset life	*Rate of inflation* (g)	*Straight line*[a]	*Sum of years' digits*[b]	*Double-declining balance*[c]
10 years	0	79	84	82
(close to the average	5	63	74	70
for producer's equipment)	10	52	64	59
20 years	0	63	74	69
(close to the average	5	43	57	52
for total producers'	10	32	46	41
investment)				
30 years	0	52	64	59
(close to the average	5	32	46	41
for producers' structures)	10	22	35	32

Sources: Values of z are computed from the general formula

$$z = \int_0^T e^{-rs} q e^{-gs} D(s)\,ds,$$

where T is the tax life of the investment, s is its age, r is the discount rate, g is the anticipated rate of inflation when firms are forced to use historical-cost depreciation (indexing of depreciation allowances for general price inflation is tantamount to setting g equal to zero), q is the initial price of the investment, and $D(s)$ is the proportion of the depreciation base for an asset of age s that may be deducted from taxable income. The specific formulas used for each depreciation method are given in the notes below. The formulas are from, or are adapted from, Robert E. Hall and Dale W. Jorgenson, "Application of the Theory of Optimum Capital Accumulation," and Charles W. Bischoff, "The Effect of Alternative Lag Distributions," both in Gary Fromm, ed., *Tax Incentives and Capital Spending* (Brookings Institution, 1971).
   a. Using $D(s) = 1/T$.
   b. Using $D(s) = 2(T-s)/T^2$, a continuous approximation worked out by Bischoff (cited above), p. 84.
   c. Using

$$z = \int_0^{T/2} e^{-(r+g)s}\, \frac{2}{T}\, e^{-2s/T}\,ds + \int_{T/2}^{T} e^{-(r+g)s}\, \frac{2}{T}\, e^{-1}\,ds,$$

an expression derived from Hall and Jorgenson (cited above), p. 19.

inflation. As a standard, if firms could expense their capital costs (deduct the entire cost in the first year), the present value of the depreciation deduction would be 100, and the question of historical versus replacement cost would be irrelevant. If depreciation must be taken over the life of the asset, the present value of the depreciation deduction declines with the life of the asset. The decline is more marked under straight-line depreciation than under either of the two accelerated depreciation methods.

The noteworthy aspect of table 10-2 is the devastating impact of inflation on the present value of historical-cost depreciation. For example, if asset lives are twenty years (close to the average for all producers' investment) and inflation at 5 percent is anticipated, even accelerated depreciation (either sum of the years' digits or double-declining balance) is worth substantially less to the firm than straight-line depreciation would be if based on replacement cost.[13] In other words, if accelerated depreciation was intended as a shortcut method of replacement-cost depreciation, it is inadequate, even for expected inflation rates as low as 5 percent.

Table 10-3 presents the required rate of return for corporate investment for different assumed rates of inflation, under various depreciation rules and other tax provisions. The required rate of return using historical-cost depreciation would have been 24.6 percent if 5 percent inflation had been anticipated and 26.3 percent if 10 percent inflation had been anticipated under the 1974 tax system. With replacement-cost depreciation, on the other hand, the required rate of return for corporate investment would have been only 21.6 percent, 3 percentage points below the required rate with anticipated inflation of 5 percent. The introduction of replacement-cost depreciation would have been more valuable to firms than either an increase in the investment credit on all corporate investment from 5 percent to 10 percent or a reduction in the corporation income tax rate from 48 percent to 40 percent would have been, and virtually the same as a reduction in tax lives from an average of 20 years to an average of 10 years. Both replacement-cost depreciation and the investment credit cut the required rate of return by about 0.4 percentage point for each billion-dollar reduction in corporate tax revenue, as opposed to a cut of about 0.2 percentage point for each billion-dollar reduction in revenues from a lowering of corporate tax rates or tax lives.[14] By these

13. Read from the table in the row corresponding to $g = 0$, since replacement cost is tantamount to depreciation with no expected price inflation. Hence this comparison is between present values of 57 or 52 percent for the acceleration methods and 63 percent for replacement cost: replacement cost is better for firms.

14. The computed values for the cost of capital are similar to those given by T. Nicolaus Tideman and Donald P. Tucker in chapter 2, except that they present the capital cost net of depreciation, while I add in depreciation and give c/q. The budgetary cost of replacement-cost depreciation is from William D. Nordhaus, "The Falling Share of Profits," *Brookings Papers on Economic Activity, 1:1974*, table 1, p. 172; that of the investment credit is the result of multiplying estimated 1973 corporate fixed investment by 0.05; that of corporate tax rate cuts is derived by multiplying

Table 10-3. Rate of Return Required to Attract Corporate Investment (c/q)
under Various Tax and Depreciation Provisions
Percent

	Depreciation provision		
	Historical cost		
Tax provision	5 percent inflation	10 percent inflation	Replacement cost
1974 system	24.6	26.3	21.6
Departures from 1974 system			
Investment credit increased from 5 to 10 percent	22.8	24.6	19.7
Tax rates lowered from 48 to 40 percent	22.7	24.0	20.6
Tax lives reduced from 20 to 10 years	21.5	23.2	19.4

Sources: The following values are assumed for the 1974 system: after-tax real interest rate (r) = 5 percent; true depreciation rate (d) = 13 percent; investment credit rate (k) = 5 percent; corporate tax rate (u) = 48 percent; and tax life for investment (T) = 20 years. The present value of the depreciation deduction is then a weighted average of the values in table 10-2 with the weights equaling 0.25 for straight-line depreciation, 0.10 for sum of years' digits, and 0.65 for double-declining balance—the approximate present proportions according to information obtained from the U.S. Department of the Treasury. The after-tax real interest rate was taken from Charles W. Bischoff, "The Effect of Alternative Lag Distributions," in Gary Fromm, ed., *Tax Incentives and Capital Spending* (Brookings Institution, 1971), pp. 61–125. The depreciation rate was computed from the formula $K = I + (1-d)K_{-1}$, where K is the capital stock and I is net investment, both for privately owned structures and equipment in constant dollars, from the national income accounts in John C. Musgrave, "New Estimates of Fixed Nonresidential Business Capital in the United States, 1925–73," *Survey of Current Business*, vol. 54 (March 1974), pp. 23–27. For d, the implied average for the past seven years was calculated, using a composite capital stock consisting of two-thirds of the double-declining-balance version and one-third of the straight-line version of the stock.

standards, then, the introduction of replacement-cost depreciation is as effective as any other commonly discussed fiscal device in stimulating investment per dollar of budgetary cost.

Replacement-cost depreciation may stimulate capital investment efficiently, but is it desirable to do so? A first argument in favor is that replacement-cost depreciation at least makes any stimulating or depressing effect on investment embodied in the tax law independent of the rate of inflation, which seems appropriate. Unless Congress wishes to tighten depreciation provisions whenever prices are expected to rise, it should not welcome a hidden tightening caused when inflationary expectations increase. Second, replacement-cost depreciation would be a satisfactory way to stimulate a currently lagging sector of the economy (producers' investment) without aggravating the budget deficit as severely as other investment incentives would. Replacement-cost investment dollars have, in a sense, one of the highest ag-

before-tax profits by 0.08; and that of cutting the tax lives comes from extrapolations based on information in "Alternative Estimates of Corporate Depreciation and Profits, 1965–73," *Survey of Current Business*, vol. 54 (May 1974), pp. 19–21.

gregate demand "bangs-for-the-buck" of any of the commonly used countercyclical actions. Computations based on estimates provided by Charles Bischoff indicate that a switch to replacement-cost depreciation would sufficiently increase GNP to *reduce* the budget deficit after about two years.[15]

Looking beyond the current recession, policymakers must decide whether they wish to increase the fraction of GNP that is invested. James Tobin, Edmund Phelps, and now Martin Feldstein have argued that the United States is and has long been investing too little—the welfare of all generations would be increased if all would agree to an increased investment ratio.[16] This welfare gain would be due to the fact that rates of return on corporate and other business investments (see table 10-3) very much exceed the rates of return at which individuals are willing to save. Any step that would increase saving— such as a larger federal surplus (or smaller deficit)—and thereby enable increased investment would advance this objective. So would the introduction of replacement-cost depreciation, provided that savings were increased to meet heightened investment demand.

But it also can be argued that measures to increase investment are not so desirable at this time. One may either question the value of growth or argue that identifiable near-term sources of investment demand—to develop new sources of energy, to provide housing, and to meet public and private commitments in areas such as pollution abatement and mass transit—are so large that, even without additional measures to stimulate investment, saving as a fraction of GNP must rise in the late seventies.[17] If policymakers accept the forecast that investment demand will be strong, they should strive to increase saving before they add further to investment demand.

ASSET INCOMES AND COSTS. Unanticipated inflation generates windfall gains for borrowers and windfall losses for lenders, gains and losses that the existing tax system ignores. As inflation becomes ex-

15. Bischoff, "The Effect of Alternative Lag Distributions," p. 117.

16. See, for example, James Tobin, "Economic Growth as an Objective of Government Policy," *American Economic Review*, vol. 54 (May 1964, *Papers and Proceedings, 1963*), pp. 1–20; Edmund Phelps, "The Golden Rule of Accumulation: A Fable for Growthmen," *American Economic Review*, vol. 51 (September 1961), pp. 638–43; and Martin Feldstein, "Social Security, Induced Retirement, and Aggregate Capital Accumulation," *Journal of Political Economy*, vol. 82 (September–October 1974), pp. 905–26.

17. See Barry Bosworth, James S. Duesenberry, and Andrew S. Carron, *Capital Needs in the Seventies* (Brookings Institution, 1975).

pected, lenders come to demand a premium to cover their losses both from inflation and from the failure of the tax system to recognize the inflationary loss; and borrowers become willing to pay this premium because they can deduct it before computing taxable income. Martin Bailey, Vito Tanzi, and Martin Feldstein have shown that if borrowers and lenders face the same marginal tax rate (t), the market interest rate (i) must be related to the interest rate that would prevail when prices are stable (i^*) by the expression

$$(2) \qquad\qquad i = i^* + g/(1-t)$$

if after-tax interest income and expense are to be unaffected by inflation when the tax system is not indexed.[18] If the tax system is indexed, the tax rate, t, on the excess of i over i^* can be considered equal to zero; that is, interest paid or received to cover the change in the real value of fixed dollar assets is untaxed. Hence if $i^* = 5$ percent, anticipated inflation, g, is 10 percent, and both borrower and lender are in the 50 percent tax bracket ($t = 0.5$), then the nominal interest rate, i, will be 25 percent in a nonindexed system and 15 percent in an indexed system. Thus the standard monetarist proposition—that the nominal interest rate equals the real interest rate plus the rate of anticipated inflation—is seen to be oversimplified, or appropriate only for a world without taxes or with inflation indexing of interest payments and receipts. If these conditions are satisfied and if all taxpayers face the same marginal tax rate, market-determined increases in interest rates eventually will adjust both to inflation and the tax code, and there are no distortions introduced by the lack of indexing.

Unfortunately, however, one cannot be confident that market interest rates will rise just the amount suggested in equation 2, that everyone will anticipate the same rate of inflation, or that borrowers and lenders will be in the same tax bracket. Consequently a nonindexed system may create undesirable distortions.

First, those who anticipate inflation incorrectly suffer multiplied

18. See chapter 11 in this volume; Vito Tanzi, "Inflation, Indexation and Interest Income Taxation," Banca Nazionale del Lavoro, *Quarterly Review*, no. 116 (March 1976), pp. 64–76; and Martin Feldstein, "Inflation, Income Taxes, and the Rate of Interest: A Theoretical Analysis," Discussion Paper 414 (Harvard Institute of Economic Research, 1975; processed). Feldstein also deals with a reason why this proposition is oversimplified: if the rate of return on money balances is fixed at zero and if the demand for money is interest elastic, the rise in nominal interest rates will cause asset holders to try to substitute capital and bonds for money, and in so doing, will affect interest rates.

windfall losses (lenders who underestimate or borrowers who overestimate inflation) or enjoy multiplied windfall gains (borrowers who underestimate or lenders who overestimate inflation).[19]

Second, not all lenders and borrowers face the same marginal tax rates. Consequently the before-tax interest rate necessary to compensate lenders subject to high marginal rates will be higher than the interest rates that borrowers subject to lower marginal rates are willing to pay. As a result some transactions that would occur if prices were stable will not occur when prices are rising. Building on the previous numerical example, assume that lenders are in the 50 percent bracket and borrowers are in the 25 percent bracket. At 10 percent inflation, the real interest rate to lenders is 5 percent if the market rate is 25 percent, but the real interest rate to borrowers is 5 percent if the market rate is 18.3 percent. At any nominal interest rate between 18.3 and 25 percent, the probable outcome of market adjustments, some loans will be made, but each will be less profitable than it would be if prices were stable, and some loans will not be negotiated, because they are now unprofitable to the borrower, the lender, or both. The same example can be turned around to cover the case where lenders (in the 25 percent tax bracket) will be willing to lend at 18.3 percent and borrowers (in the 50 percent tax bracket) willing to borrow at 25 percent: here inflation will increase the volume of loans and cause excessive use of debt finance.

Third, even if lenders and borrowers face the same tax rate, the lack of indexing increases the volatility of interest rates. If the relevant tax rate in equation 2 is 50 percent, interest rates will rise by twice the anticipated rate if the tax system is not indexed but only by the amount of inflation if it is indexed. The added instability from failure to index can be substantial with anticipated inflation of 5

19. This point can be illustrated by an example. If $i^* = 5$ percent, $g = 10$ percent, and all taxpayers face a tax rate of 0.5, the market rate of interest would be 15 percent under an indexed tax system and 25 percent under a nonindexed one. If the tax system were indexed, those unaware of the imminence of inflation would lend at 5 percent, be allowed to deduct the 10 percent inflation erosion after the fact, and have a net after-tax real loss of 2.5 percent (in contrast to those who correctly anticipated inflation, who would have a net after-tax real gain of 2.5 percent). If the system were not indexed, those unaware of inflation would still lend at 5 percent and receive 2.5 percent after tax—and −7.5 percent after considering inflation erosion (still in contrast to those who correctly anticipated inflation, who again would receive a net after-tax real return of 2.5 percent). The lack of indexing would increase the premium for correct anticipation of inflation.

percent or more. Volatility of interest rates is undesirable because convention, politics, and institutions impose limits on some nominal rates but not others. Increases in market interest rates can then cause withdrawals from savings and loan institutions and depression in the housing market, and they penalize small savers who are unable to protect their assets against erosion by inflation. They may also lead to unwise monetary policy in an attempt to forestall variation in nominal rates. The argument for reducing volatility in interest rates is strong and indexing will help do the job.

Finally, if interest income and expense are not indexed, investment demand will be reduced if depreciation deductions are limited to historical cost. In the preceding numerical example, if the real interest rate were 5 percent, expected rates of inflation were 10 percent, all tax rates were 50 percent, and nominal interest income (expense) were taxable (deductible), equation 2 shows that all lenders and borrowers would be in the same after-tax position if the nominal interest rate were 25 percent that they would be in if prices were stable and the interest rate were 5 percent. For borrowers who invest in real capital, however, this would be true *only* if the 10 percent nominal capital gain on their investment were not taxed. In that case, their real after-tax investment return would be 2.5 percent—the 25 percent borrowing rate taxed at 50 percent, with the firm willing to pay another 10 percent to reflect the fact that debt depreciates in value relative to real capital, which has an untaxed nominal gain. But if the 10 percent nominal capital gain on the borrower's investment were explicitly taxed at 50 percent, as it would be if historical-cost depreciation prevented the firm from depreciating the true value of the capital it used up, an additional tax equal to 5 percent of the amount borrowed would have to be paid, reducing net income from plus 2.5 percent to minus 2.5 percent.[20]

Thus the conditions under which the indexing of interest payments does not matter in the long run are seen to be highly restrictive and unrealistic. In real world economies such indexing undoubtedly does matter. Several desirable objectives would be accomplished by allowing depositors to claim only real interest as income, by not allowing mortgage borrowers to deduct the inflation premium in mortgage rates, by not taxing equity holders on gains that simply maintain the

20. Discussions with Arthur M. Okun were helpful in clarifying this point. Feldstein addressed similar issues in "Inflation, Income Taxes, and the Rate of Interest."

real value of the stock, by not allowing businesses to deduct inflation premiums or by allowing replacement-cost depreciation only on the equity-financed portion of investment. Such changes in the tax code would eliminate random changes in tax burdens and various potential distortions in loan and capital markets, reduce the volatility of nominal interest rates, and lessen the instability in financial markets.

Conclusions

Whether or not to index the tax and transfer system thus breaks down into a series of specific issues. The easiest to resolve is the pressing need to eliminate the overindexing of social security and civil service retirement programs. No rational argument can be made in favor of retaining these provisions, and the social security provision is important enough that it can indeed "bust the budget" if allowed to persist.

Next, the procedures for computing taxable income should be revised. Depreciation deductions should be based on replacement cost. The use of historical cost deters investment by significant but widely varying amounts, depending on the anticipated rate of inflation and the durability of assets. Interest income and expenses and capital gains and losses should also be indexed, not only for equities but also for bonds, savings deposits, mortgages, and all other assets, in order to reduce short-term inequities, distortions, and financial instability that result from a nonindexed tax treatment.

The most difficult question of all, however, concerns the desirability of indexing the dollar magnitudes in the income tax exemptions, the widths of the tax brackets, and other fixed nominal dollar provisions. This paper has been an attempt to argue that the purely economic considerations are probably unimportant and unpredictable. The political considerations seem just as unpredictable, but may be very important. Is it better for Congress to make a rule determining how taxes will be adjusted for inflation, or is it better to let inflation force Congress periodically to reconsider the rate structure exemptions and other provisions influencing the distribution of tax burdens?

CHAPTER ELEVEN

Inflationary Distortions and Taxes

MARTIN J. BAILEY

TO ASK whether the tax system should include indexing formulas to correct for the effects of inflation is equivalent to asking which set of distortions one prefers. In periods of price stability the tax system distorts the economy in various ways, some intended and some not. Inflation independently distorts both the economy and the measurement of taxable income; it also compounds or modifies economic distortions caused by the tax system. These effects are separate and distinct; only the tax-related, inflation-induced ones can be corrected by indexing. Indexing should be advocated only if the set of tax distortions associated with whatever automatic adjustments Congress will actually enact are preferred to those associated with inflation without such adjustments. It should be understood also that indexing cannot conceivably undo inflation-caused distortions that are related, not to taxes, but to wage leads and lags and to contracts negotiated on false expectations.

Expectations regarding inflation are crucial to the desirability of indexing. Most discussions of indexing seem to take for granted that inflation will be more rapid in the future than it has been in the past. But such assumptions should be explicit. If it were known that inflation would be at least 10 percent a year and would average 15 or 20 percent, indexing would seem urgently desirable to almost everyone. In contrast, if inflation were expected to average less than 2 percent, few would deem indexing worth the trouble.

Proponents of indexing usually assert that inflation distorts the accounting of incomes for tax purposes, causing some taxpayers to pay tax on more than their true incomes and some to pay tax on less. They sometimes hold that these effects are inherently bad; occasionally they merely assume it. From this perspective, indexing should undo these effects, making real tax burdens independent of inflation. Since taxable income is sometimes larger and frequently smaller than economic income, however, the standard of taxing true income has already been violated. Moreover, many effects of the present tax system are poorly understood and may be unintended. Inflation superimposes additional unintended effects, proportional in size either to the rate of inflation or to its cumulative amount. Not all of these effects are undesirable; once this possibility is admitted, one must consider which effects of inflation might be offset, first taking into account the objectives of the tax system and how inflation affects them.

The principal objectives of the tax system are (1) fiscal discipline —what the government buys must be paid for, primarily from tax revenues; (2) vertical equity, that is, progressivity; (3) horizontal equity, or the equal taxation of persons in equal circumstances (that is, with equal economic incomes); and (4) economic stabilization, especially *automatic* stabilization through the elasticity of total tax revenues. In addition the tax code is used to accomplish a number of more specific objectives: the promotion of economic efficiency in the private sector, the encouragement of home ownership, the preservation of small family farms, and a host of other purposes. In the advancement of these objectives, indexing has both important disadvantages and advantages; hence the case for it is far from clear.

Variable or intermittent inflation heightens uncertainty, but these events permit few reliable judgments and pose no special problems for tax policy. I shall comment on them briefly, however.

The effects of intermittent inflation are hard to predict. Wages, especially in highly unionized industries, initially rise more slowly than prices owing to long-term labor contracts. Buyers on long-term, fixed-price contracts enjoy windfall profits at the expense of their suppliers. Some industries fare better than others. On the average, stock prices rise less than the general price level so that the real values of corporate shares fall. The decline in the real value of stocks may have several causes. Traders may anticipate monetary and fiscal restrictions to stop the inflation. Or they may fear price controls or other regulations and the attendant uncertainty about prices and sales. Stock prices may also reflect the added burden of the corporation income tax, which is discussed below.

When inflation is higher than expected, borrowers profit at the expense of lenders because they can repay in depreciated dollars. Like other creditors, pensioners and other fixed-income recipients suffer losses that can continue over many years. If inflation persists, however, lenders demand higher interest rates, and get them as borrowers who expect more inflation compete for funds. Eventually pensioners and other fixed-income recipients benefit from high interest rates and from legislated adjustments of transfer payments. These adjustments end the transitional transfer from lenders to borrowers. When inflation subsides, high interest rates continue until borrowers and lenders lower their price expectations. During this phase lenders profit at the expense of borrowers, and pensioners do better than they anticipated.

The indexing of the tax system will neither avoid nor compensate for these effects of unanticipated changes in the rate of inflation on the distribution of income. A tax system with no indexing, however, magnifies fluctuations in interest rates. Lenders must pay taxes on that part of their interest income necessary to recover real capital. Symmetrically, borrowers may deduct from taxable income the entire interest payment, even though part of it is repayment of the original real capital. When inflation subsides, but before interest rates decline, the tax system again magnifies the transfer of income, this time from debtors to creditors. Indexing would prevent this magnifying effect.

In contrast, a steady and continuing inflation does not involve these transfers and economic uncertainties. Inflation becomes the norm, and such agreements as labor contracts and sales for future delivery will all reflect it. Relative prices and real incomes are approximately the same as with a stable price level. In this chapter, I will concentrate mainly on this case; that is, continuous inflation to which the economy fully adjusts.

Fiscal Discipline

If government expenditures rise, either taxes or the government deficit must increase. To some degree taxes increase automatically as incomes rise because the personal income tax is progressive, while the rest of the tax system is roughly proportional. Whether incomes rise because of inflation or the growth of real income is immaterial. The revenues are available to expand existing programs, to start new programs, and to reduce taxes. Therefore inflation gives Congress scope to create new programs or to expand old ones if it does not reduce taxes instead.

For those who want more and larger government programs, the effect of inflation seems desirable because it reduces the need for new taxes or tax increases. For those who want fewer and smaller government programs, this effect seems undesirable; they would favor indexing to avoid an inflation-induced fiscal dividend, to tighten fiscal discipline, and to promote a more careful review of real increases in government spending.

As a practical matter, however, it is hard to give this effect of indexing much weight. Congress has not allowed inflation to enlarge the share of national income taken by the personal income tax; instead it has periodically reduced personal income tax receipts by enacting just enough tax "reforms" to hold constant the ratio of personal income taxes to national income. The government share of national income has grown since 1953 largely because of increases in the social security program and in the state and local government sectors, all of which have required specific tax legislation. Total government as a fraction of national income rose by 8.9 percentage points from 30.9 percent to 39.8 percent (see table 11-1). Federal personal tax and nontax receipts, consisting almost entirely of the personal income tax, increased from 10.6 to 11.5 percent, less than 1 percentage point. In sharp contrast, the share of social insurance contributions more than tripled, from 2.4 to 7.8 percent, and that of state and local receipts from their own revenue nearly doubled, from 8.0 percent to 14.4 percent. Thus between 1953 and 1974, the growth in government's share of national income was fully accounted for by two areas, neither of which has a fiscal dividend.

One could argue that indexing would reduce the frequency of tax reforms that nearly always complicate the tax laws further. This bene-

Table 11-1. Total National Income and Selected Components, National Income Accounts, 1953 and 1974
Amounts in billions of dollars

Year	Total national income		Total government receipts		Federal personal tax and nontax receipts		Social insurance contributions		State and local receipts[a]	
	Amount	Percentage of total	Amount	Percentage of national income	Amount	Percentage of national income	Amount	Percentage of national income	Amount	Percentage of national income
1953	304.7	100.0	94.3	30.9	32.2	10.6	7.4	2.4	24.4	8.0
1974	1,142.2	100.0	455.0	39.8	131.2	11.5	88.7	7.8	164.0	14.4

Source: *Economic Report of the President, February 1975*, tables C-15, C-67, C-68.
a. Excludes federal grants.

Figure 11-1. **Effective Sales and Excise Tax Rates before and after Ten-Year, 100 Percent Cumulative Inflation, by Adjusted Family Income, 1975 Tax Laws**

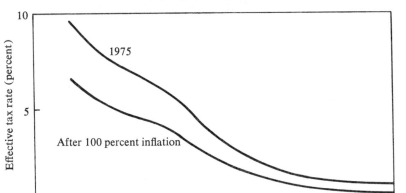

Source: Table 11-5, column 5, and sum of columns 5 and 10.

fit is at best conjectural, however. Tax reforms enacted since World War II might have been enacted even if there had been no inflation. Even if the number of tax changes is increased by inflation, the number and extent of the reforms may not be.

Vertical Equity, or Progressivity

The effect of inflation on the progressivity of the income tax system is important and noteworthy but usually overlooked. In the absence of legislation, the real burden of the most regressive taxes happens to be reduced by inflation, while that of the most progressive is increased. The decline in the value of personal exemptions and the minimum standard deduction and the compression of the rate schedule of the personal income tax are exceptions to this rule.

The burden of the most regressive taxes, the alcoholic beverage and tobacco excise taxes, is reduced exactly in proportion to inflation. Gasoline taxes are also specific excises and are probably regressive. Almost all other excises, such as the sales taxes in most states, are ad valorem taxes whose real value is unaffected by inflation. Figure 11-1 shows the reduction in real excise tax burdens caused by a doubling of prices. The share of specific excises in all sales and excise taxes is assumed to be the same for every income class. Specific excises on alcoholic beverages, tobacco, and motor fuels average about half of all sales and excises. Inflation reduces the burden of excise taxes on the lowest income class from almost 10 percent to about 7 percent of income. Both the burden and its reduction due to inflation fall steadily with rising income until they are negligible at incomes of $1 million and over.

Two important taxes, one regressive and one progressive, are little affected by inflation: the social security tax and the property tax. The wage ceiling for the social security tax is now indexed to the median earnings of covered workers and thus is affected by inflation only by the lag in the indexing formula and only for those whose earnings exceed the ceiling. This effect is minor, however, and is opposite to almost all other effects of inflation that increase progressivity.

Inflation seems to reduce real property tax collections because re-assessment cycles commonly range from three to eight years and in a few extreme cases are even longer.[1] But tax collections can be increased as readily by raising tax rates as by revaluation unless a legal ceiling prevents increases in rates, and local governments set the rates each year. Hence this tax can be disregarded when discussing the impact of inflation.

The effect of inflation on the rate structure of the personal income tax may be perceived by noting that if the price level doubles, and if the tax law is unchanged, each marginal and average tax rate becomes applicable at half the real income to which it applied before the price rise.[2] Figure 11-2 shows the impact on a family of four of cumulative inflation of 100 percent (for example, ten years of 7 percent inflation a year or two years of 41 percent inflation each year). The steps show the marginal tax rate schedules, without regard for the $30-per-person credit enacted in 1975; the smooth curves show the average rates applicable to ordinary income after reducing the tax by the personal credit.

Families with incomes between roughly $2,800 and $5,800 in 1975, whom Congress has exempted from the federal income tax by successive increases in personal exemptions and the low-income allowance, would again become taxable. Presumably tax increases on

1. Henry J. Aaron, *Who Pays the Property Tax? A New View* (Brookings Institution, 1975), pp. 3, 68–69.
2. See chapter 5.

Figure 11-2. Federal Individual Income Tax Rates and Tax as a Percentage of Income for a Family of Four, before and after Ten-Year, 100 Percent Cumulative Inflation, by Real Adjusted Gross Income, 1975 Tax Laws[a]

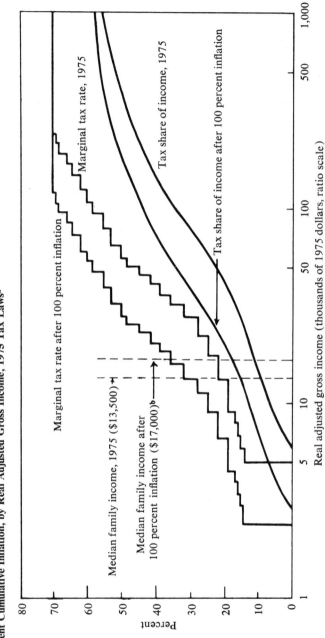

Percent

Marginal tax rate after 100 percent inflation

Marginal tax rate, 1975

Tax share of income, 1975

Tax share of income after 100 percent inflation

Median family income, 1975 ($13,500)

Median family income after 100 percent inflation ($17,000)[b]

Real adjusted gross income (thousands of 1975 dollars, ratio scale)

Sources: Median income from, or derived from, *Economic Report of the President, January 1976*, p. 194. Tax share calculated from Internal Revenue Code, individual income tax rates for 1975.
a. The effect of the $30-per-person tax credit enacted in 1975 is disregarded in the steps, but is included in the smooth curves. Deductions are assumed as either $1,900 or 16 percent of adjusted gross income, whichever is greater. Exemptions are $750 per person.
b. The figure of $17,000 for median family income after 100 percent inflation is the author's estimate of 1985 median family income.

these families and on others with incomes below the median should be deplored.

Tax increases on incomes above the median are more controversial. Even after a 100 percent inflation, average rates remain below 15 percent for half the population. But such an inflation would reduce the income at which the average tax rate schedule steepens noticeably from about $30,000 to about $15,000 (in 1975 prices). After a doubling of prices and incomes, rapid progression would begin around median income so that rates would rise steeply through the top half of the income distribution. Tax reformers who want substantial progressivity among most families with above-average incomes instead of having it concentrated, as now, on the very rich would welcome such a change.

Figure 11-2 presents a reasonably accurate picture of the impact of inflation on families whose incomes consist largely of wages and salaries. It is highly misleading, however, for families with incomes far above the median because such families receive a large part of their incomes in the form of capital gains or in other tax-privileged forms.

If shifting is disregarded, three taxes that contribute most to whatever progressivity there is in the overall tax structure are the capital gains tax, the corporation income tax, and federal and state estate taxes.[3] For distinct reasons the real burden of each increases directly with the rate of inflation.

The Capital Gains Tax

Because taxable capital gain is the monetary difference between the net sale price and the actual (historical) cost, general inflation increases taxable gains in both monetary and real terms, increasing the capital gains tax and reducing the real gain after tax. Part of the monetary gain is merely recovery of original real capital. Nevertheless, it is taxable under present law; thus the higher the rate of inflation, the lower the real gain after tax. Of course, the taxpayer may defer realization of the gain and so offset this tax increase through deferral.

---

3. For estimates of the overall pattern of tax burdens, see Joseph A. Pechman and Benjamin A. Okner, *Who Bears the Tax Burden?* (Brookings Institution, 1974), especially chap. 4; and note that the average rate of individual income tax does not exceed 16 percent of properly measured income for any income class (variant 1c, p. 59).

Figure 11-3. Capital Gains as a Percentage of Adjusted Gross Income, 1969 and 1971[a]

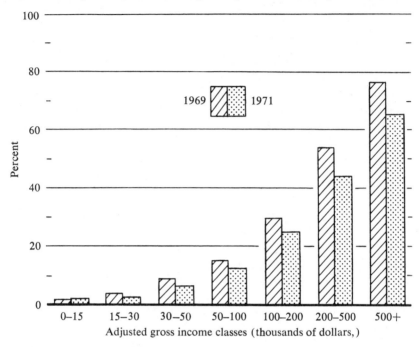

Adjusted gross income classes (thousands of dollars,)

Sources: U.S. Internal Revenue Service, *Statistics of Income—1969: Individual Income Tax Returns* (Government Printing Office, 1971), pp. 9, 33, 40, 42; and ibid., *1971* (GPO, 1973), pp. 6, 64–66.
a. The numerator of each percentage is total net capital gains, including the half of long-term gains excluded from adjusted gross income. The denominator is adjusted gross income plus the excluded half of long-term gains.

The taxation of nominal gains increases the apparent progressivity of the tax system for two reasons: first, the share of income realized in the form of capital gains is higher for high-income than for low-income taxpayers; and second, capital gains are taxed at progressive rates. Figure 11-3 illustrates the first reason. It shows the share of capital gains in total income both for 1969 and 1971, a peak and a trough of business activity, respectively. Capital gains represent less than 2 percent of income under $15,000 but range from 65 percent to 77 percent in the over-$500,000 bracket in those two years. Thus even a proportional inflation surtax on capital gains would be highly progressive.

The inflation surtax, however, is steeply progressive, not proportional (see table 11-2). As a result, the tax may exceed the real gain, leaving the taxpayer with an after-tax loss from a before-tax gain. The

Table 11-2. Inflation Surcharge on a Capital Gain, One-Year Holding Period, for Tax Rates of 10 Percent and 30 Percent, by Selected Inflation Rates and Real Rates of Gain
Rates in percent

Inflation rate per year	Sales price per dollar invested (dollars) Real rate of gain			Percentage tax per dollar of real gain Real rate of gain			Percentage inflation surcharge Real rate of gain		
	1	2	4	1	2	4	1	2	4
				Tax rate = 10					
0	1.01	1.02	1.04	10	10	10	0	0	0
3	1.04	1.05	1.07	40	25	18	30	15	8
7	1.08	1.09	1.11	81	46	28	71	36	18
				Tax rate = 30					
0	1.01	1.02	1.04	30	30	30	0	0	0
3	1.04	1.05	1.07	121	76	53	91	46	23
7	1.08	1.09	1.11	242	137	85	212	107	55

Source: Developed by author.

higher the taxpayer's marginal bracket and the smaller his rate of real gain, the more likely he is to take this kind of loss. A taxpayer facing 3 percent inflation and enjoying a 1 percent gain pays a tax equal to 30 percent of his real gain if he is in the 10 percent bracket and 91 percent if he is in the 30 percent bracket. At 7 percent inflation the tax rates rise to 71 percent and 212 percent, respectively.

Taxpayers may react to the inflation surcharge by holding assets longer, thereby deferring taxes and reducing the present value of the burden and of the inflation surcharge.[4] The larger the surcharge, the greater is the incentive to delay realization (see table 11-3). The full deferral effect can be seen in column 5, which shows the difference in the effective tax rate on two assets subject to the same cumulative increase in value but held for one and ten years respectively. The differential rises steeply with the rate of inflation. Table 11-3 is based on real gains equal to 2 percent a year (the rate implied by the 1962 capital gains study made by the Internal Revenue Service) if the average holding period was ten years.[5]

4. See Martin J. Bailey, "Capital Gains and Income Taxation," in Arnold C. Harberger and Martin J. Bailey, eds., *The Taxation of Income from Capital* (Brookings Institution, 1969), pp. 24–26.

5. U.S. Internal Revenue Service, *Statistics of Income—1962, Supplemental Report: Sales of Capital Assets Reported on Individual Income Tax Returns* (Government Printing Office, 1966). The 2 percent rate is an average of a 1 percent

Table 11-3. Tax Rate on Real Capital Gain as a Function of the Length of the Holding Period, by Selected Inflation Rates[a]
Rates in percent

Inflation rate (1)	One-year holding period, tax rate on real gain (2)	Ten-year holding period		Difference in effective rate, one- and ten-year holding period (percentage points) (5)
		Tax rate on real gain (3)	Tax on annual accrual rate (4)	
0	30	30	28	2
3	76	65	63	13
7	137	97	97	40

Sources: Column 2 is from the column in table 11-2 showing a one-year, 2 percent real gain and a 30 percent tax rate. Column 3 shows the tax rate on realization of a ten-year gain for the same real rate of gain and the same rates of inflation, computed as the ratio of tax to the cumulated real gain obtained by subtracting an inflation-adjusted cost basis from the sale price. Even viewed this way, the tax rate is lower for a ten-year gain than for a one-year gain when there is inflation—at 3 percent inflation the tax rate on the ten-year gain is 65 percent, compared with 76 percent on a one-year gain. Column 4 is the author's calculation, explained in the text. Column 5 equals column 2 minus column 4.
a. Tax rate = 30 percent on nominal gains. Although a 100 percent inflation doubles prices whether it occurs in one year or ten, the speed of inflation affects the tax impact because of the effects of compound interest.

If real gains average 2 percent a year, the holding period is ten years, and inflation is 7 percent a year, the effective capital gains rate for a taxpayer ostensibly in the 60 percent bracket (that is, one who pays 30 percent on capital gains) is 97 percent. For lower tax rates the proportionate increase in effective tax is similar. Therefore, as a rough guide, a 7 percent inflation triples capital gains rates. The effects shown in table 11-3 apply when the marginal rate applied to a capital gain remains unchanged. In addition, inflation disproportionately increases nominal gains and pushes taxpayers into higher brackets.

real annual gain for corporate stocks sold that year and a higher rate on other assets. Evidently sellers of corporate shares in 1962 realized their losses and just enough gains to have a small net gain. This pattern is likely to continue almost regardless of the average gain or loss in the stock market. No better evidence on the real rate of gain on other assets than the 1962 study is available.

The ten-year holding period results from adjusting the twelve-year average holding period for those assets for which this figure is reported. The reported items, accounting for about $6.2 billion of a total of $11 billion of gains (net of losses) in 1962, were corporate stock and other securities, real estate, residences, and livestock. No age distributions were published for assets used in trade or business, share of gain from partnerships and fiduciaries, proceeds from prior-year installment sales, and miscellaneous other items. On balance, these excluded items would seem to have shorter holding periods than those for which holding periods were published. Hence the ten-year holding period is roughly representative of all capital gains.

The Corporation Income Tax

Inflation increases the real burden of the corporation income tax in two ways. First, it leads to the understatement of depreciation costs. Second, it increases real profits of corporations at the expense of their bondholders by reducing the real value of outstanding debt. Because equity income is subject to both corporation and personal income taxes, while corporate interest payments are subject only to the personal income tax, the transfer of the real income to the corporation increases total tax revenues from income originating in corporate capital.[6]

The extra tax on equity income is less than the full 48 percent marginal rate paid by corporations. For that portion of corporate profits paid out in dividends, the rate is 48 $(1-t)$, where t is the dividend recipient's marginal tax rate. On retained earnings, which lead to capital gains, the extra tax is at most 48 $(1-t)(0.5)$, since only half of capital gains are subject to tax; in fact, a very large portion of capital gains are not taxed to individuals at all because they are transferred by gift or bequest or accrue to tax-exempt institutions. As is apparent, the lower the taxpayer's marginal tax rate, the higher the extra tax on equity is. The average individual tax rate on capital gains and dividends works out at about 50 percent for taxpayers in the 70 percent bracket[7] so that half of an increase in the corporate tax burden is offset by reduced personal taxes for top-bracket taxpayers. The offset is correspondingly smaller for lower-bracket taxpayers.

These effects are progressive to the extent that the corporation income tax reduces income from capital. On this point the best available estimates are those of J. Gregory Ballentine and Ibrahim Eris, who correct the earlier estimates of Arnold Harberger.[8] They find that capital bears most of the corporation income tax, if not all or

6. Eventually interest payments may rise sufficiently to offset this second effect, which is unexpected and therefore leaves resource allocation unchanged. When accurate expectations of inflation are built into interest payments, owning bonds and owning depreciable assets are both affected similarly by inflation and by taxation. In this case the extra corporate tax burden applies to depreciable assets and inventories financed by equity, precisely, whereas assets financed by borrowing suffer inflation-caused tax effects only through the personal income tax.

7. See Bailey, "Capital Gains and Income Taxation," pp. 27–29.

8. J. Gregory Ballentine and Ibrahim Eris, "On the General Equilibrium Analysis of Tax Incidence," *Journal of Political Economy*, vol. 83 (June 1975), pp. 633–44; and Arnold C. Harberger, "The Incidence of the Corporation Income Tax," ibid., vol. 70 (June 1962), pp. 215–40.

more than all of it. This view is still controversial.[9] To the extent that it is correct, inflation increases progressivity by increasing the corporation income tax burden on income from capital.

To find the effect of inflation on real corporate taxes, an average asset life and a typical depreciation schedule must be assumed. If asset lives are twenty years,[10] the capital stock grows 4 percent a year in real terms, and depreciation is computed by the sum-of-the-years'-digits method, inflation at 7 percent a year reduces the real value of allowable depreciation about 30 percent. For straight-line depreciation, the reduction is greater; dispersion of the service lives of assets makes it smaller. If dispersion of service lives offsets the use of less accelerated depreciation than the sum of the years' digits for some assets, 7 percent annual inflation reduces the value of depreciation allowances to about 70 percent of what they would be without inflation.

A rough estimate of the impact of inflation on the effective rate of the corporation income tax is shown in table 11-4. Columns 1 and 2 show actual depreciation, before-tax profits, and corporation income taxes as a percentage of gross corporate sales for 1966 and the years 1972–73. Depreciation deductions were liberalized in 1969 and business conditions in 1972–73 were worse than those in 1966. The estimates in column 3 assume a year of average business conditions intermediate between those of 1966 and 1972–73. The values in column 4 are derived by assuming the 30 percent decline in the real value of depreciation and the implied increase in profits and taxes. The tax increases from 6.7 percent to 8.2 percent of total receipts, a 22 percent increase and the equivalent of an 11-percentage-point increase in the present 48 percent surtax rate on corporate profits.

Consider now the offset from the decline in the value of corporate debt due to inflation. In chapter 3, Sidney Davidson and Roman L. Weil show that adjustment for net debt would offset varying amounts of the adjustment for depreciation for the tax year 1974. Most of the Dow Jones thirty industrial firms lose more from the erosion of depreciation than they gain from the reduction in real debt, but the total dollar impact of the debt adjustment is larger because the re-

9. See Joseph Stiglitz, "Taxation, Corporate Financial Policy, and the Cost of Capital," *Journal of Public Economics,* vol. 2 (February 1973), pp. 1–34.

10. Based on U.S. Department of the Treasury estimates, reported by Gramlich in chapter 10.

Table 11-4. Impact of Inflation on the Effective Rate of the Corporation Income Tax

Items affected by inflation	*Percentage of gross corporate sales*			
			Estimated future average	
	1966 (1)	*1972–73* (2)	*No inflation* (3)	*7 percent inflation* (4)
Depreciation	9.3	10.2	10.0	7.0
Profits before tax[a]	16.8	11.6	13.0	16.0
Corporate income tax	7.3	6.2	6.7	8.2

Source: Derived by author.
a. Includes inventory valuation adjustment.

sults are dominated by AT&T. T. Nicolaus Tideman and Donald P. Tucker show similar results for the short run in chapter 2, but their results indicate that over the long run most, but by no means all, firms lose more from inflation, owing to the erosion of depreciation, than they gain from the reduction in real debt. The median result for the Dow Jones thirty industrials is that the reduction in real debt offsets about two-thirds of the loss due to the erosion of depreciation, and I use this figure as representative of all corporations. The accuracy of the figure is highly conjectural, but its importance is small as will be seen in future discussion.

Estate Taxes

Estate taxes fall principally on large accumulations of capital held primarily by higher-income groups. Inflation erodes the exemptions and rate brackets of estate taxes because they are set in nominal dollar terms, thereby raising estate tax burdens on every taxable estate and pushing some estates into the taxable class. Although it is impossible to precisely calculate the incidence of these effects by income group, they are no doubt concentrated on incomes well above the median.[11]

Overall Effects

The combined effect of inflation on the burden from personal and corporation income taxes and from sales and excise taxes appears in table 11-5, columns 6 and 12, and in figure 11-4. In the lowest income

11. For a distribution by income class, see Pechman and Okner, *Who Bears the Tax Burden?* p. 106.

Table 11-5. Effective Income, Sales, and Excise Tax Rates in 1975 and Change in Effec Income, 1975 Tax Laws[a]

Adjusted family income (thousands of 1975 dollars)	Effective tax rate, 1975[b]					
	Individual income tax (1)	Capital gains tax (2)	Individual income tax less capital gains tax (3)	Corporation income tax (4)	Sales and excise taxes[c] (5)	Overall effective rate (6)
0–3	−2.5	0.1	−2.6	2.2	9.7	9.4
3–5	−3.5	0.1	−3.6	2.3	7.7	6.5
5–10	1.5	0.1	1.4	1.9	6.8	10.2
10–15	5.9	0.1	5.8	1.8	6.0	13.7
15–20	7.3	0.2	7.1	2.3	5.3	14.9
20–25	8.2	0.4	7.8	3.6	4.7	16.5
25–30	9.1	0.6	8.5	5.1	4.1	18.4
30–50	11.7	0.8	10.9	6.4	3.5	21.6
50–100	17.6	1.9	15.7	9.4	2.4	29.4
100–500	19.3	3.8	15.5	17.8	1.5	38.6
500–1,000	17.6	4.6	13.0	24.5	1.2	43.3
1,000 and over	16.4	4.7	11.7	27.1	1.1	44.6

Sources: Computed from the Brookings 1966 MERGE data file and the tax laws of 1975. Adjusted family income and the distribution of taxes conform with variant 1c in Joseph A. Pechman and Benjamin A. Okner, *Who Bears the Tax Burden?* (Brookings Institution, 1974), p. 59. See text discussion on capital gains, the corporation income tax, and household interest income in connection with the individual income tax for adjustments relating to inflation. Column 6 equals the sum of columns 2 through 5; column 11 equals the sum of columns 7 through 10; and column 12 equals the sum of columns 6 and 11. Figures are rounded.

group, below $3,000 in 1975 dollars, the fall in the real burden of sales and excise taxes (column 10) offsets the increase in personal and corporation income taxes. For higher income groups, the increases in income taxes dominate. Inflation removes the regressivity of the combined taxes over the bottom two brackets due to sales and excise taxes, and effective tax burdens become steeply progressive above the estimated median family income.

Figure 11-4 understates the increase in progressivity for reasons indicated in the text and in note *a* to table 11-5 and despite the failure to correct sales and excise taxes for the elimination of the federal excise tax on automobiles. The omission of estate and gift taxes also understates the increase in progressivity due to inflation, and this understatement is major for persons with incomes above $50,000 in 1975 dollars. The failure to allow for the reduction in the real value

tive Rates after Ten-Year, 100 Percent Cumulative Inflation, by Adjusted Family

Change in effective rate due to ten-year, 100 percent cumulative inflation

Capital gains tax (7)	Individual income tax less capital gains tax (8)	Corporation income tax[d] (9)	Sales and excise taxes[c] (10)	Overall change in effective rate (11)	Effective rate after 10-year, 100 percent cumulative inflation (12)
0.5	2.4	0.2	−3.0	0.1	9.5
1.0	7.0	0.2	−2.5	5.7	12.2
0.6	7.5	0.1	−2.2	6.0	16.2
0.6	6.1	0.1	−1.9	4.9	18.6
1.0	7.0	0.2	−1.7	6.5	21.4
1.9	8.0	0.2	−1.5	8.6	25.1
2.7	8.4	0.4	−1.3	10.2	28.6
3.2	10.1	0.5	−1.1	12.7	34.3
5.8	11.3	0.8	−0.7	17.2	46.6
9.6	8.4	1.4	−0.5	18.9	57.5
10.5	4.8	1.9	−0.5	16.7	60.0
10.4	3.0	2.2	−0.5	15.1	59.7

a. Note that estate and gift taxes are excluded from the calculations.

b. Columns 1, 2, 3, and 6 differ from the corresponding figures in Pechman and Okner, ibid., because of changes in the tax law since 1966; columns 4 and 5 are substantially the same.

c. The impact of inflation on sales and excise tax burdens was obtained by assuming that the proportion of specific excise taxes was the same as estimated by Pechman and Okner, ibid., pp. 94–95.

d. The corporation income tax burdens were increased 8 percent as explained in the text.

of depreciation allowances for unincorporated business due to inflation further understates the impact on progressivity. This omission is minor, however, because corporations account for nearly all the depreciation and because the corporation tax accounts for only a small part of the increase in progressivity. On balance the increase in progressivity shown in table 11-5 and in figure 11-4 is a conservative but roughly correct first-order estimate of the effect of inflation.

Whether this increase in progressivity should be offset by indexing the tax system depends on the intent of Congress when it enacted the present tax structure. If sufficient votes to make the rate structure more progressive cannot be mustered, is a haphazard increase in progressivity through inflation an acceptable alternative? Would so significant a change in the progressivity of the tax system from inflation stand the test of time? If Congress did not enact indexing, it might vote other changes in the tax structure with equivalent effects

Figure 11-4. Effective Tax Rates before and after Ten-Year 100 Percent Cumulative Inflation, by Adjusted Family Income, 1975 Tax Laws[a]

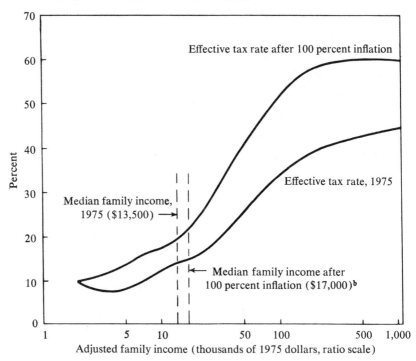

Source: Table 11-5, columns 6 and 12.

a. Combined income, sales, and excise tax rates.

b. The figure of $17,000 for median family income after 100 percent inflation is the author's estimate of 1985 median family income.

on progressivity unless inflation changes the balance of political influence. Whether the effects of inflation on progressivity should be dealt with by indexing or by other adjustments depends on numerous factors other than those already discussed.

Horizontal Equity, Efficiency, and Tax Policy

Inflation affects the relative tax burdens not only of taxpayers in different brackets but also of those in the same bracket. Both effects cause changes in behavior and in the allocation of resources that will generally moderate the direct effects of inflation on tax burdens and in some cases will eliminate them. For example, the introduction of percentage depletion would appear to favor those within any income class who have larger than average investments in petroleum extraction; but the advantage largely disappears when increased investments lower the before-tax and after-tax rates of return in favored industries. After resource shifts have equalized expected after-tax rates of return, the inequity has been converted into inefficiency.[12] When inflation increases tax discrimination, the expectation of further inflation will cause resource shifts that convert the initial inequity into inefficiency. (Also, if inflation were to cut a previous tax discrimination, then it would reduce inefficiency.)

In the case of the inflation effect on monetary assets and liabilities, changes in interest rates due to expectations of inflation eliminate the initial inequities and also eliminate any resource allocation effects associated with those specific inequities. Suppose that all loans finance investment in depreciable equipment and that the depreciation is based on historical costs. Given the loss of real value of depreciation deductions, the debtor can pay extra interest exactly equal to the rate of inflation to restore his pre-inflation real position. The extra interest, which is deductible, exactly cancels the nominal "profit" he makes on such assets; the taxability of this extra interest in the income of the creditor makes the loan equally good or bad as an investment, compared with real alternatives, where both the loan and the alternatives have become worse than before the inflation. Hence both borrower and lender reach equilibrium at a rate of interest equal to the old rate plus the expected rate of inflation if aggregate real saving remains the same. In effect, the reduced real income from owning real assets, due to the reduced real value of depreciation for tax purposes, is passed through to the creditor. The relative desirability of owning monetary or real assets is unchanged in equilibrium so that there is no incentive to change the amount of debt finance as a proportion of the total, except for the effect of heightened uncertainty, which discourages debt finance. (See chapters 2 and 10.)

When inflation is not correctly anticipated, indexing affects the distribution of income because at such times the interest rate set by borrowers and lenders will fail to reflect actual inflation. When inflation begins, industrial firms generally are net debtors and thus enjoy profits on net debt during the onset of inflation; when inflation unexpectedly declines they suffer losses on net debt.[13] Furthermore, de-

12. See Martin J. Bailey, "Progressivity and Investment Yields under U.S. Income Taxation," *Journal of Political Economy,* vol. 82 (November–December 1974), pp. 1157–75.
13. See chapters 2 and 3.

preciation deductions and net debt vary as a proportion of value added among industries, causing the impact of inflation on income to differ widely among business sectors and among stockholders, depending on the sectoral composition of their portfolios. The heightened uncertainty will make debt riskier and thus will discourage debt finance. Different firms and households will respond to uncertainty differently, with unpredictable effects on borrowing, lending, and resource allocation.

The tax system slightly increases uncertainty associated with inflation. Therefore indexing would reduce inflation-induced inefficiencies, distortions, and inequities only slightly.

Although most inflationary distortions are unsystematic and thus are hard to predict, there is a systematic efficiency effect in certain industries. It has been noted that inflation increases the tax burden on income from capital. For example, a 7 percent inflation increases the effective rate from about 40 percent when there is no inflation to about 60 percent, judging by the burden on incomes above $100,000, where the income from capital is concentrated.[14] However, such investments as those in mineral exploration, especially for petroleum, are approximately tax-exempt, and those in farming and real estate are partially tax-exempt due to such privileges as expensing and rapid depreciation of their capital expenditures and the exclusion of the imputed income from owner-occupied housing from taxable income. If inflation does not affect the value of tax provisions—such as the right to expense intangible drilling costs—then inflation sharply widens the advantage of the favored activity over investments whose income is taxed more heavily when inflation occurs. In other cases inflation has a smaller effect on the value of tax advantage; for example, investors in real estate are permitted to take depreciation deductions for tax purposes that typically exceed the decline in market value. These deductions, however, are based on historical cost and, like all depreciation, the real value is reduced by inflation. Because of the acceleration, the resulting tax increase is less than for a normally taxed investment of equal useful life; but real estate assets have longer useful lives than do most other assets. Because the inflation effect on real depreciation is greatest for assets with long useful lives, the tax advantage for commercial real estate could actually be reduced by inflation, not increased. When tax advantages are increased by price

14. The 40 percent figure agrees with unpublished U.S. Treasury estimates.

rises, inflation increases the amount of low-return, socially wasteful investment in these industries.

The tax inducements to investment in selected industries when there is no inflation reflects the intent of Congress to encourage small farms, to stimulate homeownership and residential construction, and to promote exploration in the extractive industries. If these policies are taken as given, alteration of these privileges by inflation is contrary to the intent of Congress and so constitutes an argument for indexing.

Tax incentives alter before-tax rates of return by causing more capital to flow to favored activities; accordingly, a change in the size of tax incentives due to inflation will alter before-tax rates of return. Unfortunately, the size of these changes is hard to estimate. Any such change would reduce the size of the effect of inflation on progressivity compared with that shown in figure 11-4, just as these incentives reduce the progressivity of the tax system without inflation.[15] High-income families especially would invest more in those activities whose tax advantages are increased by inflation. Those holding taxable capital gains would have added incentives to defer realization. Table 11-6 compares the effective rate of tax (from table 11-3) with the tax rate on the added real gain, when the taxpayer defers realization from ten to eleven years, as a function of the inflation rate, where eleventh-year quantities are discounted at 7 percent plus the rate of inflation. Column 3 shows the rate on eleventh-year income the taxpayer faces if he defers realization for one year; column 4 shows the rate the taxpayer faces if he realizes after ten years and then reinvests the proceeds for one year.

Comparison of columns 3 and 4 shows clearly that the incentive to defer realization is small when there is no inflation but large when inflation is as high as 7 percent a year. Even when prices are relatively stable, most capital gains remain unrealized until death and escape the capital gains tax entirely.[16] At present it seems likely that taxpayers realize gains only when they have urgent financial contingencies, such as losses that must be covered in cash, or unusual opportunities. Although the demand for ready cash might therefore seem

15. See Bailey, "Progressivity and Investment Yields."
16. In "Capital Gains and Income Taxation," I presented estimates showing this tendency for the 1950s when capital gains rates were lower than now and prices were relatively stable (p. 18).

Table 11-6. Incentive to Defer Realization of Capital Gains, by Selected Inflation Rates[a]
Percent

	Tax rate on real gain		Marginal tax rate for eleventh year[b] (3)	Tax rate on real gain for one-year holding period[c] (4)
Inflation rate	Ten-year holding period (1)	Eleven-year holding period (2)		
0	30	30	30	30
3	65	64	42	76
7	97	95	26	137

Sources: Columns 1, 2, and 4 from, or computed as described in, table 11-3; column 3 is the extra tax as a percentage of the extra gain, with eleventh-year values discounted one year at 7 percent real rate.
a. Assumes a 60 percent tax bracket on ordinary income and a 30 percent capital gains tax rate.
b. Marginal rate if realization of gains is deferred from the tenth to the eleventh year.
c. Tax rate on eleventh-year gain if gains are realized after ten years and proceeds are reinvested for one year.

inelastic with respect to taxes, most assets are acceptable collateral for loans, an alternative to realization that is now deterred by such considerations as transactions costs. Greater dispersion of asset value due to increased uncertainty would also permit covering gains with losses, despite inflation, so as to keep realization down. If inflation increases the incentive to defer enough so that net realized gains are cut in half, the rise in progressivity shown in table 11-5 and in figure 11-4 would be cut by approximately one-fourth.

Whether the increase in the effective tax rate on realized capital gains raises or lowers economic efficiency is unclear. At present realized long-term capital gains are taxed at half the rate on ordinary income in most cases. This special treatment reduces the overall burden of taxes on the income from capital and thus reduces the excise tax effect on saving and investment.[17] It also gives everyone in the higher tax brackets a strong inducement to manage his business and his portfolio so as to accrue his income from capital in the form of unrealized capital gains. It encourages the holders of such gains to defer realization. On the other hand, inflation increases the capital gains tax and the overall burden of taxes on income from capital, reducing the reward and incentive to save; in so doing it widens the gap

17. A strong case can be made that economic efficiency would be improved if income from capital (and all other sources) were taxed only if consumed but not if saved. Under such a system the rate of return upon which savings decisions are made would be closer to the rate of return upon which investment decisions are made than is true under present law. The removal of such tax wedges, or excise tax effects, generally improves economic efficiency.

between the social and private returns to investment. At the same time, inflation reduces the incentive to convert personal service income (wages, salaries, professional fees, and so forth) into capital gains and hence reduces the inefficiency involved in such conversions. At the tax rates in the second column of table 11-6, which apply to a person in the 60 percent tax bracket on ordinary income, the tax on capital gains rises sufficiently to reverse the incentive to convert personal service income into realized capital gains. But given the possibility of deferring capital gains, and despite the loss of liquidity, some incentive to convert personal service income to capital gains would remain. How much realizations would change and how much the conversion of personal service income into capital gains would be reduced is unclear.

Indexing would eliminate both the loss in efficiency from inflation-induced distortions in the economy and the tax system and the gains in efficiency from the reduced incentive to convert personal service income to capital gains. On balance the efficiency gains from indexing seem likely to outweigh the losses, and the case for indexing becomes stronger as the anticipated rate of inflation becomes higher.

Stabilization

The tax system automatically stabilizes output and employment because revenues rise and fall with the rise and fall of output and employment. It reduces economic fluctuations but cannot eliminate them.[18] If inflation occurs only when unemployment is low, the tax system may also moderate inflation by curtailing excessive demand. If inflation occurs during recession, however, the automatic rise in taxes aggravates rather than moderates declines in output and employment.

In the past, concern over output and employment motivated most interest in automatic stabilizers. That automatic stabilizers might also moderate inflation received little independent attention.

Inflation clearly reinforces the effect of automatic stabilizers on demand in an upswing but weakens or reverses their effect in a downswing. Whether automatic stabilizers moderate inflation is a more difficult question. Suppose that the increase in real revenues from in-

18. Richard A. Musgrave and Merton H. Miller, "Built-in Flexibility," *American Economic Review*, vol. 38 (March 1948), pp. 122–28.

flation does reduce demand and the rate of inflation. Indexing the tax system would eliminate this form of automatic stabilization. Is it therefore undesirable?

The answer may depend on the lag between inflation and adjustment of the tax system. Indexing the tax system without lags would eliminate the reinforcement of both the stabilizing properties of the tax system on real output at full employment and the destabilizing properties when inflation and recession coexist. Indexing would seem to make the impact of stabilizers on output and employment steadier and more reliable, but it would eliminate any contribution of the tax system to automatic stabilization of the price level.

In practice, however, indexing must lag price increases by at least one and perhaps two years. During that period indexing eliminates none of the interactions between inflation and automatic stabilizers. Because other lags in the economy—such as the lag between changes in income and those in consumption or between changes in interest rates and those in investment—are poorly understood, the desirability of indexing is hard to appraise. No analysis, including that by James L. Pierce and Jared J. Enzler in chapter 6, provides convincing evidence that indexing significantly increases or decreases the stability of the economy. Hence it appears that the decision to index should rest primarily on other grounds.

One final argument against indexing also loses its force upon close examination. To index the tax system has often been equated with a confession of defeat in the attempt to control inflation, one that threatens to open the floodgates of fiscal indiscipline. In this view, complete indexing reduces the political pressure on government to maintain monetary and fiscal discipline. Incomplete or ad hoc indexing is a lesser evil because large groups of voters remain vulnerable to inflation. In appraising this viewpoint, one must decide whether the highly uneven distribution of losses through the tax system is a desirable way to maintain the integrity of the currency. If indexing removes all harm from inflation and thereby leads to a higher and perhaps accelerating rate of inflation, should one reject it? If inflation can be rendered harmless, why worry about the political resistance to it? If in fact a major reduction in the damage done by inflation could be achieved, and if that benefit were partly undone by increased inflation, is the final result bad or good? One cannot be sure. It is hard to give this argument against indexing much weight one way or the other.

Hyperinflation

This chapter has been concerned with inflation of the type recently experienced in advanced industrial countries, seldom exceeding 20 percent a year. Preceding sections are irrelevant to runaway inflation, when price increases are measured in tens of percents a month and up. In such cases no tax system collects significant real revenues. The lag between the accrual of tax liability and actual payment to the government is sufficient to reduce real revenues to insignificance. If, say, the price level doubles each month and payments are made one month after accrual, inflation cuts real taxes in half; if payments lag accruals by three months, inflation reduces real taxes by seven-eighths. A six-month delay reduces real tax payments 98 percent. Such inflation effectively wipes out the tax system.

Ordinary indexing based on annual adjustments along the lines discussed in this volume is irrelevant to hyperinflation, unless tax is paid as accrued or liabilities are scaled up by the price change between the time of accrual and the time of payment. Even moderate rates of inflation recently experienced in the United States create a significant incentive to delay paying taxes. It is important, therefore, to charge interest for late payment of taxes based on prevailing market rates, not at some rate fixed years ago when prices were stable. In addition, it is possible to index tax liabilities for inflation between the time of accrual and the time of payment. If the threat of inflation is serious enough to warrant indexing, it is probably serious enough to require these added adjustments.

Conclusions

The case for indexing is commonly based on the misconception that indexing the tax system is desirable or necessary to assure that true economic income is taxed or to avoid misstatement of income for tax purposes.[19] The taxation of true economic income is not now, and perhaps never was, an objective of U.S. income taxation (except in those few states that have gross-income taxes). In 1972 U.S. personal income, an approximate estimate of true economic incomes, was $945 billion (see table 11-7). Barely half of true economic income was taxable. The case for indexing should rest instead on whether it will help carry out the intent of Congress better than the current law

19. For a contrasting view, see chapter 4.

Table 11-7. Derivation of Taxable Income from Personal Income, 1972
Billions of dollars

Item	*Amount*
Personal income	945
Minus: Income exempt from individual income tax[a]	120
Other exclusions from adjusted gross income[b]	49
Equals: Reported adjusted gross income	776
Minus: Exemptions, deductions, miscellaneous exclusions	298
Equals: Taxable income	478

Sources: Personal income from *Economic Report of the President, January 1975*, p. 267; other data obtained from, or estimated from, Joseph A. Pechman and Benjamin A. Okner, "Individual Income Tax Erosion by Income Classes," *The Economics of Federal Subsidy Programs*, A Compendium of Papers Submitted to the Joint Economic Committee, pt. 1: *General Study Papers*, 92:2 (Government Printing Office, 1972), pp. 13–40.

a. Income received by people who are low on the income scale and are not required to pay tax.

b. Includes imputed rent on owner-occupied homes, plus social security and other transfer payments to people with taxable incomes or to those who would become taxable if these items were included in adjusted gross income.

does when there is inflation. If current law expresses that intent for a world of stable prices, then existing tax provisions should be expressed in real terms—that is, indexed—when there is inflation. In fact, Congress shows no sign of understanding how tax policy reduces economic efficiency; and sometimes it is surprised by these effects. For example, the special accounting rules for farming were enacted as a favor to a politically powerful group without any apparent realization that these rules would attract high-bracket taxpayers into farming as a tax shelter. And just as Congress does not always anticipate the effects of tax policy, it shows little sign of understanding the effects of inflation on tax policy. The inflation of the past ten years of about 70 percent has distorted incomes for tax purposes and has compressed the rate bracket progression of the personal income tax to about two-thirds of the extent shown in figure 11-4 and table 11-5. Virtually the only response Congress has made to this change has been to increase personal exemptions, the standard deduction, and the minimum standard deduction, and to accelerate depreciation—all of which it probably would have done even had there been no inflation.

Congress would be well advised to consider indexing the tax law if it expects rapid inflation, say, at a minimum rate of 5 percent a year or more, with occasional bursts of inflation above 10 percent a year for several years. Such inflation would so distort tax policy and make business planning so uncertain due to the prospect of periodic ad hoc congressional relief that an indexing law would be well worth the trouble and the dangers that it involves.

In contrast, if Congress expects the next fifteen years to be as free of inflation as the period 1951–66 was, few would insist on the need to index now. If the future resembles the past, occasional inflationary episodes can be dealt with by ad hoc correction almost as well as by a permanent indexing provision.

Whether the future course of prices in the United States will resemble the relatively placid 1950s and early 1960s or the more tempestuous late 1960s and the 1970s is therefore central to the decision about indexing the tax system. Forecasts based on past experience have been notoriously poor. The past twenty years in international trade and finance have belied the fears of leading economists who during the 1950s worried about a chronic "dollar shortage." The widespread prediction after World War II that the United States faced another depression or stagnation due to a deficiency of aggregate demand has been refuted even more brutally by events. Current beliefs about inflation may be in for the same treatment. It would also be rash, however, to expect a return to the gold standard or anything like its comparatively strict restraints on monetary expansion. In short, it is hard to predict the future of the price level and to balance the advantages and disadvantages of indexing.

In thinking about indexing, it is important not to dwell on secondary issues. Indexing has little relevance to general fiscal management. It has much more relevance for the progressivity of the tax system, because inflation makes the overall tax burden more progressive than Congress evidently intended. Indexing would preserve the original intent of Congress, which might be preferable to an ad hoc, piecemeal approach that Congress would otherwise adopt. Similarly, inflation distorts the distribution of the tax burden among taxpayers, encourages investment in some activities more than in others, and increases economic uncertainty. The incentive effects and distortions are even greater if firms and households expect different rates of inflation.

Accurate and complete indexing of taxes can correct only for distortions that are directly tax-related; and not all of these distortions are harmful. It would prevent inflation from changing the relative advantages of tax-favored industries. It would prevent inflation from increasing the overall tax burden on saving and investment; and it would maintain the present incentive to convert personal service income to capital gains. To the extent that nominal interest rates reflect anticipated inflation, indexing of monetary interest for tax purposes is a matter of indifference to borrowers and lenders subject to the same marginal tax rates, except insofar as it reduces the volatility of realized real interest rates.

Indexing has an uncertain effect on the automatic stabilizing character of the tax system. But inflation creates a significant incentive to delay payment of taxes and reduces the real tax burden caused by delay between accrual and payment. During rapid inflation, indexing tax liabilities for the period between accrual and payment would be necessary to prevent real tax revenues from vanishing; and the interest charged on delinquent payments should be based on a market rate of interest.

The prudent advocate of indexing should also recall that actual legislation emerges from a Byzantine legislative process and may become a grotesque structure containing special favors, compromises, and modifications. Even then, the Treasury would have to write numerous new regulations to implement the legislation, another process not noted for its innocent pursuit of an economist's tax ideals. If the current interest in indexing matures into new tax laws, the result will be a complex, perhaps grotesque, addition to the present structure, possibly having little relation to theoretical ideals. For example, a provision reducing the tax-deductibility of interest payments by the decline in the real value of debt would very likely emerge from the legislative process with exceptions for homeowners and farmers. If so, the tax incentive to shift capital into residences and farming would increase with inflation to much the same extent as it does without indexing. During protracted inflation favored groups might come to realize that they had a vested interest in the continuation of inflation, making it harder to stop. Indexing per se would not be responsible for this effect, but discriminatory indexing would perpetuate it. Whereas perfect indexing would avoid the creation of vested interests that benefit from inflation (and of interests harmed by it), discriminatory indexing would perpetuate some of the interests that benefit while eliminating the most egregious harm done by inflation to other groups. Hence the political balance could shift in favor of more inflation, with a continuation of its harmful effects on resource allocation.

Actual legislation is likely to achieve only some of the hoped-for improvements and will involve appreciable costs. It may bring no improvement at all over the present process of occasional ad hoc tax reform enactments that undo some of the main impact of inflation, and could even be worse.

Whether an indexing law would improve on the present process surely depends on the future rate of inflation. Accordingly, whether Congress should start down the road of considering and enacting an indexing law depends on future inflation. Will the future rate of inflation be high enough to push the United States past the crossover point at which the advantages of an indexing law outweigh its disadvantages? It is fair to say that the United States is near the crossover point between these two positions and that reasonable men will differ about which side is right.

Comments by Martin Feldstein*

Edward Gramlich makes a number of points in his paper that are quite useful and a few that I find troublesome. He correctly stresses the importance of indexing the tax base because of the distributional consequences of inflation, but these effects of inflation are very tricky, and I will return to them shortly. He emphasizes the impact of the failure to index on capital accumulation, growth, and income distribution.

The papers presented at this conference make different assumptions about the impact of *not* indexing on interest rates and hence about the distributional effects of inflation. Assume that the economy contains one sector; that there are two factors of production—labor and capital; that the marginal product of capital equals the real interest rate in the absence of inflation, i; and that borrowers and lenders face the same marginal tax rate, t. How will inflation at the rate, π, change the market interest rate, r?

First, interest rates might remain unchanged, $r = i$. This is the assumption made by Emil Sunley and Joseph Pechman. The result of inflation is simply to push taxpayers into higher tax brackets if the rate structure is not indexed, or to leave them unaffected if the rate structure is indexed.

Second, interest rates might rise by the rate of inflation so that $r = i + \pi$. The real tax liability rises by the amount $t\pi$. If the rate of

* The final discussants ranged freely over all the issues raised at the conference and did not confine themselves to any one paper.

inflation equals the marginal productivity of capital, then both the tax on interest income and the tax deduction on interest expense double. This is approximately the assumption that T. Nicolaus Tideman and Donald Tucker and Martin Bailey make. The difference between these assumptions is also the difference between the size of the tax increases estimated by Sunley and Pechman and those estimated by Bailey.

A third possibility is that $r = i + \pi/(1 - t)$ and that real taxes rise by $t\pi/(1 - t)$. This will be the result if depreciation is adjusted for inflation, but no other change in the tax system is made.

Fourth, if all accrued capital gains were taxed, including those due to the nominal appreciation of durable goods, then the market rate of interest, r, would become $i + \pi$, as in the second possibility and the real tax liability would rise by the amount $t\pi$. Finally, if the tax base were fully indexed, the interest rate would rise to $r = i + \pi$, but that portion of the increase necessary for the maintenance of real capital would not be included in the tax base, and real tax liability would be unaffected. Keep in mind that all of these possible outcomes refer to a situation in which the capital stock is assumed to be unaffected by inflation; if the capital stock adjusts, the range of possibilities is increased correspondingly.

This taxonomy of possible outcomes leads to several important conclusions. First, the quantitative effects of the failure to index the tax base are very hard to estimate. Second, the failure to index will affect real income and prices. Third, if we do not index, Congress will find it difficult or impossible to understand the real effects of the tax system on disposable incomes. For this reason the tax base should be indexed for inflation. The case for indexing the rate structure is less clear, although I share Gramlich's intuition that the failure to do so may cause Congress to sanction changes in the rate structure that it would not choose if it were freed from the political constraints that inflation forces our elected representatives to confront.

Comments by Arthur Okun

I interpret the results reported in the paper by Joseph Pechman and Emil Sunley as evidence that indexing the rate structure is not very important. Whether to index the tax base is a much more important topic that entails analytically challenging and economically significant questions.

The basic problem arises because a tax system based on nominal income subjects to tax part of receipts necessary for the maintenance of real capital. Eventually, if nothing is done, the capital stock will grow less rapidly because of this tax until the marginal productivity of capital is higher by an amount sufficient to equate the supply of saving with demands for net investment. This effect may be large. One way to avoid it is the "anchor" proposal, discussed by Edward Gramlich, to index depreciation and make no other change in the tax system. In that case, interest rates are supposed to adjust so as to leave borrowers and lenders in the same position with inflation as they were in without it. I do not have the religious faith in the general equilibrium of asset markets required to accept that proposal.

I see a better case for a "nail-it-down" approach that adjusts every element in the tax base. We have heard several such proposals, one from the Financial Accounting Standards Board and one from John Shoven. Roger Brinner's proposal can be interpreted as a third, if generalized. In my judgment, the best nail-it-down approach is the one advanced by William Fellner. He would index the depreciation of capital goods only if financed by equity, not if financed by debt. He would also make the monetary adjustments called for by several authors here.

Before we make such changes, however, we should ask why they are necessary. In the abstract, I do not find "inflation neutrality" a compelling target for tax policy. It seems to me that the big issue is the threat to the national saving rate that comes from inflation under the present tax system. Even though I regard the interest elasticity of savings as small, sustained 10 percent inflation would almost certainly reduce private savings, perhaps even by enough to break Denison's law! I do not think we save too little, nor do I regard the rate of saving generated by the market under any tax system as necessarily a social optimum. I can see no persuasive argument that we are saving too much, however, and I would hate to see inflation reduce saving in some unplanned way.

Putting the question this way forces one to take a broader view of the taxation of property income and not constrain oneself to consider only the effects of inflation on income from capital. You should not graft inflation adjustments onto the tax system without looking at the system onto which they are being grafted. For example, Martin Bailey has argued that cumulative averaging works out better than does the inflation adjustment, but cumulative averaging is a major adjustment that transcends inflation. John Bossons has pointed out that during inflationary years many people would have large real capital losses on financial assets. So we would have to review the tax treatment of realized capital losses and hence logically of unrealized capital gains. Even after we did that, we could not stop there. We could not ignore the current expensing of research and development expenditures or the failure to capitalize and to allow depreciation deductions on human capital. Finally, problems of transitional equity from inflation adjustment could not be ignored any more than similar problems from other tax changes could be. The larger issues of taxation of property income must enter into the debate over any proposal for inflation adjustment.

While I will not dwell on it, I cannot abstract the inflation adjustment of taxation from still another issue that concerns me greatly —the value of retaining the nominal dollar yardstick for measuring economic transactions. In my judgment that constitutes the most important argument for the restoration of some measure of price stability. In short, any program to remove the implicit tax on capital levied by inflation would have a number of costs—it would encourage the abandonment of the dollar yardstick and it would require an agonizing reappraisal of other subsidies to capital, explicit and implicit.

Still, I must agree with Martin Bailey that at some rate of inflation, perhaps 10 percent a year, the benefits exceed the costs. At 5 percent inflation, I have no trouble opposing a general move to indexing, although I would see some case for offering firms the option of indexed straight-line depreciation on equity-financed physical assets as an alternative to nonindexed accelerated depreciation.

Comments by Peter Diamond

The kind of tax system we now have imposes an inflation surtax by increasing the tax base by the rate of inflation times net wealth. The surtax is imposed on this increase in the tax base at the same rates now applicable to similar incomes—at ordinary rates on interest from bonds, at half of ordinary rates on realized long-term capital gains, and at zero rate on unrealized capital gains. The absence of indexing means that inflation increases both the tax on capital incomes and the distortions caused by the tax in its current form. We cannot say whether that is good or bad until we determine whether taxes are distributed between income from labor and income from capital so as to minimize the inevitable distortions of economic decisions. In short, we would need to know something we do not know. For example, the capital gains tax produces a well-known "lock-in" effect. Inflation increases this lock-in effect and indexing would lessen it. The holder of a positive nominal gain, but a negative real gain, is locked in under the present tax system but would have an incentive to realize under an indexed system. We do not know the importance of this distortion and hence do not know what effect its removal would have on revenue.

One of Martin Bailey's points deserves to be underscored. He notes that inflation increases the relative advantage of income from those assets favored by certain tax incentives. As long as we hold that Congress did not anticipate the current rate of inflation when it introduced these tax incentives, the case for indexing gains power.

In the end, however, we are left with the simple fact that inflation results in a tax on wealth. A tax on wealth does not bother me, but its random size does. Unfortunately, undoing the effects of this tax is enormously difficult and perhaps impossible to do precisely because of taxation on both realized and accrued gains and losses. One might do better, as E. Cary Brown suggests, with a set of ad hoc adjustments. I doubt that the best feasible solution is to do as much indexing as possible on an accrual basis and to use realization only when necessary. I suspect that the best feasible answer will entail matching up assets and liabilities.

Comments by Richard A. Musgrave

Martin Bailey's paper now contains a section on horizontal equity that was not part of an earlier draft. The paper also contains some statements, however, that make the exclusion of any mention of horizontal equity easier to understand than its inclusion. These statements assert that even in the absence of inflation taxable income is not meaningfully defined. Bailey argues that inflation cannot be indicted for the demise of an ideal long since dead at the hands of our legislators. Since there is no such thing in the tax law as a meaningful definition of income, Bailey seems to be saying that we should not bring any preconceptions to the question of whether the distortions caused by inflation are good or bad.

I find this position untenable. This entire conference, and indeed most discussions of tax policy, are based on the explicit or implicit presumption that there is something meaningful in the concept of taxable income, something that is not fully realized in practice but that must be thought of in real terms to be meaningful. For this reason I think there is a strong presumption that the result of inflation—the taxation of people with equal real incomes at unequal rates —is undesirable on equity grounds. The chance that the distortions caused by inflation will just happen to offset other distortions found in the tax structure is very small. The income tax should relate to real income.

Bailey is not alone in neglecting the horizontal inequities caused by inflation. This conference has been replete with papers that dwelled on the impact of inflation on vertical equity. But the absence of even one on the differential effects of inflation on people with the same real income is a regrettable omission. I say this not to downgrade the importance of progressivity but to upgrade the importance of fairness.

I find myself in agreement with Bailey's judgment that the difference between the stabilizing effects of an indexed system and those of a nonindexed system are small and that other considerations should determine whether or not to index the tax system. But if that set of considerations is secondary, I find myself driven back to the impact of inflation on horizontal equity as the central issue in the debate on indexing. Of course, indexing will remove only a small part of the distortions caused by inflation, because tax rates are all below 100 percent of nominal income. This fact suggests that it would be profitable to consider how the government could give people a way to invest their funds free from the distortions of inflation; it might even be more profitable than discussing indexing the tax system.

Discussion of the Gramlich and Bailey Papers

The discussion of the two concluding papers, directed by Stanley Surrey, was structured around three questions. The first question concerned the desirability of indexing the personal income tax rate structure if that were the only form of inflation adjustment that would be adopted. The second question concerned the desirability of indexing the tax base if the accounting profession chose to require inflation-adjusted business accounts. The third question concerned the desirability of indexing the tax base if the accounting profession should choose not to require inflation-adjusted business accounts.

On the question of whether to index the rate structure, Martin Feldstein asserted that no one had made a strong case for or against doing so. Although the gain would not be large, it would not be difficult to index the rate structure, and he felt that it probably would be good to do so and that it would certainly be a mistake to drop the idea. Stanley Fischer, Robert Gordon, and William Fellner agreed with Feldstein's position. Fischer noted that the paper by James Pierce and Jared Enzler had removed the only economic objection to indexing—that is, that it would increase economic instability. Gordon pointed out that discretionary tax changes entailed political costs that could be avoided by indexing. Fellner observed that discretionary tax changes might come only after a lag, during which no compensation for inflation was made, and that because of the delay, adjustments would be excessively large. Formula adjustment would be superior, he said.

Edward Denison said he probably would favor indexing the rate structure because much of government expenditure is already indexed. Expenditure indexing introduces a bias toward a rising government sector unless tax schedules are indexed too. Congressional action is not required to increase expenditures to match inflation, so Congress can indulge its proclivity to vote bigger outlays only by raising real expenditures. Indexing of the rate structure is needed to prevent Congress from doing so without also voting higher taxes.

Richard Goode drew conclusions different from Denison's analysis. If transfer payments are indexed, if interest rates rise with inflation, and if the cost of goods and services purchased by the government continue to rise more than average, then indexing the rate structure might well lead to ever-increasing deficits rather than to smaller expenditures, he feared. Edward Gramlich reminded the group of the paradox reported in Martin Bailey's paper: those parts of government expenditures rose fastest that were financed by taxes that did not increase automatically but required legislative changes both to increase and to maintain real revenues, namely social security and local government.

Bailey reiterated his view that one's position should depend on one's expectations regarding inflation. But Vito Tanzi pointed out that changes in the rate structure could be set to occur only when the cumulative change in prices was sufficiently large. Feldstein expressed the judgment that while indexing would be universally supported by economists for high rates of inflation, it would be far easier to introduce during low inflation, when it would be regarded by the public as merely a technical adjustment in the system.

Joseph Pechman agreed that indexing the rate structure is not very important but opposed it on the ground that the automatic increase in taxes due to inflation and real growth required Congress periodically to reexamine the distribution of tax burdens by income classes and to alter them if it sees fit. Feldstein countered by observing that Congress has adjusted everything but the rate structure over the past decade, and that the proper indexing scheme would save Congress a lot of time and trouble. George Perry pointed out that almost all the arguments for or against indexing the rate structure were political, not economic, but reminded the group that one economic fact has considerable political significance. In reference to the paper by Pechman and Emil Sunley, he noted that indexing the rate structure would have removed the need for nearly all the discretionary reduction in taxes over the past fifteen years. He observed that almost all tax reforms involve increases in tax burdens for some previously favored group and that Congress typically balances revenue-increasing reforms with reductions in tax rates, increases in exemptions, or other tax cuts. He concluded that indexing the rate structure would doom tax reform for many years. Arnold Harberger disagreed vigorously with Perry, alleging that countries with the most inflation should have the best tax systems if Perry's argument were correct.

Peter Diamond remarked that economists are predisposed by their training to want all parts of the economy to function in real terms and that they therefore favor indexing the rate structure. But the arguments for and against indexing presented at the conference seemed to rest more on political intuition than on economics. He concluded that Congress could adjust the rate structure for the effect of inflation either by formula or through discretionary legislation, that precision was not required, and that neither he nor any of the other participants in the conference were experts on the political consequences of choosing one path or the other. Henry Aaron wondered why economists would wish to spend the limited amount of attention they could get from Congress on a matter all agreed was so unimportant. Roger Brinner supported this point with the judgment that Congress might well choose to index the rate structure and to adjust capital gains for inflation but to do nothing else. He thought that such a change would make the tax system less, rather than more, equitable.

The judgment that conference participants (1) regarded indexing the rate structure to be of secondary importance, (2) considered it an essentially political question, and (3) were roughly equally divided on its desirability provoked no objections.

Surrey then asked the participants to consider whether indexing the tax base would be desirable if the accounting profession were to require business to recognize the effects of inflation in their accounts, records, and reports. T. Nicolaus Tideman said that he would favor indexing the tax base in that case, partly because such a change would be nearly inevitable if the accounting profession enforced such changes in business accounting, but even more because he felt it would improve the tax system. He recognized that such a change would entail major redistributions of tax burdens, including large short-run increases in utility taxes that might require rate increases, but he held that it would increase economic efficiency and should be undertaken. John Bossons said that he would oppose these changes unless they were accompanied by complementary changes in the taxation of personal income from lending. Inflation correction of the personal and business tax bases should be regarded as an all-or-nothing proposition. Tideman agreed with this position. Cary Brown stated that he would favor full-scale indexing, but he was sure that Congress would not. Bailey observed that if the accountants correctly indexed business incomes, then the remaining technical problems of indexing personal incomes would be minor. Bossons also pointed out that indexing would reduce the effective rate of taxation on income from capital. Because he felt that income from capital is not taxed excessively at present, he urged that indexing be accompanied by offsetting increases in taxation of income from capital, such as repeal of the investment tax credit.

Tideman said that if the accounting profession does not require inflation-adjusted records, he would still favor indexing the tax base, but he thought the prospects for enactment would be rather slim. Goode supported Tideman's position, pointing out that what constitutes good tax policy does not depend on what rules the accounting profession chooses to enforce. Frank Weston stated that the issue in the accounting profession was not whether to abandon historical-cost accounting but whether to introduce inflation-adjusted accounting along with historical-cost accounting. He envisioned the two systems running alongside one another for some time. Only after several years might historical-cost accounting be abandoned.

A number of participants raised the possibility that indexing only some elements of the tax base might be sufficient to secure whatever advantages full indexing along the lines suggested by the Federal Accounting Standards Board would yield. No participant, however, advocated any form of inflation adjustment of the business tax base if complementary adjustments are not made in the individual income tax base as well. Feldstein pointed out that it could be proven that adjustment of depreciation for changes in the price level would be adequate in equilibrium if all investment were financed by debt and all borrowers and lenders were in the same tax bracket. Arthur Okun said that interest rates might not happen to change by just enough to leave after-tax real incomes unchanged even in such a simple and unrealistic world. Feldstein agreed that for this reason, as well as the fact that some capital is financed by equity and that the tax rates of borrowers and lenders are unequal, he would prefer complete indexing. But indexing depreciation, he maintained, is better than nothing.

Donald Tucker held that even in the simple all-debt, equal-tax-rate world described by Feldstein, the choice between indexing only depreciation and materials costs and completely indexing the tax base would affect the financial structure of firms by altering the pattern through time of the tax burdens that firms face. Brown remarked that heavily leveraged firms might be driven into bankruptcy by the advent of inflation if full indexing were introduced because such a reform would increase the present value of tax liabilities. Generous averaging provisions would cushion the blow for many firms by preventing sharp fluctuations in taxes as inflation increased and subsided. Bailey noted that debt-heavy firms had done very nicely with the unexpected acceleration of inflation but might do rather badly during the unexpected deceleration of inflation if their bonds lacked call provisions.

Okun underscored his opposition to the indexing of assets and liabilities by offering to write the brief that AT&T did not have $2 billion in additional profits due to inflation in 1974. He pointed out that such an anomaly would be avoided by provisions that merely allowed adjustment of depreciation for that part of physical capital financed by equity. Bailey noted that partial indexing of the tax base would lead to an increase in the tax advantage of homeownership because it would permit the homeowner to deduct interest payments enlarged by the impact of inflation on interest rates, but little of this extra deduction would ever be captured because most capital gains on homes escape taxation. He labeled this consequence the strongest argument for full indexing over partial indexing of the tax base.

Gramlich, Okun, and Pechman all stressed that advocates of indexing had to recognize that Congress might not do the job correctly. The blunders in attempting to index social security and civil service pensions were mentioned repeatedly as evidence that the same kinds of mistakes might plague efforts to index the tax base. Pechman feared that Congress would enact those changes that reduced tax liabilities but would fail to enact those that increased liabilities. Surrey asked how best to avoid that unfortunate outcome. Pechman replied that the best solution is to avoid inflation.

Conference Participants

Henry J. Aaron *Brookings Institution (Conference Chairman)*
Martin J. Bailey *University of Maryland*
Alan S. Blinder *Princeton University*
John Bossons *University of Toronto*
David F. Bradford *Princeton University*
Roger E. Brinner *Harvard University and Data Resources, Inc.*
E. Cary Brown *Massachusetts Institute of Technology*
Sidney Davidson *University of Chicago*
Edward F. Denison *Brookings Institution*
Peter Diamond *Massachusetts Institute of Technology*
Jared J. Enzler *Board of Governors, Federal Reserve System*
Ray C. Fair *Yale University*
Martin Feldstein *Harvard University*
William J. Fellner *Yale University (Emeritus) and American Enterprise Institute for Public Policy Research*
Stanley Fischer *Massachusetts Institute of Technology*
Joseph Gabbay *Ministry of Finance, Israel*
Richard Goode *International Monetary Fund*
Robert J. Gordon *Northwestern University*

Edward M. Gramlich *Brookings Institution*

Victor Halberstadt *University of Leyden, The Netherlands*

Arnold C. Harberger *University of Chicago*

George E. Lent *International Monetary Fund*

A. H. Lovell *British Treasury, United Kingdom*

Kenneth Messere *Organisation for Economic Co-operation and Development*

David Morgan *London School of Economics*

Richard Musgrave *Harvard University*

John Nolan *Miller and Chevalier, Attorneys at Law*

Arthur M. Okun *Brookings Institution*

Harry Olsher *Fund for Public Policy Research*

Joseph A. Pechman *Brookings Institution*

George L. Perry *Brookings Institution*

James L. Pierce *Consultant, Committee on Banking, Currency, and Housing, U.S. House of Representatives*

Eytan Sheshinski *Hebrew University, Jerusalem*

John B. Shoven *Stanford University*

Emil M. Sunley, Jr. *Brookings Institution*

Stanley S. Surrey *Harvard Law School*

Vito Tanzi *International Monetary Fund*

T. Nicolaus Tideman *Virginia Polytechnic Institute and State University*

George S. Tolley *University of Chicago*

Donald P. Tucker *Board of Governors, Federal Reserve System*

Roman L. Weil *Georgia Institute of Technology*

Frank T. Weston *Arthur Young and Company (Retired)*

James W. Wetzler *Staff Economist, Joint Committee on Internal Revenue Taxation, U.S. Congress*

Index

Aaron, Henry J., 1–31, 79, 193, 268, 269, 297n, 326

Accounting: accrual versus realization, 8, 119; adjustments for inflation, 81–83; to compute cost of materials used, 12–14; historical cost versus inflation-adjusted, 327–28; replacement-cost, 268. *See also* Financial statements; General-price-level-adjusted accounting; Tax reports

Accounting Principles Board, 84, 89n, 115

Accrual taxation: of capital gains, 40, 58, 127–28, 146, 149, 192, 320, 323; inflation and, 119; partial versus complete, 8–9

Adie, Douglas, 217n

Aid to Families with Dependent Children, 274

Allen, R. I. G., 215n

American Telephone and Telegraph Company, 18, 92, 99, 305, 328

Argentina: depreciable assets revaluation, 200, 204, 205; depreciation adjustments, 201; indexing system, 223, 224; permanent revaluation plan, 207; taxation of capital gains, 222

Assets: depreciable, 87, 200, 204–05; effect of inflation on, 2, 35; financial, 116; individual, 84; in terms of replacement cost, 84, 116. *See also* Capital assets

Australia, 204, 206

Australian Committee of Inquiry into Inflation and Taxation, 206, 211

Austria: annual revaluation adjustments, 210; business accounts revaluation, 195; depreciable assets revaluation, 204, 205; inventory revaluation, 205–06; revaluation options, 201

Bailey, Martin J., 3n, 24, 26, 133n, 149, 154, 167, 168, 192, 269, 287, 291–329

Ballentine, J. Gregory, 303

Bankruptcy, during inflation, 35, 38

Banks: effect of inflation on, 115; general-price-level-adjusted net income, 94

Base-stock method, for inventory profits taxation, 201, 205, 212

BEA. *See* Bureau of Economic Analysis

Belgium: business accounts revaluation, 195; depreciable assets revaluation, 204; reappraisal of industrial buildings, 196; revaluation plan coverage, 207, 208

Bischoff, Charles W., 282n, 286

Blechman, Barry M., 274n, 276n